McGraw-Hill Education
GRE
2021

McGraw-Hill Education
GRE
2021

Erfun Geula

New York Chicago San Francisco Athens London Madrid
Mexico City Milan New Delhi Singapore Sydney Toronto

1 2 3 4 5 6 7 8 9   LOV   24 23 22 21 20 (book alone)
1 2 3 4 5 6 7 8 9   LOV   24 23 22 21 20 (Elite)

ISBN   978-1-260-46334-7 (Elite)
MHID   1-260-46334-6

e-ISBN 978-1-260-46335-4 (e-book Elite)
e-MHID   1-260-46335-4

ISBN   978-1-260-46332-3 (book alone)
MHID   1-260-46332-X

ISBN   978-1-260-46333-0 (e-book alone)
MHID   1-260-46333-8

GRE is a registered trademark of Educational Test Service (ETS), which was not involved in the production of, and does not endorse, this product

Interior artwork by Cenveo

McGraw Hill products are available at special quantity discounts to use as premiums and sales promotions or for use in corporate training programs. To contact a representative, please visit the Contact Us pages at www.mhprofessional.com.

Contents

PART 3　GRE Quantitative Reasoning

PART 4　Math Review

McGraw-Hill Education

GRE

2021

Getting Started

CHAPTER 1

Introducing the GRE

Study this chapter to learn about:

- GRE scoring
- The section-adaptive nature of the exam
- Using the calculator
- Skipping questions and guessing
- The GRE test format

What Is the GRE?

The GRE (Graduate Record Examination) is a test required by most universities for admission to their MA, MS, and PhD programs. Increasingly, many business schools are accepting the exam as well. Unlike most tests that students may have taken in college or high school, the exam does not test knowledge or achievement in any specific areas. Instead, the exam is designed to assess the test-taker's fundamental Quantitative and Verbal Reasoning abilities.

Thus the Quantitative portion of the exam does not address "advanced" mathematical concepts such as calculus or advanced trigonometry. Instead, it assesses a student's conceptual understanding of the foundational mathematical topics from high school: algebra; fractions, decimals, and percents; arithmetic; word problems; and geometry. Many students interpret this information to mean that they simply need to re-memorize their rules from high school math to succeed on the Quantitative section. In fact, the Quantitative questions are concerned more with a student's ability to implement logic skills in conjunction with these topics rather than to regurgitate a certain set of rules.

> You should think of the Quantitative questions as puzzles to be solved using certain mathematical principles, not as questions that can be solved by straightforward application of a few principles or formulas.

Likewise, the Verbal portion of the exam does not require preexisting content knowledge. The Reading Comprehension questions do not assume or require prior familiarity with the passage's content; instead, they are designed to measure a student's ability to efficiently digest the information in a college-level text. Text Completion and Sentence Equivalence questions, however, will require knowledge of college- and graduate-level vocabulary. For students who perform below their desired score range on the Verbal Reasoning section of the diagnostic test, learning vocabulary may be the quickest way to a score improvement.

> It should be noted that even the vocabulary-based questions address verbal reasoning in the sense that they address a test-taker's ability to use the context of a sentence and logical connections among a sentence's parts to identify the word(s) that best fit in a certain context.

The GRE consists of six or seven sections: an Analytical Writing section, two scored Quantitative Reasoning sections, two scored Verbal Reasoning sections, and one unscored experimental section, which could be either Quantitative or Verbal. The computer-based version of the test is arranged as follows:

Computer-Based GRE: Test Format

SECTIONS	QUESTIONS	TIME
Analytical Writing	Issue Task Argument Task	30 minutes 30 minutes
Verbal—2 sections	20 questions per section	30 minutes per section
Quantitative—2 sections	20 questions per section	35 minutes per section
Unscored*	Varies	Varies
Research**	Varies	Varies

* The unscored section will contain an experimental Verbal or Quantitative section.
** You may not encounter a Research section but if you do, it will be at the end of the exam.

> The paper-based version of the GRE involves slightly different time limits and numbers of questions. It does not include a Research section.

GRE Scoring

For your performance on the Quantitative and Verbal sections, you will receive *raw* scores, which are calculated based on the questions you answered correctly in each section and the level of difficulty of these questions. These raw scores are then converted to scaled scores ranging from 130 to 170, going up in 1-point increments. *The conversion from the raw score to the scaled score depends on:*

- the number of questions answered correctly for a given section
- the assigned level of difficulty of all correct and incorrect questions (each question is assigned a level of difficulty ranging from 1 to 5).

Each of the two essays that you write in the Analytical Writing section is scored on a scale of 0 to 6. Your score for the Analytical Writing section will be the average of these two scores. For details, see the simplified Analytical Writing scoring rubrics on pages 56–57.

Perhaps surprisingly, a larger proportion of test-takers perform well on the Quantitative Reasoning section than on the Verbal Reasoning section. For example, according to reports published by ETS, a score of 160 on the Verbal section corresponds to the 83rd percentile, while the same score on the Quantitative section corresponds to the 81st percentile.

What Is a Section-Adaptive Exam?

In June 2011 the makers of the GRE began administering the *Revised GRE*, which substantially changed the structure and format of the exam. One of the primary changes to the exam was the switch from a *computer-adaptive* test to a *section-adaptive* test. In a computer-adaptive test, the level of difficulty of each new question is based on a student's performance on all previous questions. On a section-adaptive test, on the other hand, the content and level of difficulty of a given question is not determined by a student's performance on all previous questions. Instead, the content and difficulty of a given *section* is determined by the student's performance on a previous section. For example, test-takers can expect that their first Quantitative section will feature questions that are mostly categorized as *medium*. Based on the test-taker's performance on this first section, the next Quantitative section will have questions that are mostly *easy*, *medium*, or *difficult*. The scoring algorithm will then use data from both sections to determine a student's Quantitative or Verbal score.

One consequence of this system is that a student's score will often have a ceiling if he or she has trouble on the first Quantitative or Verbal section. Essentially, if the second section is not categorized as "difficult," then no matter how well a student performs on that second section, it is unlikely that the student will achieve a score in the upper percentiles of that measure.

While you are taking the GRE, don't try to guess how you're doing. Many students are tempted to use the perceived level of difficulty of their questions to estimate their performance on the test. This is a perilous strategy for three reasons:

1. **The questions within even the most difficult section will consist of a range of levels of difficulty.**

2. Often, a question that might appear difficult or easy to you might not be categorized in the same way for all test-takers.

3. Prematurely assessing your performance on the test will distract you from your primary goal on the exam: to get as many questions correct as possible!

Using the Calculator

You'll be happy to know that you will be provided with an on-screen calculator for the Quantitative sections. The calculator features addition, subtraction, multiplication, division, and square roots. Though this certainly eliminates the need to memorize many of the common powers and roots, you should avoid deferring to the calculator for *all* calculations. Many calculations require the use of simple mental math that you do every day. If you do not feel confident with this math or are confronted with what seems to be a complex calculation, then you should use the calculator.

Skipping Questions and Guessing

The revised GRE computer format offers certain functions that work in favor of the test-taker. At the upper right of your test screen, there will be an option to "mark" a question. Test-takers can mark up to three questions per section. So if you think you can get a question correct by spending additional time on it, just mark that question and come back to it. Unlike other standardized tests you may have taken, the GRE does not penalize students for incorrect answers. Thus you should guess and mark any questions that you're unsure of or that you feel will take too long to answer.

The GRE Test Format

Verbal Reasoning Ability

Each of the two scored Verbal sections contains 20 questions. These questions fall into three categories:

- 6 Text Completion questions
- 5 Sentence Equivalence questions
- 9 Reading Comprehension questions

Most test-takers erroneously assume that these question types test strictly your vocabulary knowledge. Though it's certainly true that a large vocabulary is helpful for these questions, you need to be equally concerned about the use of concrete textual evidence to justify your answers.

Text Completion Questions

Text Completion questions are verbal questions designed to test your vocabulary and your ability to use the context of a sentence to infer the appropriate word choice. Text Completion questions consist of a one-to-five-sentence passage with one to three blanks. You are asked to use logic and the context of the sentence to identify the best word for each blank. There is no partial credit for Text Completion questions. For Text Completion questions with one blank, there will be five choices. For Text Completion questions with two to three blanks, there will be three choices for each blank. Here is an example of a Text Completion question:

Nagel's tendency to question (i) _____ philosophical views has long drawn admiration from his peers. But ironically enough, this very rebelliousness has accounted for the (ii) _____ his new book.

Blank (i)	Blank (ii)
Ⓐ thoughtful	Ⓓ antipathy toward
Ⓑ provocative	Ⓔ embrace of
Ⓒ orthodox	Ⓕ curiosity over

SOLUTION: The clue "this very rebelliousness" indicates that the word in the first blank should match the definition of "accepted." The best choice for Blank (i) is therefore **orthodox**. The phrase "But ironically enough . . ." tells you that the reception toward Nagel's new book is the opposite of "admiration." The best choice for Blank (ii) is therefore **antipathy toward**. The correct answer is C and D.

Sentence Equivalence Questions

Sentence Equivalence questions are also designed to test your vocabulary and your ability to use the context of a sentence to infer the appropriate word choice. Sentence Equivalence questions consist of a one-sentence passage with one blank. You are given six choices and will be asked to use logic and the context of the sentence to identify *two* words that best fit in the blank. There is no partial credit for Sentence Equivalence questions. In contrast to Text Completion questions, Sentence Equivalence questions are generally more dependent on vocabulary. In addition, Sentence Equivalence questions are more amenable to strategy: almost always, the two correct answers will be synonyms (this is discussed in the Text Completion and Sentence Equivalence review chapters). The following is an example of a Sentence Equivalence question:

After Harold had endured weeks of his neighbors' blaring music, his well-known _____ finally gave way to frustration.

    A imperturbability
    B indigence
    C aestheticism
    D equanimity
    E diligence
    F virulence

SOLUTION: The phrase "finally gave way" indicates that Howard's "frustration" contrasts with his usual behavior. You should be looking for choices whose meaning is the opposite of being frustrated. The correct answer is A and D.

Reading Comprehension Questions

In Reading Comprehension questions, you are given a passage that is from one to five paragraphs in length and you are asked questions about the content of the passage, the inferences that can be drawn from the passage, and ways to strengthen or weaken claims in the passage. The following is a typical Reading Comprehension passage followed by a typical question:

When Tocqueville came to America in 1831, he expressed a sentiment that is echoed in the works of Bloom and Kennedy: that American democracy, by encouraging dissent, can lead to its own undoing. But in contrast to the pessimism that dominates Bloom's and Kennedy's thinking, Tocqueville's analysis went a step further. While acknowledging the seeming inevitability of dissent among the citizenry, he also recognized that beneath this frustration there lay a fundamental belief that democratic politics would ultimately amend the situations that aroused complaint. As Tocqueville noted, at any given point in time, democracy can appear chaotic, shallow, and contradictory. But, he noted, it was never stagnant. For Tocqueville, democracy's tendency to encourage and accommodate discontent was its greatest virtue. Because it is self-correcting, a properly run democratic system would ultimately benefit from any discontent because the system is designed to ultimately rectify the problem.

The author mentions Tocqueville's belief that democracy "was never stagnant" to

    A highlight Tocqueville's belief in the self-correcting nature of democracy
    B introduce a difference between Tocqueville's thinking and that of Bloom and Kennedy
    C explain why Tocqueville believes citizens of democratic nations are often unhappy
    D suggest ways to eliminate the frustration of the citizens of democratic nations
    E imply that many of the concerns of democratic citizens are baseless

SOLUTION: The author provides this statement to support the larger point that democracies can withstand turmoil because they are designed to correct themselves. The correct answer is A.

Quantitative Reasoning Ability

Each of the two scored Quantitative sections contains 20 questions. These questions fall into three categories:

- 8 Quantitative Comparison questions
- 9 Discrete Quantitative questions
- 3 Data Interpretation questions

Quantitative Comparison Questions

In Quantitative Comparison questions, you will see two columns and will be asked to determine which column has a greater value. Here is an example:

Each of the following questions consists of two quantities, Quantity A and Quantity B. You are to compare the two quantities. You may use additional information centered above the two quantities if additional information is given. Choose:

    Ⓐ if Quantity A is greater
    Ⓑ if Quantity B is greater
    Ⓒ if the two quantities are equal
    Ⓓ if the relationship between the two quantities cannot be determined

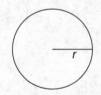

A circle has radius r

QUANTITY A	QUANTITY B	
The area of the circle	The circumference of the circle	Ⓐ Ⓑ Ⓒ Ⓓ

SOLUTION: The area of the circle can be represented as πr^2. The circumference of the circle can be represented as $2\pi r$. If the radius is 1, then Quantity B is greater. If the radius is 10, then Quantity A is greater. Thus, given the information, you cannot determine which quantity has a greater value. The correct answer is Choice D.

Discrete Quantitative Questions: Multiple Choice and Numeric Entry

These are the standard problem-solving questions that most students are familiar with. There are three types of Discrete Quantitative questions:

Multiple Choice—Select One Answer. In these questions, you are presented with one question and five answer choices. You are asked to select one answer choice. Here is an example.

If the $\sqrt{x + 9} = 5$, then $x =$

     Ⓐ −4
     Ⓑ 4
     Ⓒ 16
     Ⓓ 25
     Ⓔ 144

SOLUTION: To solve for x, first square both sides of the equation: $x + 9 = 25$. Subtract 9 from both sides. $x = 16$. The correct answer is Choice C.

Multiple Choice—Select All Applicable Answers. In these questions, you are presented with one question and 3 to 12 answer choices. You are asked to select *all* answer choices that apply. There is no partial credit. These questions can be thought of as variants of the Roman numeral questions that you may have seen on the SAT. A typical Roman numeral question looks like the following:

If $x^5 > x^3$, then which of the following could be true?

    I. $x > 0$
   II. $x < 0$
   III. $x < -1$

     Ⓐ I only
     Ⓑ I and II only
     Ⓒ I and III only
     Ⓓ II and III only
     Ⓔ I, II, and III

On the GRE, that question would take the following form:

For this question, indicate all of the answer choices that apply.

If $x^5 > x^3$, then which of the following could be true?

    Ⓐ $x > 0$
    Ⓑ $x < 0$
    Ⓒ $x < -1$

SOLUTION: Test the numbers for Choice A. If $x = 2$, then $32 > 8$. Choice A is possible. Test the numbers for Choice B. If $x = -(\frac{1}{2})$, then $-\frac{1}{3}2 > -\frac{1}{8}$. Choice B is possible. Test the numbers for Choice C. If $x = -2$, then $-32 < -8$. Choice C is not possible. The correct answer is A and B only.

Numeric Entry. No choices—these questions do not have choices. Instead, you are asked to type the correct answer into a box on the screen. Because there are no answer choices, these questions do not lend themselves to plugging in numbers or back-solving. The following is an example:

For this question, write your answer in the box.

If Jack's salary increases by 25%, then his new salary will be $40,000 greater than his original salary. What is his original salary?

SOLUTION: Let j = Jack's original salary. A 25% increase is equal to a $40,000 increase. Therefore,

$0.25j = 40,000$

$j = \$160,000$

Data Interpretation Questions

In Data Interpretation questions, you are presented with a graph, table, or chart and are asked to make calculations or inferences from the data presented to you. The questions will either be

- Multiple-Choice Questions—Select One Answer Choice
- Multiple-Choice Questions—Select One or More Answer Choices.

Here is an example.

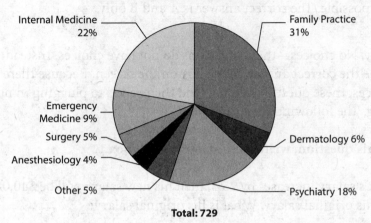

Area of Specialization for 2009 Graduates of Medical School X

Internal Medicine 22%

Family Practice 31%

Emergency Medicine 9%

Surgery 5%

Anesthesiology 4%

Other 5%

Dermatology 6%

Psychiatry 18%

Total: 729

Approximately how many 2009 graduates of Medical School X specialized in internal medicine?

- (A) 80
- (B) 160
- (C) 220
- (D) 240
- (E) 300

SOLUTION: Since there were 729 students, the number specializing in internal medicine was 22% of 729. $0.22 \times 729 = 160.38$. The closest answer is 160. The correct answer is B.

Before diving into the strategies and content review of this book, you should familiarize yourself with the different question types and the different appearances that they take on the exam. This advice is especially important for test day. You don't want to spend precious time trying to recall what a question is asking for, nor do you want to let lack of familiarity with the test structure induce anxiety. Understanding the form and structure of the GRE is an integral component to your preparation for the exam.

Information for International Test-Takers

If you are an international student who is planning to take the GRE, these pages will provide some information that can help make the process easier for you. We also suggest that you visit the official GRE website, **www.ets.org/gre**, for further details and updates. The site is maintained by Educational Testing Service (ETS), the organization that creates and administers the test.

The GRE General Test is currently offered as a computer-based test in the United States, Canada, and many other countries. The test is offered in a paper-based format in areas of the world where computer-based testing is not available.

Arranging to Take the GRE

Finding a Testing Center

With permanent testing centers located in countries all around the world, most applicants should not have trouble finding a place to take the test. If there are no centers near your home, you will need to travel to one. When you register for the GRE, you will need to schedule a test appointment at a specific testing center. Go to **www.ets.org/gre** for a complete listing of testing centers worldwide.

Registering for the Test

Register early to get your preferred test date and to receive your test preparation material in time to prepare for the test. Remember that testing appointments are scheduled on a first-come, first-served basis. Major credit cards are accepted to pay for registration. To register visit **www.ets.org/gre**.

Standby Testing

Standby testing is available at permanent test centers on a first-come, first-served, space-available basis in the United States, American Samoa, Guam, U.S. Virgin Islands, Puerto Rico, and Canada only. It is not available in Mainland China, Hong Kong, India, Iran, Korea, or Taiwan.

Canceling or Rescheduling

If you must cancel or reschedule a testing appointment, contact the GRE Program by mail or phone no later than four full days before your appointment (not including the day of your test or the day of your request). Keep in mind that you cannot reschedule between sites served by different Regional Registration Centers. See the ETS website for details.

Paper-Based Testing

You can register for the paper-based General Test either online or by mail. Use a money order or a certified check when registering by mail. Download and complete the registration form and mail the completed form with payment to the address printed on the form. ETS must receive your registration form by the registration deadline, which can be found at **www.ets.org/gre**. Allow at least four weeks for processing.

Identification

It is your responsibility to bring an acceptable form of identification to the testing center. The following documents can be used in the country in which you are a citizen:

- Passport
- National ID card
- State or Province ID card
- Official driver's license
- Military ID card

See the ETS website for further details.

Test Preparation for International Students

ETS is very careful to make sure that the GRE is not biased against international test-takers. All questions are pre-tested by being included in unscored "experimental" test sections given to both U.S. and international test-takers. If statistics prove that any of the new questions put the international test-takers at a disadvantage, those items never appear on the test. Still, international test-takers face certain challenges.

The Language Barrier

The biggest and most obvious difficulty for international test-takers is the language barrier. Many people residing outside of the United States who sign up to take the GRE are non-native English speakers. The entire test, including instructions and questions, is in English. One part of the test is focused on verbal skills and another part is a writing test, which requires not only an understanding of the language but a command of it. Your English writing, reading comprehension, and grammar skills are directly tested on the GRE. If you are a non-native English speaker, to improve your understanding of the language in the months leading up to the test, you are encouraged to:

- Read as much in English as possible, especially newspapers or journal articles
- Create flash cards with difficult English words on them
- Practice your English by speaking with others who speak the language— preferably better than you do!
- Watch television shows featuring native English speakers

Your goal should be to practice presenting evidence in a cohesive and interesting way to support your arguments in the writing section of the exam. When you read items from English-language publications, pay particular attention to how the writers gather evidence and present it because there are often subtle cultural differences at play. Remember that the quantitative part of the GRE is also in English so it's a good idea to review math formulas and glossaries in English.

Becoming Familiar with Standardized Tests

Getting acquainted with standardized tests is another must-do for international test-takers. This type of exam is a part of the average American's educational experience but is not necessarily a cultural norm in other parts of the world. Some people outside the United States may be unfamiliar with multiple-choice questions. These are questions in which you are given several choices from which to choose for the correct answer. There are strategies for choosing the best one when you're not sure. For example, you can eliminate answers that you know are incorrect and then choose among the remaining choices. This is called "taking an educated guess," and it can improve your chances of picking the correct answer. Timing is a very important part of standardized tests. Keeping calm is the first step to overcoming the pressure. Taking practice tests is key to learning how to pace yourself to maximize your performance in a limited time period. Taking practice tests will also help you become familiar with the test format. Understanding the instructions for each part of the test in advance can save you time during the exam because you won't have to spend time on the instructions in addition to the other reading you have to do.

Testing Your English-Language Skills

If you received your undergraduate degree from an institution in a country whose official language is not English, the graduate program to which you are applying will likely require you to submit proof of your English proficiency along with your GRE scores. Most institutions accept scores on either the TOEFL (Test of English as a Foreign Language) or the IELTS (International English Language Testing System); many now also accept scores on the newer PTE (Pearson Test of English). Check with the programs to which you are applying for information about their test requirements. There is no specific passing score on these tests; graduate institutions set their own requirements.

- **TOEFL:** The TOEFL iBT is an Internet-based test administered more than 50 dates a year at more than 4,500 sites around the world. A paper-based version (TOEFL PBT) is still used but only in a few locations where Internet access is not reliable. For more information including the format of the test, scoring, and registration, visit **www.ets.org/toefl**. The TOEFL iBT captures the test-taker's speech and uses this to measure English-speaking ability in a standardized manner. Multiple-choice questions are used to measure reading and listening abilities. Two essay questions are used to measure writing abilities.
- **IELTS:** The IELTS is a paper-based test created at Cambridge University in the UK. It consists of four modules—Listening, Reading, Writing, and Speaking. Question types include multiple choice, sentence completion, short answer, classification, matching, labeling, and diagram/chart interpretation. The Speaking test is a face-to-face interview with a certified examiner. IELTS has two versions: Academic and General Training.

The Academic test is for those who want to study at a tertiary level in an English-speaking country. The General Training test is for those who want to do work experience or training programs, enroll in secondary school, or migrate to an English-speaking country. For more information, visit **www.ielts.org**.

■ **PTE:** The PTE was developed by Pearson, an international educational testing and publishing company. Like the TOEFL iBT, it is administered at testing centers on a computer (there is no paper version). Visit **www.pearsonpte.com** for more information about the PTE and updated lists of the schools that accept it and the locations where it is given. Like the TOEFL, the PTE uses multiple-choice questions plus essay questions to measure reading, listening, and writing skills. A 30-second audio clip of the test-taker's speech is sent to schools along with the test scores.

One Last Hurdle: The Student Visa

Nonresidents of the United States need to obtain a visa to live in the United States. Once you have chosen a graduate program and have been accepted, you will need to begin the process of obtaining your student visa.

Getting a student visa to study in the United States is not as difficult as getting an H1-B visa to work in the country after graduation. Experts, including the U.S. government, suggest that students begin the student visa process as early as possible. Besides needing the time to complete the required forms, you will also need to schedule an appointment for the required embassy consular interview, and the waiting times for this vary and can be lengthy.

Visa Requirements

During the student visa process, you are expected to prove that you have adequate financing to study in the United States, ties to your home country, and a likelihood that you will return home after finishing your studies. In addition, you will have to participate in an ink-free, digital fingerprint scan and provide a passport valid for travel to the United States and with a validity date at least six months beyond your intended period of stay.

Your U.S. school will provide you with an I-20 form to complete. The school will use this to register you with the Student and Exchange Visitor Information System (SEVIS), an Internet-based system that maintains accurate and current information on nonimmigrant students and exchange visitors and their families. If you have a spouse and/or children who will be joining you, you must register them with SEVIS as well. You'll also need to submit a completed and signed nonimmigrant visa application with form DS-160. To download this form and for more information on the visa process, go to the U.S. Department of State website, **https://travel.state.gov/content/travel/en/us-visas/visa-information-resources/forms/ds-160-online-nonimmigrant-visa-application.html.**

Transcripts, diplomas from previous institutions, scores from standardized tests such as the TOEFL or IELTS, and proof you can afford the school (income tax records, original bank books and statements) are things you should have on hand when applying for your visa. If you have dependents, you will also need documents that prove your relationship to your spouse and children, such as a marriage license and birth certificates.

Good luck with your application process!

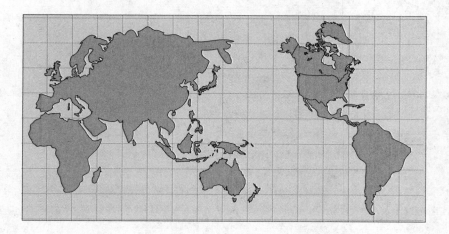

CHAPTER 2

GRE Diagnostic Test

How to Use the Diagnostic Test

This chapter presents a sample GRE diagnostic test. Its questions have been designed to match real GRE questions as closely as possible in terms of format, length, and degree of difficulty. You should use this test as a launching point to determine your strengths and weaknesses, and to identify how far your current score is from your score goal.

> You can also take this test on your tablet, smartphone, or computer. See page 2A for information.

Use the diagnostic test to plan your study by following these four steps:

1. **Take the diagnostic test under test conditions.** Find a quiet place where you will not be disturbed. Take the test as if it were the actual GRE. Work through the test from beginning to end in one sitting. Mark your answers directly on the test pages. Observe the time limit given at the start of each section. If you have not finished a section when time runs out, mark the last question you answered and note how much longer it takes you to complete the section. This information will tell you if you need to speed up your pace, and if so, by how much.

2. **Answer every question.** On the real GRE, there is no penalty for wrong answers, so it makes sense to answer every question, even if you have to guess. If you don't know an answer, see if you can eliminate one or more of the answer choices. The more choices you can eliminate, the better your chance of guessing correctly.

3. **Check your answers.** Go to the Answers and Explanations section at the end of the test. Pay particular attention to the explanations for questions you missed.

4. **Fill out the evaluation charts.** These charts are located at the end of the Answers and Explanations section. Mark the numbers of the questions you missed, and the charts will show you in which sections of this book you need to spend the most study time.

SECTION 1

Analytical Writing

Analyze an Issue

30 minutes

For this task, you will be given a brief quotation that states or implies an issue of general interest. You will also be given instructions on how to respond to that issue. You will then have 30 minutes to plan and write a response.

Be sure to follow the instructions that you are given. In writing your response, support your ideas with reasons and examples drawn from your reading, your studies, and your personal experiences. Your response will be evaluated based on how well you organize and express your ideas, how well you support your opinions with reasons and examples, and how well you follow the rules of standard English grammar and usage.

Take a few minutes to plan your response. When you are finished writing, make sure to review your work and make any necessary revisions.

ISSUE TOPIC

The purpose of an education is to prepare students for financially rewarding careers.

Write a response in which you discuss the extent to which you agree or disagree with the statement and explain your reasoning for the position you take. In developing and supporting your position, you should consider ways in which the statement might or might not hold true and explain how these considerations shape your position.

SECTION 2

Analytical Writing

Analyze an Argument

30 minutes

For this task, you will be given a brief passage that presents an argument. You will also be given instructions on how to respond to the passage. You will then have 30 minutes to plan and write a response in which you evaluate the argument according to the instructions that you are given. Be aware that you are **not** being asked to present your own personal views on the topic.

In writing your response, be sure to support your ideas with reasons and examples. Your response will be evaluated based on how well you analyze the argument presented in the prompt, how well you organize and express your ideas, and how well you follow the rules of standard English grammar and usage.

Take a few minutes to plan your response. When you are finished writing, make sure to review your work and make any necessary revisions.

ARGUMENT TOPIC

In Borlarvia, the porpoise has become endangered due to overhunting by Borlarvian fishermen. The government is attempting to preserve the porpoise by encouraging the fishermen to stop hunting and instead give paid boat tours to tourists interested in observing the porpoise. The fishermen have expert knowledge of the porpoise's habitat, and many tourists have expressed interest in these boat rides, so the plan has a good chance of ensuring that the fishermen make a good living while still preserving the porpoise.

Write a response in which you discuss what questions would need to be answered in order to decide whether the recommendation is likely to have the predicted result. Be sure to explain how the answers to these questions would help evaluate the recommendation.

GO ON TO NEXT PAGE ➤

_____

_____

_____

_____

_____

_____

_____

_____

_____

_____

_____

_____

_____

_____

_____

_____

_____

_____

_____

_____

_____

_____

_____

STOP.
This is the end of Section 2.

Verbal Reasoning

20 questions — 30 minutes

This section includes three types of questions: Reading Comprehension, Text Completion, and Sentence Equivalence. Read the following directions before you begin the section.

Directions

Reading Comprehension Questions
- *Multiple-Choice Questions—Select One Answer Choice*: Select one answer choice from a list of five choices.
- *Multiple-Choice Questions—Select One or More Answer Choices:* From a list of three answer choices, select all that are correct.
- *Select-in-Passage*. Select the sentence in the passage that meets a certain description.

Text Completion Questions
- For each blank, select one choice from the corresponding list of choices. Fill all blanks in the way that best completes the text.

Sentence Equivalence Questions
- Select the two answer choices that (1) complete the sentence in a way that makes sense and (2) produce sentences that are similar in meaning.

In Questions 1 to 6, for each blank, select the choice that best completes the text.

1. The professor regarded the student's theory with _____ , considering the overall idea creative, but the logic behind the specific details unsound.

   - (A) deliberation
   - (B) ambivalence
   - (C) indifference
   - (D) condescension
   - (E) consternation

2. Dylan's unwavering belief in the priority of self-interest was tantamount to _____ : he took it as axiomatic that, since he could never be sure of others' beliefs or desires, he should focus only on his own.

    Ⓐ selfishness

    Ⓑ solipsism

    Ⓒ fortitude

    Ⓓ determinism

    Ⓔ negligence

3. A retreat to nature appealed to Thoreau for reasons other than the solitude that it provided. Thoreau believed that (i) _____ the untamed put him in touch with an (ii) _____ that, by definition, could not be replicated by the schemings of 19th-century man.

Blank (i)	Blank (ii)
Ⓐ deflection of	Ⓓ unpredictability
Ⓑ immersion in	Ⓔ austerity
Ⓒ lionization of	Ⓕ simplicity

4. Alarmists attribute the startling rise of student debt to the greed of for-profit universities. But, in focusing on the (i) _____ of these institutions, the critics overlook the more troubling trend in American culture: the belief that education is just another (ii) _____ whose value can and should be quantified economically.

Blank (i)	Blank (ii)
Ⓐ archaism	Ⓓ pursuit
Ⓑ avarice	Ⓔ volition
Ⓒ naïveté	Ⓕ commodity

5. The inability of economists to (i) _____ the causes of financial recessions should not, as some critics believe, be taken as a commentary on the limits of economics as a science. In every science, be it physics, chemistry, or psychology, the practitioners of the field put faith not in their results but in their (ii) _____: as long as they are adhering to the appropriate mode of analysis, the scientists are confident that questions that can be answered eventually will be.

Blank (i)	Blank (ii)
Ⓐ exacerbate	Ⓓ calculations
Ⓑ mollify	Ⓔ methodologies
Ⓒ delineate	Ⓕ equivalencies

6. Scientific discovery is generally (i) _____ process, building on and supplementing the discoveries made by previous researchers. But those discoveries that tend to alter the trajectory of human thought are often made in isolation of previous (ii) _____ . Darwin's discovery of evolution, for example, though mainstream today, was not obviously (iii) _____ by the work of any naturalists before him.

Blank (i)	Blank (ii)	Blank (iii)
Ⓐ a cumulative	Ⓓ calculations	Ⓖ hindered
Ⓑ an erroneous	Ⓔ exemplars	Ⓗ contended
Ⓒ an impertinent	Ⓕ paradigms	Ⓘ anticipated

Question 7 is based on the passage below. Select <u>one</u> answer choice.

In the country of Bunrose, the government has a monopoly on tobacco products. Thirty years ago, in response to a rise in tobacco-related illnesses, the government decided to limit its sale of tobacco products. Despite the loss in tobacco-related revenue, the government's net revenue was no less this year than it was 30 years ago.

7. Which of the following, if true, best explains why the government's net revenue did not decrease since it limited the sale of tobacco products?

   Ⓐ In addition to limiting its sale of tobacco products, the government also ran advertisements highlighting the dangers of tobacco use.

   Ⓑ Many members of the government's legislature were in favor of the government's decision to limit tobacco use.

   Ⓒ Twenty years ago, most of the people using tobacco were aware of its health risks.

   Ⓓ All health care in Bunrose is government-funded.

   Ⓔ Consumers who saved money on tobacco products spent the majority of that money on private goods.

Questions 8 to 10 refer to the passage below. For each question, select <u>one</u> answer choice, unless the instructions state otherwise.

When Edward O. Wilson argued for the concept of consilience, he had in mind the unification of all the scientific disciplines under one broad theory. Wilson believed that the reducibility of psychology to biology, biology to chemistry, and chemistry to physics implied that,
5 with the proper conceptual and methodological tools, scientists would eventually be able to study all of these disparate domains within the same framework. Though most scientists agree with Wilson's basic premise, attempts at realizing his concept have been sparse and often met with a combination of amusement and scorn.
10   Why scientists have been so reluctant to pursue his project and to entertain others' attempts is due, at least partly, to the entrenched methodologies of each of these disciplines. The tools that psychologists use to study their subjects differ fundamentally from what biologists use to study their subject matter, and these tools differ just as
15 drastically from what chemists use to study theirs. Any attempt to bridge the gap between fields necessitates a break with orthodoxy and, by extension, an introduction of tools and concepts that the established thinkers in a field are simply unfamiliar with.

8. According to the passage, what accounts for most scientists' reactions of "amusement and scorn"?

   Ⓐ Doubt about the plausibility of Wilson's theory

   Ⓑ Concern that attempting to achieve consilience would undermine the credibility of their given field

   Ⓒ Lack of familiarity with the approach necessary to achieve consilience

   Ⓓ An inability to reach a consensus about what would constitute consilience

   Ⓔ Ambivalence toward the approaches of scientists in other fields

9. Select the sentence that explains why Wilson was in favor of consilience.

    ┌─────────────────────────┐
    │   │
    │   │
    └─────────────────────────┘

10. It can be inferred from the passage that scientists would be more open to attempts at consilience if which of the following was true?

    (A) Scientists in other fields also accepted consilience.
    (B) The approach necessary to achieve consilience was part of the repertoire of each scientist's given field.
    (C) Evidence was discovered that definitively proved the reducibility of one science to another science.
    (D) Consilience was limited to only certain fields.
    (E) The realization of consilience did not rely on empirical data.

In Questions 11 to 14, select the two answer choices that (1) complete the sentence in a way that makes sense and (2) produce sentences that are similar in meaning.

11. The coffee shop's business plan, though _____ in the short-term, would ultimately undermine the owner's goal of maximizing profits.

    [A] lucrative
    [B] venal
    [C] deliberate
    [D] profitable
    [E] profligate
    [F] felonious

12. Though not without some justification, the athlete's decision to forgo college only reinforced the widely held belief of his _____ .

    [A] impetuosity
    [B] recklessness
    [C] miserliness
    [D] diligence
    [E] consilience
    [F] denigration

13. Offering only loose guidelines, the recipe gave cooks the opportunity to practice _____ when creating the dishes.

    [A] indolence
    [B] creativity
    [C] thoughtfulness
    [D] ingenuity
    [E] expertise
    [F] haphazardness

14. Despite the strides made in contemporary neuroscience over the past 50 years, knowledge of certain brain processes is incomplete and, in some cases, downright _____ .

[A] lackadaisical

[B] negligible

[C] porous

[D] fleeting

[E] interminable

[F] anachronistic

Questions 15 to 17 refer to the passage below. For each question, select <u>one</u> answer choice, unless the instructions state otherwise.

It is a belief so common as to be hackneyed: There exists a linear and continuous relationship between the themes and characters of a novelist's works and the life of the novelist himself. We need not look far to find rebuttals to this theme, but in the case of Dostoevsky, we
5 find a counterpoint to this broader cynicism. An obvious example is *The Gambler,* wherein the main character's tragic gambling addiction closely parallels Dostoevsky's own lifelong travails with the roulette wheel and the subsequent financial consequences. But more broadly, the redemptive and existential overtones of his great novels, *Crime*
10 *and Punishment* and *The Brothers Karamazov,* have their antecedent in Dostoevsky's infamous encounter with the firing squad. Though Dostoevsky was reprieved from death at the last minute, the experience laid the foundations for the themes that characterized his more mature works: mortality, salvation, and compassion.

15. The passage is primarily concerned with

Ⓐ debating likelihood that a novelist will introduce real-life experiences into his fiction

Ⓑ analyzing the effect that Dostoevsky's experience with the firing squad had on his novels

Ⓒ arguing for a commonly held belief about the relationship of an author's experiences and the content of the author's novels

Ⓓ evaluating Dostoevsky's ability to make his characters' lives believable

Ⓔ highlighting the impact that intense personal experiences have on novelists

GO ON TO NEXT PAGE ➤

16. The author most likely mentions *Crime and Punishment* and *The Brothers Karamazov* in line 9–10 in order to

    A. provide examples of novels that were influenced by actual events in Dostoevsky's life

    B. emphasize the "existential and redemptive" elements in Dostoevsky's work

    C. suggest that the themes in *The Gambler* are not representative of Dostoevsky's mature novels

    D. illustrate the influence that Dostoevsky's experience with the firing squad had on his novels

    E. correct a misconception about the similarities between the two novels

17. In the context of the passage, *hackneyed* in line 1 most nearly means

    A. controversial
    B. cliché
    C. exotic
    D. forgettable
    E. ill-conceived

Question 18 is based on the passage below. Select <u>one</u> answer choice.

From 1980 to 2000, overall expenditures on prescription drugs in Centerville had increased. To curb this increase, the government of Centerville banned pharmaceutical companies from increasing the prices of their drugs. Nonetheless, ten years following the ban, per capita expenditure on prescription drugs in Centerville had increased.

18. Which of the following, if true, most likely explains why the government's action did not achieve its desired effect?

    A. Citizens aged 65 or older, who are the greatest consumers of prescription drugs in Centerville, accounted for a larger percentage of the population in 2010 than they did in 2000.

    B. To offset the potential loss in revenues caused by the ban, pharmaceutical companies decreased their advertising budgets.

    C. The population of Centerville increased from 2000 to 2010.

    D. During the time period, the government passed laws that loosened restrictions on more affordable generic drugs.

    E. Because of the ban, several foreign prescription drug manufacturers limited their advertising in Centerville.

Questions 19 to 20 refer to the passage below. For each question, select <u>one</u> answer choice, unless the instructions state otherwise.

What are we to make of Beethoven's Ninth Symphony? The fact that Beethoven created this masterpiece while battling with encroaching deafness has given this work a prominent place in the canon of Western music. And even when considered in a vacuum, the first three
5   movements of the symphony rightfully receive nearly universal praise from music critics and composers alike. But then there is that fourth movement, at once groundbreaking for its use of words and off-putting with its straightforward text and sentimentality. One wonders about the impetus behind this decision to use Schiller's *Ode to Joy*, a text that
10   praises the divine that is always implicit in Beethoven's work, but that does so in such an overt way that the previous movements are almost rendered superfluous. Unfortunately, it seems as though Verdi was on to something when he made the following claim about the symphony: "No one will ever surpass the sublimity of the first movement, but it
15   will be an easy task to write as badly for voices as is done in the last movement."

19. The passage is primarily concerned with

    Ⓐ explaining why Beethoven wrote his Ninth Symphony
    Ⓑ evaluating Beethoven's Ninth Symphony
    Ⓒ identifying the differences between the first three movements of Beethoven's Ninth Symphony and the last movement of his Ninth Symphony
    Ⓓ analyzing the context in which Beethoven wrote his Ninth Symphony
    Ⓔ questioning the text that Beethoven used in the fourth movement of his Ninth Symphony

20. Which of the following can be inferred about the author's opinion toward Beethoven's Ninth Symphony? (Indicate <u>all</u> that apply.)

    Ⓐ He agrees with most music critics' interpretation of the first three movements.
    Ⓑ He considers the fourth movement largely unnecessary.
    Ⓒ He believes that the fourth movement offers nothing of merit to those studying Beethoven's symphonies.

———————————— **STOP.** ————————————
This is the end of Section 3.

SECTION 4

Verbal Reasoning

20 questions — 30 minutes

This section includes three types of questions: Reading Comprehension, Text Completion, and Sentence Equivalence. Read the following directions before you begin the section.

Directions

Reading Comprehension Questions
- *Multiple-Choice Questions—Select One Answer Choice*: Select one answer choice from a list of five choices.
- *Multiple-Choice Questions—Select One or More Answer Choices*: From a list of three answer choices, select all that are correct.
- *Select-in-Passage*. Select the sentence in the passage that meets a certain description.

Text Completion Questions
- For each blank, select one choice from the corresponding list of choices. Fill all blanks in the way that best completes the text.

Sentence Equivalence Questions
- Select the <u>two</u> answer choices that (1) complete the sentence in a way that makes sense and (2) produce sentences that are similar in meaning.

In Questions 1 to 6, for each blank, select the choice that best completes the text.

1. By taking the mental lives of animals as his subject matter, the author presents himself with the _____ task of explicating something that is, in many ways, inaccessible.

   - Ⓐ impossible
   - Ⓑ meandering
   - Ⓒ feckless
   - Ⓓ pugnacious
   - Ⓔ felicitous

2. The contradictions inherent in Bernie's worldview were apparent to everyone but him: while always quick to point out the importance of moral _____, in his personal dealings, he considered _____ to be somehow unproblematic.

Ⓐ malingering		Ⓓ dissembling
Ⓑ equivocation		Ⓔ mischievousness
Ⓒ rectitude		Ⓕ fastidiousness

3. Although the politician's well-considered declaration could hardly be thought of as_____, it somehow still elicited murmurs of _____ from the electorate.

Ⓐ ephemeral		Ⓓ quiescence
Ⓑ offensive		Ⓔ disapproval
Ⓒ trivial		Ⓕ solicitousness

4. The new book obscures in _____ material that would be beneficial for all audiences, not just the academic circles that the author traffics in. Such inaccessibility, while lamentable for any book with general relevance, is particularly _____ in this case, given the author's oft-stated desire to make his research available to a wider audience.

Ⓐ jargon		Ⓓ irksome
Ⓑ malevolence		Ⓔ enervating
Ⓒ disinterestedness		Ⓕ disheartening

5. To his acquaintances, his _____ might seem effortful, so consistently and unfailingly does he demonstrate it. But those who know him well know his vehement opposition to all forms of _____ and so take his good-naturedness at face value

Ⓐ geniality		Ⓓ objectivity
Ⓑ stolidity		Ⓔ subterfuge
Ⓒ vivacity		Ⓕ venality

GO ON TO NEXT PAGE ➤

6. Her frenetic intellectual energy lent itself to (a)n _____ that, while usually frowned upon in a discipline so focused on hyper-specialization, gave her the opportunity to come up with novel syntheses that challenged prevailing views in the field.

- (A) divergence
- (B) acuity
- (C) miserliness
- (D) eclecticism
- (E) virtuosity

Questions 7 to 10 refer to the passage below. For each question, select one answer choice, unless the instructions state otherwise.

Long the orthodox position in all sciences of the mind, materialism is revealing itself to be a porous, internally-inconsistent philosophical position, one that cannot withstand the implications of cutting edge of physics. At the heart of materialism is the belief that all phenomena
5 can ultimately be explained in physical terms. The intuitive appeal of such a position has contributed to its vaunted status among the sciences, and rightfully so, given how much progress has been made in various scientific disciplines. But what are we to make of consciousness? The last frontier in neuroscience, the question of
10 how our physical brain can give rise to subjective experience, has been deferred indefinitely; leaving one to wonder not *when* but *if* the question can be resolved. Quantum physics has an answer: the question is senseless. Quantum physics shows us that the fundamentals of matter are only probability, wave-like functions. Subatomic
15 particles, the very constituents of everything that scientists investigate, do not behave like matter at all, and so the metaphysical foundation of so much scientific inquiry is found to be irreparably, tragically cracked. If we continue operating under the assumption that consciousness can be reduced to physical terms, we'll find ourselves in a dead-end.
20 To understand this most mysterious, most human of phenomena, we need to reorient our metaphysics, taking the elusive, slippery nature of matter as a starting point, not as an inconvenience.

7. As used in line 2, "porous" most nearly means

    (A) inscrutable
    (B) indefensible
    (C) problem-plagued
    (D) irrefutable
    (E) meaningless

8. Select the sentence in which the author explains an answer to a question.

    [   ]

9. The author most likely mentions "how much progress has been made in various scientific disciplines" in order to

    (A) question the reasonableness of materialism
    (B) show why it would be beneficial to abandon materialism
    (C) provide a reason for materialism's popularity
    (D) suggest that some components of materialism can be salvaged
    (E) undermine the position that materialism is flawed

10. The passage is primarily concerned with

    (A) arguing in favor of a certain position
    (B) showing that consciousness will never be explained
    (C) explaining the shortcomings of a position and a consequence of these shortcomings
    (D) describing the significance of certain scientific findings
    (E) highlighting the differences between two phenomena

Question 11 is based on the passage below. Select <u>one</u> answer choice.

The cost of producing computers in Ertrulia is significantly greater than in Kantanistan. To stimulate domestic business, the Ertrulian government imposes a 20 percent tax on all computers purchased from foreign manufacturers. However, an economic analyst recently
5 suggested that the government can drop the 20 percent tax without harming overall purchases from domestic computer manufacturers.

GO ON TO NEXT PAGE ➤

11. Which of the following, if true, would strengthen the analyst's suggestion?

- Ⓐ The manufacturer of Orange, the world's most popular and highest-quality computers, is based in Ertrulia.
- Ⓑ Kantanistan manufacturers have recently been able to reduce their costs in creating computers.
- Ⓒ Kantanistan's government threatened levying a similar tax on Ertrulian computers.
- Ⓓ Most computer users in Ertrulia state cost as the primary factor in their computer-purchasing decisions.
- Ⓔ Kantanistan has fewer computer manufacturers than does Ertrulia.

In Questions 12 to 15, select the two choices that (1) complete the sentence in a way that makes sense and (2) produce sentences that are similar in meaning.

12. The executive's _____ nature was a source of vexation to the employees, leaving them guessing about the vicissitudes of his mood at every moment.

- Ⓐ belligerent
- Ⓑ pacific
- Ⓒ mercurial
- Ⓓ temperamental
- Ⓔ bellicose
- Ⓕ stoic

13. To perceive her occasional air of genuine confusion as a general quality was to risk overlooking her even more noteworthy _____.

- Ⓐ perspicacity
- Ⓑ malevolence
- Ⓒ insincerity
- Ⓓ bemusement
- Ⓔ falsity
- Ⓕ acuity

14. The author's purpose in overlooking the shortcomings of the industry can be characterized as nothing short of disingenuous; while such _____ can sometimes be charitably interpreted as done in the service of economy and readability, the shortcomings are so fundamental to the book's main point that leaving them out distorts the picture that the author presents.

- Ⓐ denials
- Ⓑ elisions
- Ⓒ dishonesty
- Ⓓ omissions
- Ⓔ bifurcations
- Ⓕ deceptiveness

15. The _____ between many major scientific discoveries and the original intent of the studies that led to these discoveries is a commentary on the serendipity at the heart of much scientific research.

    A complexity
    B convolutedness
    C synchrony
    D discordance
    E incongruity
    F fallibility

Question 16 is based on the passage below. Select <u>one</u> answer choice.

Research shows that partners whose sleep-and-wake cycles are at least three hours apart tend to express less closeness with their partners than do couples with more closely-aligned sleep-and-wake cycles. Since mismatched sleep-and-wake cycles probably make partners less likely
5 to share common activities, counseling these couples to have better-matched sleep-and-wake cycles would help alleviate their relationship discord.

16. Which of the following, if true, would best weaken the argument?

    Ⓐ Couples who do not have different sleep-and-wake cycles argue sometimes.
    Ⓑ Sleep-and-wake cycles are related to serotonin levels, which can change with proper habit modification.
    Ⓒ Research shows that partners often develop different sleep-and-wake cycles as a way to express frustration with one another.
    Ⓓ Different personality types can often create irreconcilable differences in relationships.
    Ⓔ The research cited in the argument only refers to couples who have been together for at least a year.

GO ON TO NEXT PAGE ➤

Questions 17 to 19 refer to the passage below. For each question, select <u>one</u> answer choice, unless the instructions state otherwise.

Determining whether an extinct species was bipedal has plagued anthropologists for decades. While the structure of an organism's limbs and the arch of its feet are often noteworthy clues, the difficulty of finding intact fossils of limbs and identifying the species to which the limbs belong has limited the use of such inferences. Skulls, on the other hand, can serve as an ideal proxy, since they are more commonly found in the wild and because they provide a wealth of useful data to determine their species of origin. However, the question of whether skulls can actually provide useful data about bipedalism has been a point of contention for decades. The most compelling evidence in favor of this position comes from the foramen magnum, the large hole at the base of the human skull through which the spinal cord passes. Since Dart's discovery of the "Taung Child," there has been speculation that a forward-shifted foramen magnum is an indicator of bipedalism, since such a shift would have helped to balance the head atop the spinal cord. But most of the arguments to date have been speculative, drawing on just-so theories about the conditions that led to bipedalism rather than empirical studies.

Fortunately, a new investigation by Russo and Kirk has lent additional support to this link. To support the link between bipedalism and a forward-shifting foramen magnum, Russo and Kirk first identified the primary obstacle for proponents of their position: lack of evidence across different species. So, instead of focusing only on humans, they used advanced statistical methods to sample a wealth of mammalian species. They discovered that the foramen magnum in all bipedal mammals was, on average, more forward-positioned than in quadrupedal mammals. Importantly, the researchers used multiple tools and forms of measurements to draw their conclusion, thereby eliminating possible objections about sample size or biased methodology. Though not conclusive, the discovery of such a link should strengthen anthropologists' confidence in using skulls to determine bipedalism. Future research should focus on investigating ways to conduct controlled experiments on the benefits of a forward-shifted foramen magnum.

17. The primary purpose of the passage is to

    (A) explain a conflict and a resolution to that conflict
    (B) explain the significance of a study
    (C) question a standard scientific view
    (D) describe the function of an anatomical feature
    (E) provide a history of a debate

18. It can be inferred that Russo and Kirk's study is useful for which of the following reasons? (Indicate all that apply)

    A It used multiple tools and measurements

    B Skulls can more easily be used to identify a member of a species than can limbs

    C It eliminates other potential functions of the foramen magnum

19. According to the passage, which of the following is true about the foramen magnum? (Indicate all that apply)

    A It was necessary for bipedalism to evolve

    B It can be found in the skulls of all mammals

    C It was first articulated by Dart

Question 20 is based on the passage below. Select one answer choice.

Broomtown's subway system is undergoing a severe budget deficit. Analysts project that the only way to avoid a budget crisis is to increase subway revenue by at least 40 percent. Currently, subway riders pay a flat fare for each ride. The city's chairwoman proposes increasing this fare by 40 percent as an effective way to stave off a budgetary crisis.

20. Which of the following, if true, weakens the likelihood that the chairwoman's proposal will achieve its goal?

    Ⓐ Tokens purchased for subway rides expire after 90 days.

    Ⓑ Based on the current system, fares for subways on the express track are 20 percent greater than fares for subways on the local track.

    Ⓒ On most of the city's major subway routes, bus fares are 20 percent greater than current subway fares.

    Ⓓ Suburban areas, which are not served by many subways, are growing faster than the urban areas that most of the subways serve.

    Ⓔ Part of the reason analysts project a crisis is that the major subways need to be updated.

—————————————————— **STOP.** ——————————————————
This is the end of Section 4.

SECTION 5

Quantitative Reasoning

20 questions — 35 minutes

This section includes four types of questions: Multiple-Choice Questions—Select One Answer, Multiple-Choice Questions—Select One or More Answers, Numeric Entry Questions, and Quantitative Comparisons. Read the following directions before you begin the section.

General Information

- Numbers: All the numbers shown in this section are real numbers.
- Figures: Assume that the position of all points, angles, and so on are in the order shown and the measures of angles are positive.
- All figures lie in a plane unless otherwise stated.
- All straight lines can be assumed to be straight.
- Note that geometric figures are *not necessarily drawn to scale*. Do not try to estimate lengths and sizes of figures in order to answer questions.

Directions

Multiple-Choice Questions—Select One Answer
- Select one answer choice from a list of five choices.

Multiple-Choice Questions—Select One or More Answers
- Select one or more answer choices following the directions given.
- You must select all of the correct answer choices and no others in order to earn credit for the question.
- If the question specifies how many answer choices to select, you must select that number of choices.

Numeric Entry Questions
- Indicate your answer in the box provided with the question.
- Equivalent forms of an answer, such as 1.5 and 1.50, are all correct.
- You do not have to reduce fractions to lowest terms.

Quantitative Comparisons
- These questions present two quantities, Quantity A and Quantity B. Information about one or both of the quantities may be provided in the space between the two quantities. You must compare the two quantities and choose

  - (A) if Quantity A is greater
  - (B) if Quantity B is greater
  - (C) if the two quantities are equal
  - (D) if the relationship between the two quantities cannot be determined

Each of the following questions consists of two quantities, Quantity A and Quantity B. You are to compare the two quantities. You may use additional information centered above the two quantities if additional information is given. Choose

- Ⓐ if Quantity A is greater
- Ⓑ if Quantity B is greater
- Ⓒ if the two quantities are equal
- Ⓓ if the relationship between the two quantities cannot be determined

	QUANTITY A	QUANTITY B	
1.	2^{60}	8^{20}	Ⓐ Ⓑ Ⓒ Ⓓ

$$x^2 - 5x = 6$$
$$-y^2 + 3y = 9y + 9$$

	QUANTITY A	QUANTITY B	
2.	x	y	Ⓐ Ⓑ Ⓒ Ⓓ

Working at a constant rate, Bob can produce $\frac{x}{3}$ widgets in 8 minutes. Working at a constant rate, Jack can produce $2x$ widgets in 40 minutes, where $x > 0$.

	QUANTITY A	QUANTITY B	
3.	The number of minutes it will take Bob to produce $5x$ widgets	The number of minutes it will take Jack to produce $6x$ widgets	Ⓐ Ⓑ Ⓒ Ⓓ

$$t > 1$$

	QUANTITY A	QUANTITY B	
4.	$1/(1 + \frac{3}{2^t})$	$1/(1 + \frac{3}{3^t})$	Ⓐ Ⓑ Ⓒ Ⓓ

From 1992 to 1993, the price of a home increased by x%.
From 1993 to 1994, the price of the home then decreased by x%.

	QUANTITY A	QUANTITY B	
5.	The price of the home at the beginning of 1992	The price of the home at the beginning of 1994	Ⓐ Ⓑ Ⓒ Ⓓ

	QUANTITY A	QUANTITY B	
6.	The product of the consecutive integers from 20 through 73, inclusive.	The product of the consecutive integers from 18 through 72, inclusive.	Ⓐ Ⓑ Ⓒ Ⓓ

GO ON TO NEXT PAGE ➤

Line p is defined by the equation $2y + 3x = 6$

	QUANTITY A	QUANTITY B	
7.	The y-intercept of line p	The x-intercept of line p	Ⓐ Ⓑ Ⓒ Ⓓ

The length of rectangle x is 20% greater than the length of rectangle y.
The width of rectangle x is 20% less than the width of rectangle y.

	QUANTITY A	QUANTITY B	
8.	The area of rectangle x	The area of rectangle y	Ⓐ Ⓑ Ⓒ Ⓓ

For Questions 9 to 14 select one answer choice, unless the instructions state otherwise.

9. If the function $f(x)$ is defined as $f(x) = 3(x + 2) + 5$, then $f(a - 2) =$

Ⓐ $3a$
Ⓑ $3a + 5$
Ⓒ $3a + 11$
Ⓓ $3a - 1$
Ⓔ $3a - 6$

10. If the ratio of stocks to bonds in a certain portfolio is 5:3, then which of the following CANNOT be the total number of stocks and bonds?

Ⓐ 8
Ⓑ 50
Ⓒ 120
Ⓓ 160
Ⓔ 200

For Question 11, write your answer in the box.

11. What is the greatest integer, x, such that $(125^x/25^6) < 1$?

For this question, indicate all of the answer choices that apply.

12. If $(x^3)(y^5) > 0$, and $(x^2)(z^3) < 0$, which of the following must be true?

   A $x > 0$
   B $z < 0$
   C $xy > 0$
   D $yz < 0$
   E $\frac{(x^2)}{z} < 0$
   F $xyz < 0$

13. Five friends agree to split the cost of a lunch equally. If one of the friends does not attend the lunch, the remaining four friends would each have to pay an additional $6. What is the cost of the lunch?

   A $20
   B $24
   C $80
   D $100
   E $120

14. If a six-sided die is rolled three times, what is the probability that the die will land on an even number exactly twice and on an odd number exactly once?

   A $\frac{1}{8}$

   B $\frac{1}{4}$

   C $\frac{3}{8}$

   D $\frac{1}{2}$

   E $\frac{7}{8}$

Questions 15 to 17 are based on the data below. For each question, select one answer, unless the instructions state otherwise.

Revenue and Expenses (in U.S. Dollars) for Company Z, 2000–2009

Note: Gross Profit = Revenue – Expenses

15. For how many years did expenses exceed revenue?

 (A) 1
 (B) 2
 (C) 3
 (D) 7
 (E) 8

16. The percent change in gross profit from 2007 to 2008 is approximately what percent greater than the percent change in gross profit from 2008 to 2009?

 (A) 500%
 (B) 600%
 (C) 1,500%
 (D) 1,600%
 (E) 1,700%

17. If the revenues in 2009 were $3 million less, and the expenses for 2009 were $4 million more, then the average (arithmetic mean) annual profit for the 10 years shown would be approximately how much less?

 (A) $300,000
 (B) $400,000
 (C) $600,000
 (D) $700,000
 (E) $1,000,000

For Questions 18 to 20, select one answer choice, unless the instructions state otherwise.

18. In 1998, the list price of a home was $\frac{1}{3}$ greater than the original price. In 2008, the list price of the home was $\frac{1}{2}$ greater than the original price. By what percent did the list price of the home increase from 1998 to 2008?

    (A) 10%

    (B) 12.5%

    (C) $16\frac{2}{3}$%

    (D) $33\frac{2}{3}$%

    (E) 50%

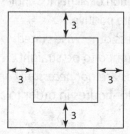

19. The figure above represents a square photograph bordered by a frame that has a uniform width of 3 inches. If the frame and the picture have the same area, and each of the photograph's sides measures x inches, which of the following equations is true?

    (A) $(x + 6)^2 = 2x^2$
    (B) $(x + 3)^2 = 2x^2$
    (C) $(x + 9)^2 = 2x^2$
    (D) $(x + 3)^2 = 4x^2$
    (E) $(x + 6)^2 = 4x^2$

20. On the xy-plane, the center of circle O is at point (3,2). If the point (10,2) lies outside of the circle and the point (3,8) lies inside of the circle, which of the following could be the radius of the circle?

    (A) 5
    (B) 5.5
    (C) 6
    (D) 6.5
    (E) 7

STOP.
This is the end of Section 5.

SECTION 6

Quantitative Reasoning

20 questions — 35 minutes

This section includes four types of questions: Multiple-Choice Questions—Select One Answer, Multiple-Choice Questions—Select One or More Answers, Numeric Entry Questions, and Quantitative Comparisons. Read the following directions before you begin the section.

General Information

- Numbers: All the numbers shown in this section are real numbers.
- Figures: Assume that the position of all points, angles, and so on are in the order shown and the measures of angles are positive.
- All figures lie in a plane unless otherwise stated.
- All straight lines can be assumed to be straight.
- Note that geometric figures are *not necessarily drawn to scale*. Do not try to estimate lengths and sizes of figures in order to answer questions.

Directions

Multiple-Choice Questions—Select One Answer
- Select one answer choice from a list of five choices.

Multiple-Choice Questions—Select One or More Answers
- Select one or more answer choices following the directions given.
- You must select all of the correct answer choices and no others in order to earn credit for the question.
- If the question specifies how many answer choices to select, you must select that number of choices.

Numeric Entry Questions
- Indicate your answer in the box provided with the question.
- Equivalent forms of an answer, such as 1.5 and 1.50, are all correct.
- You do not have to reduce fractions to lowest terms.

Quantitative Comparisons
- These questions present two quantities, Quantity A and Quantity B. Information about one or both of the quantities may be provided in the space between the two quantities. You must compare the two quantities and choose

      (A) if Quantity A is greater
      (B) if Quantity B is greater
      (C) if the two quantities are equal
      (D) if the relationship between the two quantities cannot be determined

Each of the following questions consists of two quantities, Quantity A and Quantity B. You are to compare the two quantities. You may use additional information centered above the two quantities if additional information is given. Choose

   Ⓐ if Quantity A is greater
   Ⓑ if Quantity B is greater
   Ⓒ if the two quantities are equal
   Ⓓ if the relationship between the two quantities cannot be determined

x is a positive integer such that 2^x is a factor of 1,000.

	QUANTITY A	**QUANTITY B**	
1.	the greatest value for x	9	Ⓐ Ⓑ Ⓒ Ⓓ

	QUANTITY A	**QUANTITY B**	
2.	$\sqrt[4]{255}$	4	Ⓐ Ⓑ Ⓒ Ⓓ

$$x > 0$$

	QUANTITY A	**QUANTITY B**	
3.	$\dfrac{27x^{-2}}{9x^{-4}}$	$\dfrac{12^{-1}x^3}{36^{-1}x^2}$	Ⓐ Ⓑ Ⓒ Ⓓ

At a certain company, the average age of the men is 24.7 and the average age of the women is 25.9. The average age of all the employees is 25.5.

	QUANTITY A	**QUANTITY B**	
4.	The percentage of employees at the company who are female	75%	Ⓐ Ⓑ Ⓒ Ⓓ

8 years ago, Jack's age was double Linda's age. In 4 years, Jack's age will be 50% greater than Linda's age.

	QUANTITY A	**QUANTITY B**	
5.	Jack's age 8 years ago	Linda's age in 4 years	Ⓐ Ⓑ Ⓒ Ⓓ

GO ON TO NEXT PAGE ➤

The side lengths of triangle RST are 3, 4, and 6, respectively.

	QUANTITY A	QUANTITY B	
6.	The degree measurement of the largest angle in triangle RST	90	Ⓐ Ⓑ Ⓒ Ⓓ

---

a, b, and c represent the side lengths of a certain triangle.

	QUANTITY A	QUANTITY B	
7.	$2a + 3b$	$2b + c$	Ⓐ Ⓑ Ⓒ Ⓓ

Line l is defined by the equation $y = 2x + 3$.
Line m intersects line l at the point (6, 9).

	QUANTITY A	QUANTITY B	
8.	the slope of line l	the slope of line m	Ⓐ Ⓑ Ⓒ Ⓓ

For question 9, select <u>one</u> answer choice.

9. If x is a positive integer, what is the remainder when 3^{4x+2} is divided by 10?

Ⓐ 1
Ⓑ 3
Ⓒ 5
Ⓓ 7
Ⓔ 9

For question 10, write your answer in the boxes.

10. At a certain company, there are $\frac{3}{5}$ as many managers as there are directors, and each manager earns $\frac{4}{3}$ as much money per week as each director does. Last week, what was the ratio of the total amount earned by managers to the total amount earned by directors?

For question 11 select <u>one</u> answer choice.

11. If $2^a 8^b = 64$ and $9^a 3^b = 27$, then what is the value of a?

   Ⓐ $\frac{1}{2}$

   Ⓑ $\frac{3}{5}$

   Ⓒ $\frac{2}{3}$

   Ⓓ 1

   Ⓔ $\frac{3}{2}$

For this question, indicate all of the answer choices that apply.

12. If $0 < x/y < 1$, then which of the following must be true?

   Ⓐ $\frac{x^2}{y^2} < \frac{x}{y}$

   Ⓑ $\frac{x^2}{y} > \frac{x}{y}$

   Ⓒ $(x+5)/(y+5) < 1$

For question 13, select <u>one</u> answer choice.

13. Working independently at the same constant rate, 9 machines can fill an order in 20 hours. How many of these machines, working independently, would be needed to fill the same order in 45 hours?

   Ⓐ 3

   Ⓑ 4

   Ⓒ 5

   Ⓓ 6

   Ⓔ 7

Questions 14 to 16 refer to the following table. For each question, select <u>one</u> answer, unless the instructions state otherwise.

Shirt Sales for Company		
YEAR	NUMBER OF SHIRTS SOLD	TOTAL REVENUE FROM SHIRTS
2011	25,000	1.1 million
2012	43,000	2.4 million
2013	48,000	2.6 million
2014	46,000	2.7 million
2015	63,000	3.8 million
2016	67,000	4.4 million

For question 14, write your answer in the box.

14. The average revenue per t-shirt was what percent greater in 2012 than in 2011?

   [   ] %

   Round your answer to the nearest tenth of a percent

15. If the total revenue in 2012 had been 50% greater, the average revenue from 2011–2016 would have been approximately how much greater?

   (A) $150,000
   (B) $200,000
   (C) $220,000
   (D) $240,000
   (E) $280,000

16. If, in 2013, the company sold 75% of its shirts for $30, and the rest of the shirts for x dollars, which of the following is closest to the value of x?

   (A) $120
   (B) $125
   (C) $130
   (D) $135
   (E) $140

For questions 17 to 20, select one answer, unless the instructions state otherwise.

17. Last week, Janet worked x hours and earned y dollars per hour. If she plans to reduce the number of hours she works this week by 20%, by what percent would her hourly wage have to increase for her total wage this week to equal her total wage last week?

   (A) 15%
   (B) 20%
   (C) 25%
   (D) 33.3%
   (E) 40%

18. If a fair-sided die is rolled three times, what is the probability that the die will land on a prime number each time?

    Ⓐ 0.0625
    Ⓑ 0.125
    Ⓒ 0.25
    Ⓓ 0.375
    Ⓔ 0.5

For question 19, write your answer in the box.

19. If each edge of a certain cube is tripled in length, the volume of the resulting cube will be how many times the volume of the original cube?

20. In a certain basket, there are 50 apples and 30 bananas. If the same number of apples and bananas is removed, how many of each fruit would have to be removed for the resulting ratio of the new number of apples to the new number of bananas to equal 5:1?

    Ⓐ 5
    Ⓑ 10
    Ⓒ 15
    Ⓓ 20
    Ⓔ 25

—————————————— **STOP.** ——————————————
This is the end of Section 6.

Answers and Explanations

Section 1. Analytical Writing: Analyze an Issue

Use the following scoring rubric to grade your essay. Grade yourself as honestly as possible regarding the organization, structure, fluency, and accuracy of your writing. Then compare your essay to the sample high-scoring response that follows.

	Analyze an Issue: Scoring		
SCORE	FOCUS	ORGANIZATION	CONVENTIONS
0	Does not address the prompt. Off topic.	Incomprehensible. May merely copy the prompt without development.	Illegible. Nonverbal. Serious errors make the paper unreadable. May be in a foreign language.
1	Mostly irrelevant to the prompt.	Little or no development of ideas. No evidence of analysis or organization.	Pervasive errors in grammar, mechanics, and spelling.
2	Unclear connection to the prompt.	Unfocused and disorganized.	Frequent errors in sentence structure, mechanics, and spelling.
3	Limited connection to the prompt.	Rough organization with weak examples or reasons.	Occasional major errors and frequent minor errors in conventions of written English.
4	Competent connection to the prompt.	Relevant examples or reasons develop a logical position.	Occasional minor errors in conventions of written English.
5	Clear, focused connection to the prompt.	Thoughtful, appropriate examples or reasons develop a consistent, coherent position. Connectors are ably used to mark transitions.	Very few errors. Sentence structure is varied and vocabulary is advanced.
6	Insightful, clever connection to the prompt.	Compelling, convincing examples or reasons develop a consistent, coherent position. The argument flows effortlessly and persuasively.	Very few errors. Sentence structure is varied and vocabulary is precise, well chosen, and effective.

Sample Response with a Score of 6

Wherever there are successful entrepreneurs, there will be individuals who argue that education is not a necessary component of financial success. It is certainly true that there are cases of individuals who succeeded in the business world and became quite wealthy without the benefit of an extensive education. Heavyweight boxer George Foreman is one such individual, who went on to have great financial success despite dropping out of high school. Hairstylist Vidal Sassoon and media mogul Walt Disney also dropped out of high school, going on to earn fortunes in their respective fields. And steel magnate Andrew Carnegie gained his enormous financial success without even finishing elementary school!

Admittedly, these individuals were all able to build large businesses and earn great financial rewards without the benefit of an extended formal education, so clearly education is not necessary for a financially-rewarding career. Yet, the Bureau of Labor Statistics records show a distinct positive correlation between educational attainment levels and annual earnings, so it is safe to say that for most people who are not blessed with a stroke of entrepreneurial genius, a good education will result in a better paying job.

One purpose of education is to earn more money, to be sure, but this is not the only goal. Education brings so many more benefits than simply monetary ones. One of its purposes, simply put, is to help us become more fulfilled and live happier lives. On a strictly materialistic level, an educated person with a better paying job is likely to be more satisfied with her standard of living and lifestyle. Education is also critical for helping individuals develop the skills to do work they truly enjoy, which further increases happiness.

Along with helping us lead happier lives, education helps us to develop relationship skills and the emotional maturity to handle life's setbacks. Individuals who play on school sports teams have to learn to deal with other players as they bask in the glory of victory or suffer the agony of defeat. Physical education classes include as part of a curriculum teach students the value of teamwork and how to manage conflicts with other players. Teacher-student interactions can also reveal valuable lessons about how to deal with authority, lessons different from those a student might learn at home. Finally, the friendships inevitably forged as part of the school community's social structure help students to deal with relationships in ways that prepare them for what is to come later in life.

Another important purpose of education is to help students become better problem solvers. This skill may be developed in math courses, where numbers are used to work out problems. It may also be taught in science courses like engineering, where structural queries are posed and students must find ways to work out solutions. Students in the social sciences learn to problem-solve from investigating historical and present-day situations involving human interactions. Even in literature and other humanities courses, problem-solving techniques can be modeled through the messages some literary works convey.

In addition to improving problem-solving, education further serves to build self-confidence. A student who must research data for a school science project will become more adept at navigating through the maze of available information to find concrete facts that address a scientific question. The student who must give an oral presentation in history class strengthens his or her ability to speak in front of peers. Through composition courses and the requirements of essay tests, students become more confident as writers and learn to hone their written skills. Simply the process of answering questions in class can help students to become more confident speakers, skills that may benefit them enormously in later job interviews.

Education also helps individuals to become more valued contributors, in whatever realm they choose to interact. A more educated worker will often have additional skills that enable him to gain not only financial rewards, but also more responsibility in his work. This individual is able to use his judgment more often and to contribute his expertise. He makes leadership decisions based on his own unique perspective, an opportunity that might have been lost had he not had the necessary training for advancement.

Without the education that he obtained before becoming president, for instance, John F. Kennedy might not have been in a position during the Cuban Missile Crisis to make the decisions he did to respond to Russian leader Nikita Khrushchev, and the U.S. might not have avoided a catastrophic war with the Soviet Union. Nobel Prize–winning scientists Marie and Pierre Curie might never have discovered radium or developed their theory of radioactivity without obtaining their educations in science. Their training brought them to a level of skill where they could know enough to experiment and finally succeed, making contributions for which history will always remember them.

Not many of us will be remembered in history for our contributions. But even the first-grade teachers or school social workers who help in a circumscribed community will, due in part to their educations, make contributions that change student's lives. Those students will go on to positively affect others, as Jimmy Stewart's character, George Bailey, recognized about his own contributions in the Christmas movie *It's a Wonderful Life*. Education helps provide individuals with better financial prospects in their jobs, certainly, but that is only part of what it does. Its greater purpose lies in helping empower us as thriving individuals by increasing our own personal happiness, relationship skills, emotional maturity, problem-solving abilities, self-confidence, and societal contributions.

Section 2. Analytical Writing: Analyze an Argument

Use the following scoring rubric to grade your essay. Grade yourself as honestly as possible regarding the organization, structure, fluency, and accuracy of your writing. Then compare your essay to the sample high-scoring response that follows.

Analyze an Argument: Scoring

SCORE	FOCUS	ORGANIZATION	CONVENTIONS
0	Does not address the prompt. Off topic.	Incomprehensible. May merely copy the prompt without development.	Illegible. Nonverbal. Serious errors make the paper unreadable. May be in a foreign language.
1	Little or no analysis of the argument. May indicate misunderstanding of the prompt.	Little or no development of ideas. No evidence of analysis or organization.	Pervasive errors in grammar, mechanics, and spelling.
2	Little analysis. May instead present opinions and unrelated thoughts.	Disorganized and illogical.	Frequent errors in sentence structure, mechanics, and spelling.
3	Some analysis of the prompt, but some major flaws may be omitted.	Rough organization with irrelevant support or unclear transitions.	Occasional major errors and frequent minor errors in conventions of written English.
4	Important flaws in the argument are touched upon.	Ideas are sound but may not flow logically or clearly.	Occasional minor errors in conventions of written English.
5	Perceptive analysis of the major flaws in the argument.	Logical examples and support develop a consistent, coherent critique. Connectors are ably used to mark transitions.	Very few errors. Sentence structure is varied and vocabulary is advanced.
6	Insightful, clever analysis of the argument's flaws and fallacies.	Compelling, convincing examples and support develop a consistent, coherent critique. The analysis flows effortlessly and persuasively.	Very few errors. Sentence structure is varied, and vocabulary is precise, well chosen, and effective.

Sample Response with a Score of 6

The Borlarvia government proposes that fisherman give paid boat tours as a way of ensuring their own livelihood while also preserving the porpoise. To support this recommendation, the government explains that the porpoise has become endangered due to overhunting, that fishermen have a high degree of knowledge about the porpoise's habitat, and that tourists have shown interest in the boat tours. The government's proposal also relies on the central assumption that boat tours, if offered, would earn fisherman enough money to make a good living. To evaluate whether the recommendation is likely to have its predicted result, we must examine several questions pertaining this assumption of the government's plan.

The first question that would need to be answered is: will the tourists pay for boat tours? The government's proposal mentioned that tourists have expressed interest in the boat rides, but expressing interest does not necessarily equate to a willingness to pay for the tours. If the tourists would compensate the tour guides monetarily, then the plan might have a greater chance of succeeding. If it turns out, however, that the tourists aren't willing to pay for the tours and would only attend them if they were free, then the government's plan would not help fishermen earn their living.

A second question to be asked, in addition to knowing whether tourists will pay for the tours, is how much revenue is likely to be generated by the boat tours consistently, on an annual basis? If the projected earnings are sufficient to replace or exceed the fishermen's normal earnings throughout the course of the year, then the boat tour plan would be more likely to achieve its intended result. If the annual revenue would be too low, on the other hand, or if perhaps tour income might be too seasonal to cover what the fishermen would need to earn over a full year, then the government's plan would not provide enough income for the fisherman and would be ineffective.

Along with investigating revenue-related questions, we must also ask about the likely impact of weather and other external factors on the tours. If the weather in Borlarvia is steady year-round, boat tours would be more likely to succeed. If the weather is unpredictable, often rainy, or otherwise problematic, then the boat tour plan would be less effective. Other external factors might also come into play, such as the potential setbacks posed by economic downturns and the risks of water pollution by Borlarvian manufacturing firms or petroleum companies. Economic slow-downs tend to result in people spending less money on non-essential expenses, meaning that fewer tourists would schedule boat rides, and business revenue would diminish. Large-scale pollution could also prevent boat tours during the waste clean-up process, reducing the overall income to the fisherman and thwarting the plan's success.

One final question regarding whether the fishermen could make a good living giving boat tours concerns the fishermen themselves. Do Borlarvian fishermen have the skills and the willingness to successfully conduct boat tours? Knowing a great deal about the habitat of a species does not automatically translate into making a person a good tour guide. Running a successful tour business requires skills that the fisherman might not be accustomed to using on a daily basis, such as dealing with the general public--including children--and managing safety concerns for passengers on their boats. Tour guides would have to be adept at public speaking as well. If the fisherman did have the skills and the willingness to perform this type of job, the government's plan would stand a better chance of succeeding. Otherwise, the plan would not work, because the fishermen would not be effective as tour guides.

The Borlarvian government makes the claim that conducting boat tours will enable fisherman to make a good living while preventing the porpoise from becoming extinct. If this is to be the case, the answers to several key questions will need to be obtained first, to determine whether it would be possible for fisherman to make a good living from this endeavor. The willingness of tourists to pay, the amount of expected revenue, the impact of weather and external factors, and the skill and willingness of the fishermen themselves would all need to be assessed to evaluate whether the plan proposed by the government would be likely to have the predicted result.

Section 3. Verbal Reasoning

1. **B** The word in the blank describes how the professor regarded the student's theory. The clause after the comma provides the clue. Since the professor views parts of the theory as "creative" and parts as "unsound," the professor's view is *conflicted*. Of the choices, the word that best matches *conflicted* is **ambivalent**.

2. **B** The word in the blank clarifies Dylan's "belief in the priority of self-interest." The clause after the colon further clarifies this belief, telling you that "he could never be sure of others' beliefs or desires." **Solipsism**, which is the philosophical belief that we cannot be sure of the existence of other minds, is the best choice.

3. **B and D** There are more clues for the first blank, so start there. Since "a retreat to nature appealed to Thoreau," he most likely *absorbed* himself in the untamed. The word closest in meaning to *absorbed* is **immersion**. What did "immersion in the untamed" put Thoreau in touch with? A good guess would be the word *untamed*. Of the choices, the word closest in meaning to *untamed* is **unpredictability**.

4. **B and F** Since there are more clues for the first blank, start there. The word in the blank describes what component of the institutions the critics focus on. Since the critics are focused on the "greed" of the institutions, a good prediction for the blank is *greed*. The word closest in meaning to greed is **avarice**. Now look at the second blank. The word in the blank is described as something "whose value can and should be quantified economically." A good prediction is *good*. Of the choices, the word closest in meaning to *good* is **commodity**.

5. **C and E** Since there are more clues for the first blank, start there. The word in the blank describes what economists are unable to do, with respect to the causes of recessions. The fact that critics are wrong about this inability implies that, on its face, the inability might be something negative. What would economists be *expected* to do? A good prediction is *explain*. Of the choices, the word closest in meaning to *explain* is **delineate**. Now move to the second blank. The clause after the colon indicates that economists put their faith in "the appropriate mode of analysis." A good prediction for the blank is *approach*. Of the choices, the word closest in meaning to *approach* is **methodologies**.

6. **A, F, and I** There are the most clues for the first blank, so start there. The first blank describes the type of process that most scientific discoveries are. Since they "build on and supplement" previous discoveries, the process is most likely **cumulative**. Now move to the second blank. The contextual clue *but* indicates that discoveries that "alter the trajectory of human thought" are made in a process that is the opposite of *cumulative*. These processes must thus not build on previously established *models*. Of the choices, the word closest in meaning to *models* is **paradigms**. Now look at the third blank. The contextual clue "for example" indicates that Darwin's discovery will provide an example of the previous fact. Since such a discovery must have been made in isolation of previous scientific work, the work of others must not have **anticipated** Darwin's work.

7. **D** First, understand the situation. By limiting the sale of tobacco products, the government decreased a revenue source. Despite that, the government's net

revenues stayed the same since the laws limiting tobacco sales were put into effect. The correct answer will provide a piece of information that explains how the government ended up making more money, despite the ban.

> **Choice A:** If the government ran advertisements, then it spent money, meaning its net revenue would have been even *less*. You want to explain why the revenue went up. Choice A is incorrect.

> **Choice B:** How members of the legislature felt about the law would not affect the government's net revenues. Choice B is incorrect.

> **Choice C:** People's awareness of the health risks of tobacco is irrelevant. Choice C is incorrect.

> **Choice D:** If tobacco use went down, then there were probably fewer tobacco-related illnesses. Fewer tobacco-related illnesses would result in an overall decline in the country's health care expenditures. If all health care in the country is government funded, then Bunrose's loss in tobacco-related revenue would be offset by the decrease in its health care expenses. Choice D explains the discrepancy.

> **Choice E:** If consumers spent the money they saved on private goods, then that money was not going back to the government. Thus no information is given about how the government could have recouped the money it lost by limiting tobacco sales. Choice E is incorrect.

8. **C** This is a *detail* question. To answer the question, find textual evidence that explains the "amusement and scorn." The evidence is in paragraph two. At the end of the paragraph, the author explains why the "entrenched methodologies" explain the resistance. The reason given is that the thinkers of a field will be "unfamiliar with" the new tools and concepts needed to achieve consilience. The correct answer is thus C.

> **Choice A:** A contradicts information in the passage. You are told that "most scientists agree with Wilson's basic premise."

> **Choice B:** B is not supported by the passage.

> **Choice D:** D is not supported by the passage.

> **Choice E:** E is not supported by the passage.

9. **Sentence 2** The first sentence explains what *consilience* is, not why Wilson believed it. In the second sentence, the author provides an explanation for Wilson's belief, that is, the reducibility of all the sciences.

10. **B** To answer an *inference* question, you must draw a conclusion from text in the passage. The passage tells you that scientists are reluctant to accept approaches toward *consilience* because they are "unfamiliar" with the tools necessary to achieve it. Thus it can be concluded that if they were familiar with the tools, they would be more likely to accept *consilience*.

11. **A and D** The contrast signal *though* indicates that the effect of the business plan on the short-term goals of the coffee shop contrasts with the effect on the long-term goals. Since you are told that the plan will "undermine" the

long-term goal of maximizing the coffee shop's profit, it most likely has a *beneficial* effect in the short-term. Of the choices, the words that best match *beneficial* are **profitable** and **lucrative**.

12. **A and B** The contrast signal *though* indicates that the perceptions of the athlete's decision contrast with the fact that it had "some justification." The prediction should thus be a word related to actions done without justification. A good prediction is *impulsive*. Of the choices, the words closest in meaning to *impulsive* are **impetuosity** and **recklessness**.

13. **B and D** The opportunity given to the cooks is described by the fact that the recipe offered "only loose guidelines." If the guidelines were loose, then the cooks were able to practice *flexibility*. Of the choices, the words closest in meaning to *flexibility* are **creativity** and **ingenuity**.

14. **B and C** The contrast signal *despite* indicates that the meaning of the word in the blank contrasts with the fact that there have been "strides" in neuroscience. The word *downright* indicates that this description is more extreme than "incomplete." A good prediction would be *lacking*. Of the choices, the words closest in meaning to *lacking* are **porous** and **negligible**.

15. The author begins the passage by introducing a commonly held belief ("There exists a linear and continuous relationship between the themes and characters of a novelist's works and the life of the novelist himself") and then moves on to mention that this belief is not *always* valid. The author then uses Dostoevsky's life and novels to show that though not always valid, the belief has merit. The answer that best captures the main point of the passage is C.

    Choice A: A is not supported by any information in the passage.

    Choice B: B is too narrow. Though the author does discuss the impact of the firing squad on Dostoevsky, he does this to make the larger point that Dostoevsky's experiences influenced his novels.

    Choice D: D is incorrect because the passage is not concerned with the "believability" of Dostoevsky's novels.

    Choice E: E is too narrow. The author suggests that intense experiences affected Dostoevsky, but this idea is not the main point of the passage.

16. To answer a *purpose* question, you should determine *why* the author provides the given information. In this case, you want to know why the author mentions *Crime and Punishment* and *The Brothers Karamazov*. The author mentions Dostoevsky to show that a novelist's experiences are reflected in the novelist's works. The author uses these novels as examples of novels whose themes were influenced by events in Dostoevsky's life. The best answer is thus A.

    Choice B: B is incorrect because it does not address *why* the author mentions these novels. Though the author does suggest that they have "existential and redemptive" themes, the author's concern is how Dostoevsky's experiences led to his development of these themes.

    Choice C: C is incorrect because the passage does not suggest any concern with a contrast between the different themes of Dostoevsky's novels.

Choice D: D is incorrect because it is too narrow. Though the author suggests that Dostoevsky's experience with the firing squad influenced the themes of his novels, the author mentions the novels to support his main point.

Choice E: E is incorrect because the choice is not supported by anything mentioned in the passage.

17. **B** When answering a *vocabulary in-context* question, use clues in the sentence to make your own prediction for the correct answer. The first sentence states that "It is a belief so common as to be hackneyed." *Hackneyed* must thus have a definition similar in meaning to *common*. Of the choices, the word closest in meaning to *common* is **cliché**.

18. **A** First, identify the situation: The government banned price increases on prescription drugs, but per capita expenditure on prescription drugs went up. The correct choice will provide information that resolves these apparently contradictory facts.

    Choice A: If this choice is true, then it can be inferred that, per person, the amount spent on prescription drugs increased. This information thus helps to explain the discrepancy. The correct answer is A.

    Choice B: The actions that the pharmaceutical company took to offset losses in revenue are irrelevant to the situation.

    Choice C: If the population increased, you would expect per capita expenditures to have *decreased*, not increased.

    Choice D: More affordable generic drugs would more likely lead to a decrease in per capita expenditure, not to an increase.

    Choice E: The source of the drugs is irrelevant.

19. The main point is expressed in the passage's first sentence. The author spends the rest of the passage evaluating the pros and cons of the symphony. The best answer is B.

    Choice A: Though the author "wonders about the impetus behind this decision to use Schiller's *Ode to Joy*," nowhere else in the passage does the author consider Beethoven's motivations.

    Choice C: The author does discuss the differences between the first three movements and the last movement, but the author discusses these differences in the context of criticizing the fourth movement.

    Choice D: The author mentions Beethoven's deafness as one of the reasons for the symphony's positive reception. However, this issue of deafness is not addressed anywhere else in the passage. This choice is thus too narrow in scope.

    Choice E: The author does discuss the text of Beethoven's Ninth Symphony, but he does so to make a larger point about what he considers the symphony's flaws.

20. **A and B**

> **Choice A:** The author states: "the first three movements of the symphony rightfully receive nearly universal praise from music critics and composers alike." The use of the word *rightfully* implies that the author agrees with these critics.
>
> **Choice B:** The author states: "One wonders about the impetus behind this decision to use Schiller's *Ode to Joy*, a text that praises the divine that is always implicit in Beethoven's work, but that does so in such an overt way that the previous movements are almost rendered superfluous." The use of the word *superfluous* implies that the author believes the movement is unnecessary.
>
> **Choice C:** Though the author questions the use of text in the fourth movement, he says nothing to imply that the movement is of no scholarly value. Thus this choice cannot be inferred.

Section 4. Verbal Reasoning

1. **A** How would we characterize the task of explaining something that we can barely access? A good prediction is "impossible." The answer is A.

2. **C and D** The trigger is the colon, which indicates that the second part of the sentence will clarify the "contradictions…in his worldview." The contradiction concerns his moral positions and his behavior. While he was willing to make claims about morality, he was less willing to practice them. The correct answers are thus C and D.

3. **B and E** Start with the first blank. If the declaration was "well-considered" then what it "could hardly be thought of as" (in other words, what it is *not*) is negative—eliminate A and C. The answer is B. For the second blank, the signal "still" indicates that the types of murmurs are the opposite of what you'd expect from an inoffensive statement. The best answer is "disapproval."

4. **A and F** Start with the first blank: What kind of material would the book be obscured in if it were only accessible to academic circles? The best answer is "jargon." Move on to the second blank. The author feels that the inaccessibility is always lamentable, but particularly now, so he considers the case "upsetting." The best answer is "disheartening."

5. **A and E** Start with the second blank. If his friends take his good-naturedness at face value, then he is probably opposed to "inauthenticity." The best match is "subterfuge." Now go to the first blank. The characteristic being referred to is his good-naturedness. The best match for that is "geniality."

6. **D** The key clue here is that whatever characteristic she had was frowned upon in the "hyper-specialized" discipline. We can thus predict that her characteristic is the opposite of hyper-specialization. A good prediction is "wide." The best match is "eclecticism."

7. **C** "Porous" is used in a negative context, so eliminate A and D. The author mentions that "materialism" has merit, so eliminate B. The author does not indicate that materialism is meaningless, so eliminate E. The answer is C.

8. **Sentence 7** "Quantum physics shows us…" The only question in the passage is, "But what are we to make of consciousness?" The answer comes two lines later, "Quantum physics has an answer: the question is senseless." The explanation for this answer is the following sentence.

9. **C** The author mentions "how much progress has been made in various scientific disciplines" when explaining its "vaunted status among the sciences." The clue "but" tells us that the author's point in this sentence is in contrast to the point of the following sentence. The question, "But what about consciousness?" serves to highlight materialism's shortcomings, so the mention of progress is most likely meant to "explain materialism's popularity."

10. **C** The passage discusses the shortcomings of the materialist position to show that, as long as neuroscientists are committed to this position, they will never be able to explain consciousness. The best answer is C.

11. **A** We want to find the answer showing that the relatively lower price of Kantanistan computers won't stimulate Errulian computer buyers to switch over to Kantanistan computers. Choice A does this by showing a competing reason for Errulians to buy Errulian computers. Though the computers made in Errulia might be more expensive, they are also higher quality, thus justifying the higher price that Errulians would have to pay.

12. **C and D** How would you characterize someone who leaves you guessing about his mood at every moment? A good, simple guess is "moody." The best answers are C and D.

13. **A and F** If you view occasional confusion as a general quality, then you risk overlooking the opposite of confusion. A good guess would be "mental clarity." The best matches are A and F.

14. **B and D** The word in the blank refers to the act of "overlooking shortcomings," or in other words, not mentioning something. When someone fails to mention something, that person is "ignoring" that fact. The best matches are B and D. Notice that A doesn't quite fit since the author doesn't deny the shortcomings; she simply fails to mention them.

15. **D and E** The characteristic the blank describes is "a commentary on the serendipity" of research. If many findings are serendipitous, then the outcomes are different from what was expected. A good prediction for the blank would thus be "difference." The best matches are "discordance" and "incongruity."

16. **C** The basis of the conclusion is a correlation between sleep cycles and expressed closeness in a relationship. From this correlation, the author concludes that the sleep cycles *cause* the lack of closeness. To weaken the argument, we want to identify a different explanation for the correlation. Choice C does this by showing that lack of closeness leads to different sleep cycles, rather than the reverse.

    Choice A is incorrect because couples without such misaligned cycles are irrelevant to the argument.

    Choice B is incorrect because it strengthens rather than weakens the argument.

    Choice D is incorrect because it is irrelevant to the argument.

    Choice E is incorrect because the length of the relationship is not necessarily relevant to the argument.

17. **B** The author structures the passage by providing an introduction to a debate and then presenting a study that supports one side of the debate. While choice A might be tempting, the study does not provide a resolution. The best answer is B.

18. **A and B** In line 27, the author says, "Importantly, the researchers used multiple tools and forms of measurements to draw their conclusion," so choice A is true. In the third sentence, the author says, "Skulls, on the other hand, can serve as an ideal proxy, since they are more commonly found in the wild and because they provide a wealth of useful data to determine their species of origin." The author mentions this as a reason it would be beneficial to use skulls to infer whether a species is bipedal. Since Russo and Kirk's study strengthens the relationship between skulls and bipedalism, we can infer that this fact makes their study useful. There is no support for choice C.

19. **B** Let's go through each choice:

   Choice A Though there is a link between the foramen magnum and bipedalism, nothing in the passage indicates that the foramen magnum was necessary for bipedalism to evolve.

   Choice B The author says, "They discovered that the foramen magnum in all bipedal mammals was, on average, more forward-positioned than in quadrupedal mammals." The phrasing of this sentence implies that all mammals have a foramen magnum.

   Choice C The passage says, "Since Dart's discovery of the 'Taung Child,' there has been speculation that a forward-shifted foramen magnum is an indicator of bipedalism." From this sentence, it may be tempting to conclude that Dart was the first to present the theory, but such an inference is not warranted by the information in the passage.

20. **C** To weaken the argument, we want to show that increasing subway fare by 40 percent won't lead to the necessary increase in subway revenue. Choice C does this by showing that, after the increase, people can just use the cheaper buses instead of the more expensive subways.

   Choice A is incorrect because the relatively fast expiration date means that people wouldn't be able to hoard tokens before the increase, thus strengthening her plan.

   Choice B is incorrect because the argument concerns all subway fares, not express versus local.

   Choice D is incorrect because it's a fact that we need to increase subway revenue by 40 percent. Whether a larger percentage of people aren't taking subways in the near future is irrelevant.

   Choice E provides a reason for the crisis, but doesn't address the logic of the chairwoman's proposal.

Section 5. Quantitative Reasoning

1. **C** The simplest way to simplify the comparison is to rewrite the value of Quantity B using a base of 2: $8 = 2^3$, so $8^{20} = (2^3)^{20} = 2^{60}$.

2. **A** When working with quadratic equations, you should manipulate them to be in the form: $x^2 + bx + c = 0$. The first quadratic equation will thus read: $x^2 - 5x - 6 = 0$, and the second equation will read: $y^2 + 6y + 9 = 0$. Next, factor both equations. The first equation factors to: $(x - 6)(x + 1) = 0$, so $x = 6$ or $x = -1$. The second equation factors to $(y + 3)^2 = 0$, so $y = -3$. When $x = 6$, quantity A is greater. When $x = -1$, quantity A is greater.

3. **C** Using the $R = \frac{W}{T}$ formula, you know that Bob's rate is: $\frac{x}{3}/8 = \frac{x}{24}$, and Jack's rate is $\frac{2x}{40} = \frac{x}{20}$. To arrive at an expression for Quantity A, use $R \times T = W$. $\frac{x}{24}t = 5x$. Solve for t:

$$t = \frac{5x}{\frac{x}{24}}$$
$$t = 5x \times \frac{24}{x}$$
$$t = 120$$

To arrive at an expression for Quantity B, use $R \times T = W$. $(\frac{x}{20})t = 6x$. Solve for t:

$$t = \frac{6x}{\frac{x}{20}}$$
$$t = 6x \times \frac{20}{x}$$
$$t = 120$$

The values in the quantities are equal.

4. **B** Since the fractions in the two columns have the same numerator, the fraction with the smaller denominator will yield the larger quantity. Thus the comparison is:

$$1 + \frac{3}{2^t} \text{ versus } 1 + \frac{3}{3^t}$$

Subtract 1 from both sides:

$$\frac{3}{2^t} \text{ versus } \frac{3}{3^t}$$

Since $t > 1$, $\frac{3}{3^t}$ will be smaller than $\frac{3}{2^t}$, which means that the denominator in Quantity B is smaller than the denominator in Quantity A. Therefore, the value of Quantity B is greater than the value of Quantity A. If one were to plug in a value of 2 for t then one would see that Quantity A is 0.5714 while Quantity B is 0.7518.

5. **A** It might be tempting to choose C here since the percent increase and decrease are the same. However, note that since the price of the home is greater in 1993 than in 1992, the percent decrease will be taken from a bigger whole than will the percent increase. This means that the decrease from 1993 to 1994 will be greater than the increase from 1992 to 1993. Thus the price of the home in 1994 will be less than the price of the home in 1992.

6. **B** It might be tempting to use your calculator to determine the value of both columns. However, it is important to recognize that Quantitative Comparison questions will almost never require such time-intensive calculations. The more efficient approach is to see how the factors in the two columns differ. Rewrite the following as:

Quantity A → $(20 \times 21 \times 22 \ldots 72) \times 73$

Quantity B → $18 \times 19 \times (20 \times 21 \times 22 \ldots 72)$

Note that the two quantities share the factors of 20–72, inclusive. Thus the real quantities to be compared are 73 in Column A and 18×19 in Column B. (18×19) is greater than 73.

7. **A** To determine the y-intercept of the line, substitute 0 for x and solve for y. Thus:

$$2y + 3(0) = 6$$

$$2y = 6$$

$$y = 3$$

To determine the x-intercept of the line, substitute 0 for y and solve for x. Thus:

$$2(0) + 3x = 6$$

$$3x = 6$$

$$x = 2$$

The y-intercept of the line is 3 and the x-intercept is 2. Quantity A is greater.

8. **B** Substitute values. Let the length of rectangle $y = 10$. The length of rectangle x is thus $1.2(10) = 12$. Let the width of rectangle $y = 10$. The width of rectangle x is thus $0.8(10) = 8$. The area of rectangle x is thus $12 \times 8 = 96$. The area of rectangle y is thus $10 \times 10 = 100$. The area of rectangle y is greater.

9. **B** Substitute $(a - 2)$ for x in the function and arrive at:

$$f(a - 2) = 3(a - 2 + 2) + 5$$

$$= 3a + 5$$

10. **B** If the ratio of stocks to bonds is 5:3, then you can represent the number of stocks as $5x$, where x is an integer, and the number of bonds as $3x$. Therefore, the total number of stocks and bonds will be $8x$. Since x is an integer, the sum must be a multiple of 8. Of the choices, 50 is the only value that is not a multiple of 8.

11. **3** Since you are solving for x, isolate the variable by multiplying both sides of the inequality by 25^6. The inequality now reads: $\frac{125^x}{25^6} < 1$. Next, rewrite 125^x as $(5^3)^x = 5^{3x}$, and rewrite 25^6 as $(5^2)^6 = 5^{12}$. The inequality now reads: $125^x < 25^6$. Because the bases are the same:

$$3x < 12$$

$$x < 4$$

If $x < 4$, the greatest possible integer value for x is 3.

12. **B, C, E, and F** Interpret the given information using properties of positives and negatives. In the first inequality, the exponents are odd, meaning that the sign of the bases is preserved. Thus if $(x^3)(y^5) > 0$, then $xy > 0$. If $xy > 0$, then x and y are *both positive or both negative*. In the second inequality, you know that x^2 is always positive. Thus, $z^3 < 0$. If $z^3 < 0$, then $z < 0$. Now look at the choices. Based on the inferences you made, B, C, E, and F must be true.

13. **E** Let c represent the cost of the lunch. The original cost per person for the lunch is: $\frac{c}{5}$. After a friend drops out, the cost per person is $\frac{c}{4}$. The prompt tells you that the cost per person after a friend drops out is $6 more than the original cost per person. You can express this relationship algebraically as:

$$\frac{c}{4} = \frac{c}{5} + 6$$

To get rid of the denominator, multiply through the equation by 20, the least common multiple of 4 and 5. Arrive at:

$$5c = 4c + 120$$

$$c = 120$$

14. **C** The outcome you are looking for is any combination of even-even-odd. Since all three conditions must be met, you should calculate each individual probability and multiply them. The probability of landing on even $= \frac{1}{2}$, and the probability of landing on odd $= \frac{1}{2}$. Thus, the probability of the outcome even-even-odd $= (\frac{1}{2})(\frac{1}{2})(\frac{1}{2}) = \frac{1}{8}$. However, note that $\frac{1}{8}$ represents the ordering even-even-odd. The outcome in the question can be satisfied when the order is even-even-odd, even-odd-even, or odd-even-even. Since there are three arrangements that satisfy what the question is asking for, multiply $\frac{1}{8}$ by $3 = \frac{3}{8}$.

15. **B** The point corresponding to expenses is above the point corresponding to revenues for two of the years (2000 and 2001). The correct answer is B.

16. **D** First, calculate the percent change in profit for the two time periods. In 2007, the profit was approximately $18 million − $15 million = $3 million. In 2008, the profit was approximately $26 million − $12 million = $14 million. The approximate percent change in profits from 2007 to 2008 was thus:

$$\frac{14 \text{ million} - 3 \text{ million}}{3 \text{ million}} \times 100 = 366.66\%$$

In 2009, the profit was approximately $29 million − $18 million = $11 million. The approximate percent change in profit from 2008 to 2009 was thus:

$$\frac{14 \text{ million} - 11 \text{ million}}{14 \text{ million}} = 21.4\%$$

Now the question is, 366.66 is approximately what percent greater than 21.4? Use the percent change formula:

$$\text{percent change} = \frac{\text{change in value}}{\text{original value}} \times 100$$

Plug the values into the formula:

$$\text{percent change} = \frac{366.66 - 21.4}{21.4} \times 100 = 1{,}613\%$$

The closest answer is choice D.

17. **D** profit = revenue – cost. The change in profit during this time period would be: –$3 million – $4 million = –$7 million. Since the change would distribute evenly throughout the 10-year period, the change in the average would be:

    change in profit/number of years = $7 million/10 = $700,000

18. **B** When working with questions that provide only fractions or percents and *no* given amounts, the best strategy is to plug in numbers. Since the list price increases by $\frac{1}{3}$ and by $\frac{1}{2}$, choose an original value for the list price that is divisible by 2 and 3: 600. The price in 1998 was thus 600 + $\frac{1}{3}$(600) = 800. The price in 2008 was 600 + $\frac{1}{2}$(600) = 900. Now use the percent change formula:

    $$\frac{change}{original} \times 100$$

    The change is 900 – 800 = 100. The original value is the price of the home in 2008, which was 800. Arrive at: $\frac{100}{800} \times 100 = 12.5\%$.

19. **A** If the frame has a uniform width of 3 inches, then each side of the frame must measure $x + 6$ inches. The area of the larger square is thus $(x + 6)^2$. Since each side of the photograph measures x inches, the area of the photograph is x^2.

    the area of the frame = the area of the larger square – the area of the photograph

    Thus the area of the frame = $(x + 6)^2 – x^2$. Since the area of the frame equals the area of the photograph, you can arrive at the following equation: $(x + 6)^2 – x^2 = x^2$. Add x^2 to both sides: $(x + 6)^2 = 2x^2$.

20. **D** With a "could be true" question, you need to identify a property for the given unknown that is satisfied by only one of the choices. The distance between the center of the circle and the point (10,2) is 7. Since (10,2) lies outside of the circle, the radius must be less than 7. The distance between the center of the circle and the point (3,8) is 6. Since the point (3,8) lies inside of the circle, the radius of the circle must be greater than 6. The radius of the circle is thus between 6 and 7. Of the choices, the only value between 6 and 7 is 6.5.

Section 6. Quantitative Reasoning

1. **B** x represents the number of times that 2 appears in the prime factorization of 1,000. So to determine possible values for x, let's break 1,000 down into its prime factors and determine how many 2s appear. $1,000 = 4 \times 250 = 4 \times 2 \times 125 = 2 \times 2 \times 2 \times 5 \times 5 \times 5$. So 1,000 has three 2s, which means the greatest value for x is 3.

2. **B** Don't solve! Since quantity A is so ugly, we should manipulate the quantities to get rid of the radical.

   To eliminate the fourth-root, take both sides to the power of 4. Now, quantity $A = 255$, and quantity $B = 4^4 = 256$. Therefore, quantity B is larger.

3. **D** As a general rule, you should try to eliminate negative exponents within a fraction. To do so, we can use the following rule: $a^{-x}/b^{-x} = b^x/a^x$. Let's apply this rule to each quantity.

   Quantity A will come out to: $\frac{27x^4}{9x^2}$

   Quantity B will come out to: $\frac{36x^3}{12x^2}$

   Now, let's simplify both quantities further:

   Divide Quantity A to arrive at $\frac{3x^4}{x^2} \to 3x^2$

   Divide Quantity B to arrive at $\frac{3x^3}{x^2} \to 3x$

   You may be tempted to choose Quantity A, since x is raised to a larger exponent than in Quantity B, but don't forget to consider "weird" numbers!

   If $x = 1$, then Quantity A = 3 and Quantity B = 3, in which case the quantities are equal. If $x = 2$, then Quantity A = 12, and Quantity B = 6, in which case Quantity A is greater. Since there is more than one relationship, the answer is D.

4. **B** Don't solve! Assume that the value of Quantity A is 75% and determine how that value would relate to the given information. Let's use the weighted average formula to understand this relationship.

   If 75% of the company is female, then 25% is male, in which case the "weight" of the female employees is 0.75 and the weight of the male employees is 0.25. Plugging these values into the weighted average formula, we arrive at:

   $$0.25(24.7) + 0.75(25.9) = 25.6$$

   Since 25.6 > 25.5, we know that the actual percentage of female employees needs to be smaller. Therefore, Quantity B is greater.

5. **C** Set up the given information algebraically. Let j = Jack's current age and l = Linda's current age. 8 years ago, Jack's age was thus $j - 8$, and Linda's age was $l - 8$. Now, use this information to create an algebraic relationship: $j - 8 = 2(l - 8)$. The second relationship concerns their ages in 4 years. At that point, Jack's age will be $j + 4$, and Linda's age will be $l + 4$. We can create the relationship: $j + 4 = 1.5(l + 4)$.

Now, we have a system of equations:

$$j - 8 = 2(l - 8)$$

$$j + 4 = 1.5(l + 4)$$

Simplify the first equation to arrive at: $j - 8 = 2l - 16 \rightarrow j = 2l - 8$. Now, substitute $2l - 8$ for j in the second equation and simplify:

$(2l - 8) + 4 = 1.5(l + 4) \rightarrow 2l - 4 = 1.5l + 6 \rightarrow .5l = 10 \rightarrow l = 20$. Now we can use $l = 20$ to solve for Jack's age. $j = 2l - 8 = 2(20) - 8 = 32$.

So Jack's current age is 32, and Linda's current age is 20. Therefore, 8 years ago, Jack's age was 24, and, in 4 years, Linda's age will be 24. The quantities are equal.

6. **A** A property of a triangle with sides of length a, b, and c, where c is the longest side, is that, if $a^2 + b^2 < c^2$, then the triangle is obtuse, meaning one angle has a measurement greater than 90 degrees. Since the above inequality applies to triangle RST, we can infer that it is obtuse. Therefore, Quantity A is greater.

7. **A** First, simplify the comparison by subtracting $2b$ from both quantities to arrive at:

Quantity A: $2a + b$

Quantity B: c

Now, we can use the rule: the length of any given side of a triangle must be greater than the difference of the other two sides and less than the sum of those two sides. From this rule, we can conclude that $c < a + b$. Since $c < a + b$ and $2a + b > a + b$, we can conclude that $2a + b > c$.

8. **D** We know that the slope of line l is 2, but knowing the point of intersection is not enough to learn anything about the slope of line m. Therefore, a relationship between the two quantities cannot be determined.

9. **E** When any number is divided by 10, the remainder is determined by the units digit of that number, so our real goal is to determine the units digit of 3^{4x+2}. To do so, let's choose a simple value for x: $x = 1$.

Thus, $3^{4x+2} = 3^6 = 729$.

In this case, the units digit is 9. Since there's only one answer to this question, the fact that the units digit now is 9 means that the units digit will always be 9. The answer is thus E.

10. $\frac{4}{5}$ Since this question has only fractions and no actual values, we should choose smart numbers. Let the number of directors = 5. In that case, the number of managers = 3. Let the amount earned per week by each director = 3. In that case, the amount earned per week by each manager is 4. The total

amount earned last week by all the managers is thus: amount per manager * number of managers = 3 * 4 = 12. The total amount earned last week by all the directors is thus: amount per director * number of directors = 3 * 5 = 15. The resulting ratio is thus $\frac{12}{15}$, which reduces to $\frac{4}{5}$.

11. **B** When dealing with exponential terms, it's usually a good idea to express the bases in their prime form, after which we can employ any relevant exponent rules. Start with the first equation: 2^a is already in prime form, so let's express 8^b in its prime factorization: $8 = 2^3$, so $8^b = (2^3)^b = 2^{3b}$. Let's also express 64 in its prime factorization. $64 = 2^6$. Now, the equation reads:

$$2^a 2^{3b} = 2^6$$

Simplify: $2^a 2^{3b} = 2^{a+3b} = 2^6$. Since both sides are expressed in base 2, the exponents must be equal. Thus, $a + 3b = 6$.

Now, let's do the same thing for the second equation: $9^a = (3^2)^a = 3^{2a}$, and $27 = 3^3$. So the second equation reads: $3^{2a} * 3^b = 3^3$. Since both sides are expressed in base 3, the exponents must be equal. Thus, $2a + b = 3$.

We now have a system of equations:

$a + 3b = 6$

$2a + b = 3$

Since we want to solve for a, let's isolate b in the second equation: $b = 3 - 2a$. Now substitute $3 - 2a$ for b in the first equation:

$$a + 3(3 - 2a) = 6 \rightarrow a + 9 - 6a = 6 \rightarrow -5a = -3 \rightarrow a = \frac{3}{5}$$

12. **A and C**

   Choice A: From the given information, we know that x/y is a positive proper fraction. If you multiply a positive proper fraction by itself, the result will be smaller than the original fraction. Thus, choice A must be true.

   Choice B: Choose values: If $x = 3$ and $y = 4$, then $x^2/y = 3^2/4 = \frac{9}{4}$, which is greater than $\frac{3}{4}$. However, if $x = \frac{1}{2}$ and $y = 2$, then $x^2/y = \frac{1}{4}/2 = \frac{1}{8}$, which is not greater than $\frac{1}{4}$. Thus, choice B doesn't have to be true.

   Choice C: Choose values: If $x = 1$ and $y = 2$, then $x + \frac{5}{y} + 5 = \frac{6}{7}$, which is less than 1. Now try fractions: if $x = \frac{1}{2}$, and $y = \frac{2}{3}$, then $x + \frac{5}{y} + 5 = \frac{1}{2} + 5/\frac{2}{3} + 5 = \frac{11}{2}/\frac{17}{3}$, which is less than 1. Choice C must be true.

13. **B** The fastest way to answer this question is to think about the job in terms of the unit machine-hours. If 9 machines need 20 hours to do the job, then the job requires 9 machines * 20 hours = 180 machine-hours. This is a fixed amount, so, to do the same job, any change in the number of machines will cause an inverse change in the number of hours, and vice versa. So, to solve for the number of machines, n, needed to do the job in 45 hours, we can create the equation: n machines * 45 hours = 180 machine-hours. Solve for n: $n = \frac{180}{45} = 4$.

14. **26.8%** To determine the average revenue per t-shirt in a given year, use the formula: total revenue/number of t-shirts. For 2012, this comes out to $2.4 million/43,000 = ~$55.81. For 2011, this comes out to $1.1 million/25,000 = $44. Now, use the percent greater formula: (larger − smaller)/smaller * 100. Plugging in the values, we arrive at: [(55.81 − 44)/44] * 100 = ~26.8%.

15. **B** A 50% increase in the 2012 revenue would equal 0.5($2.4 million) = $1.2 million. To determine how this increase would affect the average for all 6 years, divide the total increase by the number of years: $1.2 million/6 years = $200,000.

16. **B** The total revenue from the shirts priced at $30 was 0.75(48,000)($30) = $1.08 million. The total revenue from the other 12,000 shirts thus equals $2.6 million − $1.08 million = $1.52 million. The revenue per shirt for the remaining 25% of the shirts thus equals total revenue/ number of shirts = $1.52 million/12,000 = $126.66. The closest answer is B.

17. **C** A simple way to answer this question is to choose values. Let $x = 20$, and let $y = 100$. Based on these values, her income last week was $2,000. If she reduces her hours by 20%, then the new number of hours worked will equal 20(0.8) = 16. The new hourly wage, h, will be such that $16h = 2,000$. Solve for h: 2,000/16 = $125. $125 is 25% greater than $100. Her hourly wage will thus have to increase by 25%.

18. **B** The prime numbers from 1-6 are 2, 3, and 5. The probability that the die will land on a prime number on any one roll is thus $\frac{3}{6} = \frac{1}{2}$. For the die to land on a prime number on 3 consecutive rolls, multiply the probability that each individual event will occur: 0.5 * 0.5 * 0.5 = 0.125.

19. **27** The fastest way to answer this question is to choose a value for the edge of the original cube. Let's assign the value 2. In that case, the volume of the original cube = $2^3 = 8$. If the edge length of the original cube was 2, then the edge length of the new cube = 2 * 3 = 6. The volume of the new cube thus = $6^3 = 216$. Finally, to determine how many times greater the volume of the new cube is, divide 216 by 8 to arrive at 27.

20. **E** Let the number of apples and bananas removed = x. In that case, we can create the proportion: (new number apples)/(new number bananas) = $(50 − x)/(30 − x) = \frac{5}{1}$. Cross-multiply to arrive at:

$50 − x = 150 − 5x$. Isolate x: $4x = 100 \rightarrow x = 25$.

Sample Scaled Scores

The following table gives an approximate idea of the scaled score that you would receive for your performance on the diagnostic test. The figures are approximations because the scaling is different for every form of the GRE test. (This process is necessary to ensure that scores on each test form are equivalent to scores on every other test form.) So do not assume that the scaled scores shown below are exactly the ones that you would receive on the real GRE. Use this information only to get a general idea of how your performance would be rated.

Sample Scoring for Quantitative and Verbal Sections			
NUMBER OF CORRECT QUESTIONS	SCALED SCORE	NUMBER OF CORRECT QUESTIONS	SCALED SCORE
0	130	21	151
1	131	22	152
2	132	23	153
3	133	24	154
4	134	25	155
5	135	26	156
6	136	27	157
7	137	28	158
8	138	29	159
9	139	30	160
10	140	31	161
11	141	32	162
12	142	33	163
13	143	34	164
14	144	35	165
15	145	36	166
16	146	37	167
17	147	38	168
18	148	39	169
19	149	40	170
20	150		

Evaluation Charts

Once you have reviewed the answers and explanations to the GRE diagnostic test and scored your performance, use that information to help you plan your GRE study program.

Two charts follow, one for the Verbal Reasoning section of the test and one for the Quantitative Reasoning section. For each question that you missed, find the item number in one of these two charts. Check the column on the left to see the test content area for that item. If you missed questions in a particular content area, you need to focus on that area as you prepare for the GRE. The chapters that cover that content area are listed in the column on the right.

GRE Diagnostic Test: Verbal Reasoning, Section 3

CONTENT AREA	ITEM NUMBER	CHAPTERS TO REVIEW
Text Completion	1, 2, 3, 4, 5, 6	4
Sentence Equivalence	11, 12, 13, 14	5
Reading Comprehension	7, 8, 9, 10, 15, 16, 17, 18, 19, 20	6

GRE Diagnostic Test: Verbal Reasoning, Section 4

CONTENT AREA	ITEM NUMBER	CHAPTERS TO REVIEW
Text Completion	1, 2, 3, 4, 5, 6	4
Sentence Equivalence	11, 12, 13, 14	5
Reading Comprehension	7, 8, 9, 10, 15, 16, 17, 18, 19, 20	6

GRE Diagnostic Test: Quantitative Reasoning, Section 5

CONTENT AREA	ITEM NUMBER	CHAPTERS TO REVIEW
Number Properties	1, 2, 3	9
Part-to-Whole Relationships	4, 14, 18	10
Algebra	9, 12	11
From Words to Algebra	5, 6, 11, 13	12
Geometry	7, 8, 19, 20	13
Data Interpretation	10, 15, 16, 17	14

GRE Diagnostic Test: Quantitative Reasoning, Section 6

CONTENT AREA	ITEM NUMBER	CHAPTERS TO REVIEW
Number Properties	1, 9	9
Part-to-Whole Relationships	10, 12, 17, 20	10
Algebra	2, 3, 11	11
From Words to Algebra	4, 5, 13, 18	12
Geometry	6, 7, 8, 19	13
Data Interpretation	14, 15, 16	14

PART 2

GRE Analytical Writing and Verbal Reasoning

CHAPTER 3

The Analytical Writing Measure

Study this chapter to learn about:

- How analytical writing is scored
- How to approach the Analyze an Issue task
- How to approach the Analyze an Argument task

The first two sections of the GRE consist of two separately timed 30-minute writing tasks: Analyze an Issue and Analyze an Argument. The **Analyze an Issue** task will present you with an opinion and ask you to articulate your perspective on the opinion expressed. To do so, you are expected to draw on personal experiences and knowledge to support your point. There is no correct answer to these questions, and you should not feel compelled to take a stance that you agree with. Instead, you should focus on crafting an argument for which you have the most evidence to reinforce your point.

The **Analyze an Argument** is complementary to the Analyze an Issue task. Whereas, the Analyze an Issue task expects you to bring in outside information to support your point, the Analyze an Argument task provides you with an argument and asks you to address its cogency. To do so, your focus should be on identifying assumptions within the argument and evidence that would be necessary to strengthen or weaken the argument. The argument provided will *always* have logical flaws in it, and your task is to critically analyze the argument, identify these flaws, and identify ways to eliminate these flaws.

Scoring Analytical Writing

Two graders will score each essay, with each grader assigning a score from 0 to 6. The average of these two scores will determine your score for each writing task. The score for each writing task will then be averaged to yield your overall Analytical Writing score.

For example, if one grader gives you a score of 5 on your first essay and the second grader gives you a score of 6, your score for the first essay is 5.5. If one grader gives you a score of 4 for your second essay and the second grader gives you a 5, then your score for the second essay is 4.5. Your overall score will then be the average of 5.5 and 4.5, which is 5.

What Are the Graders Looking For?

Essays that receive high scores tend to have several consistent features: fluid writing, complex sentence structure, organization, and sound reasoning.

Fluid Writing

To achieve fluid writing, you must create smooth and logical transitions among the different components of your essay. Doing so requires the use of rhetorical devices that link components of the essay together. Words such as *indeed, furthermore, however, despite, nonetheless, since,* and *due to* create internal logic among the different parts of the essay. They facilitate the reader's ability to understand the information that you present and the point you are trying to make with this information. When you are writing, you should be concerned with making sure that you use the appropriate words or phrases to create a logical and smooth flow among the different parts of your essay.

Complex Sentence Structure

If you tend to write in short, choppy sentences, you will need to revise your writing to incorporate sentences that convey multiple thoughts at once. Though it's not necessarily true, most readers tend to interpret short sentences as representative of shallow thinking and will grade your essays accordingly. One way to create more complex sentences is to introduce subordinate clauses into your writing. For example, a choppy writer might write the following:

> The above argument is wrong. It makes a lot of assumptions. We need to know a few things to make the argument stronger.

Writing with more complex sentence structures would rephrase the preceding into the following sentence:

> Due to its several unfounded assumptions, the above argument is flawed. To strengthen the argument, several facts need to be addressed, otherwise the argument of the logic is porous.

Organization

You can have a groundbreaking idea, but if you don't present the idea in a clear and logical way, then the reader will never grasp the point you are trying to make. As will be discussed later, organizing your thoughts into discrete paragraphs will be an essential component of achieving a good score on the essays.

Sound Reasoning

Remember: these are *analytical* tasks. To do well, you need to think critically about the information presented to you and provide arguments and insights that would not be obvious to someone who only superficially analyzes the information. As explained later, a large component of your essay-writing process will be the development of clear and logical arguments.

Simplified Scoring Rubrics

Here is a simplified version of the rubric used by the graders to score responses to the Analyze an Issue task:

Analyze an Issue: Scoring			
SCORE	FOCUS	ORGANIZATION	CONVENTIONS
0	Does not address the prompt. Off topic.	Incomprehensible. May merely copy the prompt without development.	Illegible. Nonverbal. Serious errors make the paper unreadable. May be in a foreign language.
1	Mostly irrelevant to the prompt.	Little or no development of ideas. No evidence of analysis or organization.	Pervasive errors in grammar, mechanics, and spelling.
2	Unclear connection to the prompt.	Unfocused and disorganized.	Frequent errors in sentence structure, mechanics, and spelling.
3	Limited connection to the prompt.	Rough organization with weak examples or reasons.	Occasional major errors and frequent minor errors in conventions of written English.
4	Competent connection to the prompt.	Relevant examples or reasons develop a logical position.	Occasional minor errors in conventions of written English.
5	Clear, focused connection to the prompt.	Thoughtful, appropriate examples or reasons develop a consistent, coherent position. Connectors are ably used to mark transitions.	Very few errors. Sentence structure is varied and vocabulary is advanced.
6	Insightful, clever connection to the prompt.	Compelling, convincing examples or reasons develop a consistent, coherent position. The argument flows effortlessly and persuasively.	Very few errors. Sentence structure is varied and vocabulary is precise, well chosen, and effective.

Here is a simplified version of the rubric the graders use to score responses to the Analyze an Argument task:

Analyze an Argument: Scoring			
SCORE	FOCUS	ORGANIZATION	CONVENTIONS
0	Does not address the prompt. Off topic.	Incomprehensible. May merely copy the prompt without development.	Illegible. Nonverbal. Serious errors make the paper unreadable. May be in a foreign language.
1	Little or no analysis of the argument. May indicate misunderstanding of the prompt.	Little or no development of ideas. No evidence of analysis or organization.	Pervasive errors in grammar, mechanics, and spelling.
2	Little analysis. May instead present opinions and unrelated thoughts.	Disorganized and illogical.	Frequent errors in sentence structure, mechanics, and spelling.
3	Some analysis of the prompt, but some major flaws may be omitted.	Rough organization with irrelevant support or unclear transitions.	Occasional major errors and frequent minor errors in conventions of written English.
4	Important flaws in the argument are touched upon.	Ideas are sound but may not flow logically or clearly.	Occasional minor errors in conventions of written English.
5	Perceptive analysis of the major flaws in the argument.	Logical examples and support develop a consistent, coherent critique. Connectors are ably used to mark transitions.	Very few errors. Sentence structure is varied and vocabulary is advanced.
6	Insightful, clever analysis of the argument's flaws and fallacies.	Compelling, convincing examples and support develop a consistent, coherent critique. The analysis flows effortlessly and persuasively.	Very few errors. Sentence structure is varied and vocabulary is precise, well chosen, and effective.

How to Approach the "Analyze an Issue" Task

The Analyze an Issue task will present you with a one- or two-sentence claim and ask you to evaluate that claim by using outside evidence. The essay will be graded on your ability to:

- Understand the implications of the statement
- Develop a well-reasoned and organized line of thought
- Use relevant examples to support your point
- Present your ideas clearly and intelligibly

Here is a sample Analyze an Issue task:

> The attention popular culture gives to celebrities has had a negative effect on the members of that culture.

Discuss the extent to which you agree or disagree with the statement and explain your reasoning for the position you take. In developing and supporting your position, you should consider ways in which the statement might or might not hold true and explain how these considerations shape your position.

Follow these steps to tackle the Analyze an Issue task. Spending the amount of time indicated next to each step will help you pace yourself for each assignment.

Step 1: Brainstorm (3 Minutes)

Once you read the task, you should spend time determining what stance you will take on the issue and what evidence you will use to support that stance. *It is important to note that you need not take a stance that you agree with!* Because evidence is *vital* to the issue task, you should consider both sides of the issue and adopt the stance that you can provide more evidence for. A typical brainstorm for the preceding prompt might look like the following:

Agree → Teenagers develop bad habits

People out of touch with high art

Disagree → Celebrities expose us to important ideas and issues, e.g., Magic Johnson, Angelina Jolie

Celebrity mistakes help us avoid our own mistakes, e.g., Amy Winehouse

In this brainstorm, the writer has come up with more evidence to argue against the statement in the task, so the writer should adopt that stance.

Step 2: Create Your Outline (3 Minutes)

A good issue essay should consist of (1) an introductory paragraph that states your main point, (2) body paragraphs providing examples that reinforce this main point, and (3) a concluding paragraph that summarizes your point and its implications. Your next step should be to draft an outline that follows this structure. In your outline, you should develop a rough sketch of what point you will make in each paragraph and how you will support that point. For example:

<u>Paragraph 1: Thesis:</u> Attn to celebrities = good thing. Why?

1. Makes us aware of issues

2. Brings attn to important causes

3. Teaches us mistakes of others

Paragraph 2: Topic sentence: Makes us aware of issues

Example: Angelina Jolie helping malnourished children in Africa

Paragraph 3: Topic sentence: Brings attn to important causes

Example: Magic Johnson diagnosed with HIV led to more public awareness.

Paragraph 4: Topic sentence: Teaches us mistakes of others

Example: Amy Winehouse and drug abuse

Paragraph 5: Conclusion: Restate main ideas. Food for thought: even though so many people think social media is a bad thing, maybe it's good for the above reasons.

Step 3: Write Your Body Paragraphs (5 Minutes per Paragraph)

Start with your body paragraphs because these constitute the most important part of your essay. Each body paragraph should take the following structure:

- **Sentence 1: Topic sentence:** State the point that you are trying to convey in the paragraph.
- **Sentences 2 to 4: Example:** Go into detail with the example that you are using to support your main point.
- **Sentences 5 to 6. Reasoning:** Explain how your example supports the topic sentence.

Here is a sample body paragraph for the prompt.

The attention our culture gives celebrities often highlights causes that society at large might otherwise be unaware of. For example, Angelina Jolie's numerous trips to malnourished villages in Africa have been highly publicized by the news media. When this actress makes these trips, she focuses on the chronic impoverishment of these countries and the absence of many basic necessities that we take for granted in the Western world, such as readily available food, lodging, and sanitation. Because Jolie is so famous and her travels receive so much attention, the problems in these countries are broadcast to a wider audience than they would be through just a late-night infomercial or news segment. Thus it is evident that Jolie's fame has had a positive impact on society. She has used the constant attention from the media to bring awareness to an important social issue that might otherwise have gone ignored by much of Western society. And though the problems that she addresses have certainly not been eradicated, her focus on them has put society in a better position to address some of the world's inequalities.

Step 4: Write Your Introductory and Concluding Paragraphs (6 Minutes)

The goal of your introductory paragraph is twofold:

1. Give context for the issue you are discussing.
2. Clearly state your *thesis*—the stance that you will be trying to support in the essay.

To give context, you should first explain the larger relevance of the issue. To do so, it is oftentimes helpful to *address the counterargument*, a rhetorical strategy in which you provide the opposite side of the argument and then segue into your own opinion. Once you have addressed the counterargument and transitioned into your opinion, you should write a concluding sentence that clearly illustrates what you will be arguing in your essay.

Here is a sample introductory paragraph:

With society's increasing emphasis and glorification of celebrity culture, it has become commonplace to regard this attention with suspicion and sometimes even downright derision. The constant barrage of reality TV shows has made everyone skeptical of the actual value that celebrity culture provides to society and has caused many critics to lament what they believe is the deterioration of American cultural life. Nonetheless, despite some apparent drawbacks of the attention that we give celebrities, this behavior has numerous benefits to our society. Specifically, the attention we give celebrities increases our awareness of societal problems, gives a large audience to important issues, and helps us learn from the publicized mistakes of celebrities.

The goal of your concluding paragraph is to summarize the points you made in your essay and to discuss the implications of your main point. When discussing the implications, you should focus on addressing the relevance of your thesis to issues outside the scope of the essay. Let's look at an example of a concluding paragraph:

> *The examples illustrate the beneficial effects that our attention to celebrities can provide society. Because news and media coverage are so pervasive in our lives, and because these outlets so often cover celebrity life, celebrities can often use these outlets to advance social and cultural causes that the general population might otherwise neglect. Though many worry that the development of social media and the proliferation of celebrity websites have made celebrities into only a spectacle, the point still stands that celebrities can leverage their popularity to achieve goals that supersede their immediate self-interest and benefit society as a whole.*

Step 5: Proofread (3 Minutes)

You should make sure to always leave yourself time at the end to proofread your essay. When proofreading, you should reread the essay carefully, focusing on any grammatical mistakes or typos you may have made. At this point, it's often too late to dramatically alter the substance of the essay (hopefully, you would have done so during one of the earlier steps). So worry less about the content and more about the technical aspects of your writing—the grammar, spelling, and fluidity of the sentences.

How to Approach the "Analyze an Argument" Task

The Analyze an Argument task addresses your ability to understand and deconstruct an argument. The prompt for this essay will provide evidence and a claim drawn from that evidence. Your task is to critique the argument by identifying the major assumptions that the author makes. In writing the essay, you will be tested on your:

- Logical reasoning skills
- Ability to analyze the components of an argument
- Mastery of technical English
- Ability to articulate your thoughts

Here is a sample Analyze an Argument task:

> Ever since our company downsized in 2009 by reducing the number of customer support staff, we have seen a decrease in revenue. Customers have expressed frustration over the lack of available staff members, and customer surveys have shown that these customers wish we were available to help them outside of normal business hours. The obvious solution to our problem of decreasing revenues is to increase the size of the customer support staff to what it was before we downsized in 2009.

Write a response in which you examine the stated or unstated assumptions of the argument. Be sure to explain how the argument depends on the assumptions and what the implications are if the assumptions prove unwarranted.

Here's how to tackle the Analyze an Argument task. Again, spending the amount of time indicated next to each step will help you pace yourself for each assignment.

Step 1: Read the Argument and Identify the Claim and Evidence (2 Minutes)

When reading the argument, your goal is to identify the main conclusion the author draws and the evidence that he or she uses to support this conclusion. It is *essential* that you identify the claim, because without doing so, you will not be able to analyze the cogency of the author's argument. In the preceding example, the claim is, *The obvious solution to our problem of decreasing revenues is to increase the size of the customer support staff to what it was before we downsized in 2009.*

Step 2: Identify the Major Assumptions and Create Your Outline (3 Minutes)

Your next step is to think about the *assumptions* of the argument. An assumption is an unstated piece of information that *must* be true for an argument to be valid. The more assumptions the author makes, the more open to scrutiny the argument is. In the preceding example, some major assumptions are:

- The loss in revenue was not caused by factors other than the decrease in customer support.
- Customer service is an important consideration that potential clients make when using the business.
- Repeat business is an important source of revenue for the business.
- The previous customer support staff was available outside of business hours.
- Any new customer support staff the business adds would provide a level of service comparable to that of the old staff.

Once you have identified the assumptions, draft your outline. In the outline, you should list the key assumptions you will address. A typical outline might look like the following:

Paragraph 1: Argument flawed b/c many assumptions. Not obvious that more cust. supp. = more revenue

Paragraph 2: First assumption: How important is customer service to getting business? If people still give business despite bad customer service, then new support staff won't matter.

Paragraph 3: Second assumption: Could the loss in revenue have been due to other factors? Was the economy bad? Did other parts of the company decline during this time period?

Paragraph 4: Third assumption: What was the previous customer support staff like? Were they better than the current ones? If so, would new ones be as good as the old ones? If new hires are not as good as the old staff, then hiring new personnel might not solve the problem.

Paragraph 5: Conclusion: Even though there's a correlation b/w loss in staff and revenue, it's not obvious that the loss in staff led to the loss in revenue. Need to address a lot of other factors before deciding that they should hire more customer support staff.

Step 3: Write Your Body Paragraphs (5 Minutes per Paragraph)

In each body paragraph, you should examine a major assumption in the argument. Start by introducing the assumption. Then state why the argument actually depends on this assumption. Here is a writer's paragraph 3 based on the preceding outline:

The author uses the correlation between the loss of revenue and decrease in customer support during the same time period to conclude that the business will benefit by hiring additional customer service employees. However, the author commits a logical fallacy by equating correlation and causation. The fact that the loss of revenue coincided with this decrease in staff is not enough to conclude that the loss in revenue was caused by the decrease in staff. Perhaps the economy was bad during this time period, and the company lost revenues because its clientele did not have as much disposable income. Or perhaps there were other segments of the company that were underperforming during this time period. Or perhaps one of its competitors had introduced a new product or service that took away some of the company's business. Because the author leaves so many external variables unaddressed, it is not possible to draw a firm causal connection between the data in the argument.

Step 4: Write Your Introduction and Conclusion (7 Minutes)

In the introduction, focus on restating the author's main point, and briefly summarize why you think the argument is flawed. You do not need to list the major assumptions that you will address. Just make it obvious that there are important assumptions and flaws in the argument. Here is an example:

Though it would appear that the company's declining revenues would be bolstered by the addition of customer support staff, the author does not make a logical case for adding more customer support staff. On its face, it might appear that the provided data lead to the author's conclusion, but there are several unwarranted assumptions that must be addressed to establish the soundness of the author's case.

Your conclusion does not need to be long, nor does it need to include a restatement of the assumptions listed in your argument. Simply write a paragraph showing that you understand the author's perspective but find it lacking. Here is an example:

When addressing a loss in revenue, a desire to revert to previous structures and strategies is certainly reasonable and oftentimes beneficial. However, the author's current plan, as based on the given data, suffers from too many flaws to be worthwhile. The existence of so many outside variables calls into question the soundness of the author's reasoning. Until such variables are addressed, it cannot be established whether the addition of customer support staff will lead to an increase in revenue.

Step 5: Proofread (3 Minutes)

You should make sure to always leave yourself time at the end to proofread your essay. When proofreading, you should reread the essay carefully, focusing on any grammatical mistakes or typos you may have made. At this point, it is often too late to dramatically alter the substance of the essay (hopefully, you would have done so during one of the earlier steps). So worry less about the content and more about the technical aspects of your writing—the grammar, spelling, and fluidity of the sentences.

For 10 more practice Analytical Writing assignments and high-scoring sample essays, go to the interactive practice tests. (See pages 2A–3A).

CHAPTER 4

Text Completion

Study this chapter to learn about:

- Single-blank Text Completion questions
- Double- and triple-blank Text Completion questions

Text Completion questions consist of a one-to-five-sentence passage with one to three blanks. You are asked to use logic and the context of the sentence to identify the best word for each blank. There is no partial credit for Text Completion questions. For Text Completion questions with one blank, there will be five choices. For Text Completion questions with two to three blanks, there will be three choices for each blank

Single-Blank Text Completion Questions

Single-blank Text Completion questions will always have five choices. Your task is to use the *context* of the sentence to select the choice that best fits in the blank. When most people do Text Completion questions, they take the word in each choice and insert it back into the sentence. Though this approach will sometimes lead to the right answer, the better method is to *predict the answer* and then see which choice matches your prediction.

How will you predict the answer? By identifying the *contextual clues*. Contextual clues are words or phrases that link elements of a sentence. These clues help provide a logical structure for understanding the relationship between the sentence's different components. Though the terminology might seem foreign, you use contextual clues whenever you infer the meaning of a sentence. Take a look at the following sentence and choose your own word for the blank.

> In contrast to his earlier _____, Jack is now extremely diligent.

What word did you put into the blank? Was it something like *laziness* or *apathy*? If so, why? Chances are, you recognized that the phrase "in contrast" indicated that the word in the blank should be the opposite of Jack's current "diligent" behavior. In the preceding example, "in contrast" is the contextual clue. It tells us that how Jack is now will be the opposite of how Jack was before.

Contextual clues will typically fall into three categories:

- **Contrast signals:** but, yet, nonetheless, nevertheless, despite, in spite of, in contrast, contrasted with, opposed to, although, however, on the contrary, rather than, still, though
- **Continuity signals:** indeed, and, also, moreover, furthermore, in addition, in fact, semicolon (;), colon (:)
- **Cause-effect signals:** thus, therefore, consequently, due to, because, since, as a result, hence, so

Now that you have looked at contextual clues, let's look at the steps for answering a typical Text Completion question.

> Due to an insatiable _____, the business executive felt no qualms about employing unethical means to generate profits.
>
> (A) benevolence
> (B) curiosity
> (C) ambiguity
> (D) deliberateness
> (E) avarice

Step 1: Identify the Contextual Clue

In the previous sentence, the phrase "due to" is a cause-effect signal.

Step 2: Determine the Contextual Clue's Relationship with the Rest of the Sentence

Determine the relationship that the contextual clue creates between the blank and the different parts of the sentence. In the example, the phrase "due to" indicates that the word in the blank will characterize someone willing to pursue unethical means to generate profits.

Step 3: Predict Your Own Word for the Blank

From Step 2, you know that the word in the blank will describe someone who will take extreme measures to make money. What would be an appropriate word to describe this behavior? *Greed* comes to mind.

Step 4: Select the Answer That Best Matches Your Prediction

Among the five choices, the closest synonym for *greed* is **avarice**. The correct answer is E.

Double- and Triple-Blank Text Completion Questions

In double- and triple-blank questions, you will be given one to five sentences with two to three blanks and asked to select the appropriate word for each blank. In these questions, there are only three choices for each blank, and there is no partial credit. Let's look at an example:

> The writer's deft mastery of the novelistic form was not, as commonly thought, a function of (i) _____: he spent years (ii) _____ his skills until his previous weaknesses became applauded virtues.

Blank (i)	Blank (ii)
(A) innate abilities	(D) genuflecting
(B) artistic sensibilities	(E) honing
(C) overarching perspicacity	(F) deriding

When working with double and triple blanks, many of the strategies for single blanks will apply. However, you must keep the following rule in mind: *you don't have to start with the first blank.* Instead, identify which blank will be easier to work with, and use the methods already discussed to determine the word for the blank. Then move on to the remaining blank, and use contextual clues to determine the appropriate word for that blank.

In the previous example, the word in the first blank depends on what comes after the colon. You should thus determine the word for the second blank first, and then use that word to determine the word for the first blank.

To determine the word for the second blank, you can use the process outlined earlier. The contextual clue "until" indicates that the writer did something to his skills to change them from "weaknesses" to "virtues." Now make your prediction. If the writer made weaknesses into virtues, then he probably *refined* his weaknesses. Now find the word in the choices that most closely matches *refined*. Of the choices, the word that most closely matches refined is **honing**. Thus the correct answer for the second blank is E.

Now to determine the word for the first blank, assume that *honing* is in the second place, and go through the same process as before. The word in the blank refers to an erroneous belief about the author's "mastery of the novelistic form." If the writer "spent years honing his skills," then the talent took time to develop. It would thus be erroneous to believe that the talents were based on "instinct." Of the choices, the phrase that most closely matches "instinct" is **innate abilities**. The correct choice for the first blank is A.

Exercise: Text Completion Set 1

For the following questions, complete the text by picking the best entry for each blank from the corresponding column of choices.

1. The essayist believes that the _____ of the university's English department could be ameliorated only by an overhaul in the school's management.

    - (A) prosperity
    - (B) denigration
    - (C) deterioration
    - (D) proliferation
    - (E) consternation

2. Successful expansion of a business is as much a matter of _____ as of hard work: the greatest work ethic will be useless if it is not performed in the service of a concrete plan.

    - (A) foresight
    - (B) persistence
    - (C) insight
    - (D) talent
    - (E) parsimony

3. Despite its obvious flaws, the economist's plan to increase employment found many _____, mostly because a better alternative did not seem feasible.

    - (A) detractors
    - (B) confounders
    - (C) proponents
    - (D) derivatives
    - (E) expungers

4. The inherent _____ of David Foster Wallace's novels is apparent in the proliferation of guides and supplements to his novels.

    Ⓐ density

    Ⓑ beauty

    Ⓒ aesthetics

    Ⓓ unconventionality

    Ⓔ misanthropy

5. The novelist's _____ tone puzzled readers expecting the straightforward and terse prose that characterized his previous works.

    Ⓐ philosophical

    Ⓑ meandering

    Ⓒ jovial

    Ⓓ progressive

    Ⓔ melancholy

6. The belief that professional athletes can become financially _____ after signing lucrative contracts motivated the league's commissioner to institute a mandatory financial-planning course.

    Ⓐ enthusiastic

    Ⓑ haughty

    Ⓒ reckless

    Ⓓ opulent

    Ⓔ diminutive

7. The discovery that the brain's connections can change even during old age
_____ previous beliefs that the basic configuration of the brain is
fixed by middle age.

    Ⓐ undermined

    Ⓑ highlighted

    Ⓒ determined

    Ⓓ implied

    Ⓔ validated

8. The politician's newly developed tendency to (i) _____
underrepresented groups surprised colleagues who remembered him as
(ii) _____ these groups' economic plight.

Blank (i)	Blank (ii)
Ⓐ sympathize with	Ⓓ curious about
Ⓑ mimic	Ⓔ indifferent to
Ⓒ deride	Ⓕ hopeful for

9. By adopting a(n) (i) _____ tone in lieu of a more moderate one,
the author produces arguments based more on (ii) _____ than
sound reasoning.

Blank (i)	Blank (ii)
Ⓐ incendiary	Ⓓ rhetoric
Ⓑ well-reasoned	Ⓔ displacement
Ⓒ conservative	Ⓕ analysis

10. Greene's discussion of the nuances of particle physics, though
seemingly _____, actually serves a purpose. Indeed, without
this background, the reader would be unable to _____ the
significance of the evidence presented later in the book.

Blank (i)	Blank (ii)
Ⓐ incomprehensible	Ⓓ obstruct
Ⓑ tangential	Ⓔ synthesize
Ⓒ deliberate	Ⓕ appreciate

Exercise: Text Completion Set 2

For the following questions, complete the text by picking the best entry for each blank from the corresponding column of choices.

11. In certain regions of Mars, the weather _____ so wildly that you can feel as though you are experiencing winter and summer in the same day.

   - (A) navigates
   - (B) buffers
   - (C) crests
   - (D) diminishes
   - (E) fluctuates

12. The claim that all life on earth originated from Mars is far from (i) _____. There are gaps in the evidence that must be addressed before the scientific community can even begin to (ii) _____ the theory's plausibility.

Blank (i)	Blank (ii)
(A) substantiated	(D) coalesce
(B) contradictory	(E) entertain
(C) antagonizing	(F) delineate

13. In the convict's case, the axiom that "Still waters run deep" finds (i) _____: his apparent façade of (ii) _____ should not imply a lack of remorse.

Blank (i)	Blank (ii)
(A) credence	(D) contrition
(B) antagonism	(E) bemusement
(C) ambiguity	(F) stoicism

14. For the start-up, the (i) _____ stresses of the economic downturn seemed to have a silver lining. Though the persistent concern about attaining new clients taxed the employees' psyches, it also taught them the necessity of (ii) _____ to weather cyclical fluctuations.

Blank (i)	Blank (ii)
Ⓐ unmitigated	Ⓓ confabulation
Ⓑ miserly	Ⓔ serendipity
Ⓒ conciliatory	Ⓕ resourcefulness

15. It is the (i) _____ nature of technology that most alarms cultural critics. Though they find many of its features (ii) _____ and even beneficial, they worry that its ubiquity can be (iii) _____ .

Blank (i)	Blank (ii)	Blank (iii)
Ⓐ insidious	Ⓓ salutary	Ⓖ nourishing
Ⓑ understated	Ⓔ tolerable	Ⓗ incidental
Ⓒ ominous	Ⓕ irreproducible	Ⓘ alienating

16. His inherent (i) _____ leisure proved beneficial to his finances but (ii) _____ his personal development, since he never gave himself time to pursue hobbies.

Blank (i)	Blank (ii)
Ⓐ consumption with	Ⓓ deleterious to
Ⓑ ignorance of	Ⓔ fortuitous to
Ⓒ aversion to	Ⓕ derivative of

17. Because Kundera's novels take place during a time of upheaval in Eastern Europe, critics believe that Kundera's use of the social (i) _____ in which his characters' lives occur implies political commentary. However, the novelist has been clear that his works are meant to (ii) _____ all elements of human living, not just the political.

Blank (i)	Blank (ii)
Ⓐ confluence	Ⓓ reflect
Ⓑ milieu	Ⓔ vindicate
Ⓒ isolation	Ⓕ derogate

18. Unlike the composers of previous eras, Beethoven demonstrated not only a mastery of music's technical aspects, but also an artistic (i) _____ that was difficult to replicate. This was obvious in the emotional undercurrents in many of his works, and this (ii) _____ at least partly explains the enduring popularity of his compositions.

Blank (i)	Blank (ii)
Ⓐ accessibility	Ⓓ dilettantism
Ⓑ passion	Ⓔ miserliness
Ⓒ aestheticism	Ⓕ unconventionality

19. One of Garcia Marquez's most acclaimed abilities is his (i) _____ insertion of the supernatural into his characters' everyday lives. Most novelists who attempt to introduce such plot elements are rightfully accused of heavy-handedness, but Garcia Marquez can weave absurdities into his plots without straining our (ii) _____.

Blank (i)	Blank (ii)
Ⓐ encumbered	Ⓓ literacy
Ⓑ painstaking	Ⓔ credulity
Ⓒ organic	Ⓕ probity

20. Though offended by his competitor's (i) _____ characterization, the politician sought to address this misrepresentation without stooping to his competitor's (ii) _____ tactics.

Blank (i)	Blank (ii)
Ⓐ accusatory	Ⓓ unscrupulous
Ⓑ libelous	Ⓔ pandering
Ⓒ prescient	Ⓕ conciliatory

Exercise: Text Completion Set 3

For the following questions, complete the text by picking the best entry for each blank from the corresponding column of choices.

21. The salesmen subscribed to the belief that the surest way to selling a product was to coax someone with (i) _____. In fact, most people were skeptical enough to detect such (ii) _____.

Blank (i)	Blank (ii)
Ⓐ meticulousness	Ⓓ disingenuousness
Ⓑ deliberation	Ⓔ authenticity
Ⓒ blandishments	Ⓕ ebullience

22. The disgraced scientist was unable to approach his studies with the requisite level of (i) _____: instead of simply observing and characterizing the phenomena, he (ii) _____ the evidence to match his predictions.

Blank (i)	Blank (ii)
Ⓐ disinterest	Ⓓ objectified
Ⓑ indifference	Ⓔ supplanted
Ⓒ alacrity	Ⓕ distorted

23. Emerson emphasized the distinction between (i) _____ and obsession. While he believed that the scholarly life afforded its adherents a fresh perspective, he warned against the perils of becoming (ii) _____ such a pursuit.

Blank (i)	Blank (ii)
Ⓐ erudition	Ⓓ adept at
Ⓑ consummation	Ⓔ consumed with
Ⓒ misanthropy	Ⓕ inured to

24. (i) _____ his contemporaries' dismissal of his (ii) _____ approach, Barry continued implementing the effective but unconventional shooting strategy.

Blank (i)	Blank (ii)
Ⓐ Incensed by	Ⓓ cantankerous
Ⓑ Perpetuated by	Ⓔ inchoate
Ⓒ Nonplussed by	Ⓕ unorthodox

25. Deriving wonderment from novelty is relatively commonplace; far more difficult is the ability to find beauty in the _____.

Ⓐ plebeian
Ⓑ malevolent
Ⓒ prosaic
Ⓓ ecstatic
Ⓔ unknown

26. There was a (i) _____ agreement among the employees about the leadership hierarchy. Though no one made explicit mention of it, they all (ii) _____ that Johnson, because of both his experience and mathematical (iii) _____, was best-suited to head the numbers-based project.

Blank (i)	Blank (ii)	Blank (iii)
Ⓐ tacit	Ⓓ acknowledged	Ⓖ diminution
Ⓑ illicit	Ⓔ disputed	Ⓗ acumen
Ⓒ convivial	Ⓕ coalesced	Ⓘ consternation

27. Mathematician Poincaré lived a stereotypically (i) _____ existence. Like many of his contemporaries, he (ii) _____ the messiness of human engagement for the precision of mathematical concepts.

Blank (i)	Blank (ii)
Ⓐ hermetic	Ⓓ mollified
Ⓑ dilettantish	Ⓔ considered
Ⓒ conciliatory	Ⓕ forsook

28. Constant exposure to our public figures' foibles and flaws is at once humanizing and _____; as we become sympathetic to their plights, we also become increasingly wary of their motives.

    (A) disillusioning

    (B) emboldening

    (C) honoring

    (D) humbling

    (E) condescending

29. (i) _____ Congress' pleas, the stubborn clique of politicians prevented the passage of a well-regarded bill, thereby (ii) _____ the patience of even its most loyal allies.

Blank (i)	Blank (ii)
(A) Unamenable to	(D) instigating
(B) Consigned to	(E) taxing
(C) Castigated by	(F) perseverating

30. The patient was warned that the medical treatment, though proved to be effective, would be _____, inducing an unshakable sense of lethargy.

    (A) discouraging

    (B) unendurable

    (C) enervating

    (D) incommensurate

    (E) frivolous

Exercise Answers

Text Completion Set 1

1. **C** If the "overhaul" will "ameliorate" the situation in the English department, then the English department's current state must be negative. Prediction: *worsening*. The choice that best matches *worsening* is **deterioration**.

2. **A** The word in the blank describes what is necessary for "successful expansion of a business." The phrase after the colon provides the clue for the blank. The phrase indicates that a concrete plan is necessary. Thus a good prediction would be a word that deals with developing a plan: *planning*. The word that best matches *planning* is **foresight**.

3. **C** The word in the blank describes the people reacting to the economist's plan. The contextual clue "despite" indicates that the plan's reception was in contrast to what would be expected from a plan with "flaws." A good prediction would be *supporters*. The word that best matches *supporters* is **proponents**.

4. **A** The word in the blank describes David Foster Wallace's novels. The word "apparent" indicates that the many "guides and supplements" is a clue to the description of his novels. If his novels have given rise to guides and supplements, then they must be *difficult*. The word in the choices that most closely matches *difficult* is **density**.

5. **B** The word in the blank describes the novelist's tone. Since this tone "puzzled" readers of his previous works, it must be different from the tone of his previous works. If his previous works were "straightforward and terse," then his new work must be the opposite of "straightforward and terse." A good prediction is *long-winded*. The word among the choices that most closely matches *long-winded* is **meandering**.

6. **C** The word in the blank describes what can happen to athletes after they sign "lucrative contracts." This belief explains why the commissioner "institute[d] a mandatory financial-planning course." The most likely reason the commissioner instituted such a course is that the athletes are financially *irresponsible* with their money. The word in the choices that best matches *irresponsible* is **reckless**.

7. **A** The discovery in the first part of the sentence is in contrast to "previous beliefs" about the brain. Prediction: What did this discovery do to previous beliefs? A good word is *overthrew*. The word in the choices that best matches *overthrew* is **undermined**.

8. **A and E** Since the politician's current behavior "surprises" colleagues, the word in the first blank and second blanks should convey opposing attitudes toward "underrepresented groups."

9. **A and D** The easier blank to address in this sentence is the first. "In lieu of" indicates contrast, so the author's tone is in contrast to "moderate." A good prediction is *extreme*. Of the choices in Column 1, the word closest in meaning to *extreme* is **incendiary**. Now, substitute **incendiary** into the first blank and solve for the second blank. The argument's content is in contrast to "sound reasoning." Thus it must be without substance. A good prediction is *style*. The word in the choices that best matches *style* is **rhetoric**.

10. **B and F** The first blank is simpler, so start there. The first blank describes a false view of "Greene's discussion of the nuances of particle physics." The discussion "served a purpose," so since the word in the blank comes after "though," it should convey a meaning opposite of serving a purpose. A good prediction is *irrelevant*. In Column 1, the closest word to *irrelevant* is **tangential**. The second blank describes why a reader needs this information. Since the information "served a purpose," the reader must need it to *understand* the evidence. In Column 2, the closest word to *understand* is **appreciate**.

Text Completion Set 2

11. **E** The word in the blank describes what the weather does. The idiom "so . . . that . . ." implies that the feeling of "experiencing winter and summer in the same day" is because of what the weather does. Prediction: if it feels like you're experiencing different times of year on the same day, then the weather *varies*. The choice closest in meaning to *varies* is **fluctuates**.

12. **A and E** There are more clues for the second blank, so start there. The word in the blank describes what the scientists will do once certain conditions about the theory are met. Since gaps must be addressed, once these gaps are addressed, scientists will most likely *consider* the theory's plausibility. The choice closest in meaning to *consider* is **entertain**. Now look at the first blank. If there are so many gaps that scientists have yet to **entertain** the theory's plausibility, then the claim must be far from *supported*. The choice closest in meaning to *supported* is **substantiated**.

13. **A and F** Start with the second blank. The convict's external appearance does not imply a lack of remorse. What kind of appearance would seem to imply a lack of remorse? An *emotionless* one. Of the choices, the word closest in meaning to *emotionless* is **stoicism**. Now look at the first blank: if his stoicism does not imply remorse, then the axiom finds *validation*. Of the choices, the word closest in meaning to validation is **credence**.

14. **A and F** Start with the first blank. If there was "persistent concern about attaining new clients," then the stresses must have been *unrelenting*. Of the choices, the word closest in meaning to *unrelenting* is **unmitigated**. Now look at the second blank. The word in the second blank describes a positive skill that the employees obtained in response to the economic downturn. The only positive word in the second column is **resourcefulness**. Since there are more clues for the second blank, start there.

15. **A, E, and I** There are the most clues for the third blank, so start there. The word in the blank describes a concern that cultural critics have about technology. Thus the word in the blank must be negative. Of the choices, the word with the most clearly negative connotation is **alienating**. Now look at the second blank. The contextual clue "and even" indicates that the word in the blank is a milder form of "beneficial." A good prediction is *acceptable*. Of the choices, the word closest in meaning to *acceptable* is **tolerable**. Finally, look at the first blank. What about technology most alarms cultural critics? Its *ubiquity* alarms most. Of the choices, the word closest in meaning to *ubiquitous* is **insidious**.

16. **C and D** There are more clues for the second word, so start there. The contextual clue "but" indicates that the effect of the first blank on his finances is opposite of the effect on "his personal development." If it is "beneficial" to his finances, then it is *harmful* to "his personal development." Of the choices, the word closest in meaning to *harmful* is **deleterious**. Now, look at the first blank: If he never gave himself time to pursue hobbies, then how did he feel about leisure? A good prediction is *opposition to*. Of the choices, the word closest in meaning to *opposition to* is **aversion to**.

17. **B and D** There are more clues for the word in the first blank, so start there. Critics' beliefs about his work are based on the social *context* of his novels. Of the choices, the word closest in meaning to *context* is **milieu**. Now, look at the second blank. The word "however" indicates that Kundera believes his works touch on all aspects of human living. A good prediction is *represent*. Of the choices, the word closest in meaning to *represent* is **reflect**.

18. **B and F** There are more clues for the first blank, so start there. The word in the blank describes an element of Beethoven's compositions. In the next sentence, the phrase "emotional undercurrents" provides a clue for this element. If there were "emotional undercurrents" in his compositions, then the compositions must have been *emotional*. Of the choices, the word closest in meaning to *emotional* is **passion**. Now look at the second blank. The word in the blank describes Beethoven's music. Since Beethoven was "unlike" previous composers, his approach must have been *unusual*. Among the choices, the word that best matches *unusual* is **unconventionality**.

19. **C and E** There are more clues for the first blank, so start there. The contextual clue "but" indicates that Garcia Marquez's approach differs from that of his contemporaries. If the contemporaries approach is characterized as "heavy-handed," then Marquez's approach must be the opposite of "heavy-handed." A good prediction is *natural*. Of the choices, the word closest in meaning to *natural* is **organic**. Now look at the second blank. If Garcia Marquez can organically use supernatural elements, then he does not strain our *belief*. Of the choices, the word closest in meaning to *belief* is **credulity**.

20. **B and D** There are more clues for the word in the first blank, so start there. The word in the blank describes the competitor's characterization of the politician. In the second sentence, we are told that this was a "misrepresentation." Thus the characterization must have been *false*. Of the choices, the word closest in meaning to *false* is **libelous**. Now look at the second blank. The word in the blank describes the competitor's tactics. Since the competitor made **libelous** characterizations, his tactics were *dishonest*. Of the choices, the word closest in meaning to *dishonest* is **unscrupulous**.

Text Completion Set 3

21. **C and D** Start with the first blank. If the salesman is "coaxing" people, then he is using a dishonest tactic. The word in the blank should be anything that implies dishonesty. Of the choices, the best word is **blandishments**. Now solve for the second blank. People are detecting the salesman's tactic, and his tactic is characterized by dishonesty. A good word for the blank would be *dishonesty*. Of the choices, the word closest in meaning to *dishonesty* is **disingenuousness**.

22. **A and F** There are more clues for the first blank, so start there. The word in the first blank indicates the approach that the scientist did not take. The contextual clue "instead of" indicates that the scientist did not simply observe and characterize what he saw. If he did not simply observe and characterize, then what did he lack? A good prediction would be *objectivity*. Of the choices, the word closest in meaning to *objectivity* is **disinterest**. Now look at the second blank. The word in the second blank tells us what the scientist did "instead of simply observing and characterizing the phenomena." A good prediction is *manipulated*. Of the choices, the word closest in meaning to *manipulated* is **distorted**.

23. **A and E** Start with the first blank. If the distinction is between the blank and "obsession," Emerson must view moderate amounts of the blank favorably. The second sentence says that Emerson believed "the scholarly life afforded its adherents a fresh perspective," so he must have a favorable view of *scholarliness*. Of the choices, the word that most closely matches *scholarliness* is **erudition**. Now look at the second blank. If Emerson "emphasized the distinction between **erudition** and obsession," then he warned against becoming *obsessed with* the pursuit. Of the choices, the word closest in meaning to *obsessed with* is **consumed with**.

24. **C and F** There are more clues for the second blank, so start there. The word in the second blank describes Barry's approach. You are told in the second sentence that Barry's shooting strategy is "unconventional." Thus a good prediction for the second blank is *unconventional*. Of the choices, the word closest in meaning to *unconventional* is **unorthodox**. Now look at the first blank: if Barry continued using the strategy, then how did he feel about "his contemporaries' dismissal"? A good prediction would be *unconcerned with*. Of the choices, the word closest in meaning to *unconcerned with* is **nonplussed by**.

25. **C** The phrase "far more difficult" indicates that the word in the blank will be the opposite of where "beauty" normally comes from. If it is usually found in "novelty," then the word in the blank should be the opposite of "novelty." A good prediction would be *mundane*. Of the choices, the word closest in meaning to *mundane* is **prosaic**.

26. **A, D, and H** The easiest blank to start with is the first. If "no one made explicit mention of" the leadership hierarchy, then the agreement must have been *unspoken*. Of the choices, the word closest in meaning to unspoken is **tacit**. The next easiest blank is the third blank. If Johnson "was best-suited to head the numbers-based project," then he must have been adept at math. A good prediction would be *aptitude*. Of the choices, the word closest in meaning to *aptitude* is **acumen**. Finally, go to the second blank. If the agreement was tacit, then the employees *recognized* it without stating it. Of the choices, the word closest in meaning to *recognized* is **acknowledged**.

27. **A and F** Start with the second blank. The contextual clue "in favor of" indicates that Poincaré preferred "the precision of mathematical concepts" to "human engagement." A good prediction for the second blank is: *bypassed*. Of the choices, the word closest in meaning to *bypassed* is **forsook**. Now look at the first blank. If he **forsook** human engagement, then what kind of existence

did he lead? A good prediction would be *solitary*. The word in the choices that best matches *solitary* is **hermetic**.

28. **A** The word in the blank characterizes the public figures. The contextual clue (;) indicates that what comes after the semicolon will clarify this description. The clause after the semicolon states that "we also become increasingly wary" of politicians' motives. If we are becoming wary, then we are becoming *disenchanted*. Among the choices, the word closest in meaning to *disenchanted* is **disillusioning**.

29. **A and E** Start with the first blank. Since the clique of politicians is "stubborn," it is most likely *unswayed by* Congress' pleas. The closest match to *unswayed by* is **unamenable to**. Now look at the second blank. The contextual clue "thereby" indicates that the effect that the politicians' actions had on the "patience" of their allies is a result of their prevention of the bill. Since the bill is "well-regarded," their allies were most likely unhappy with the actions. The word that best conveys this meaning is **taxing**.

30. **C** The word in the blank describes the medical treatment. The clue is provided at the end of the sentence: "inducing an unshakable sense of lethargy." If something induces lethargy, then it is *sapping*. The word closest in meaning to *sapping* is **enervating**.

CHAPTER 5

Sentence Equivalence

Study this chapter to learn about:

- How to approach sentence equivalence questions
- Looking for synonyms

Sentence Equivalence questions consist of a single-sentence passage with one blank. You will be given six choices and asked to use logic and the context of the sentence to identify *two* words that best fit in the blank. There is no partial credit for Sentence Equivalence questions.

How to Approach Sentence Equivalence Questions

The approach to Sentence Equivalence questions is very similar to the approach to Text Completion questions. Your goal should be to identify contextual clues, understand the relationship they create between the blank and the rest of the sentence, make a prediction for the word in the blank, and then identify the words that best match your prediction. Let's look at a sample question and the steps to take.

Despite their obvious hostility toward each other, the two teammates remained silent on the issue since they both believed that verbalizing these feelings would undermine the _____ necessary for the team's long-term success.

    A harmony
    B imbalance
    C malevolence
    D tacitness
    E cooperation
    F diligence

The causal word "since" indicates that the teammates' feelings about verbalizing their feelings explains why they remained silent. You know that the feelings were "hostile" and the teammates were afraid that these feelings would "undermine" something necessary for the team's success. So to make the prediction, ask the following question: What component of team success would "hostile" feelings most likely "undermine"? A good prediction is *unity*. Now look at the choices, and find the two words closest in meaning to *unity*. The best choices are **harmony** and **cooperation**. The correct answer is A and E.

Look for Synonyms

As shown previously, the general strategy for Sentence Equivalence questions is very similar to the general strategy for single-blank Text Completion questions. However, one key difference between the two question types is the fact that you must select *two* words for the blank in Sentence Equivalence questions. Though it might appear that this format makes Sentence Equivalence questions more difficult, you can take advantage of this fact by recognizing that *the correct answers will almost always be synonyms*.

This strategy is beneficial because you can usually eliminate answer choices that have no synonyms. For illustration, let's block out the sentence in the Sentence Equivalence question below and only show the choices. Look at which choices you can eliminate:

██
████████████████████████

- A determined
- B morose
- C dejected
- D apathetic
- E exaggerated
- F motivated

Since *determined* and *motivated* have similar meanings, you can keep A and F. Since *morose* and *dejected* have similar meanings, you can keep C and D. But notice that there is no synonym for *apathetic* and no synonym for *exaggerated*. *Thus without even seeing the sentence, you can eliminate choices D and E!*
This strategy could have helped you in the original question in this section. Perhaps you chose *diligence* as one of your answers. However, if you look back at the choices, you'll notice that there are no synonyms for *diligence*. Thus diligence could not have been correct.

Exercise: Sentence Equivalence Set 1

For the following questions, select <u>two</u> answer choices that (1) complete the sentence in a way that makes sense and (2) produce sentences that are similar in meaning.

1. It is a common _____ that most scientific discoveries are simply moments of genius: in fact, the discoveries we hear of usually take years of painstaking work.

   A myth
   B verity
   C curiosity
   D misconception
   E trope
   F theme

2. Success in this business requires constant _____ of one's reputation, since even one negative perception can often undo years of hard work.

   A neglect of
   B knowledge of
   C curiosity about
   D monitoring of
   E oversight of
   F consideration of

3. That she was occasionally late to class did not concern the professor; instead, it was only when her tardiness became _____ that the professor decided to chastise her.

   A well-known
   B offensive
   C habitual
   D sensitive
   E commonplace
   F infrequent

4. Even in football, where violence is considered part of the game, the player's brutish playing style was _____.

   A contrived
   B excessive
   C overlooked
   D gratuitous
   E ambivalent
   F forsaken

5. The character's trademark cynicism was evident in his obvious _____ the loving couple.

   A disdain for
   B contempt for
   C enthrallment with
   D amusement at
   E encouragement of
   F sensitivity to

6. Despite the website's large audience, financially minded critics have been skeptical of the website's ability to _____ this popularity.

   A understand
   B develop
   C monetize
   D undermine
   E capitalize on
   F elicit

7. Because it prioritizes theory over evidence, serious philosophical thinking takes empirical support as irrelevant, or at least, _____.

   A tangential
   B mitigating
   C amorphous
   D inconsequential
   E disparaging
   F intellectual

8. Supporters of the company believe that its negative valuation is _____ the founders' often childish behavior rather than the company's merits as a sustainable business.

    A attributable to
    B a consequence of
    C preceded by
    D obscured by
    E eliminated by
    F despite

9. The belief that the increasing use of electronic elements in music detracts from the artistic value of that music is flawed as such a view _____ the aesthetic abilities necessary to use electronics effectively.

    A emphasizes
    B determines
    C trivializes
    D neglects
    E underscores
    F undermines

10. Far from being dejected by the setback, the _____ employee used the challenge as motivation to work even harder.

    A tenacious
    B ambivalent
    C plucky
    D circumspect
    E morose
    F understated

Exercise: Sentence Equivalence Set 2

For the following questions, select <u>two</u> answer choices that (1) complete the sentence in a way that makes sense and (2) produce sentences that are similar in meaning.

11. Given the _____ reputation that Picasso has attained in Western culture, the lukewarm reactions to his early work, *Les Demoiselles d'Avignon* were more the exception than the norm.

    [A] anomalous
    [B] maligned
    [C] misunderstood
    [D] legendary
    [E] acclaimed
    [F] mediocre

12. For a nation known for its populace's belief in self-reliance, the United States' increased consumption of self-help books and deference to self-help gurus is _____.

    [A] anticipated
    [B] ironic
    [C] calculated
    [D] pervasive
    [E] unexpected
    [F] embraced

13. Any investigation that focuses only on television's negative impacts on people's attention spans is _____: the popular shows of a given time period serve as a cultural barometer highlighting the reigning norms and beliefs of that period.

    [A] shortsighted
    [B] prescient
    [C] illuminating
    [D] limited
    [E] critical
    [F] condescending

14. Notwithstanding the _____ boss, the employees at the small firm are known for their amicability.

   A cantankerous
   B jovial
   C intelligent
   D serious
   E frigid
   F diligent

15. More _____ than stingy, the accountant will willingly spend money on purchases that he believes justify the cost.

   A miserly
   B withholding
   C frugal
   D thrifty
   E profligate
   F excessive

16. The heroine reacted with uncharacteristic _____ to her town's tragedy: prior to that point in the novel, she had been defined by her sentimentality.

   A stoicism
   B emotion
   C aplomb
   D concern
   E zealousness
   F indifference

17. The conclusion to be drawn from the football game is that the outcomes of sporting events are, as a recent commentator accurately stated, _____: even the best prognostications are flawed.

   A exciting
   B retaliatory
   C enthralling
   D unforeseen
   E competitive
   F unpredictable

18. The lecturer projected an authoritativeness that all too often was undermined by the _____ nature of his claims.

   A vacuous
   B insipid
   C dilettante
   D illuminating
   E surprising
   F superficial

19. As subtle as it is _____, the new novel bears little resemblance to the heavy-handedness and superficiality that characterized her previous works.

   A artificial
   B supernatural
   C profound
   D probing
   E paradoxical
   F relevant

20. Far from being problematic, the _____ nature of scientific knowledge explains much of its appeal: most scientists implicitly recognize that their field's given theories will eventually be supplanted or amended as new data comes to light.

   A fluid
   B benevolent
   C systematic
   D tempestuous
   E dynamic
   F convoluted

21. The politician's controversial educational reform policy was _____ by the record number of high school graduates during his term.

   A elaborated
   B underscored
   C justified
   D calcified
   E vindicated
   F questioned

Exercise: Sentence Equivalence Set 3

For the following questions, select <u>two</u> answer choices that (1) complete the sentence in a way that makes sense and (2) produce sentences that are similar in meaning.

22. The fact that the Board cannot reach a resolution on such an urgent issue is a reflection of the _____ beliefs that underpin the objectives of the various members.

    A divergent
    B paradoxical
    C intimidating
    D tacit
    E hyperbolic
    F discrepant

23. Oftentimes, entrepreneurs are so blinded by the potential _____ of a successful business that they neglect attention to details necessary for the day-to-day operations of the business.

    A meticulousness
    B tangibility
    C negligence
    D implications
    E consequences
    F derivatives

24. With a plot featuring passionate romantic affairs and far-fetched tragedies, the new novel only reinforces the belief that the author's flair for the dramatic has devolved into the _____.

    A maudlin
    B surreal
    C sentimental
    D immutable
    E torrid
    F lachrymose

25. The director's decision to omit certain scenes from the film seemed uncharacteristically _____, marked by neither consistency nor, apparently, logic.

    A arbitrary
    B selective
    C discriminating
    D premeditated
    E haphazard
    F fecund

26. The actor's excitement over the new role was _____ when he discovered that the role was only for a minor character.

    A tempered
    B delivered
    C intensified
    D embellished
    E heightened
    F diminished

27. Amicable and inclined toward harmony, the artist _____ all forms of violence: the very idea of harm inspired a shudder.

    A ignored
    B pontificated
    C eschewed
    D glorified
    E shirked
    F curated

28. Her belief in his inherent sincerity _____ the thought that he could sometimes be deceptive.

    A precluded
    B doubted
    C manifested
    D clouded
    E confused
    F eliminated

29. Though laudable, Lakoff's account of Dostoevsky's influences is
_____, focusing only on his Christian background at the
expense of Dostoevsky's concern with the social milieu that he inhabited.

    A punctuated
    B impervious
    C misleading
    D insufficient
    E penetrating
    F inadequate

30. A common misconception about the practice of yoga is that it is
_____ for all of one's physical maladies; unfortunately, yoga
instructors exaggerating the benefits of the practice do nothing to dispel
this myth.

    A a panacea
    B an antecedent
    C a decrement
    D an elixir
    E a toxin
    F an elegy

31. With the _____ of capitalism comes the implication that the
accumulation of resources is a contributing factor to, if not a precondition
of, psychological well-being.

    A apotheosis
    B reduction
    C persistence
    D perniciousness
    E deification
    F vilification

Exercise Answers

Sentence Equivalence Set 1

1. **A and D** The word in the blank describes common beliefs about scientific discoveries. The contextual clue is "in fact," which indicates that the following clause is in contrast to what is currently believed about scientific discoveries. If the discoveries actually "take years of painstaking work," then the common belief is wrong. A good prediction for the blank would be *false belief*. Of the choices, the words that most closely match *false belief* are **myth** and **misconception**.

2. **D and E** The word in the blank describes what is necessary to ensure "success in this business." The contextual clue is the causal clue "since." If "one negative perception can often undo years of hard work," then a business would need to *maintain* its reputation. The words that most closely match *maintain* are **monitoring** and **oversight**.

3. **C and E** The word in the blank describes the level of tardiness that caused the professor to chastise the student. The contextual clue "instead" indicates contrast. When the student was "occasionally late," it did not bother the professor. The word in the blank should thus be the opposite of "occasional." A good prediction would be *constant*. The choices that best match *constant* are **habitual** and **commonplace**.

4. **B and D** The word in the blank describes the player's "brutish playing style." The contextual clue "even" indicates that the player's style was extreme for football. Since "violence is considered part of the game," and the player's style was extreme, a good prediction would be *overboard*. The choices that best match *overboard* are **excessive** and **gratuitous**.

5. **A and B** The word in the blank describes the character's attitude toward the "loving couple." Since the character is "cynical," his attitude toward the couple would most likely be negative. A good prediction would be *distaste for*. The words in the choice that most closely match *distaste for* are **disdain for** and **contempt for**.

6. **C and E** The word in the blank tells us what the "financially minded critics have been skeptical" of. The contrast signal "Despite" indicates that their skepticism contrasts with the popularity of the website. If the critics are financially minded, then they would most likely be skeptical of the website's ability to make money. A good prediction would be *take advantage of*. The choices that best match *take advantage of* are **monetize** and **capitalize on**.

7. **A and D** The word in the blank describes the attitude that philosophical thinking takes toward empirical support. The contextual clue "or at least" indicates that this attitude is similar to the belief that "takes empirical support as irrelevant." A good prediction would be a synonym of "irrelevant": *unimportant*. The words in the choices that most match *unimportant* are **tangential** and **inconsequential**.

8. **A and B** The word in the blank describes the company's negative valuation. The contextual clue "rather" indicates contrast. Supporters of the company believe that the company is worthwhile, so they most likely have a positive view of the company. Thus they do not think the merits of the company explain its negative valuation. To predict a word we can conclude that the

supporters *assign* the negative valuation to the behavior of the founders instead of to the company itself. Of the choices, the words that best match *assign* are **attributable to** and **a consequence of**.

9. **C and D** The contextual clue "as" indicates that the word in the blank will explain why the belief in the first part of the sentence is flawed. If "the belief that the increasing use of electronic elements in music detracts from the artistic value of that music is flawed," then the view most likely *ignores* the aesthetic abilities displayed by that music. Of the choices, the words that most closely match *ignores* are **neglects** and **trivializes**. The correct answer is C and D.

10. **A and C** The word in the blank describes the employee. The contrast clue "far from" indicates that the employee behaved in a manner that contrasts with the way someone "discouraged" behaves. A good prediction would be *persistent*. The words that most closely match *persistent* are **tenacious** and **plucky**.

Sentence Equivalence Set 2

11. **D and E** The blank describes Picasso's reputation. The logical structure "Given *x* then *y*" is a causal clue, indicating that the first part of the sentence will determine the content of the second part of the sentence. If Picasso's current reputation leads to the conclusion that the lukewarm reactions to his early works were "the exception," then his reputation must be positive. A good prediction would be *celebrated*. Of the choices, the words closest in meaning to *celebrated* are **legendary** and **acclaimed**.

12. **B and E** The word in the blank will describe the "United States' increased consumption of self-help books and deference to self-help gurus." The contrast clue "for" indicates that this description is in spite of the US reputation for self-reliance. To make a prediction, if the United States is known for self-reliance, then its focus on self-help is *surprising*. Of the choices, the words that most closely match *surprising* are **ironic** and **unexpected**.

13. **A and D** The word in the blank describes "any investigation that focuses only on television's negative impacts on people's attention spans." The contextual clue (:) indicates that what comes after the colon will clarify what the author believes about these investigations. To make a prediction: if the investigations provide cultural insights, then ones that focus only on the negative impacts on attention span will be *narrow*. Of the choices, the words closest in meaning to *narrow* are **shortsighted** and **limited**.

14. **A and E** The word in the blank describes the boss. The word "notwithstanding" indicates contrast. Thus the description of the boss will contrast with the description of the other employees. If the other employees are amicable, the description of the boss will be the opposite of amicable. Now select your own word. A good word for "opposite of amicable" is *unfriendly*. The answer choices closest in meaning to *unfriendly* are **cantankerous** and **frigid**.

15. **C and D** The word in the blank will characterize the accountant. The structure "More *x* than stingy" implies that the characterization of the accountant will have a different connotation than the word "stingy." This characterization will match a description of someone who "will willingly spend money." A good word here would be *thrifty*. The words closest in

meaning to *thrifty* are **frugal** and **thrifty**. (Notice that sometimes the word you predict will show up in the choices!)

16. **A and F** The word in the blank describes the heroine's "uncharacteristic" response to the tragedy. The colon is the important contextual clue in the sentence. In this case, what comes after it will clarify how the heroine typically responds. Her typical response is marked by "sentimentality." Thus her current "uncharacteristic" response will be the opposite of sentimentality. A good predictor is *emotionless*. The choices closest in meaning to *emotionless* are **stoicism** and **indifference**.

17. **D and F** The word in the blank characterizes the outcome of sporting events. The colon is the contextual clue in this sentence. What comes after the colon will clarify the description of the outcomes of sporting events. If "even the best prognostications are flawed," then a good word for the blank would be *surprising*. The words in the choices that best match *surprising* are **unforeseen** and **unpredictable**.

18. **A and F** The word in the blank will describe the lecturer's claims. The word "undermined" implies that there is a contrast between the lecturer's claims and the "authoritativeness" that he projected. The word in the blank should thus be the opposite of what would be expected from someone who projects "authoritativeness." A good prediction would be *shallowness*. The words in the choices that best match *shallowness* are **vacuous** and **superficial**.

19. **C and D** The word in the blank is a characteristic of the new novel. The phrase "bears little resemblance" indicates that the new novel's characteristics will be the opposite of those of the original novel. "Subtle" is the opposite of "heavy-handed," so the word in the blank will be the opposite of "superficiality." Now choose your own word: a good word would be *deep*. Of the choices, the words that most closely match *deep* are **profound** and **probing**.

20. **A and E** The word in the blank will describe "scientific knowledge." The contextual clue in the sentence is the colon. What comes after it will clarify what was stated before it. In this case, what comes after the colon will provide a clue for what the description of scientific knowledge will be. Since scientists recognize that their theories will be "supplanted or amended," the nature of scientific knowledge is that it is *changing*. The words in the choices that best match *changing* are **fluid** and **dynamic**.

21. **C and E** The word in the blank provides a description of the controversial policy. What impact would the record number of high school graduates have on the policy? It would most likely *redeem* it. Of the choices, the words closest in meaning to *redeem* are **vindicated** and **justified**.

Sentence Equivalence Set 3

22. **A and F** The word in the blank describes the beliefs of the various members of the Board. Since the members cannot reach a resolution, their beliefs must be *different*. The words that best match the choices are **divergent** and **discrepant**.

23. **D and E** What potential element of a successful business would "blind" an entrepreneur from attending to the "day-to-day operations of the business"?

The most likely candidate is the *results*. Of the choices, the words closest in meaning to *results* are **implications** and **consequences**.

24. **A and C** The word in the blank describes what the author's "flair for the dramatic" has "devolved" into. The describing phrase at the beginning of the sentence serves as a contextual clue by telling us what the novel now features. The combination of the clue at the beginning of the sentence and the word "devolved" tells us that the word in the blank is an extreme version of "dramatic." A good predictor would be *melodramatic*. The words that best match *melodramatic* are **maudlin** and **sentimental**.

25. **A and E** The word in the blank describes the director's decision. The contextual clue is the describing phrase after the comma. This phrase clarifies the meaning of the author's decision. If the decision is "marked by neither consistency nor, apparently, logic," then a good predictor word would be *random*. The words that best match *random* are **arbitrary** and **haphazard**.

26. **A and F** The word in the blank describes what happened to the actor's excitement after the discovery. Since he discovered that the role was only for a minor character, something negative must have happened to his excitement. A good prediction here would be *decreased*. The words that best match *decreased* are **tempered** and **diminished**.

27. **C and E** The blank describes the author's attitude toward violence. The contextual clues are the description that the author is "amicable and inclined toward harmony" and the phrase after the colon that says the "idea of harm inspired a shudder." A good predictor word to select from these characterizations is *avoided*. Of the choices, the words closest in meaning to *avoided* are **eschewed** and **shirked**.

28. **A and F** The word in the blank explains the relationship between "her belief in his inherent sincerity" and the possibility that "he could sometimes be deceptive." Since she believed him to be sincere, the possibility of his insincerity must have been nonexistent. A good verb to predict is *eliminated*. Of the choices, the words closest in meaning to *eliminated* are **precluded** and **eliminated**.

29. **D and F** The word in the blank describes "Lakoff's account of Dostoevsky's influences." The clause after the comma explains what will go in the blank. Since Lakoff's account did not address "Dostoevsky's concern with the social milieu that he inhabited," the account must have been *limited*. Of the choices, the words closest in meaning to *limited* are **insufficient** and **inadequate**.

30. **A and D** The word in the blank describes the common misconception about yoga. Since "exaggerating the benefits . . . do nothing to dispel this myth," the myth must concern an extreme belief about yoga's benefits. An extreme belief would be the belief that it is a *cure-all*. Of the choices, the words closest in meaning to *cure-all* are **panacea** and **elixir**.

31. **A and E** The word in the blank describes how capitalism is viewed. If the word in the blank implies the belief that capital increases well-being, then capitalism must be *glorified*. Of the choices, the words closest in meaning to *glorified* are **apotheosis** and **deification**.

Reading Comprehension

O f the 20 questions that you will see in each scored Verbal section, approximately 9 will be Reading Comprehension questions. Reading Comprehension questions can be divided into two categories:

- **Information-based passages.** These passages can be classified as "long" or "short." A long passage is generally three to four paragraphs and 500+ words. Each long passage will have four associated questions. You can expect to see one long passage on your test. A short passage is generally one to two paragraphs and 100 to 300 words. Each short passage will have one to four associated questions, though most of the time there will be two or three questions. You can expect to see five to six short passages on your test.

    For both long and short passages, the questions concern the meaning of the passage, the author's purpose, details about the passage, inferences that can be drawn from the passage, and application of the passage's information to other contexts.

- **Argument-based passages.** Each of these passages has a single associated question. An argument-based passage will always be one paragraph (and sometimes as short as a sentence) and will always have one associated multiple-choice question. You can expect to see four to six argument-based passages on your test.

For argument-based passages, the questions concern the logic and structure of an argument. Typical questions will ask you to find an assumption in the argument, to find ways to strengthen or weaken the argument, and to identify the logical structure of the passage. The content for the passages will generally come from the *humanities* (e.g., art, literature, and philosophy), *sciences* (e.g., biology, ecology, astrophysics, and geology), and from the *social sciences* (e.g., economics, psychology, and sociology). No previous familiarity with the information in the passages is assumed or required.

Question Formats

Reading comprehension questions have three formats.

Multiple-Choice Questions—Select One Answer Choice

These are standard multiple-choice questions. You will be given five answer choices and will be asked to select one. Note that argument-based passages will *always* be "multiple choice, choose one."

Multiple-Choice Questions—Select One or More Answer Choices

In these questions, you will be given a question and three answer choices. (In these questions, the answer choice letters will be in square boxes rather than ovals, as a signal that you may choose more than one.) You are to select all the choices that provide a correct answer to the question. In these questions, at least one of the choices will always be correct. There is no partial credit. These questions are inherently more difficult, so if you are short on time, you should guess on these questions.

Select-in-Passage

In these questions, you will be asked to highlight the sentence in the passage that best answers the question. The suggested approach for argument-based passages is fundamentally different from the approach for information-based passages, so let's consider the two groups separately.

Information-Based Passages

Many test-takers preparing for the Reading Comprehension section are intimidated by both the length and scope of the passages. Though the content of the passages is certainly not straightforward (most of them are graduate-level texts), the following strategies will equip you with the proper mind-set and approach for both the passages and accompanying questions. A large component of this section will focus on how to be an *efficient, active reader*. Throughout this section, the focus will be on the necessity of asking yourself *big-picture* questions about the passage and identifying concrete, *textual* evidence in support of your answers. After all, the test-makers need to justify whichever answer they deem correct, so you should be able to do so as well.

Developing the appropriate approach for GRE passages largely requires the development of the mind-set that the test-makers are addressing in the passages and associated questions. These passages are written by academics and are about academic topics, so you will want to view the passages with a keen, analytical eye. Because of this, there are no foolproof methods for tackling Reading Comprehension. Many companies and books suggest reading the questions and then the passage, but assuming you have budgeted your time correctly, *you should always read the passage first*. Why? Because properly answering the questions and eliminating wrong choices requires an understanding of the passage's structure and the author's tone and main purpose, all of which cannot be fully understood unless you've read the passage first.

This section will look at how you should best approach the passages to align your mind-set with that of the test-makers.

Principle 1: Engage Yourself with the Text

Most of the time when you read, you tend to passively absorb the information without questioning what it's telling you or even what its relevance is to the author's main point. On GRE passages, you need to read *actively*, with an eye toward the passage's *structure*. As you read through the passage, you should always be asking yourself questions. What's the author's main point? Why is she telling me this? How does this detail relate to the passage's overall purpose? Oftentimes, there's a tendency for readers to get bogged down in the content of the passage and to lose sight of the bigger picture, but by asking yourself *Why?* instead of *What?*, you'll be able to efficiently absorb the passage's content without wasting time on minor details.

Principle 2: Slow Down, Then Speed Up

The beginning of a passage always introduces essential information. It will introduce key people or terms, important phenomena, the background for a theory, or in many cases, *the passage's main point*. Since this information is so important, you should slow down when reading the first few sentences of a short passage and the first paragraph of a long passage. *Make sure that you understand all the terms and information introduced at the beginning of the passage.* Even if this means losing time at the beginning, you'll make up for it later in the passage by speeding up when you're only looking at minor details.

Principle 3: Identify the Main Purpose

When you are reading a passage, your initial goal should be to identify the author's purpose. This means asking yourself: "*Why did the author write the passage?*"

Many test-takers tend to answer this question by giving a list of *what* the author said, but this is not the answer that you're looking for. *In one sentence, you should be able to say why the author wrote the passage:*

Incorrect: "The author says A, B, C, D, and then switches to say E."

Correct: "The author wants to show that a perspective on human evolution is flawed."

The incorrect response only identifies information in the passage without understanding it in the larger context of the author's *goal*. The correct response identifies a reason the author has for writing the passage.
Generally, the author's purpose will fall into four categories:

- **Explain.** The author's goal is to explain a concept or phenomenon.
- **Resolve/reconcile.** The author's goal is to resolve two or more competing viewpoints.
- **Introduce.** The author's goal is to introduce a surprising discovery, phenomenon, or perspective
- **Solve.** The author's goal is to provide a solution or answer to a question presented in the passage.

To identify a passage's main idea, you should focus on *contrast signals* and *continuity signals* similar to the ones discussed in Chapter 4.

In the context of reading passages, these clues are essential because they provide pivots for the direction of the passage. When you see a contextual signal, you should slow down and identify the importance of that sentence to the passage. Usually, that sentence will either determine the main purpose of the passage or provide a transition into the passage's main purpose. Look at the following excerpt from a passage:

> . . . Because the volume of shipments during the 16th and 17th centuries was so low compared to modern standards, most historians contend that colonial era trade is irrelevant to the origins of the modern corporation. *However*, despite the relatively low volume of trade, the hierarchical structure of these organizations is an edifying antecedent to today's high-volume companies.

If you were asking yourself *why* as you read the first sentence, you probably couldn't arrive at an answer. The real purpose doesn't manifest itself until the contextual clue *however*. Once you see this word, you know that the author is introducing a point of emphasis, and you should slow down to understand what this point is, how it relates to the previous sentence, and what type of information might come after it.

In the preceding excerpt, you see that the claim "the hierarchical structure of these organizations is an edifying antecedent to today's high-volume companies" contrasts with what most historians think about the role of 16th- and 17th-century trade in the development of the modern corporation. You can thus infer that the author's goal is probably to *introduce*: the author believes that the 16th- and 17th-century trading companies are relevant to the development of the modern corporation, and he will most likely go on to clarify that surprising new idea in the rest of the passage.

Principle 4: Understand the Role of Evidence

Once you have identified the main purpose, the next step is to understand the role that the rest of the information in the passage plays. To do so, you must keep the following point in mind: *everything the author says will somehow relate to his main point.*

In a short passage, this information may constitute only a few sentences, whereas in a longer passage, it may comprise several paragraphs, but the general point still stands: as you read through the rest of the passage, you want to understand *why* the author is presenting the information that he does. For example, is he trying to qualify a claim? Is he trying to provide evidence for his theory? Is he trying to address a rebuttal to his theory?

This advice is especially helpful for long passages and for dense scientific passages. For long passages, where time constraints can prevent you from reading the entire passage, focus on the first and last sentence of each paragraph, and use those sentences to understand the role the paragraph plays in the overall passage. If a question refers you to the details of that paragraph, you can go back and read it more carefully.

For dense scientific passages (or any passage that contains information that is difficult to absorb), do not read and reread the supporting information. Instead, make sure that you have an idea of why the author is introducing that content, and if necessary, go back to that information later if a question addresses it.

So how can you identify when the author is providing supporting evidence? Just as there are important contextual clues for identifying main purpose, there are also important contextual clues for the introduction of evidence.

Clues to Introducing Evidence

For example
For instance
Indeed
Because of
As a result of
Since
Illustrated by
Shown by
Evidence for

Let's extend the previous excerpt to see these contextual clues in action.

. . . Because the volume of shipments during the 16th and 17th centuries was so low compared to modern standards, most historians contend that colonial era trade is irrelevant to the origins of the modern corporation. However,

despite the relatively low volume of trade, the hierarchical structure of
5   these organizations was an edifying antecedent to today's high-volume
companies. *For example*, the complexity of the trans-Atlantic tea trade
required the development of tiered management structures to coordinate
the consolidation of tea from disparate sources and to ensure its proper
distribution to the American colonies. *Indeed*, to safeguard against potential
10   pilfering, the owners of these trading companies established bases in both
the United States and England, a transnational corporate structure that sees
its full realization in today's multinational conglomerates.

Recall that you identified that the author's main purpose is to show that 16th-
and 17th-century trading companies are relevant to the development of the
modern corporation. When reading the rest of the paragraph, you should focus on
how that information relates to the main point. The contextual clues *for example*
and *indeed* are essential to understanding the role of this supporting evidence.
You know that what comes after *for example* will *support* the author's main point.
Because *indeed* indicates continuity, you know that the last sentence will serve
to further reinforce this main point. Thus when reading these sentences, you can
understand the structure of the paragraph and the role of each of the sentences
even if you haven't digested all of the minor information. And this is not a problem:
minor information should not concern you. The reason the author mentions it is
the larger concern.

Principle 5: Identify the Author's Tone

Tone refers to the author's attitude toward the subject matter in the passage. For
example, an author can be *pessimistic*, *slightly hopeful*, *objective*, *skeptical*, and
so on. To identify tone, look for *valenced* words in the passage. If the author uses
words like *fortunately* or *thankfully*, you know that the author feels positively
about whatever he is discussing, whereas words like *regrettably* indicate that the
author feels negatively about the content matter of the passage. However, note that,
while the author might *regret* a situation, he will rarely *abhor* it. Why? Because
the author's tone in a GRE passage will almost never be extreme. *Identifying* tone
is important not only because some questions explicitly ask about tone, but also
because you can use the author's tone to eliminate wrong answer choices.
Now let's put these strategies into action with a full passage and associated
questions.

Scientists have long acknowledged that the deterioration of the ocean's
coral reef ecosystems is at least partly due to the effects of global climate
change. One of the primary consequences of this change in climate has
been the disruption of the symbiotic relationship between the polyps that
5   compose coral reefs and the algae that feed on these polyps. Researchers have
identified that the culprit for much of this disruption is coral "bleaching,"
which occurs when the algae feeding on the polyps die and therefore lose
their green pigmentation. The prevailing explanation for coral bleaching
has been that the increase in the ocean's temperature disrupts the process of
10   photosynthesis—the conversion of light into energy—and thereby kills the

algae. However, recent research has shown that such bleaching occurs even in the absence of light.

Tolleter and his team of scientists showed that bleaching still occurs even if the algae are heat-stressed in the dark. This finding is significant
15 because during the dark, the algae's photosynthetic machinery is turned off, meaning that the heat's effect on the algae must occur by disrupting cellular processes other than photosynthesis. Tolleter's findings, though keeping intact the belief that ocean temperatures affect bleaching, question the exact mechanism through which this bleaching occurs. Future research
20 is necessary to identify the other routes by which bleaching occurs, but these findings, by implicating additional mechanisms in the process of bleaching, should point scientists toward new directions in identifying ways to decelerate this bleaching process.

As you probably recognized, there are a lot of details in this passage, along with terminology that may not be completely familiar to you. But let's try to take a big-picture approach toward the passage. In the beginning of the passage, the author introduces an important term: "bleaching." An efficient reader would *slow down* to understand this term. Once you understand what bleaching is, your next step is to *identify the author's main purpose.* He gives you "the prevailing theory" for why bleaching occurs, but is the author's main purpose to describe this theory? No. In the last sentence of the first paragraph, the contextual clue "However" indicates that the author's purpose is to show that bleaching can happen for reasons other than disrupting photosynthesis. Now that you know why the author has written the passage, your next step is to *identify the role of the evidence*—in this case, why the author wrote the second paragraph.

The last sentence of the first paragraph questions the prevailing theory, and the second paragraph is spent providing evidence for why this theory has been questioned. Though the terminology and processes might be difficult to follow, you know that the role of this paragraph is to *explain why the prevailing theory of the disruption of photosynthesis is not adequate to account for the phenomenon of bleaching.* Now that you have a big-picture understanding of the passage, you can move on to the questions.

Question Types

This section reviews common GRE question-types by seeing how they relate to the previous passage. But before that, keep in mind two important guidelines you should follow when answering any Reading Comprehension question:

- Eliminate any choices that contradict the passage.
- Eliminate any choices that are irrelevant to the question being asked.

Main-Point Questions

Main-point questions can be phrased as:

- "The primary purpose of the passage is to . . ."
- "The author's primary purpose is to . . ."
- "The author is primarily concerned with . . ."
- "Which of the following would be an appropriate title for the passage?"

The primary purpose of the passage is to

- (A) question the validity of "ocean bleaching"
- (B) explain why "bleaching" occurs
- (C) explain the role of photosynthesis in the process of "bleaching"
- (D) introduce an alternate explanation for "bleaching" and its implications
- (E) identify the effect of global warming on coral reefs

How to Tackle a Main-Point Question

The answer to any main-point question will encompass the entire scope of the passage. Oftentimes, there will be choices that provide information that is true about the passage but that does not fully address the entire purpose of the passage. To avoid these answers, ask yourself: Does this choice explain the passage as a whole or just part of the passage?

Let's review the possible choices with this advice in mind:

- **Choice A.** Remember the importance of *evidence*. The author does not question whether bleaching occurs. → Incorrect
- **Choice B.** This is a trap answer. In the third sentence, the author states: "Researchers have identified that the culprit for much of this disruption is coral 'bleaching,' which occurs when the algae feeding on the polyps die and therefore lose their green pigmentation." Thus the author does explain the process of bleaching. However, the point of the passage is not to discuss this process. → Incorrect
- **Choice C.** The author does more than just *explain* the role of photosynthesis in bleaching; he provides evidence that refutes it. → Incorrect
- **Choice D.** This answer successfully addresses the scope of the passage. The author spends the second paragraph refuting the view that bleaching occurs because of a disruption of photosynthesis, and concludes by saying that "these findings . . . should point scientists toward new directions in identifying ways to decelerate this bleaching process." → Correct
- **Choice E.** This choice is too broad. Though the author does state that bleaching is due to global warming, the passage is not primarily concerned with the effects of global warming. → Incorrect

Detail Questions

Detail questions can be phrased as:

- "According to the passage . . ."
- "Based on the passage, which of the following is true . . ."
- "The author mentions which of the following . . ."

According to the passage, the primary difference between Tolleter's findings and the "prevailing explanation" (line 8) is that Tolleter's findings

- (A) de-emphasize the role of climate change in coral bleaching
- (B) provide a new explanation for the mechanism behind coral bleaching
- (C) show that coral bleaching is initiated by means other than the disruption of photosynthesis
- (D) resolve the debate over the causes of coral bleaching
- (E) reinforce the role that temperature change has on coral bleaching

How to Tackle a Detail Question

To answer a *detail* question, you should focus on finding specific text from the passage that answers the question. For *detail* questions, you do not need to make any inferences and should avoid making assumptions. Instead, look at each choice, and identify which choice is best supported by concrete evidence from the passage. Let's review the previous choices with this advice in mind.

- **Choice A.** The passage states that Tolleter's team focused on the cellular mechanisms behind coral bleaching. The role of climate change is not questioned. → Incorrect
- **Choice B.** At first glance, this answer might appear correct. However, the author explicitly states that Tolleter's findings "question the exact mechanism through which this bleaching occurs." Questioning the mechanism is different from "providing a new explanation." Since there is no evidence that Tolleter's team has provided a new explanation, eliminate Choice B. → Incorrect
- **Choice C.** This choice restates the author's description of the significance of Tolleter's findings. The author states that Tolleter's findings "question the exact mechanism through which this bleaching occurs." Choice C is a restatement of this fact and is thus supported by the passage. → Correct
- **Choice D.** There is no evidence that Tolleter's team has "resolved" the debate; instead, they have questioned the "prevailing explanation." → Incorrect
- **Choice E.** The role of temperature change is not an issue in the passage. → Incorrect

Inference Questions

Inference questions can be phrased as:

- "The passage suggests . . ."
- "The passage implies" . . ."
- "Which of the following can be inferred from the passage . . ."
- "Which of the following can be concluded from the passage . . ."

Consider each of the choices separately and select all that apply.

The passage suggests which of the following about photosynthesis?

- A   It can sometimes occur in the absence of light.
- B   Tolleter's findings call into doubt its role in coral bleaching.
- C   It is not the only cellular mechanism implicated in coral bleaching.

How to Tackle an Inference Question

Inference questions are very similar to detail questions. As is the case with detail questions, with inference questions you should focus on identifying concrete textual evidence to justify your answer. The primary difference is the following: *To answer an inference question, you must draw a conclusion based on information in the passage.* With inference questions, the actual answer will never be *explicitly* stated in the passage. Instead, it will be *implied* by what the author says. To answer these questions, look for which choices can be directly inferred from the given information in the passage.

Let's review the previous choices with this advice in mind. The passage suggests which of the following about photosynthesis?

- **Choice A.** The passage questions the role of photosynthesis in coral bleaching by providing evidence that coral bleaching occurs even when the algae are heat-stressed in the dark. Since being heat-stressed in the dark is used as evidence against the role of photosynthesis in coral bleaching, it can be inferred that photosynthesis does *not* occur in the absence of light. Choice A states the opposite of what can be inferred and is thus incorrect. → Incorrect
- **Choice B.** The passage states that "the heat's effect on the algae must occur by disrupting cellular processes other than photosynthesis." The author discusses the effect of heat on algae in the absence of light to show that bleaching occurs even when the photosynthesis machinery is turned off. → Correct
- **Choice C.** In the last sentence, the author states that Tolleter's findings suggest that additional mechanisms must be implicated as causes for coral bleaching. The term "additional" implies "in addition to photosynthesis." → Correct

Select-in-Passage Questions

In Select-in-Passage questions, you will be asked to highlight a sentence in the passage that corresponds to the information that the question asks for. These questions will usually be phrased as "Select the sentence in which the author . . ."

> Select the sentence in which the author introduces a theory that Tolleter's research rejects.

How to Tackle a Select-in-Passage Question

Use the context of the question to determine where to turn to in the passage. In the first paragraph, the author introduces the background of coral bleaching and previous explanations for it, so you should look there. Since Tolleter's team rejects photosynthesis as an explanation for coral bleaching, find the sentence that introduces the previous belief that photosynthesis was responsible for coral bleaching. The sentence is "The prevailing explanation for coral bleaching has been that the increase in the ocean's temperature disrupts the process of photosynthesis—the conversion of light into energy—and thereby kills the algae."

Vocabulary Questions

Vocabulary questions are usually phrased in the following way: *In the context in which it appears, ". . ." most nearly means . . . .*

On the computer-based test, the word being referred to will always be highlighted.

> In the context in which it appears, "implicating" (line 21) most nearly means
>
> - (A) suggesting
> - (B) accusing
> - (C) questioning
> - (D) undermining
> - (E) neglecting

How to Tackle a Vocabulary Question

Treat reading-based vocabulary questions the same way you treat Sentence Equivalence and Text Completion questions: use the context to make your own prediction; then find which word in the choices most closely matches your prediction.

Let's review the previous question with this advice in mind: "Implicating" appears in the following sentence: "Future research is necessary to identify the other routes by which bleaching occurs, but these findings, by implicating additional mechanisms in the process of bleaching, should point scientists toward new directions in identifying ways to decelerate this bleaching process." The word is used in reference to the discovery of mechanisms other than photosynthesis that are responsible for coral bleaching. A good prediction would thus be *discovering*. Of the choices, the word closest in meaning to *discovering* is **suggesting**. The correct answer is Choice A.

Argument-Based Passages

In an argument-based passage, you will be given one paragraph and one associated question. Though ETS groups these passages with other types of Reading Comprehension passages, your approach toward these passages should differ from the approach you take toward a typical Reading Comprehension passage. Usually, the passage will present information and a claim drawn from that information. Your task will be to identify information that most impacts the argument by strengthening it, weakening it, providing an assumption, or resolving an apparent discrepancy. Let's take a look at a sample question and how to approach it:

> Two software producers, DigiCom and EverDrop, recently launched new word processors. The two word processors are comparably priced, and each received highly favorable reviews during independent consumer tests. Nonetheless, since DigiCom has spent more money than EverDrop on advertising, sales of the DigiCom word processor will greatly exceed those of the EverDrop word processor.
>
> Which of the following, if true, most strongly supports the author's prediction?
>
> (A) DigiCom's production team spent twice as many hours refining the usability of its current word processor as it did refining the usability of its previous word processor.
> (B) Any large differences between the two word processors are obvious only to users with specific experience in software engineering.
> (C) News and media outlets have not extensively publicized the release of DigiCom and EverDrop's software.
> (D) DigiCom's advertising budget for the new word processor is greater than its advertising budget for any of its other lines of software.
> (E) EverDrop's advertising team is well-known for perfectly tailoring the company's ads to its target demographic.

How to Tackle Questions on an Argument-Based Passage

First, read and categorize the question. The sample question is a "strengthen" question. The correct answer should provide a fact that will support the author's argument.

Next, understand the situation in the passage. Think of the situation as a summary of all the background **facts** presented in the passage. In this case, the situation can be paraphrased as the following: two companies have released new software that is about equally priced and that has generated positive reviews.

Next, identify the argument. The *argument* is an opinion drawn in the passage based on certain evidence. The *evidence* used to support the opinion is called the *premise* or *premises*, and the opinion the author draws is called the *claim*.

To identify the claim of the passage, look for words such as:

as a result
belief
consequently
hypothesis
in conclusion
may
might
nevertheless
nonetheless
predicts
probably
therefore
thus
will

These are good claim signals because such words generally introduce a belief that *can be disputed*. If something in the passage can be disputed, then it is a claim, not a fact.

To identify the premises of the passage, look for words such as:

since
because
due to
owing to
as a result of

All of these phrases play the role of providing evidence that leads to a conclusion. Thus when you see these phrases, you should be on the lookout for the author's main claim.

Now that you know what the argument, premises, and claim are, let's identify them in the passage. In the previous passage, the argument is the following:

Nonetheless, since DigiCom has spent more money than EverDrop on advertising, the sales of the DigiCom word processor will greatly exceed those of the EverDrop word processor.

The *claim* is that sales of the DigiCom word processor will greatly exceed those of the EverDrop word processor. This claim is based on the *premise* that "DigiCom has spent more money than EverDrop on advertising."

Once you have identified the claim and premises of the passage, your next step is to think about *assumptions* made in the argument. You can think of an *assumption* as the glue that holds the premises and claim together. Basically, it is a piece of evidence that is *necessary* for the conclusion to logically follow from the premises. Though any argument can have infinite assumptions, some will be more obvious than others. A major assumption in the previous argument is that *increased advertising will actually lead to increased sales.*

Finally, go through the choices. When going through the choices, your goal is to identify the choice that *best* addresses the link between the premises and the claim:

- In a **strengthen** question, you are looking for a piece of information that strengthens the link.
- In a **weaken** question, you are looking for a piece of information that *breaks* the link between premise and conclusion.
- In an **assumption** question, you are looking for a piece of information that is *necessary* for the conclusion to be drawn from the premises.

Since this is a strengthen question, you should look for a choice strengthening the argument that increased advertising will lead to additional sales for the DigiCom word processor.

Now let's look at the choices.

- **Choice A.** The argument of the passage concerns the link between increased advertising and increased sales. The usability of the software is *irrelevant* to the passage's argument. → Incorrect
- **Choice B.** The argument of the passage concerns the link between increased advertising and increased sales. The ability of users to differentiate between the word processors is *irrelevant*. → Incorrect
- **Choice C.** This choice strengthens the link between the premise and the conclusion. You want an answer choice showing that increased advertisements will lead to increased sales for DigiCom. If the given statement in Choice C is true, then the possibility that the advertising will be ineffective due to prior publicizing of the software is eliminated. By eliminating a potential weakness, Choice C strengthens the argument. → Correct
- **Choice D.** This choice might be tempting since it addresses DigiCom's advertising budget. However, it does *not* address the gap between advertising and increased revenues. You are already told that DigiCom will spend more money than EverDrop on advertising. The fact that this advertising budget is greater than for any other DigiCom line of software is *irrelevant*. → Incorrect
- **Choice E.** In contrast to the other three wrong choices, this choice *does* impact the argument. However, it does so by *weakening* the argument instead of strengthening it. Recall that you are looking for information that supports the claim that DigiCom's increased advertising of its product will lead to an increase in sales of that product. If Choice E is true, then the link between increased advertising and increased revenue is broken. Why? Because the choice provides evidence showing that DigiCom's increase in advertising might *not* lead to an increase in revenue. Thus Choice E impacts the argument, but does so by weakening the argument rather than strengthening it. → Incorrect

Exercise: Reading Comprehension

Questions 1 to 2 refer to the following passage.

When Tocqueville came to America in 1831, he expressed a
sentiment that is echoed in the works of Bloom and Kennedy: that
American democracy, by encouraging dissent, can lead to its own
undoing. But in contrast to the pessimism that dominates Bloom's
5 and Kennedy's thinking, Tocqueville's analysis went a step further.
While acknowledging the seeming inevitability of dissent among
the citizenry, he also recognized that beneath this frustration there
lay a fundamental belief that democratic politics would ultimately
amend the situations that aroused complaint. As Tocqueville noted, at
10 any given point in time democracy can appear chaotic, shallow, and
contradictory. But, he noted, it was never stagnant. For Tocqueville,
democracy's tendency to encourage and accommodate discontent
was its greatest virtue. Because it is self-correcting, a properly run
democratic system would ultimately benefit from any discontent
15 because the system is designed to rectify the problem.

1. The author mentions Tocqueville's belief that democracy "was never
   stagnant" (line 11) to

   (A) highlight Tocqueville's belief in the self-correcting nature of
       democracy
   (B) introduce a difference between Tocqueville's thinking and that of
       Bloom and Kennedy
   (C) explain why Tocqueville believes citizens of democratic nations are
       often upset
   (D) suggest ways to eliminate the frustration of the citizens of
       democratic nations
   (E) imply that many of the concerns of democratic citizens are baseless

2. It can be inferred from the passage that Tocqueville agrees with Bloom
   and Kennedy about which of the following?

   (A) Democracy is the ideal form of government.
   (B) Discontent is inherent in any democracy.
   (C) Democracy can only function when its citizens express concern over
       important issues.
   (D) Democracy's greatest virtue is its adaptability.
   (E) If not properly run, democracy can undermine itself.

Questions 3 to 5 refer to the following passage:

One of the key necessities for understanding an organism's evolutionary history is the identification of the habitats in which the organism's ancestors thrived. Biologists have developed such techniques as radiocarbon dating and biochronology to date fossils and
5 thereby arrive at an approximate range for an organism's existence. But knowing that an organism existed during a certain time period says little about the environment that the organism inhabited. Since the earth periodically goes through heating and cooling periods, biologists cannot simply assume that a region's current climate is the same as it
10 was for, say, a lemur that inhabited that region six million years ago.

To get past this quandary, biologists study the fossils of foraminifera, which are microscopic organisms suspended in the waters of the world's oceans. Foraminifera consume two types of oxygen isotope: oxygen-16 and oxygen-18. Oxygen-16 is lighter
15 than oxygen-18, and as global temperatures rise, more oxygen-16 than oxygen-18 evaporates. By studying the fossils of foraminifera, researchers are able to identify the concentrations of these two isotopes at a given time. Researchers can then use the different ratios of the two isotopes during different time periods to make highly educated
20 inferences about the global climate during a specific time period.

3. In the context in which it appears, "quandary" (line 11) most nearly means

   Ⓐ investigation
   Ⓑ dilemma
   Ⓒ conjecture
   Ⓓ approximation
   Ⓔ surprise

4. The passage is primarily concerned with

   Ⓐ introducing a problem and explaining a technique for addressing it
   Ⓑ highlighting the different ways that two types of chemicals can be used
   Ⓒ evaluating the usefulness of a scientific strategy
   Ⓓ introducing a scientific finding and discussing its implications
   Ⓔ explaining a difficulty faced by scientists

For this question, consider each of the choices separately and select all that apply.

5. Which of the following can be inferred from the passage?

A During a heating period, the ratio of oxygen-16 to oxygen-18 in the ocean decreases.

B Foraminifera can be useful in identifying the age of various fossils.

C Radioactive dating and biochronology use similar mechanisms to draw their conclusions.

Questions 6 to 9 refer to the following passage:

A detailed look into the past 13,000 years of human history reveals an important trend. The ascent of European civilization and its conquest of other cultures is not a result of some sort of inborn superiority on the part of the European conquerors. Rather, this cultural "success" is
5 attributable to the confluence of favorable environmental conditions and fortuitous cultural events. Or so argues Diamond, in his well-received analysis of the Western world's rise to dominance.

Diamond provides a wealth of data to support his point. Citing variables as varied as the mineral composition of a local region,
10 fluctuations in weather, and access to docile animals, he argues that the development and evolution of any civilization is contingent on external variables. Since these variables are inherently uncontrollable, the civilizations for which these factors were aligned favorably were the ones that were most likely to thrive. Though Diamond's use of detailed
15 evidence is refreshing, and his ability to use such disparate information to draw broad conclusions is creative, it is the sweeping nature of his conclusions that makes his argument problematic. The very act of making inferences about local environments thousands of years ago is fraught with the potential for error, but Diamond gives little weight to
20 these concerns. Indeed, by placing excessive emphasis on this data, he paints a simplistic portrait of the past 13,000 years of human history that only passingly acknowledges the roles of the individual human actors and their cultures. Paradoxically, in rightfully trying to debunk myths about Eurasian supremacy, Diamond marginalizes the cultures
25 that he is attempting to defend.

6. The author of the passage is primarily concerned with

A highlighting the importance of certain cultural trends
B introducing and evaluating a theory about why civilizations thrive
C explaining the role of data in making predictions
D discussing the factors that shape the evolution of a civilization
E analyzing the critical reception of a recent theory

7. The author most likely mentions "the mineral composition of a local region, fluctuations in weather, and access to docile animals" (lines 9–10) in order to

   Ⓐ provide examples that Diamond uses to support his theory
   Ⓑ suggest that Diamond's theory is simplistic
   Ⓒ analyze the logical cohesiveness of Diamond's theory
   Ⓓ highlight the factors relevant to a civilization's ascent
   Ⓔ rebut Diamond's central thesis

8. In the context in which it appears, "fraught" (line 19) most nearly means

   Ⓐ defined
   Ⓑ regarded
   Ⓒ determined
   Ⓓ rife
   Ⓔ coincided

9. Select the sentence in the passage in which the author introduces a position that Diamond's book challenges.

Questions 10 to 11 refer to the following passage:

Lucian Freud famously remarked that anything he might say about his art is as relevant to the art as the noise a tennis player emits when hitting a ball. Freud presented this analogy as a way of capturing his belief about the relationship between artist and art: It is the art that
5 lends significance to the artist, and not the other way around. Such a view, while unorthodox for any epoch, was especially so for the time period in which Freud created his major works. In the 20th-century, the lines between art and consumer culture became blurred, and self-promotion became *de rigueur* for most major artists of the period.
10 Freud's tendency to deflect attention is not, as some commentators have stated, wholly a by-product of a desire to prevent encroachments into his personal life. Rather, it is predominantly a function of his deep-seated belief that if one's art is given a place of prominence, the careful critic will be able to discern the thought processes and
15 motivations of the artist.

10. Which of the following situations is most in line with Freud's belief about "the relationship between artist and art" (line 4)?

   Ⓐ A sculptor who refuses to be interviewed because she values her anonymity.

   Ⓑ A potter who refers to her creations when asked personal questions.

   Ⓒ A muralist who uses scenes from her own life in her creations.

   Ⓓ A composer who acknowledges others' influences on her compositions.

   Ⓔ A novelist who writes novels that take place several centuries ago.

For this question, consider each of the choices separately and select all that apply.

11. The information in the passage supports which of the following as reasons for Freud's rejection of self-promoting techniques?

   Ⓐ A desire to maintain his privacy

   Ⓑ A desire to rebel against what was considered conventional behavior of 20th-century artists

   Ⓒ The belief that the art held more significance than the artist who created it

Question 12 refers to the following passage:

Gorland is considering a law that will allow the advertising of prescription medications. Critics of the practice worry that people who see these advertisements will seek out inappropriate prescriptions and thereby endanger their health. However, advertisers believe that since doctors ultimately decide whether to prescribe a given medication to a patient, these concerns are unfounded.

12. In responding to the critics' concerns, which of the following is an assumption that the advertisers must make?

   Ⓐ The majority of people seeking medical care have seen advertisements for prescriptions.

   Ⓑ The advertisements for prescription medications are designed to deceive consumers.

   Ⓒ People seeking health care often attempt to diagnose themselves before seeing a doctor.

   Ⓓ Doctors will not be swayed by patients seeking inappropriate prescriptions.

   Ⓔ Not all doctor visits are for the purpose of obtaining medication.

Question 13 refers to the following passage:

Business has always been a popular major for students at four-year universities. However, over the past 20 years, the percentage of students at four-year universities who major in business has decreased from 35% to 23%. Clearly, fewer students are majoring in business now than they did 20 years ago.

13. Which of the following, if true, most weakens the conclusion?

   (A) Many students who consider majoring in business end up majoring in related disciplines.
   (B) When surveyed, most students state that they major in business because it is lucrative.
   (C) The percentage of students majoring in disciplines related to business has decreased over the past 20 years.
   (D) Fewer employers seek students with business degrees now than was the case 20 years ago.
   (E) The number of students enrolled at four-year universities has increased over the past 20 years.

Question 14 refers to the following passage:

Executives at company X are wrong to conclude that the company will see an increase in profits over the next several years. **Though it is true that the company's profits increased each of the past five years**, many competitors have entered the market during this time period. **The competitors have used these past few years to develop products that will directly compete with company X's products during the next several years.**

14. In the preceding argument, the two portions in boldface play which of the following roles?

   (A) The first provides a consideration that argues against the main conclusion of the argument; the second is that conclusion.
   (B) The first provides evidence for the main conclusion of the argument; the second supports an intermediate conclusion in the argument.
   (C) The first provides a consideration that argues against the main conclusion of the argument; the second provides evidence that supports the argument's main conclusion.
   (D) The first provides an intermediate conclusion in the argument; the second provides evidence that supports the argument's main conclusion.
   (E) The first provides an intermediate conclusion in the argument; the second provides evidence against that intermediate conclusion.

Question 15 refers to the following passage:

Analyst: Sepoma, a major furniture manufacturer, had a large decline in sales revenue last year. However, this report is unexpected. Furniture retailers have stated that although overall sales of furniture decreased last year, sales of Sepoma furniture actually increased.

15. Which of the following, if true, best explains the unexpected situation above?

   Ⓐ Much of Sepoma's revenue comes from making parts for other furniture manufacturers.

   Ⓑ Last year, Sepoma spent more on advertising than it usually does.

   Ⓒ Sepoma's decline in revenue was less than the average decline in revenue for its major competitors.

   Ⓓ When revenues are weak, Sepoma is reluctant to find ways to cut costs.

   Ⓔ In a survey, potential buyers of furniture indicated that they thought Sepoma furniture was superior to that of most other brands on the market.

Exercise Answers

1. **A** The author uses this line when elaborating on Tocqueville's argument that democracy would benefit from dissent. Tocqueville believed that democracy could tolerate and benefit from dissent because it is self-correcting. The fact that it is "never stagnant" is in support of its self-correcting nature.

2. **B** All three authors agree that there will be dissent in a democracy. However, they disagree on the consequences of this dissent.

3. **B** The author refers to "this quandary" when discussing the problem confronting biologists who want to determine the environmental habitat of the species whose fossils they have discovered. A good prediction for the answer would thus be *problem*. Of the choices, the word closest in meaning to *problem* is **dilemma**.

4. **A** In the first paragraph, the author introduces a problem that scientists face (namely, determining the climate of the habitats of ancient species). In the second paragraph, the author discusses a technique developed to address this problem.

5. **A** The author states that "as global temperatures rise, more oxygen-16 than oxygen-18 evaporates." This statement implies that during heating periods, there is relatively less oxygen-16 in the ocean. It thus follows that the ratio of oxygen-16 to oxygen-18 must decrease.

6. **B** In the first paragraph, the author introduces Diamond's theory. In the second paragraph, the author evaluates the theory by noting its logical shortcomings.

7. **A** The author mentions these data as examples of what Diamond uses to support his point.

8. **D** The author uses the word "fraught" in reference to what the author believes is an erroneous assumption made by Diamond. Since the author is conveying his belief that Diamond's thinking is flawed, he probably thinks that Diamond's thinking is *full* of error. Of the choices, the word closest in meaning to *full* is **rife**.

9. **Sentence 2** Although the author devotes much of the passage to evaluating Diamond's theory, he starts off by mentioning the line of thought that Diamond challenges. This line of thought is found in sentence 2.

10. **B** Freud believes that "it is the art that lends significance to the artist, and not the other way around." He uses this fact as justification for giving his art prominence over his personal life. The situation that most closely matches the this notion is Choice B.

11. **A and C**

    Choice A: The author states "Freud's tendency to deflect attention is not, as some commentators have stated, wholly a by-product of a desire to prevent encroachments into his personal life." The use of the word "wholly" implies that his rejection of self-promotion is *somewhat* motivated by a desire to maintain his privacy. Thus Choice A is correct.

    Choice B: Though Freud's beliefs about art were unorthodox for a 20th-century artist, nothing in the passage suggests that a desire to be unorthodox motivated his rejection of self-promotion. Thus Choice B is incorrect.

Choice C: The passage implies that Freud rejected self-promotion because he wanted to give his art "a place of prominence." Thus Choice C is correct.

12. **D** The author argues that "these concerns are unfounded" based on the fact that doctors have the ultimate say on whether to prescribe medication to a patient. For this argument to be valid, it must be assumed that the patients seeking inappropriate medications will not be able to convince the doctor to prescribe the unnecessary medications. If these patients *were* able to convince the doctor, then even though the doctor has the ultimate say, the critics' concerns would be legitimate.

13. **E** The passage's conclusion is that "fewer students are majoring in business now than they did 20 years ago." This claim is based on the fact that the *percentage* of students majoring in business has decreased over the past 20 years. The claim uses a percentage to draw a conclusion about an actual value. If it turns out that the number of students enrolled at these colleges had also increased, then the decrease in the percentage would not necessarily lead to a decrease in the number of students majoring in business. The correct answer is thus E.

14. **C** The main conclusion of the argument is "Executives at company X are wrong to conclude that the company will see an increase in profits over the next several years." This conclusion is supported by the evidence that competitors have recently entered the market and have developed products that will compete with Company X. A consideration against the conclusion is that profits increased in each of the five years. The first boldface is thus against the main conclusion, and the second boldface is in support of the main conclusion. The correct answer is Choice C.

15. **A** First, identify what is unexpected about the situation. Sepoma's revenues decreased even though sales of its furniture increased. How could this be the case? Sepoma must have sources of revenue other than its own furniture. Choice A is the correct answer because it shows that Sepoma makes money by selling parts to other manufacturers. If the revenue for the furniture of those other manufacturers decreased, then Sepoma's revenue would have decreased as well.

GRE Quantitative Reasoning

CHAPTER 7

Two Essential Quantitative Reasoning Strategies

Study this chapter to learn about:

- Strategy 1: Plug in numbers
- Strategy 2: Back-solve

The following strategies are meant to apply generally to all content areas. Though no GRE question is "designed" for you to use these strategies, they can be effective in situations where no algebraic or conceptual solution is immediately apparent. When working through the questions later in the book, focus on mastering all approaches toward the question—both the algebraic, content-based approach and the "strategic" approach, where possible.

Strategy 1: Plug In Numbers

One of the primary difficulties test-takers have with algebra is its abstract nature. **Plugging in numbers** helps you get past the abstract by using concrete values in place of variables. *You can plug in numbers any time there are variables in the answer choices.* This does not mean that you always *should* plug in numbers in these situations, but it is always an option. Since plugging in numbers requires variables in the answer choices, it can only be used on multiple-choice Discrete Quantitative questions. Let's look at a sample question and how to answer it by plugging in numbers:

Which of the following equals the average (arithmetic mean) of $(a - 2)^2$ and $(a + 2)^2$?

(A) a^2
(B) $a^2 + 2$
(C) $a^2 + 4$
(D) $a^2 + 2x$
(E) $a^2 + 8x$

STEP 1: Choose a value for the variable in the question. When choosing a value for a variable, keep in mind the following recommendations:

- Never choose 0 or 1.
- Never choose a value that will yield a 0 or 1.
- Avoid repeating the same value throughout the question.
- Always work with integers.

So what value should you choose for a? Based on number 1, you won't choose 0 or 1. Based on number 2, you won't choose 3. Why? Because if you plug in 3 for a, $(3 - 2)^2 = 1^2$, so 3 yields a value of 1. Based on number 3, you won't choose 4: $(4 - 2)^2 = 2^2$. 2 will appear multiple times in the question. So you can't choose 1, 2, 3, or 4. Go with 5. It does not violate any of the rules given earlier, and it is a prime number, which you generally want. Once you have chosen the value, label it on your paper: $a = 5$.

STEP 2: Answer the question using the value that you chose. Since you let $a = 5$, the question now becomes: Which of the following equals the average (arithmetic mean) of $(5 - 2)^2$ and $(5 + 2)^2$? Solve:

$(5 - 2)^2 = 3^2 = 9$ and $(5 + 2)^2 = 7^2 = 49$.

The average of 9 and 49 is:

$\frac{9 + 49}{2} = \frac{58}{2} = 29$

The value above is called the "goal." Write that answer on your paper and circle it.

STEP 3: Plug the value you chose for the variable into the choices. The choice that yields a value that matches the goal will be the correct answer. This step is straightforward, except for the following caveat: *Check all the choices!* Occasionally, more than one choice will yield the correct answer, in which case you will need to choose a new value for the variable. This is obviously not an ideal situation, which is why you want to follow the rules in Step 1 about which numbers to avoid.

Here's the question again:

Which of the following equals the average (arithmetic mean) of $(a - 2)^2$ and $(a + 2)^2$?

- (A) a^2
- (B) $a^2 + 2$
- (C) $a^2 + 4$
- (D) $a^2 + 2x$
- (E) $a^2 + 8x$

SOLUTION: Plug in 5 for a, and identify which choice yields a value of 29.

- (A) $5^2 = 25$ → No
- (B) $5^2 + 2 = 27$ → No
- (C) $5^2 + 4 = 29$ → Yes
- (D) $5^2 + 2(5) = 35$ → No
- (E) $5^2 + 8(5) = 65$ → No

The only choice that yields a value that matches the goal is C, so C is the correct answer.

Plugging In Numbers with Multiple Variables

Sometimes, you will have a candidate for plugging in numbers, but there will be more than one variable in the question. Look at the following example:

If $a + b = 11c$, what is the average of a, b, and c, in terms of c?

- (A) $3c$
- (B) $3c + 1$
- (C) $4c$
- (D) $5c$
- (E) $5c - 1$

When there are multiple variables in a plug-in question, *you must choose values that satisfy the restrictions in the question.* For example, in the previous question, you cannot simply choose 2 for a, 3 for b, and 5 for c. When you plug those values into the equation, you will arrive at $2 + 3 = 11(5) = 55$. This is not a true equation. Instead of arbitrarily choosing values, you must let the values for one or more of the variables determine the other variable. In the previous example, let's choose values for a and b and let those values determine c.

STEP 1: Choose values for the variables in the question. What values should you choose for a and b? You can choose anything that does not violate the rules outlined in Step 1 of the previous section, but keep in mind that you want c to be an integer. If c = an integer, then $11c$ must be a multiple of 11. Thus to yield an integer for c, you should choose values for a and b that will sum to a multiple of 11. Let's choose 9 for a and 13 for b. Those values sum to 22, which is a multiple of 11. Now use these values to solve for c:

$$a + b = 11c$$
$$9 + 13 = 22 = 11c$$
$$11c = 22$$
$$c = 2$$

So your values are $a = 9$, $b = 13$, $c = 2$.

STEP 2: Answer the question using the values you chose for the variables. What is the average of 9, 13, and 2?

$$\frac{9 + 13 + 2}{3} = \frac{24}{3} = 8$$

Circle the "goal": ⑧

STEP 3: Plug the values into the choices and see which choice yields a value that matches your goal. Here's the original question again:

If $a + b = 11c$, what is the average of a, b, and c, in terms of a and b?

    Ⓐ $3c$
    Ⓑ $3c + 1$
    Ⓒ $4c$
    Ⓓ $5c$
    Ⓔ $5c - 1$

Now substitute 2 for c in all the choices and identify which choice matches the target of 8.

    Ⓐ $3(2) = 6$ → No
    Ⓑ $3(2) + 1 = 7$ → No
    Ⓒ $4(2) = 8$ → Yes
    Ⓓ $5(2) = 10$ → No
    Ⓔ $5(2) - 1 = 9$ → No

The only choice that yields a value that matches the target is C.

Strategy 2: Back-Solve

Like plugging in numbers, *back-solving* is specific to Discrete Quantitative questions. Back-solving is an option when the choices provide values for a variable in the question. Again, back-solving is a way to avoid algebra. Instead of working out the manipulations in the question, you can work backward to determine which choice provides a value that matches the restrictions in the question. Let's look at an example:

> After a 20% decrease, the price of a shirt was $120. What was the original price of the shirt?
>
> Ⓐ $100
> Ⓑ $144
> Ⓒ $150
> Ⓓ $160
> Ⓔ $180

Though you can certainly answer this question algebraically, let's focus on back-solving.

STEP 1: Start with Choice B. Take the value in Choice B and determine how it relates to the information in the question. If the original price of the shirt was $144, then the new price of the shirt would be $144 − 0.2($144) = $115.20. When the original price of the shirt is $144, the reduced price of the shirt ($115.20) is less than $120. Thus $144 is too small a value for the original price of the shirt. Since the value in B is too small, the value in A must be too small as well. The correct answer is C, D, or E.

STEP 2: Back-solve with Choice D. Why Choice D? There are three possibilities: Either D is the answer, D is too small, or D is too big. If D is too small, then the answer must be choice E. If D is too big, then the answer must be choice C. No matter what happens, you won't have to test choices C and E. Thus by testing B and then D, you ensure that you will never have to test more than two choices.

Let's see how the value in D relates to the given information. If the original price of the shirt was $160, then the reduced price of the shirt would be $160 − 0.2(160) = $128. $128 is greater than the reduced price in the question. You can thus infer that $160 is too large of a value for the original price of the shirt. The value in Choice D is too large. If the value in Choice D is too large, then the value in Choice E must be too large as well. The correct answer must be C.

Exercise: Two Essential Quantitative Reasoning Strategies

Discrete Quantitative Questions

1. The cost for a phone call is $0.75 for the first minute and $0.50 per minute after the first minute. If a phone call lasted x minutes, what was the cost of the phone call in terms of x?

   (A) $0.75
   (B) $0.75 + x$
   (C) $0.75 + 0.5x$
   (D) $0.75 + 0.5(x - 1)$
   (E) $1.25x$

2. If $2x + 3y = z$, what is x in terms of y and z?

   (A) $z - 3y$
   (B) $2z - 3y$
   (C) $\frac{z - 3y}{2}$
   (D) $\frac{z}{2} - 3y$
   (E) $z + 3y$

3. Walking at a constant rate of x miles per hour, it took Jack y hours to travel from his home to his school. In terms of x and y, which of the following is equivalent to half of the distance that Jack traveled?

   (A) xy
   (B) $2xy$
   (C) $\frac{xy}{2}$
   (D) $2(x + y)$
   (E) $\frac{2x}{y}$

4. The total price for a equally priced shirts was b dollars. In terms of b and a, what is the total price for six of these shirts?

   (A) $\frac{ab}{6}$
   (B) $\frac{6}{ab}$
   (C) $\frac{6a}{b}$
   (D) $\frac{6b}{a}$
   (E) $6ab$

5. Traveling at a constant rate of 15 miles per hour, it took Bob x hours to go from his home to his school. Traveling at a constant rate of 20 miles per hour, it took Bob $x - 1$ hours to travel the same route. What is the value of x?

   (A) 2
   (B) 3
   (C) 4
   (D) 5
   (E) 6

For this question, indicate all of the answer choices that apply.

6. If $xy = 12$, and $x + y = 7$, then y could equal which of the following?

   [A] 3
   [B] 4
   [C] 5
   [D] 6
   [E] 7

7. If $a^2 + b = 7$, then b could equal which of the following?

   (A) 6
   (B) 8
   (C) 9
   (D) 10
   (E) 11

8. A group of x friends agreed to equally split the bill for a meal that cost y dollars. If z friends decide not to pay how much will each of the remaining friends have to pay, in terms of x, y, and z?

   (A) $\frac{y}{x-z}$
   (B) $\frac{y}{z}$
   (C) $\frac{y}{x}$
   (D) $\frac{y}{z-x}$
   (E) $\frac{y-x}{z}$

9. A retailer originally bought 50 equally priced phones for a total of z dollars. If he sold each phone for 25% more than he paid for it, then in terms of z, how much was each phone sold for?

   Ⓐ $\frac{z}{50}$

   Ⓑ $\frac{z}{40}$

   Ⓒ $\frac{5z}{4}$

   Ⓓ $\frac{4z}{5}$

   Ⓔ $62.5z$

10. Sam has y tapes, which is three times as many as Bob and half as many as Tom. In terms of y, how many tapes do Sam, Bob, and Tom have combined?

   Ⓐ $\frac{3y}{2}$

   Ⓑ $\frac{5y}{2}$

   Ⓒ $\frac{7y}{3}$

   Ⓓ $3y$

   Ⓔ $\frac{10y}{3}$

11. A basketball team averaged z points per game for q games. If the team scored 100 points its next game, what was the team's average in terms of z and q?

   Ⓐ $\frac{z+100}{q}$

   Ⓑ $\frac{zq+100}{q+1}$

   Ⓒ $\frac{zq+100}{q}$

   Ⓓ $\frac{zq}{q+1}$

   Ⓔ $\frac{z+100}{q+1}$

12. If $\frac{ab}{a+b} = 2$, then what is a in terms of b?

   Ⓐ $\frac{b-2}{2b}$

   Ⓑ $\frac{2b}{b+2}$

   Ⓒ $\frac{2b}{b-2}$

   Ⓓ $\frac{b}{2b-2}$

   Ⓔ $\frac{b+2}{2b}$

Exercise Answers

Discrete Quantitative Questions

1. **D**

   Step 1: Choose a smart value for x: Let $x = 3$.

   Step 2: Substitute 3 for x in the question and determine the "goal": The cost of the first minute = $0.75. The cost for the next two minutes = $0.50(2) = $1. The total cost = $1.75. Goal: $1.75

   Step 3: Substitute 3 for x in the choices, and identify which choice yields a value that matches your goal: $1.75

   The only choice that yields a value of $1.75 is D.

2. **C**

   Step 1: Choose smart values: Let $x = 5$ and $y = 15$. Substitute these values to determine a value for z: $2(5) + 3(15) = 60$. Thus when $x = 5$ and $y = 15$, $z = 60$.

   Step 2: Substitute 5 for x in the question and determine the "goal": In this case, you want to solve for x, so the goal is simply the value that you chose for x: 5.

   Step 3: Substitute 15 for y and 60 for z in the choices, and identify which choice yields a value that matches your goal: 5. The only choice that yields a value of 5 is C.

3. **C**

   Step 1: Choose smart values for x and y: Let $x = 10$ and $y = 5$.

   Step 2: Substitute 10 for x and 5 for y in the question and determine the "goal." Since you want half the distance to the school, let's use these values to get the entire distance, and then divide by 2. In this case, the total distance to the school is (miles/hour) x # of hours = $xy = 10 \times 5 = 50$. Half of the distance is thus $50/2 = 25$. The goal is 25.

   Step 3: Substitute 10 for x and 5 for y in the choices, and identify which choice yields a value that matches your goal: 25. The only choice that yields a value of 25 is C.

4. **D**

   Step 1: Choose smart values: Let $a = 5$ and $b = 20$.

   Step 2: Substitute 5 for a and 20 for b in the question and determine the goal: If 5 shirts cost $20, then each shirt is $20/5 = $4. The cost of six shirts will thus be $6 \times $4 = 24$. The goal is 24.

   Step 3: Substitute 5 for a and 20 for b in the choices, and identify which choice yields a value that matches your goal: 24. The only choice that yields a value of 24 is D.

5. **C** Since the distance for both trips is the same, the answer should provide a value of x that yields the same distance for both trips. You can determine the

value of x by back-solving. First, start with 3. If $x = 3$, then traveling at 15 mph, Bob traveled a distance of 15(3) = 45. Traveling 20 mph for (3 − 1) hours, Bob traveled 40 miles. 3 is too small for the distances to match. Eliminate A and B. Now go to Choice D. If $x = 5$, then traveling at 15 mph, Bob traveled a distance of 15(5) = 75. Traveling 20 mph for (5 − 1) hours, Bob traveled 80 miles. 5 is too large for the values to match. Eliminate D and E. The answer is C.

6. **A and B** Back-solving is a good strategy here, but make sure to check all the choices. Try Choice A. If $y = 3$, then $3x = 12 \rightarrow x = 4$. These values satisfy the equation: $x + y = 7$. Thus 3 is a potential answer. Go through this process for all the choices. The only other choice that provides a value that will yield a value for x that satisfies both equations is 4. The answer is A and B.

7. **A** Back-solve by starting with Choice B. If $b = 8$, then

$$a^2 + 8 = 7$$

$$a^2 = -1$$

A number raised to an even exponent never yields a negative result. Thus 8 is too large for B. The correct answer must be A.

8. **A**

   Step 1: Choose smart values: Let $y = 100$, $x = 25$, and $z = 5$.

   Step 2: Substitute 100 for y, 20 for x, and 5 for z in the question and determine the "goal": If there were originally 25 people and 5 people dropped out, then the bill will be split among 25 − 5 = 20 people. The total bill is $100, so after the friends drop out, the cost per person will be 100/20 = 5. The goal is 5.

   Step 3: Substitute 100 for y, 20 for x, and 5 for z in the choices, and identify which choice yields a value that matches your goal: 5. The only choice that yields a value of 5 is A.

9. **B**

   Step 1: Choose a smart value: Let $z = 200$.

   Step 2: Substitute 200 for z in the question and determine the "goal": If the retailer paid $200 for 50 phones, then each phone cost $4. If the dealer charged 25% more than he paid for it, he sold each phone for $4 + 0.25(4) = 5$. The goal is 5.

   Step 3: Substitute 200 for z in the choices, and identify which choice yields a value that matches your goal: 5. The only choice that yields a value of 5 is B.

10. **E**

    Step 1: Choose a smart value: To ensure that the number of tapes that Bob has is an integer, choose a multiple of 3 for y: 6.

    Step 2: Substitute 6 for y in the question and determine the "goal": If Sam has 6 tapes, then Bob has 2 tapes, and Tom has 12 tapes. In total, they have 6 + 2 + 12 = 20 tapes.

Step 3: Substitute 6 for y in the choices, and identify which choice yields a value that matches your goal: 20. The only choice that yields a value of 20 is E.

11. **B**

Step 1: Choose smart values for z and q: Let $z = 80$ and $q = 5$.

Step 2: Substitute 80 for z and 5 for q in the question and determine the "goal": If the team averaged 80 points per game for 5 games, then its total number of points for those 5 games was $80 \times 5 = 400$. After the team scored 100 points, its total was 500 and the number of games played was 6. Thus the new average is $\frac{500}{6} = \frac{250}{3}$. The goal is $\frac{250}{3}$.

Step 3: Substitute 80 for z and 5 for q in the choices, and identify which choice yields a value that matches your goal: $\frac{250}{3}$. The only choice that yields a value of $\frac{250}{3}$ is B.

12. **C**

Step 1: Choose smart values for a and b: Since there is a restriction in the question, choose a value for a and let that value determine b: Let $a = 6$. Substitute 6 into the given equation to solve for b:

$$\frac{6b}{6 + b} = 2$$

$$6b = 2(6 + b)$$

$$6b = 12 + 2b$$

$$4b = 12$$

$$b = 3$$

So $a = 6$, and $b = 3$.

Step 2: Substitute 6 for a and 3 for b in the question and determine the "goal": Since the question asks to solve for a, the goal is simply the value of a: 6.

Step 3: Substitute 3 for b in the choices, and identify which choice yields a value that matches your goal: 6. The only choice that yields a value of 6 is C.

CHAPTER 8

Quantitative Comparison Strategies

Study this chapter to learn about:

- Quantitative Comparison format

- Strategy: Play devil's advocate

- Strategy: Plug in numbers with interesting properties

- Strategy: Make comparisons, not calculations

- Strategy: Make the columns comparable

- Strategy: Use the implied relationship between the quantities

- Strategy: Work backward

Quantitative Comparison Format

Each of the following questions consists of two quantities, Quantity A and Quantity B. You are to compare the two quantities. You may use additional information centered above the two quantities if additional information is given. Choose

(A) if Quantity A is greater
(B) if Quantity B is greater
(C) if the two quantities are equal
(D) if the relationship between the two quantities cannot be determined

Though the choices on the test do not state it explicitly, your concern is whether there is a *constant* relationship between the quantities. Specifically, if you can determine that in some instances, Quantity A is greater, but in other instances, Quantity B is greater, then the answer is Choice D: the relationship cannot be determined. To choose A, B, or C, you need to show that the given relationship is *always* true. Let's look at a sample question:

QUANTITY A	QUANTITY B	
$x^2 + 7x$	$x^2 + 14$	Ⓐ Ⓑ Ⓒ Ⓓ

Choose:

Ⓐ if Quantity A is greater
Ⓑ if Quantity B is greater
Ⓒ if the two quantities are equal
Ⓓ if the relationship between the two quantities cannot be determined

SOLUTION: If x is greater than 2, then Quantity A is always greater. For example, if $x = 3$, then the value of Quantity A is 30, and the value of Quantity B is 23. Thus you can eliminate choices B and C. Why? Because if Quantity A is greater in this instance, then it is not possible for Quantity B to *always* be greater or for the two quantities to *always* be equal. Now that the choice is between A and D, determine whether Quantity A will *always* be greater. Substitute 1 for x. Quantity A = 8, and Quantity B = 15. In this case, Quantity B is greater. Since different values yield different relationships, the relationship cannot be determined, so the correct answer is Choice D.

Strategy: Play Devil's Advocate

The example question illustrates the type of reasoning fundamental to Quantitative Comparison questions. The best way to think about the quantities is to ask yourself: "Will this relationship *always* be true?" Often, it will turn out that the value in one column is *sometimes* larger than the value in the other column, and *sometimes* smaller than the value in the other column. In such cases, the answer will be D, not A or B. For the answer on Quantitative Comparison to be A, B, or C, that relationship must *always* be true. If you find contradictory relationships between the columns, then the answer is Choice D.

As you might expect, many tougher Quantitative Comparison questions will expect you to identify situations in which there is an indeterminate relationship between the columns. To identify that this is the case, your ultimate goal should be to *arrive at Choice D!* For example, if you determine that Quantity A is greater in one situation, your next step should be to determine whether there are other situations in which the relationship between the two quantities is different. Look at the following examples:

QUANTITY A	QUANTITY B	
$3(x + 25)$	75	Ⓐ Ⓑ Ⓒ Ⓓ

Choose:

> Ⓐ if Quantity A is greater
> Ⓑ if Quantity B is greater
> Ⓒ if the two quantities are equal
> Ⓓ if the relationship between the two quantities cannot be determined

SOLUTION: When $x = 1$, the value of Quantity A = 3(26) = 78. In this case, the value of Quantity A is greater. Since it is not possible for Quantity B to *always* be greater or for the two quantities to *always* be equal, you can eliminate choices B and C.

Now that you have determined that Quantity A is sometimes greater, the next step is to see whether any values will provide a counterexample to that relationship. For reasons that will be further explained in the next chapter, a good number to choose is 0.

When $x = 0$, the value of Quantity A will equal 3(25) = 75. In this case, the values in the two columns are equal. You have now found a counterexample to the relationship that was obtained when $x = 1$. Since different values for x give different relationships for the columns, the relationship cannot be determined. The answer is Choice D.

QUANTITY A	QUANTITY B	
$17y$	$20y$	Ⓐ Ⓑ Ⓒ Ⓓ

Choose:

> Ⓐ if Quantity A is greater
> Ⓑ if Quantity B is greater
> Ⓒ if the two quantities are equal
> Ⓓ if the relationship between the two quantities cannot be determined

When $y = 1$, the value of Quantity A = 17, and the value of Quantity B = 20. Thus in this case, Quantity B is greater, and the answer must be Choice B or D. When $y = 0$, Quantity A = 0, and Quantity B = 0. In this case, the columns are equal. You have found contradictory relationships, so the answer is D.

Strategy: Plug In Numbers with Interesting Properties

When plugging in numbers for variables in Quantitative Comparison questions, it might be difficult to determine where to start. After all, there are literally infinite possibilities! However, because your ultimate goal is to prove Choice D, you should choose numbers that will most likely give you contradictory relationships. The best numbers to choose will therefore be numbers that have interesting properties. Of all numbers, the *best* to choose are **0, 1,** and **–1**.

However, the test-makers will throw nuances at you that will force you to test other types of numbers. The following is a list of other types of numbers you should consider when plugging in numbers in Quantitative Comparisons:

- Numbers less than −1
- Numbers between −1 and 0 (i.e., negative proper fractions)
- Numbers between 0 and 1 (i.e., positive proper fractions)
- Numbers greater than 1

Though it might seem like plugging in so many different values will be time-consuming, it's important to remember the following:

- You only need to find one contradictory relationship to prove Choice D.
- Many Quantitative Comparison questions provide constraints on the variables that will eliminate some of the types of numbers mentioned previously.

x is an integer

QUANTITY A	QUANTITY B	
2^x	$(-1)^x$	Ⓐ Ⓑ Ⓒ Ⓓ

SOLUTION: Let $x = 1$. When $x = 1$, the value of Quantity A will be $2^1 = 2$, and the value of Quantity B will be $(-1)^1 = -1$. In this case, the value of Quantity A is greater, so the answer must be A or D. Now plug in a new value for x. Since x is an integer, you cannot choose a fraction. A smart number here would be the strangest-behaving integer: 0. When $x = 0$, the value of Quantity A will be $2^0 = 1$, and the value of Quantity B will be $(-1)^0 = 1$. In this case, the values of the two quantities are equal. Since different values give different relationships between the quantities, the relationship cannot be determined. The answer is Choice D.

Strategy: Make Comparisons, Not Calculations

When doing Quantitative Comparison questions, it is essential to step out of the problem-solving mind-set that you're accustomed to. Quantitative Comparison questions are designed to test mathematical intuition and quick, efficient mathematical reasoning, and this fact should dictate your approach. One key consequence of this fact is that you should *always look at both columns before you begin any calculations.* In many situations, doing so will help you reduce or even completely avoid any calculations. Look at the following examples:

QUANTITY A	QUANTITY B	
0.98(576)	0.92(574)	Ⓐ Ⓑ Ⓒ Ⓓ

SOLUTION: You want to not only get this question right, but to do so *quickly*. With your calculator, you can of course get a value for both columns. But before diving into the calculations, look to see whether you can make a quick comparison. You should notice that 0.98 > 0.92 and that 576 > 574. Since both values in Quantity A are greater than both values in Quantity B, the product of the two values in Quantity A must be greater. Thus the answer is A.

QUANTITY A	QUANTITY B	
$\frac{1}{2} - \frac{1}{3} + \frac{1}{4} - \frac{1}{5} + \frac{1}{6}$	$\frac{1}{2}$	Ⓐ Ⓑ Ⓒ Ⓓ

SOLUTION: Your first step should be to look at both columns. Since Quantity B is $\frac{1}{2}$, you should look to see whether adding and subtracting the fractions in Column A will make the ultimate value greater than or less than $\frac{1}{2}$. Again, you can do the calculations here, but a better use of time is to look at the different fractions being added in pairs. $\frac{1}{3}$ is greater than $\frac{1}{4}$, so subtracting $\frac{1}{3}$ from a number and then adding $\frac{1}{4}$ will result in a value smaller than the original number. $\frac{1}{5}$ is greater than $\frac{1}{6}$, so subtracting $\frac{1}{5}$ from a number and then adding $\frac{1}{6}$ will also result in a number smaller than the original value. Thus the cumulative result of the operations in Quantity A will be a value less than $\frac{1}{2}$, and the correct answer is Choice B.

It is important to note that you were able to arrive at this answer without actually calculating the value of Quantity A. This is a point essential to Quantitative Comparison questions. If you look at a column and find yourself intimidated by all the calculations you think you should do, take a step back and determine whether you can arrive at the relationship without doing all the math. In many cases, you will be able to do so.

Strategy: Make the Columns Comparable

An extension of the preceding principle is the following: if the columns do not appear comparable, manipulate one or both columns to make the comparison simpler. Look at the following question:

QUANTITY A	QUANTITY B	
2^{50}	8^{20}	Ⓐ Ⓑ Ⓒ Ⓓ

As it stands, it would not be possible to draw a comparison between the two quantities in a reasonable amount of time. So instead of attempting to calculate, you should attempt to manipulate one or both columns to make the comparison easier. It is important to keep in mind that when manipulating the columns, you are *not* changing their values. You are simply rewriting them to make the question simpler. In this case, you should manipulate the value in Quantity B to have a base of 2:

$(2^3)^{20} = 2^{60}$

Now the values in both quantities are expressed with a base of 2. To determine which quantity is greater, you simply need to determine which quantity has the larger exponent. In this case, the exponent in Quantity B is greater, and the correct answer is thus Choice B.

Strategy: Use the Implied Relationship Between the Quantities

The nature of Quantitative Comparisons is that there exists an implied algebraic relationship between the two quantities. Because of this fact, when you are working with Quantitative Comparisons, you can perform the same operations to both columns, as long as the operation satisfies one of the following conditions:

- Add or subtract the same value or variable to both columns.
- Divide or multiply both columns by a *positive* value or variable.
- Square or square root both columns, as long as you know that *all the values in the columns are positive.*

$$3x + 5y = 22$$

QUANTITY A	QUANTITY B	
$6x + 10y + 6$	52	Ⓐ Ⓑ Ⓒ Ⓓ

SOLUTION: Since the given information concerns the sum $3x + 5y$, you should manipulate the two columns to isolate $3x + 5y$. First, subtract 6 from both columns:

$$
\begin{array}{ll}
6x + 10y + 6 & 52 \\
\underline{\qquad -6} & \underline{-6} \\
6x + 10y & 46
\end{array}
$$

Next divide both columns by 2:

$$
\begin{array}{cc}
\frac{6x + 10y}{2} & \frac{46}{2} \\
\downarrow & \downarrow \\
3x + 5y & 23
\end{array}
$$

Since you are told that $3x + 5y = 22$, Quantity B is greater.

Strategy: Work Backward

In some Quantitative Comparison questions, you will be asked to compare an unknown to a given value. In these situations, it is often helpful to use the given value as a baseline for comparison. Look at the following examples:

$$2^x < 100$$

QUANTITY A	QUANTITY B	
The greatest integer value for x	6	Ⓐ Ⓑ Ⓒ Ⓓ

SOLUTION: Instead of solving for x, you should see whether the value in Column B will satisfy the given information, and make inferences about x from that relationship. If $x = 6$, then $2^6 = 64$. Since $64 < 100$, you know that **6** is a possible value for x. The correct answer is Choice C or D. Now to determine whether you can identify a counterexample, plug in an integer value larger than 6 for x. If $x = 7$, then $2^x = 2^7 = 128$. $128 > 100$, so 7 is too large of a value for x. Thus the greatest integer value for x must be 6. The answer is Choice C.

After a 20% reduction, the price of a shirt is more than $100.

QUANTITY A	QUANTITY B	
The original price of the shirt	120	Ⓐ Ⓑ Ⓒ Ⓓ

SOLUTION: Doing this question algebraically is certainly an option, but an alternative approach is to plug the value in Quantity B into the original equation and see how it compares to the given information. If the original price of the shirt was $120, then after a 20% reduction, the price of the shirt would be $0.8(120) = \$96$. Since the reduced price of the shirt must be more than $100, the original price of the shirt must be more than $120. Thus the value in Quantity A is greater.

Exercise: Quantitative Comparison Questions

Each of the following questions consists of two quantities, Quantity A and Quantity B. You are to compare the two quantities. You may use additional information centered above the two quantities if additional information is given. Choose

- Ⓐ if Quantity A is greater
- Ⓑ if Quantity B is greater
- Ⓒ if the two quantities are equal
- Ⓓ if the relationship between the two quantities cannot be determined

	QUANTITY A	QUANTITY B	
1.	$10a^2$	$25a^3$	Ⓐ Ⓑ Ⓒ Ⓓ

	QUANTITY A	QUANTITY B	
2.	$a + 7$	$a - 12$	Ⓐ Ⓑ Ⓒ Ⓓ

	QUANTITY A	QUANTITY B	
3.	$(c + d)^2$	$c^2 + d^2$	Ⓐ Ⓑ Ⓒ Ⓓ

x does not equal 0

	QUANTITY A	QUANTITY B	
4.	$2/x$	$7/x$	Ⓐ Ⓑ Ⓒ Ⓓ

x is an integer, and $x > 1$

	QUANTITY A	QUANTITY B	
5.	$x^2 + 5$	$x^3 + 1$	Ⓐ Ⓑ Ⓒ Ⓓ

	QUANTITY A	QUANTITY B	
6.	$0.25 \times 15\%$	$\frac{3}{80}$	Ⓐ Ⓑ Ⓒ Ⓓ

$c > 0$

	QUANTITY A	QUANTITY B	
7.	$5c$	$5/c$	Ⓐ Ⓑ Ⓒ Ⓓ

$x < 0$

	QUANTITY A	QUANTITY B	
8.	x^3	x^5	Ⓐ Ⓑ Ⓒ Ⓓ

a and b are positive integers
$$\frac{a}{b} = \frac{3}{1}$$

	QUANTITY A	QUANTITY B	
9.	3a	9b	Ⓐ Ⓑ Ⓒ Ⓓ

	QUANTITY A	QUANTITY B	
10.	The area of a circle whose radius is 18	The area of a circle whose diameter is 40.	Ⓐ Ⓑ Ⓒ Ⓓ

Set A contains all the integers from 1–1,000, inclusive.

	QUANTITY A	QUANTITY B	
11.	The number of multiples of 3 in set A	The number of multiples of 4 in set A	Ⓐ Ⓑ Ⓒ Ⓓ

The radius of Circle O is greater than 2.

	QUANTITY A	QUANTITY B	
12.	The area of Circle O	The circumference of Circle O	Ⓐ Ⓑ Ⓒ Ⓓ

x and y are integers such that $x > y > 0$ and $x + y$ is even

	QUANTITY A	QUANTITY B	
13.	$x - y$	1	Ⓐ Ⓑ Ⓒ Ⓓ

	QUANTITY A	QUANTITY B	
14.	The product of the integers from 5–25, inclusive.	The product of the integers from 1–24, inclusive.	Ⓐ Ⓑ Ⓒ Ⓓ

$$x^2 < 36$$

	QUANTITY A	QUANTITY B	
15.	x	7	Ⓐ Ⓑ Ⓒ Ⓓ

A merchant paid $200 for a coat. His profit on the coat was more than 20%.

	QUANTITY A	QUANTITY B	
16.	The selling price of the coat	$240	Ⓐ Ⓑ Ⓒ Ⓓ

Exercise Answers

1. **D** Plug in numbers:

	A	B	Comparison
$a = 1$	$10(1)^2 = 10$	$25(1)^3 = 25$	B
$a = -1$	$10(-1)^2 = +10$	$25(-1)^3 = -25$	A

Since there are contradictory relationships between the columns, a relationship cannot be determined.

2. **A** Subtract a from both quantities. Quantity A thus equals: $(a + 7) - a = 7$. Quantity B thus equals: $(a - 12) - a = -12$. $7 > -12$, so Quantity A is greater.

3. **D** Substitute values for c and d.

	A	B	Comparison
$c = 1$ $d = 1$	$(1 + 1)^2 = 4$	$1^2 + 1^2 = 2$	A
$c = 0$ $d = 0$	$(0 + 0)^2 = 0$	$0^2 + 0^2 = 0$	C

Since a relationship cannot be determined, the correct answer is D.

4. **D** Substitute values.

	A	B	Comparison
$x = 1$	$\dfrac{2}{1}$	$\dfrac{7}{1}$	B
$x = -1$	$\dfrac{2}{-1} = -2$	$\dfrac{7}{-1} = -7$	A

When x is positive, Quantity B is greater. When x is negative, Quantity A is greater. The relationship cannot be determined.

5. **D** Since you are given a range for x, you should choose extremes. Let $x = 2$, and then let $x = 10$.

	A	B	Comparison
$x = 2$	$2^2 + 5 = 9$	$2^3 + 1 = 9$	C
$x = 10$	$10^2 + 5 = 105$	$10^3 + 1 = 1{,}001$	B

Since different values yield different relationships between the quantities, the correct answer is D.

6. **C** Make the columns comparable by manipulating Quantity A to be a fraction. $0.25 = \frac{1}{4}$. $15\% = \frac{15}{100} = \frac{3}{20}$. The value in Quantity A is thus $\frac{1}{4} \times \frac{3}{20} = \frac{3}{80}$. The two quantities are equal.

7. **D** Manipulate the quantities:

$$C > 0$$

A	B
$5C$	$\dfrac{5}{C}$

Multiply by C: $5C^2$ 5

Divide by 5: C^2 1

Note that you were able to multiply by c because you were told that $c > 0$.

The comparison is c^2 versus 1. If $c > 1$, then Quantity A is greater. If c is a fraction, then Quantity B is greater.

8. **D** Choose values for x. If $x = -1$, then the two quantities are equal. If $x = -2$, then Quantity A $= -8$, and Quantity B $= -32$, in which case Quantity A is greater. Since a relationship cannot be determined, the correct answer is D.

9. **C** First, cross-multiply the given proportion: $\frac{a}{b} = \frac{3}{1} \rightarrow a = 3b$. Next, to make the quantities comparable, substitute $3b$ for a in Quantity A. Thus Quantity A $= 3(3b) = 9b$. The values in the quantities are equal.

10. **B** Don't calculate! If the diameter of the circle in Quantity B is 40, then the radius of that circle is $\frac{1}{2}(40) = 20$. Since the radius of the circle in Quantity B is greater than the radius of the circle in Quantity A, the area of the circle in Quantity B must be greater.

11. **A** Both quantities concern the same set. Within any finite set of numbers, there are fewer multiples of 4 than there are multiples of 3. For example, from 1–12, inclusive, there are four multiples of 3 (3, 6, 9, 12), but only three multiples of 4 (4, 8, 12). Thus Quantity A is greater.

12. **A** Since you are not given a value for the radius, assign a variable. Let the radius = r. In terms of r, Quantity A = πr2. In terms of r, Quantity B = 2πr. Now manipulate the columns to simplify the comparison:

	QUANTITY A	QUANTITY B
Divide by π:	πr^2	$2\pi r$
	↓	↓
	r^2	$2r$
	↓	↓
Divide by r:	r	2

Since you are told that the radius is greater than 2, Quantity A must be greater.

13. **A** Substitute values for x and y that satisfy the given information. Let $x = 13$ and $y = 1$. In this case, both are integers, $x > y > 0$, and their sum is even. Now, substitute these values into Quantity A: $13 - 1 = 12$. In this case, Quantity A is greater. Choose new values for x and y that satisfy the given information. To prove Choice D, you want to make the difference between x and y as small as possible. Let $x = 3$ and $y = 1$. In this case, all the restrictions are satisfied. $3 - 1 = 2$. Thus Quantity A is still greater.

14. **A** Don't calculate! Identify what the quantities have in common. Since both quantities share the product $(5 \times 6 \times 7 \times \ldots 24)$, you can divide both quantities by the product of the integers from 5–24, inclusive. After doing so, the real comparison becomes:

QUANTITY A	QUANTITY B
25	$1 \times 2 \times 3 \times 4$

$1 \times 2 \times 3 \times 4 = 24$. Thus Quantity A is greater.

15. **B** Since the comparison is between a value and a variable, you can work backward. If $x = 7$, then $x^2 = 49 < 36$. Thus to satisfy the given inequality, x must be less than 7.

16. **A** Since the quantities compare a value to an unknown, work backward with Quantity B. If the selling price of the coat were \$240, then the profit on the coat would be $240 - 200 = 40$. Now determine 40 as a percentage of 200. $\frac{40}{200} \times 100 = 20\%$. Since you know that the profit must be *greater* than 20%, the selling price must have been greater than \$240.

Math Review

CHAPTER 9

Number Properties

Study this chapter to learn about:

- Factors and multiples
- Odds and evens
- Positives and negatives
- Evenly spaced sets

On a broad level, you can think of properties of numbers as the branch of math concerned with how numbers behave in certain situations. Though this is an enormous field in formal mathematics, the GRE will be concerned with properties of numbers in the following contexts: divisibility, odds and evens, positives and negatives, and evenly spaced sets. Because these areas are all concerned with concrete mathematical rules and what you can deduce from these rules, questions testing these concepts will often appear in Quantitative Comparison questions or a "must be true" or "could be true" format in Discrete Quantitative questions.

Factors and Multiples

Any whole number is an **integer**. For example, 2 and –9 are integers, but $\frac{3}{2}$ and –7.2 are not. The **factors** (or **divisors**) of an **integer** are the integer values that divide evenly into that number. 2 is a factor of 12 because $\frac{12}{2} = 6$, which is an integer. But 5 is not a factor of 12, because $\frac{12}{5} = 2.4$, which is not an integer. To determine the factors of a number, you can create a factor table. For example, the factors of 12 are:

12	1
6	2
4	3

The **multiples** of an integer are the products that result when that integer is multiplied by another integer. For example, the multiples of 12 are 12(1) = 12, 12(2) = 24, 12(3) = 36, ...

Note that multiples and factors are essentially opposites of each other. Since 6 is a factor of 24, 24 is a multiple of 6.

The GRE expresses the preceding relationships in several ways. All of the following sentences mean the same thing:

2 is a factor of 12   12 is a multiple of 2
2 is a divisor of 12   12 is divisible by 2
2 divides evenly into 12   12 divided by 2 yields an integer

Many test-takers tend to confuse factors and multiples. If this is the case, think to yourself that there are *finite factors* and *many multiples*. The factors are what create a number and the multiples are what result from that number.

Prime Factors and the Factor Tree

Any number will always have 1 and itself as divisors. If an integer is divisible *only* by 1 and itself, then it is a **prime number**. Examples of prime numbers are 2, 3, 5, 7, 11, 13, and so on.

---

1 is *not* a prime number, and 2 is the *only* even prime number!

A **prime factor** is any factor of an integer that is also prime. For example, 2 and 3 are prime factors of 12, but 4 is not. There are two important properties about prime factors:

1. **Any integer can be expressed as the product of its prime factors.** For example: $12 = 2 \times 2 \times 3$.
2. **The factors of any integer will be completely determined by the prime factors of that integer.** For example, $12 = 2 \times 2 \times 3$. The factors of 12 are 1, 2, 3, (2×2), (2×3), $(2 \times 2 \times 3)$.

To determine the prime factors of a number, you should create a factor tree. The following is the factor tree for 240.

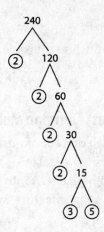

The prime factorization of 240 is thus: $(2^4) \times 3 \times 5$. From Property 2 earlier, you can infer that 40 is a factor of 240 but that 32 is not. Why? Because the prime factors of 40 ($2 \times 2 \times 2 \times 5$) are contained in the prime factorization of 240, but the prime factors of 32 ($2 \times 2 \times 2 \times 2 \times 2$) are not contained in the prime factorization of 240. One important principle that extends from the preceding explanation is the following:

If *a* is a factor of *b*, and *b* is a factor of *c*, then *a* must be a factor of *c*.

For example, since 40 is a factor of 240, 8 and 5 (which are factors of 40) must also be factors of 240.

Generally, when doing questions that concern divisibility, you should focus on prime factorization.

If *y* is divisible by 12, which of the following must be true? *Indicate all that apply.*

- A *y* is divisible by 24
- B *y* is divisible by 6
- C *y* is divisible by 4

SOLUTION: If *y* is divisible by 12, then the prime factors of 12 must be prime factors of *y*. Create a factor tree to determine the prime factors of 12.

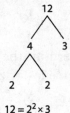

$12 = 2^2 \times 3$

You can therefore infer that y has 2, 2, and 3 in its prime factorization. Since y has 2×2 in its prime factorization, y must be divisible by 4. Since y has 2×3 in its prime factorization, y must be divisible by 6. The correct answer is B and C.

Greatest Common Factor and Least Common Multiple

The **greatest common factor (GCF)** of a set of numbers is the largest integer that divides evenly into all the numbers. To determine the greatest prime factor of a set of numbers, break each of the numbers down into their prime factors and circle the shared factors. The product of the shared factors will be the GCF.

For this question, write your answer in the box.

What is the greatest common factor of 12, 72, and 88?

SOLUTION: Determine the prime factors of each of the numbers and circle their common prime factors:

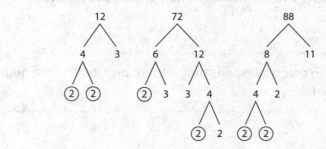

12, 72, and 88 each have two 2s in their prime factorizations. The GCF of the three numbers is thus $2 \times 2 = 4$.

The **least common multiple (LCM)** of a set of numbers is the smallest integer that is divisible by all the numbers in the set. The LCM must therefore contain the prime factors of each number in the set. As with the GCF, prime factorization is important for LCM questions.

If x is the smallest integer that is divisible by 9, 12, and 15, what is the value of x?

SOLUTION: You are asked to determine the LCM of 9, 12, and 15. First, break each number down into its prime factorization:

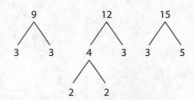

Since x is a multiple of 9, x must have two 3s in its prime factorization. Thus $x = 3 \times 3 \dots$. Since x is a multiple of 12, x must have two 2s and one 3 in its prime factorization. You know that x already has a 3 in its prime factorization, so to make x a multiple of 12, you only need to add two 2s to its prime factors. Thus $x = 3 \times 3 \times 2 \times 2 \dots$. Since x is a multiple of 15, it must have one 3 and one 5 in its prime factorization. You know from earlier that x already has a 3 in its prime factorization, so to make x a multiple of 15, you only need to add one 5 to its prime factors. Thus $x = 3 \times 3 \times 2 \times 2 \times 5 = 180$.

Remainders

Recall that 15 is a multiple of 5 since 5 divides evenly into 15. What about 16? 16 is not a multiple of 5, because $\frac{16}{5} = 3.2$, which is a noninteger. When doing division, if the numerator is not divisible by the denominator, the value left over after the denominator divides into the numerator is called the **remainder**.

$$5\overline{)16} \quad \begin{array}{r} 3 \\ -15 \\ \hline 1 \end{array} \leftarrow \text{Remainder}$$

The remainder essentially tells you how many units the numerator is past a given multiple of the denominator. It follows that the remainder must always be smaller than the divisor. Look at the remainders yielded by each of the following:

$\frac{4}{4} = 1 \text{ r } 0$

$\frac{5}{4} = 1 \text{ r } 1$

$\frac{6}{4} = 1 \text{ r } 2$

$\frac{7}{4} = 1 \text{ r } 3$

$\frac{8}{4} = 2 \text{ r } 0$

Once you come to $\frac{8}{4}$, the remainder cycles back to zero.

Unknowns and Remainders

It helps to express remainders algebraically, especially when the numerator of the fraction is an unknown. For example: When x is divided by 7, the remainder is 2. You can translate this to mean: x is two units to the right of a multiple of 7.

As illustrated in the diagram, x can equal 9, 16, 23, 30, 37, and so on. There are infinite values for x, but they are all two units to the right of a multiple of 7. You can also express the previous mathematical sentence algebraically. Any given multiple of 7 can be expressed as $7I$, where I = any integer. Since x is two units to the right of a multiple of 7, it follows that: $x = 7I + 2$.

When x is divided by 6, the remainder is 2. Which of the following could be a value of x?

    (A) 10
    (B) 12
    (C) 14
    (D) 16
    (E) 18

SOLUTION: Express x algebraically: $x = 6I + 2$. Determine which of the choices will yield an integer value for I.

A: $10 = 6I + 2 \rightarrow 8 = 6I \rightarrow 8/6 = I$.   *I* is not an integer. $\rightarrow$ Eliminate A.

B: $12 = 6I + 2 \rightarrow 10 = 6I \rightarrow 10/6 = I$.   *I* is not an integer. $\rightarrow$ Eliminate B.

C: $14 = 6I + 2 \rightarrow 12 = 6I \rightarrow 2 = I$.   *I* is an integer. $\rightarrow$ The answer
                                                                             is C.

D: $16 = 6I + 2 \rightarrow 14 = 6I \rightarrow 14/6 = I$.   *I* is not an integer. $\rightarrow$ Eliminate D.

E: $18 = 6I + 2 \rightarrow 16 = 6I \rightarrow 16/6 = I$.   *I* is not an integer. $\rightarrow$ Eliminate E.

SOLUTION: The correct answer is C.

Exercise: Factors and Multiples

Discrete Quantitative Questions

For each question, select one answer, unless the instructions state otherwise.

1. What is the greatest common factor of 16, 24, and 72?

    A) 2
    B) 4
    C) 8
    D) 12
    E) 16

For this question, write your answer in the box.

2. What is the least common multiple of 6, 8, and 15?

For Questions 3 and 4, indicate all the answer choices that apply.

3. If x is divisible by 12 and y is divisible by 8, then which of the following must be true?

    A) xy is a multiple of 48
    B) 64 is a factor of xy
    C) xy is not divisible by 5
    D) 32 is a factor of xy

4. If a is divisible by 6 and by 8, which of the following must be true?

    A) a is divisible by 4
    B) a is divisible by 12
    C) a is divisible by 48

5. What is the greatest integer, k, such that 5^k is a factor of the product of the integers from 1 through 24, inclusive?

    A) 1
    B) 2
    C) 3
    D) 4
    E) 5

Quantitative Comparison Questions

Each of the following questions consists of two quantities, Quantity A and Quantity B. You are to compare the two quantities. You may use additional information centered above the two quantities if additional information is given. Choose

Ⓐ if Quantity A is greater
Ⓑ if Quantity B is greater
Ⓒ if the two quantities are equal
Ⓓ if the relationship between the two quantities cannot be determined

x is a multiple of 12

	QUANTITY A	QUANTITY B	
1.	The remainder when x is divided by 3	The remainder when x is divided by 6	Ⓐ Ⓑ Ⓒ Ⓓ

18 is a factor of x

	QUANTITY A	QUANTITY B	
2.	The number of unique prime factors of x	2	Ⓐ Ⓑ Ⓒ Ⓓ

x is an integer

	QUANTITY A	QUANTITY B	
3.	The remainder when x is divided by 4	4	Ⓐ Ⓑ Ⓒ Ⓓ

When the integer y is divided by 6, the remainder is 1.

	QUANTITY A	QUANTITY B	
4.	The remainder when y is divided by 5	2	Ⓐ Ⓑ Ⓒ Ⓓ

Exercise Answers

Discrete Quantitative Questions

1. **C** Determine the prime factorization of each of the numbers.

    $16 = 2 \times 2 \times 2 \times 4$

    $24 = 2 \times 2 \times 2 \times 3$

    $72 = 2 \times 2 \times 2 \times 3 \times 3$

    Each term contains three 2s. The greatest common factor is thus $2 \times 2 \times 2 = 8$.

2. **120** The LCM of a set must contain the prime factorization of each term in the set. First, find the prime factorization of each term in the set:

    $6 = 2 \times 3$

    $8 = 2 \times 2 \times 2$

    $15 = 5 \times 3$

    The LCM must thus have the factors of 6: 2×3. The LCM must have the factors of 8: $2 \times 2 \times 2$. Since 6 contains a 2, the LCM will contain all the factors of 8 and 6 when it has $2 \times 2 \times 2 \times 3$ in its prime factorization. For the LCM to contain the factors of 15, an additional 5 is required. Thus the LCM is: $2 \times 2 \times 2 \times 3 \times 5 = 120$.

3. **A and D** Since x is divisible by 12, it must contain the prime factors of 12. The prime factorization of 12 is $2 \times 2 \times 3$. Since y is divisible by 8, it must contain the prime factors of 8. The prime factorization of 8 is $2 \times 2 \times 2$. xy must contain all the prime factors of x and all the prime factors of y. Thus the prime factorization of xy *must* contain $2 \times 2 \times 2 \times 2 \times 2 \times 3$. *Note that* xy *can contain other prime factors as well, but the ones just given are the only prime factors that it* has to *contain.*

    Choice A: Since the prime factors of xy can be combined to yield 48, 48 must be a factor of xy, which means xy is a multiple of 48. → Choice A is true.

    Choice B: The prime factorization of 64 is $2 \times 2 \times 2 \times 2 \times 2 \times 2$. The factorization $2 \times 2 \times 2 \times 2 \times 2 \times 3$ does not contain the prime factorization of 64. Thus 64 is not necessarily a factor of xy. → Eliminate Choice B.

    Choice C: The information in the question tells you which prime factors xy *must* have, but it does not eliminate the possibility that xy has other factors. Thus it cannot be determined whether 5 is a factor of xy. → Eliminate Choice C.

    Choice D: The prime factorization of 32 is $2 \times 2 \times 2 \times 2 \times 2$. The factorization $2 \times 2 \times 2 \times 2 \times 2 \times 3$ contains the prime factorization of 32. Thus 32 is a factor of xy. → Choice D is true.

    The correct answer is A and D.

4. **A and B** Since this is a "must be true" question, identify only what is necessarily true about a. Since a is a multiple of 6 and 8, a must contain the

prime factors of 6 and 8. Though a *could* equal $6 \times 8 = 48$, a must equal the LCM of 6 and 8, which is 24. Since a must be a multiple of 24, it must contain the factors of 24. 4 is a factor of 24, so Choice A is true. 12 is a factor of 24, so Choice B is true. 48 is not a factor of 24, so Choice C is not necessarily true. The correct answer is A and B.

5. **D** For the purpose of this question, let's express "the product of the integers from 1 through 24, inclusive" as 24!. For 5^k to be a factor of 24!, 5^k must divide evenly into 24!. For this to be true, the value of k cannot exceed the number of times 5 appears in the prime factorization of 24!. The greatest value for k will thus equal the number of times that 5 appears in the prime factorization of 24!. To determine the number of times that 5 appears in the prime factorization of 24!, look at the multiples of 5 from 1–24, inclusive: $5 = 5(1)$. $10 = 5(2)$. $15 = 5(3)$. $20 = 5(4)$. There are thus four 5s in the prime factorization of 24!. The maximum value for k is thus 4. The correct answer is D.

Quantitative Comparison Questions

1. **C** If x is a multiple of 12, then the factors of 12 must be factors of x. Since 3 is a factor of 12, 3 is a factor of x. Thus x divided by 3 yields a remainder of 0. Since 6 is a factor of 12, 6 is a factor of x. Thus x divided by 6 yields a remainder of 0.

2. **D** Since 18 is a factor of x, the prime factors of 18 must be prime factors of x. The prime factorization of 18 is $3 \times 3 \times 2$. Thus 18 has two unique prime factors, meaning x must have *at least* two unique prime factors. However, since you have no additional information about x, you do not know whether it has additional prime factors. For example, x could equal 90, which has a prime factorization of $3 \times 3 \times 2 \times 5$. In this case, x has three unique factors. The relationship cannot be determined.

3. **B** The remainder must always be smaller than the divisor. Thus the value in quantity A must be less than 4.

4. **D** Plug in the numbers. If $y = 7$, the value in Quantity A is 2. In this case, the two quantities are equal. If $y = 13$, the value in Quantity A is 3. In this case, Quantity A is greater. The relationship cannot be determined.

Odds and Evens

An even number is any integer that has 2 as a factor; for example, 4, 28, –12, –6, and so on.

Zero is an *even* number!

An odd number is simply the opposite: any number that does *not* have 2 as a factor, for example, 1, 9, –13, and so on. The GRE will expect you to know the following rules. Though testing numbers is certainly helpful on these questions, you will ultimately save time on the test by committing these rules to memory!

Addition and Subtraction

Property 1: In addition or subtraction, the result will be even if the numbers being added or subtracted are the same (both odd or both even), and the result will be odd if the numbers being added or subtracted are different (one odd and one even).

PROPERTY	EXAMPLE
odd +/– odd = even	$3 + 5 = 8$
even +/– even = even	$4 + 10 = 14$
even +/– odd = odd	$8 – 3 = 5$
odd +/– even = odd	$5 + 8 = 13$

Multiplication

Property 2: For a product to be even, at least one of the factors must be even.

PROPERTY	EXAMPLE
even × even = even	$4 \times 6 = 24$
even × odd = even	$6 \times 5 = 30$
odd × even = even	$3 \times 8 = 24$
odd × odd = odd	$7 \times 5 = 35$
even × . . . = even	$4 \times 5 \times 7 \times 11 = 1{,}540$
$(even)^x$ = even	$4^3 = 64$
$(odd)^x$ = odd	$3^3 = 27$

Let's look at a sample question that tests these properties:

For this question, indicate all of the answer choices that apply.

If x and y are integers and $3x + 2y$ is even, then which of the following must be true?

- [A] x is even
- [B] x is odd
- [C] xy is even
- [D] $x + y$ is even
- [E] x^2 is odd

SOLUTION: Use properties of odds and evens to deduce what must be true about the variables.

$$3x + 2y = \text{even}$$

Look at each term separately: you don't know whether $3x$ is odd or even, since you don't know whether x is odd or even. However, whether y is odd or even, $2y$ will always be even since $2y$ has 2 as a factor. So think of the equation as:

$3x$ + even = even

From the addition and subtraction rules, you know that even + even = even. Therefore, $3x$ must be even. For the product $3x$ to be even, the term must have an even factor. 3 is not even, *so* x *must be even.*

SOLUTION: The correct answer is A and C

Exercise: Odds and Evens

Discrete Quantitative Questions

1. If x is an integer, and $3x^2$ is even, then which of the following must be true?

   (A) $x + 3$ is even
   (B) $x^2 - 1$ is even
   (C) $x + 4$ is even
   (D) $\frac{x}{2}$ is even
   (E) $\frac{x}{2}$ is odd

2. If $-x/7$ is even, then which of the following must be true?

   (A) x is odd
   (B) x is even
   (C) x is negative
   (D) x is positive
   (E) x is a prime number

For Questions 3 to 6, indicate all of the answer choices that apply.

3. If x and y are integers, and $x^2 - y^2$ is even, then which of the following must be true?

   A $x - y$ is even
   B $x + y$ is even
   C $(x + y)^2$ is even
   D xy is even
   E $\frac{x}{y}$ is even
   F $x^2 - xy$ is even

4. If x is an even integer, then which of the following must be true?

   A $x^2 + 2$ is even

   B $\frac{x}{2}$ is even

   C $\frac{4}{x}$ is even

   D x^7 is even

   E x^2 is a multiple of 4

5. If x and y are both integers and $x(y +3)$ is odd, then which of the following must be true?

    A x is even

    B y is even

    C xy is odd

    D xy is even

    E x is odd

    F y is odd

6. If a, b, and c are positive integers, $a + b = 12$, and $bc = 15$, then which of the following must be true?

    A $b + c$ is even

    B ab is even

    C ac is odd

    D $a - c$ is even

    E abc is odd

Exercise Answers

1. **C** Exponents are irrelevant when considering properties of odds and evens. So if $3x^2$ is even, then $3x$ is even. If $3x$ is even, then $3x$ must have an even factor. 3 is not even, so x must be even. If x is even, then $x + 4$ is *always* even. You may be wondering about Choice D: note that even when x is even, $\frac{x}{2}$ is not always even. For example, if $x = 6$, $\frac{x}{2} = 3$, which is not even.

2. **B** Plug in values for x that would satisfy the given information. Try $x = 14$. In this case, $\frac{-14}{7} = -2$. -2 is even, so 14 is a possible value for x. Thus choices B and D are possibilities. However, if $x = -14$, the given information will still be true: $\frac{-(-14)}{7} = 2 =$ even. Thus x can be positive or negative. Eliminate Choice D. The correct answer is B. An important takeaway from this question is that *the sign is irrelevant in odd and even questions.*

3. **A, B, C, and F** Since exponents are irrelevant when working with odds and evens, the fact that $x^2 - y^2$ is even implies that $x - y$ is even. If the difference between two numbers is even, then x and y must both be odd or both be even. For cases where they are both odd or both even, A, B, C, and F will always be true. (You can plug in numbers to confirm.)

4. **A, D, and E** Evaluate each choice.

    Choice A: An even number to any power yields an even. An even + even = even. → A is true.

    Choice B: If x is 4, then $\frac{x}{2} = 2 =$ even. If $x = 6$, then $\frac{x}{2} = 3$, which is odd. → B is not always true.

    Choice C: If x is 4, then $\frac{4}{x} = 1$, which is odd. → C is not always true.

    Choice D: An even to any power yields an even. → D is true.

Choice E: If x is 2, then $x^2 = 4$. 4 is a multiple of 4. If x is 8, then $x^2 = 64$. 64 is a multiple of 4. Both cases lead to the conclusion that x^2 is a multiple of 4. → E is true.

5. **B, D, and E** For a product to be odd, all factors must be odd. Thus x and $(y + 3)$ must be odd. If $y + 3$ is odd, then y is even. Now evaluate the choices:

   Choice A: As previously shown, x is odd. → A is not true.

   Choice B: As previously shown, y is even. → B is true.

   Choice C: For a product to be odd, all factors must be odd. As previously shown, y is even. Thus xy is even. → C is not true.

   Choice D: See the explanation for C. → D is true

   Choice E: See the explanation for A. → E is true

   Choice F: See the explanation for B. → F is not true

6. **A, C, D, and E** Since $a + b$ is an even integer, a and b must both be odd or both be even. Since bc is an odd integer, b and c must both be odd. If $a + b = $ even and $b = $ odd, then $a = $ odd. Thus a, b, and c are all odd. Evaluate the choices:

   Choice A: odd + odd = even → A is true.

   Choice B: odd × odd = odd → B is not true.

   Choice C: odd × odd = odd → C is true.

   Choice D: odd – odd = even → D is true.

   Choice E: odd × odd × odd = odd → E is true.

Positives and Negatives

All About Zero

A number's position in relation to zero determines its sign. If a number is greater than zero, then it is **positive**. If a number is less than zero, it is **negative**.

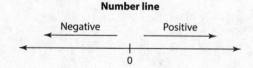

Number line

Negative   Positive

0

Generally, when you are told or asked whether a term is greater than zero or less than zero, you should interpret it using properties of positives and negatives. For example, if you are told that $xy > 0$, think of this information as "xy is positive," and proceed to use the rules covered in this chapter. As with odds and evens, you will need to know certain properties of positive and negative numbers.

Multiplication and Division

When multiplying or dividing two terms, the result will be positive if the terms are the *same* sign (both positive or both negative) and negative if the two terms are different signs (one positive and one negative).

$$+ \times + = + \qquad + \div + = +$$
$$- \times - = + \qquad - \div - = +$$
$$- \times + = - \qquad - \div + = -$$
$$+ \times - = - \qquad + \div - = -$$

If $\dfrac{1}{y-x} < 0$, then which of the following must be true?

- (A) $y > 0$
- (B) $x > 0$
- (C) $xy > 0$
- (D) $y > x$
- (E) $x > y$

SOLUTION: If $\dfrac{1}{y-x}$ is negative, then the numerator and denominator must have different signs. Since the numerator is positive, $y - x$ must be negative. Algebraically $y - x < 0$. Add x to both sides: $y < x$. Of the choices, the only one matching what you have deduced is E.

Many positive/negative questions will raise the terms to an exponent. For such questions, it's important to remember a property that is covered in Chapter 11 on quadratics: *When a variable is raised to an even exponent, the result will always be positive. When a variable is raised to an odd exponent, the sign of the result will always be the same as the sign of the base.*

If $a^4 b^3 c^7 > 0$, then which of the following must be true? (Indicate all the apply.)

- [A] $a > 0$
- [B] $b > 0$
- [C] $bc > 0$
- [D] $b/c > 0$
- [E] $ab > 0$
- [F] $abc > 0$

SOLUTION: You are not told the sign of any of the unknowns, but since a is raised to an even exponent, you know that a^2 is positive. Thus you have: $(+) \times (b^3) \times (c^7) > 0$. Since $+ \times + = +$, it must be true that $b^3 \times c^7$ is positive. Since b and c are each raised to odd exponents, the signs of b^3 and c^7 will be the same as the signs of b and c, respectively. Thus you know that $bc > 0$. If $bc > 0$, then b and c must have the same sign, meaning that their product and their quotient are positive. The correct answer is C and D.

Many test-takers mistakenly assume that since $a^4 > 0$, a must be greater than zero. However, remember that even exponents *hide* the sign of the base. Whether the base is positive or negative, the result of a variable raised to an even exponent will always be positive. Thus F is not necessarily true.

Quantitative Comparison Strategy: Positives and Negatives

The GRE loves testing properties of positives and negatives in Quantitative Comparison questions. One important building block of success for the savvy test-taker is to identify situations in which these properties are being tested.

> **Situation 1**   You are told that an unknown is greater than or less than zero.

If the stem says that $x > 0$, then you know that x is positive. If it says that $xy < 0$, then you know that xy is negative. Once you recognize that these properties are being tested, you can then start using the rules that have been covered.

> **Situation 2**   One of the quantities has a value of zero.

If you are comparing an unknown to zero, your ultimate goal is to determine the sign of that unknown. Remember that you can determine its sign *without* knowing its actual value.

$$x \neq 0$$

QUANTITY A	QUANTITY B	
$x^{16} + 1$	0	Ⓐ Ⓑ Ⓒ Ⓓ

SOLUTION: Since you are comparing $(x^{16} + 1)$ to zero, you should focus on determining the sign of Quantity A. Since the exponent on x^{16} is even, $x^{16} > 0$. Thus $x^{16} + 1 > 0$. The correct answer is Quantity A.

> **Situation 3**   One of the quantities has an even exponent, and the other quantity has an odd exponent.

Since the result of an even exponent hides the sign of the base, and the result of an odd exponent preserves the sign of the base, these properties are fertile ground to test your knowledge of positives and negatives.

q is an integer

QUANTITY A	QUANTITY B	
$(-4{,}012)^{2q}$	$(-4{,}012)^{2q+1}$	Ⓐ Ⓑ Ⓒ Ⓓ

SOLUTION: In both quantities, the base is negative. Since the exponent in Quantity A is even, the value in Quantity A must be positive. Since the exponent in Quantity B is odd, the value in Quantity B must be negative. The correct answer is A.

Finally, when testing numbers for Quantitative Comparison questions testing positives and negatives, *you should always test at least one negative case and one positive case.* You want to play devil's advocate, and the best way to do so is by choosing numbers with different signs.

$$x > y; xy \neq 0$$

QUANTITY A	QUANTITY B
x^2	y^2

Ⓐ Ⓑ Ⓒ Ⓓ

SOLUTION: The even exponents in the quantities should clue you in that the question might be addressing properties of positives and negatives. Let's thus choose positive and negative cases for x and y:

Case 1: $x = 3$ and $y = 2$. Quantity A: $3^2 = 9$. Quantity B: $2^2 = 4$. Quantity A is greater. The answer is A or D.

Case 2: $x = 3$ and $y = -2$. Quantity A: $3^2 = 9$. Quantity B: $-2^2 = 4$. Quantity A is *still* greater. Though you might be tempted to stop here and select A, notice that you have not looked at situations where *both* values are negative.

Case 3: $x = -5$ and $y = -6$. Quantity A: $-5^2 = 25$. Quantity B: $-6^2 = 36$. In this case, Quantity B is greater. A relationship cannot be determined, so the answer is D.

Exercise: Positives and Negatives

Discrete Quantitative Questions

1. If $a < b < 0$, then which of the following must be true?

   Ⓐ $ab < 0$

   Ⓑ $a + b > 0$

   Ⓒ $\frac{a}{b} < 0$

   Ⓓ $b - a > 0$

   Ⓔ $a - b > 0$

2. If $xy > 0$ and $yz < 0$, then which of the following must be negative?

   Ⓐ xyz

   Ⓑ xy^2z

   Ⓒ x^2y^2z

   Ⓓ $x^2y^2z^2$

   Ⓔ $\frac{xy}{z}$

3. If $ab^2 > 0$ and $ac < 0$, then which of the following must be true?
   (Indicate all the apply.)

   Ⓐ $ab > 0$
   Ⓑ $b > 0$
   Ⓒ $\frac{a}{c} < 0$
   Ⓓ $b^2c < 0$
   Ⓔ $a(c^2) > 0$

4. If $0 > x > y$, then which of the following must be true? (Indicate all
   that apply.)

   Ⓐ $x^2 - y^2 < 0$
   Ⓑ $y - x < 0$
   Ⓒ $\frac{1}{x^2} < 1$
   Ⓓ $\frac{x+y}{x} > 0$
   Ⓔ $y^2 - x^2 < 0$

5. If $\frac{x-a}{z^2+1} > 0$, then which of the following must be true?

   (A) $x > 0$
   (B) $x < a$
   (C) $x > a$
   (D) $xa > 0$
   (E) $x + a > 0$

6. If $xy > 0$ and $x + y > 0$, then which of the following must be true? (Indicate all that apply.)

   [A] $x < 0$

   [B] $|x| > |y|$

   [C] $x > 0$

   [D] $\frac{x}{y} > 0$

   [E] $y > 0$

Quantitative Comparison Questions

Each of the following questions consists of two quantities, Quantity A and Quantity B. You are to compare the two quantities. You may use additional information centered above the two quantities if additional information is given. Choose

   (A) if Quantity A is greater
   (B) if Quantity B is greater
   (C) if the two quantities are equal
   (D) if the relationship between the two quantities cannot be determined

$$0 > a > b$$

	QUANTITY A	QUANTITY B	
1.	a^2	b^4	(A) (B) (C) (D)

$$|x| > |y|$$

	QUANTITY A	QUANTITY B	
2.	x^2	y^2	(A) (B) (C) (D)

a and b do not equal zero

	QUANTITY A	QUANTITY B	
3.	$-(a^2)(b^4)$	$(-a)^2(-b)^4$	(A) (B) (C) (D)

$$\frac{a}{b} = 4$$

	QUANTITY A	QUANTITY B	
4.	a	b	Ⓐ Ⓑ Ⓒ Ⓓ

$$\frac{a}{b} > 0$$

	QUANTITY A	QUANTITY B	
5.	ab	0	Ⓐ Ⓑ Ⓒ Ⓓ

$$p^2q^3 > 0$$
$$p^3q^2 > 0$$

	QUANTITY A	QUANTITY B	
6.	pq	0	Ⓐ Ⓑ Ⓒ Ⓓ

$$a^2b^3c^5 > 0$$
$$a^3b^4c^5 < 0$$

	QUANTITY A	QUANTITY B	
7.	ab	0	Ⓐ Ⓑ Ⓒ Ⓓ

Exercise Answers

Discrete Quantitative Questions

1. **D** Since a and b are negative, their product and quotient must be positive. Thus eliminate A and C. The sum of two negatives is a negative. Thus eliminate B. For D and E, choose values. Let $a = -4$ and $b = -3$. Evaluate the expression in D: $-3 - (-4) = -3 + 4 = 1$. $1 > 0$, so D is true. Evaluate the expression in E: $-4 - (-3) = -4 + 3 = -1$. -1 is not greater than zero. Eliminate E.

2. **B** If xy is positive, then x and y must have the same sign. If yz is negative, then y and z must have different signs. If x and y have the same sign and y and z have different signs, then x and z must have different signs, meaning $xz < 0$. Use this information in each choice. For A, you know that $xz < 0$, but you do not know the sign of y, so you do not know whether the product is negative. In B, you know that $y^2 > 0$ (because of the even exponent) and that $xz < 0$. $(-)(+) = (-)$, so Choice B is negative. In C, you know that x^2y^2 must be positive because of the even exponents, but you do not know the sign of z. In D, all the variables are raised to even exponents, so the result must be positive. In E, you know that $xy > 0$, but you do not know the sign of the denominator. The only choice that *must* be negative is B.

3. **C, D, and E** In the first inequality, you know that a must be positive since b^2 is positive. In the second inequality, you know that a and c must have different signs. If $a > 0$, and a and c have different signs, then $c < 0$.

4. **A, B, and D** Since this is a "must be true" question, it is helpful to plug in values for x and y. First, plug in integers, and then fractions.

    Case 1: $x = -0.5$ and $y = -0.75$. Plug these values into the choices:

    A: $-0.5^2 - (-0.75)^2 < 0 \rightarrow$ True

    B: $-0.75 - (-0.5) < 0 \rightarrow$ True

    C: $\frac{1}{-0.5^2} < 1 \rightarrow$ False

    D: $\frac{-0.5 + -0.75}{-0.5} > 0 \rightarrow$ True

    E: $-0.75^2 - (-0.5)^2 < 0 \rightarrow$ False

    Now plug in integers for the choices that yielded true in Case 1. Let $x = -2$ and $y = -3$.

    A: $-2^2 - (-3)^2 < 0 \rightarrow$ True

    B: $-3 - (-2) < 0 \rightarrow$ True

    D: $\frac{-2 + -3}{-2} > 0 \rightarrow$ True

    Since 1, 2, and 4 remain true for both conditions, those are the answers.

5. **C** For a fraction to be positive, the numerator and denominator must have the same sign. Since z is raised to an even exponent, you know that z^2 must equal at least zero. Therefore, $z^2 + 1$ must be positive. If the denominator of this fraction is positive, then the numerator is also positive. Thus $x - a > 0$. Add a to both sides: $x > a$.

6. **C, D, and E** If $xy > 0$, then x and y are both positive or both negative. If x and y are both negative, then $x + y < 0$. The condition that x and y are both negative does not satisfy the given information. Thus to satisfy the given information, x and y must both be positive. If x and y are both positive, then choices C, D, and E are true.

Quantitative Comparison Questions

1. **D** Choose values: First, select an integer value for each variable. Let $a = -1$ and $b = -2$. In this case, Quantity A = 1, and Quantity B = 16. In this case, Quantity B is greater. Next, choose values that are likely to yield a relationship different than the relationship that the first pair of numbers yielded. To do so, select "weird" numbers. In this case, a good type of "weird" number is a fraction. Let $a = 0.25$ and let $b = 0.5$. In this case, Quantity A = 0.0625, and Quantity B = 0.0625. In this case, both quantities are equal. Therefore, a relationship cannot be determined.

2. **A** Plugging in numbers is a good strategy here. Since the columns have even exponents, the signs will not matter. So choose fractions and integers.

   Case 1: $x = \frac{1}{2}$ and $y = \frac{1}{3}$. In this case, the value of column A is $\frac{1}{4}$ and the value of column B is $\frac{1}{9}$. Quantity A is greater, so the answer is A or D.

   Case 2: Plug in new values to prove D: $x = 3$ and $y = 2$. In this case, the value of column A is 9, and the value of column B is 4. Quantity A is still greater.

3. **B** Though it would appear that you do not have sufficient information about a and b, keep in mind that the even exponents and the signs will help you make inferences. In Quantity A, a^2 and b^4 must be positive (because of the even exponents). Thus their product is positive. Multiply this product by -1, and the result is negative. In Quantity B, $-a^2$ and $-b^4$ are both positive. Thus their product is positive. The value in Column B is greater.

4. **D** Since $\frac{a}{b}$ equals a positive number, a and b must have the same sign. However, you do not know what the signs are. If $a = 8$, then $b = 2$, and Quantity A is greater. But if $a = -8$, then $b = -2$, and Quantity B is greater. There is more than one relationship, so the answer is D.

5. **A** If $\frac{a}{b} > 0$, then a and b must have the same sign. If a and b have the same sign, then their product must be positive. Thus $ab > 0$, and the correct answer is A.

6. **A** Your first step should be to make inferences from the stem. Inequality 1: you know that $p^2q^3 > 0$. Because of the even exponent, p^2 must be positive. Thus q^3 must be positive. If q^3 is positive, then $q > 0$ (remember, odd exponents preserve the sign of the base). Inequality 2: you know that $p^3q^2 > 0$. Because of the even exponent, q^2 must be positive. Thus p^3 must be positive. If p^3 is positive, then $p > 0$. Positive × positive = positive, so $pq > 0$.

7. **B** Your first step should be to make inferences from the stem. Inequality 1: because of the even exponent, you know that $a^2 > 0$. Thus $b^3c^5 > 0$. Because of the odd exponents, b^3 and c^5 will have the same signs as b and c, respectively. Thus $bc > 0$. Inequality 2: because of the even exponent, you know that $b^4 > 0$. Thus $a^3c^5 < 0$. Because of the odd exponents, a^3 and c^5 will have the same signs as a and c, respectively. Thus $ac < 0$. Now you know that $bc > 0$ and $ac < 0$.

If $bc > 0$, then b and c must have the same sign. If $ac < 0$, then a and c must have different signs. Therefore, a and b must have different signs, and their product must be negative.

Evenly Spaced Sets

An evenly spaced set is any series of numbers in which the spacing between consecutive terms is constant. The most basic example of an evenly spaced set is consecutive integers. In the set 1, 2, 3, 4, 5, the spacing between successive terms is 1. Other examples are:

2, 4, 6, 8 . . .
10, 15, 20 . . .
3, 8 13, 18 . . .

> Note that you can describe the first example as consecutive even integers and the second example as consecutive multiples of 5. Though the items in the third set are not multiples of the same number, the set is still evenly spaced since the increment between successive terms is 5.

Properties of Evenly Spaced Sets

The GRE will expect you to know certain properties of evenly spaced sets.

Property 1: All the terms in an evenly spaced set can be expressed using one of the terms in the set.

> If the sum of three consecutive multiples of 4 is 60, what is the value of the smallest term?

> **SOLUTION:** Approaching this algebraically, you can let a = the smallest term, b = the middle term, and c = the largest term. Therefore, $a + b + c = 60$. But notice that you have additional information about these variables! Since you are dealing with consecutive multiples of 4, you can let $b = a + 4$ and $c = b + 4 = a + 8$. Thus using substitution, you can arrive at one equation with one variable:

$$a + (a + 4) + (a + 8) = 60$$

$$3a + 12 = 60$$

$$3a = 48$$

$$a = 16$$

Property 2: The average (arithmetic mean) of an evenly spaced set = the median of the set = the average of the endpoints.

What is the average of x, $x + 4$, $x + 8$, $x + 12$, and $x + 16$?

SOLUTION: Recognize that each term is 4 greater than the previous term. You thus have an evenly spaced set. To find the average, you need the median, which in this case, is $x + 8$.

What is the average of the integers from 15–21, inclusive?

SOLUTION: Since average = median for an evenly spaced set, you could list out all the terms and find the median. But a faster approach would be to take the average of the endpoints: $\frac{15 + 21}{2} = 18$. The average is 18.

Property 3: Use the following formula to determine the number of terms in an evenly spaced set:

$$\frac{(\text{last item in the set} - \text{first item in the set})}{\text{increment}} + 1$$

Example: How many integers are there from 6–10, inclusive?

SOLUTION: Note that **inclusive** means that you will include both endpoints of the set when determining the answer. You might be tempted to simply take the difference of 10 and 6 and arrive at 4 as your answer, but this would omit one of the items. If you list out the numbers, you will see that there are five (6, 7, 8, 9, and 10). Using the preceding formula, you arrive at:

$$\frac{10 - 6}{1} + 1 = 5$$

How many multiples of 15 are there from 40–160, inclusive?

SOLUTION: Before using the formula, note that the endpoints of this set are not multiples of 15. To use the formula, you need the endpoints to have the property that the formula specifies (in this case, multiples of 15). Your endpoints will thus be 45 (the smallest multiple of 15 that is greater than 40) and 150 (the greatest multiple of 15 that is less than 160). Now you know that your endpoints are 45 and 150, and the increment between each term in the set is 15. Plug these values into the formula:

$$\frac{150 - 45}{15} + 1 = \frac{105}{15} + 1 = 7 + 1 = 8$$

Property 4: To determine the sum of the values in an evenly spaced set, use the average formula: $A \times N = S$.

Properties 2 and 3 specified how to determine the average and number of items in a set, so using these properties, you can determine the sum of a set.

What is the sum of the even integers from 4–180, inclusive?

SOLUTION: Based on Property 4, you should multiply the average and the number of items in the set. From Property 2, you know that the average of an evenly spaced set equals the average of the endpoints: $\frac{180+4}{2} = 92$. Using Property 3, you can determine the number of items:

$$\frac{180-4}{2} + 1 = 89$$

SOLUTION: $A \times N = S$, so $92 \times 89 = S = 8{,}188$.

Quantitative Comparison Strategy: Evenly Spaced Sets

Many Quantitative Comparison questions testing evenly spaced sets will give you large sets of values. As is always the case with Quantitative Comparison questions, you should minimize calculations by *comparing* the quantities and identifying what terms they have in common:

QUANTITY A	QUANTITY B	
The sum of the integers from 1–28, inclusive	The sum of the integers from 7–29, inclusive	Ⓐ Ⓑ Ⓒ Ⓓ

SOLUTION: Instead of calculating, identify similarities between the two columns.

Quantity A can be rewritten as: $(1 + 2 + 3 \ldots 6) + (7 + 8 \ldots 28)$.

Quantity B can be rewritten as: $(7 + 8 \ldots 28) + 29$.

SOLUTION: The two quantities share the sum of the terms from 7–28, inclusive. You can thus subtract this sum from both quantities. The new comparison is:

QUANTITY A	QUANTITY B	
$1 + 2 + 3 + 4 + 5 + 6$	29	Ⓐ Ⓑ Ⓒ Ⓓ

SOLUTION: The value in Quantity A = 21. 21 < 29, so Quantity B is greater.

Exercise: Evenly Spaced Sets

Discrete Quantitative Questions

1. If the sum of four consecutive even integers is 44, what is the value of the second-largest integer in the set?

   (A) 10
   (B) 12
   (C) 14
   (D) 16
   (E) 18

2. What is the median value of the integers from 14–80, inclusive?

   (A) 43
   (B) 44
   (C) 45
   (D) 46
   (E) 47

For this question, write your answer in the box.

3. How many integers from 1–120, inclusive, are multiples of 3 or 4?

   ┌─────────────────┐
   │   │
   └─────────────────┘

4. How many even multiples of 9 are there from 1–1,000, inclusive?

   (A) 55
   (B) 56
   (C) 109
   (D) 110
   (E) 111

5. In a series of six consecutive integers, the sum of the first three integers is 93. What is the sum of the last three integers?

   (A) 96
   (B) 99
   (C) 102
   (D) 105
   (E) 108

6. What is the sum of the multiples of 3 from 11–110, inclusive?

   (A) 1,980
   (B) 2,057
   (C) 3.228
   (D) 4,573
   (E) 6,050

For this question, write your answer in the box.

7. How many integers from 5–100 yield a remainder of 1 when divided by 6?

   [   ]

8. In a series of eight consecutive integers, the third term is 7. What is the sum of the eight integers?

   (A) 42
   (B) 56
   (C) 64
   (D) 68
   (E) 72

9. What is the difference between the sum of the even integers from 1–100 and the sum of the odd integers from 1–100?

   (A) 0
   (B) 25
   (C) 26
   (D) 50
   (E) 52

10. What is the difference between the number of integers from 50–60, inclusive, and the sum of the integers from 50–60, inclusive?

   (A) 11
   (B) 44
   (C) 55
   (D) 594
   (E) 605

11. In a series of twenty consecutive integers, the sum of the first two integers
     is 37. What is the sum of the last three integers in the set?

     Ⓐ 107
     Ⓑ 108
     Ⓒ 109
     Ⓓ 110
     Ⓔ 111

Quantitative Comparison Questions

Each of the following questions consists of two quantities, Quantity A and Quantity
B. You are to compare the two quantities. You may use additional information
centered above the two quantities if additional information is given. Choose

Ⓐ if Quantity A is greater
Ⓑ if Quantity B is greater
Ⓒ if the two quantities are equal
Ⓓ if the relationship between the two quantities cannot be determined

A series of consecutive integers has more positive
integers than negative integers.

	QUANTITY A	QUANTITY B	
1.	The sum of the integers in the series	0	Ⓐ Ⓑ Ⓒ Ⓓ

	QUANTITY A	QUANTITY B	
2.	The product of the integers from 6–61, inclusive	The product of the integers from 2–60, inclusive	Ⓐ Ⓑ Ⓒ Ⓓ

	QUANTITY A	QUANTITY B	
3.	The average of all the integers from 2–20, inclusive	12	Ⓐ Ⓑ Ⓒ Ⓓ

	QUANTITY A	QUANTITY B	
4.	The sum of the integers from 8–25, inclusive	The sum of the integers from 1–24, inclusive	Ⓐ Ⓑ Ⓒ Ⓓ

	QUANTITY A	QUANTITY B	
5.	The number of even integers from 2–20, inclusive	9	Ⓐ Ⓑ Ⓒ Ⓓ

Exercise Answers

Discrete Quantitative Questions

1. **B** Let the smallest integer = x. Therefore:

$$x + (x + 2) + (x + 4) + (x + 6) = 44$$

$$4x + 12 = 44$$

$$4x = 32$$

$$x = 8$$

The second-largest integer is $x + 4$. Substitute 8 for x: $8 + 4 = 12$.

2. **E** Use Property 2: The average (arithmetic mean) of an evenly spaced set = the median of the set = the average of the endpoints. In this question, the fastest way to determine the median is to take the average of the endpoints: $\frac{14 + 80}{2} = \frac{94}{2} = 47$.

3. **60** Use Property 3 to determine how many multiples of 3 there are from 1–120, inclusive. The lower bound is 3 and the upper bound is 120. Thus the number of multiples of $3 = \frac{120 - 3}{3} + 1 = 40$. Now use Property 3 to determine how many multiples of 4 there are from 1–120, inclusive. The lower bound is 4 and the upper bound is 120. Thus the number of multiples of $4 = \frac{120 - 4}{4} + 1 = 30 \rightarrow 40 + 30 = 70$. But there's an issue: You have double-counted the multiples of 12. You thus need to determine how many multiples of 12 there are from 1–120, inclusive, and subtract that value from 70. Use Property 3 again: The number of multiples of 12 from 1–120, inclusive, is $\frac{120 - 12}{12} + 1 = 10$. Thus the answer is $70 - 10 = 60$.

4. **A** An even multiple of 9 is any number that has 9 and 2 as factors, in other words, a multiple of 18. You are thus looking for the number of multiples of 18 from 1–1,000, inclusive. The smallest value in the set is 18. The largest value in the set is 990. Substitute these values into the formula from Property 3:

$$\frac{990 - 18}{18} + 1 = 55$$

5. **C** In an evenly spaced set, median = average, so the median of the first three terms will equal $\frac{\text{sum}}{\text{number of items}} = \frac{93}{3} = 31$. Since each set has three terms, and all the values are consecutive, the median of the next three terms will be 3 greater than the median of the first three terms: $31 + 3 = 34$. Use Property 4 to determine the sum of the last three terms:

average × number of items = sum

$$\downarrow \qquad \qquad \downarrow \qquad \qquad \downarrow$$

$$34 \quad \times \quad 3 \quad = \quad 102$$

6. **A** Before using any of the relevant formulas, recognize that since the question concerns multiples of 3, the endpoints are 12 and 108. Based on Property 4: average × number of items = sum. From Property 2, you know that the average of an evenly spaced set equals the average of the endpoints: $\frac{108 + 12}{2} = 60$. Using Property 3, you can determine the number of items:

$$\frac{108 - 12}{3} + 1 = 33$$

Plug these values into the formula:

average × number of items = sum

↓	↓	↓
60	× 33	= 1,980

7. **16** Though it might be difficult to see, the numbers in this set are evenly spaced. Think of numbers that yield a remainder of 1 when divided by 6: 7, 13, 19, and so on. The spacing is thus 6. Use Property 3 to determine the number of items in the set:

$$\frac{last - first}{spacing} + 1$$

The last term will be the greatest number smaller than 100 that yields a remainder of 1 when divided by 6: 97. The first term will be the smallest number greater than 5 that yields a remainder of 1 when divided by 6: 7. Now plug these values into the formula:

$$\frac{97 - 7}{6} + 1 = 16$$

8. **D** Use Property 4 to determine the sum:

average × number of items = sum

You are told that the set contains eight consecutive integers, so to calculate the sum, you must determine the average. The average of an evenly spaced set = the median. Since the given set has an even number of terms, the median will be the average of the two middle terms (in this case, the 4th and 5th terms). If the third term is 7, then the 4th term is 8 and the 5th term is 9. The average of these two terms is 8.5. Now substitute 8.5 for the average and 8 for the number of items:

average × number of items = sum

↓	↓	↓
8.5	× 8	= 68

9. **D** Though you can use the previously discussed formulas, it would be faster to recognize that from 1–100, there are an equal number of odd integers and even integers. Since there are 100 terms in the set, 50 will be odd and 50 will be even. Each even term will be 1 greater than each corresponding odd term. Since there are 50 terms, the sum of the even terms will be 50 more than the sum of the odd terms.

10. **D** Use Property 3 to determine the number of integers from 50–60, inclusive:

$$\frac{last - first}{spacing} + 1$$
$$\frac{60 - 50}{1} + 1 = 11$$

Use Property 4 to determine the sum of the integers in the set:

average × number of items = sum

The average of an evenly spaced set = the average of the endpoints. The endpoints of the set are 50 and 60. Their average is $\frac{50-60}{2}$ = 55. You know from earlier that the number of items in the set is 11. Plug these values into the formula:

average × number of items = sum

$$\downarrow \qquad\qquad \downarrow \qquad\qquad \downarrow$$
$$55 \quad \times \quad 11 \quad = \quad 605$$

Subtract the sum from the number of items: 605 − 11 = 594.

11. **B** Let x be the first integer in the set and $x + 1$ be the next integer. You know:

$$x + (x + 1) = 37$$
$$2x + 1 = 37$$
$$2x = 36$$
$$x = 18$$

To find the sum of the last three integers, determine the value of the last integer and work from there to get the value of the previous two integers. If the first integer is 18, then the 20th term in the set will be 18 + 19 = 37. The values of the 2nd-to-last and 3rd-to-last terms are 36 and 35, respectively. 35 + 36 + 37 = 108.

Quantitative Comparison Questions

1. **A** If a series of consecutive integers has more positive than negative numbers, the positive numbers must all offset the negative numbers. Thus the sum of the series will be positive. You can also see this by testing numbers. Try −2, −1, 0, 1, 2, 3. The sum is greater than zero. Try −4, −3, −2, −1, 0, 1, 2, 3, 4, 5. The sum is still greater than zero.

2. **B** Don't calculate! Determine how the two columns differ.

   Column A can be rewritten as (6 × 7 × 8 . . . 60) × 61.

   Column B can be rewritten as: 2 × 3 × 4 × 5 × (6 × 7 × 8 . . . 60).

   Divide both columns by (6 × 7 × 8 . . . 60). The new comparison is 61 versus (2 × 3 × 4 × 5). 2 × 3 × 4 × 5 = 120. 120 > 61. Thus the value in Column B is greater.

3. **B** If given the endpoints of an evenly spaced set, the fastest way to determine the average of the set is to take the average of the endpoints. The average of the integers from 2–20, inclusive is (20 + 2)/2 = 11. Quantity B is greater.

4. **B** Don't calculate! Determine how the two quantities differ.

   Quantity A can be rewritten as: (8 + 9 + 10 . . . 24) + 25.

   Quantity B can be rewritten as: 1 + 2 + 3 + 4 + 5 + 6 + 7 + (8 + 9 + 10 . . . 24).

Subtract (8 + 9 + 10 . . . 24) from both columns. The new comparison is: 25 versus (1 + 2 + 3 + 4 + 5 + 6 + 7). 1 + 2 + 3 + 4 + 5 + 6 + 7 = 28. 28 > 25. Thus Quantity B is greater.

5. **A** Use the formula from Property 3:

$$\frac{20 - 2}{2} + 1 = 10$$

Part-to-Whole Relationships

The following sections all concern part-to-whole relationships. A part-to-whole relationship can be expressed as a fraction, decimal, percent, or ratio. It may seem simplistic, but envisioning a pie in these questions often helps conceptualize the situation. It's equally important that you remember that the part must always refer to a whole. People often have a tendency to say things like, "I have one-fourth," or "Jack has 20%." But these statements beg the question: one-fourth *of what*? 20 percent *of what*? When expressing these relationships algebraically, remember that the part must always be a piece of some *quantity*.

Fractions

This section discusses fractions. A fraction is a way to represent a piece of a whole. Fractions look like the following:

$\dfrac{1}{4}$ → **numerator**

    → **denominator**

When thinking of fractions, imagine one pie. The denominator tells you how many slices the pie is broken into, and the numerator tells you how many of those slices you have. So the fraction $\frac{1}{4}$ means you have 1 slice of a pie that has been cut into 4 slices.

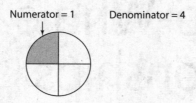

Numerator = 1   Denominator = 4

Now let's look at what happens when the numerator and denominator of a fraction change. Let's compare $\frac{1}{8}$ to $\frac{1}{4}$.

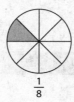

$\frac{1}{8}$

In this case, you are still dealing with one pie, but now the pie is broken up into 8 slices instead of 4. One slice out of 8 is less than 1 slice out of 4. From this, you can derive a general rule:

> As the denominator of a positive fraction increases, the value of the fraction decreases.

Now let's compare $\frac{2}{4}$ to $\frac{1}{4}$.

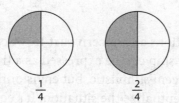

$\frac{1}{4}$ $\frac{2}{4}$

Again, each fraction represents one pie, and in both cases, the number of slices is the same. Two slices from a 4-slice pie is more than 1 slice from a 4-slice pie. Thus $\frac{2}{4}$ is greater than $\frac{1}{4}$. From this, you can derive a general rule:

> As the numerator of a positive fraction increases, the value of the fraction increases.

Quantitative Comparison Strategy: Fractions

When the quantities in a Quantitative Comparison question are fractions, focus on the relationships between numerator and denominator. If the denominators are the same, the fraction with the larger numerator will be greater. If the numerators are the same, the fraction with the smaller denominator will be greater.

<u>QUANTITY A</u>   <u>QUANTITY B</u>
$\frac{7}{100}$ $\frac{7}{100^2}$

SOLUTION: Since the numerators of the fractions are the same, the fraction with the smaller denominator will be greater. $100 < 100^2$. Thus Quantity A is greater.

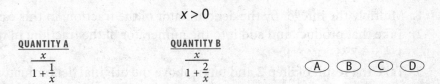

$$x > 0$$

QUANTITY A	QUANTITY B
$\dfrac{x}{1+\frac{1}{x}}$	$\dfrac{x}{1+\frac{2}{x}}$

Ⓐ Ⓑ Ⓒ Ⓓ

SOLUTION: The fractions in the two quantities have the same numerator. Thus the fraction with the smaller denominator will be greater. Since the numerator in $\left(\frac{1}{x}\right)$ is smaller than the numerator in $\left(\frac{2}{x}\right)$, $\left(\frac{1}{x}\right)$ is a smaller fraction, which means the denominator in Quantity A is smaller. Since the denominator in Quantity A is smaller, the value of the fraction in Quantity A is greater. The correct answer is A.

What if the fractions are negative? The opposite relationships apply:

As the denominator of a negative fraction increases, the value of the fraction increases.

As the numerator of a negative fraction increases, the value of the fraction decreases.

To understand why this is the case, compare $-\left(\frac{3}{5}\right)$ and $-\left(\frac{2}{5}\right)$. You know that $\frac{3}{5}$ is a larger piece of a pie than is $\frac{2}{5}$. But since $\frac{3}{5} > \frac{2}{5}$, the negative version of $\frac{3}{5}$ will be more negative than the negative version of $\frac{2}{5}$. If $-\left(\frac{3}{5}\right)$ is more negative than $-\left(\frac{2}{5}\right)$, then $-\left(\frac{3}{5}\right)$ must be smaller. See the number line below for illustration:

$$\frac{-3}{5} < \frac{-2}{5} \qquad\qquad \frac{3}{5} > \frac{2}{5}$$

<—————•————•————|————•————•—————>
$\frac{-3}{5}$ $\frac{-2}{5}$ 0 $\frac{2}{5}$ $\frac{3}{5}$

Improper Fractions

Any fraction in which the numerator is larger than the denominator is an **improper fraction**. Look at the fraction $\frac{7}{4}$. In this case, the denominator is 4, which means the pie you are working with is cut up into 4 slices. The numerator tells you that you have 7 slices of this pie. If you have 7 slices of a 4-slice pie, then you have more than one pie. In fact, you have one 4-slice pie $\left(\frac{4}{4}\right)$ and 3 additional slices of that pie $\left(\frac{3}{4}\right)$.

$$\frac{4}{4} \quad + \quad \frac{3}{4} \quad = \quad \frac{7}{4}$$

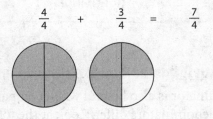

You can write this as a **mixed number**: $1\frac{3}{4}$. A mixed number is any number that is written as an integer and a fraction. To convert from a mixed number to an improper fraction, do the following:

1. Multiply the integer by the denominator of the fraction: in this case, $1 \times 4 = 4$
2. Take that product and add it to the numerator of the fraction: in this case, $4 + 3 = 7$
3. Take the result of Step 2 and put it above the original denominator: $\frac{7}{4}$.

Skills Check: Improper Fractions

Write each of the following as an improper fraction. See the end of this section for the answers.

(A) $3\frac{2}{3}$

(B) $7\frac{1}{5}$

(C) $-2\frac{2}{3}$

Adding and Subtracting Fractions

When adding or subtracting fractions, your goal is to manipulate the fractions to have the same denominator. If you are asked to solve for $\frac{1}{4} + \frac{2}{4}$, the answer would be $\frac{3}{4}$ since you are adding 1 slice of a 4-slice pie to 2 slices of a 4-slice pie. You will end up with 3 slices of a 4-slice pie, which means you will have $\frac{3}{4}$.

However, addition and subtraction of fractions will not always be so straightforward. Sometimes the fractions you are adding or subtracting will have different denominators, for example, $\frac{2}{3} - \frac{1}{4} = ?$. When adding or subtracting fractions with different denominators, you must first find a **common denominator**. To do so, find the smallest number that is a multiple of both denominators. In this case, the smallest number that is a multiple of 3 and 4 is 12. Now you need to manipulate both fractions to have a denominator of 12. To do so, you will multiply.

$$\frac{2 \times 4}{3 \times 4} - \frac{1 \times 3}{4 \times 3} = \frac{8}{12} - \frac{3}{12} = \frac{8-3}{12} = \frac{5}{12}$$

Note that when you multiply the denominator of the fraction by a value, you must multiply the numerator of the fraction by the same value. By doing so, you are essentially multiplying the fraction by 1, which means that the value of the fraction will not change.

Comparing Fractions with Different Numerators and Denominators

Using a common denominator is also helpful when comparing fractions whose numerators and denominators differ. Look at the following Quantitative Comparison question.

QUANTITY A	QUANTITY B	
$\frac{7}{8}$	$\frac{8}{9}$	Ⓐ Ⓑ Ⓒ Ⓓ

SOLUTION: Express both fractions with a denominator of 72. Quantity A: $\frac{7}{8} = \frac{7 \times 9}{8 \times 9} = \frac{63}{72}$. Quantity B: $\frac{8}{9} = \frac{8 \times 8}{9 \times 8} = \frac{64}{72}$. Now the comparison is $\frac{63}{72}$ to $\frac{64}{72}$. The fractions have the same denominator, but the numerator of the second fraction is greater. Thus Quantity B is greater.

Multiplying Fractions

The product of two positive fractions will always be smaller than either of the factors, for example, $\frac{2}{5} \times \frac{1}{4} = \frac{2}{20} = \frac{1}{10}$.

Why is this the case? *When you multiply fractions, you are essentially taking a piece of a piece.* In other words, multiplying $\frac{1}{4}$ by $\frac{2}{5}$ means that you are looking for $\frac{2}{5}$ of $\frac{1}{4}$. Or it can mean that you are taking $\frac{1}{4}$ of $\frac{2}{5}$. In either case, the result is a piece of both original fractions, meaning that the result will be smaller than either fraction. Look at the following Quantitative Comparison question.

$$1 > x > y > 0$$

QUANTITY A	QUANTITY B	
xy	$\frac{1}{x} \times \frac{1}{y}$	Ⓐ Ⓑ Ⓒ Ⓓ

SOLUTION: Since x and y are between 0 and 1, their product must be a fraction. Thus the value in Quantity A must be a fraction. Since x and y are between zero and 1, their respective reciprocals must be greater than 1. Thus the factors of the product in Quantity B are each greater than 1. Since both factors are greater than 1, the product must be greater than 1. Thus Quantity B is greater.

Generally, when multiplying fractions, you should multiply all the numerators and all the denominators. For example:

$$\frac{3}{7} \times \frac{5}{4} = \frac{3 \times 5}{7 \times 4} = \frac{15}{28}$$

However, sometimes you will be able to reduce the fractions before multiplying:

$$\left(\frac{2}{5}\right)\left(\frac{15}{6}\right) = ?$$

SOLUTION: Before multiplying, cancel out the common factors:

$$\frac{2}{5} \times \frac{15}{6} = \frac{\cancel{2}}{\cancel{5}} \times \frac{\cancel{3} \times \cancel{5}}{\cancel{3} \times \cancel{2}} = 1$$

The answer is 1.

Dividing Fractions

When dividing by a fraction, multiply the numerator by the **reciprocal** of the fraction in the denominator. To find the reciprocal of a fraction, simply switch the terms in the numerator and denominator.

$$\frac{\frac{7}{3}}{\frac{14}{9}} = ?$$

SOLUTION: Multiply $\frac{7}{3}$ by the reciprocal of $\left(\frac{14}{9}\right)$:

$$\left(\frac{7}{3}\right)\left(\frac{9}{14}\right) = \frac{7}{3} \times \frac{3 \times 3}{7 \times 2} = \frac{3}{2}$$

Fractions in Word Problems

Many word problems will test your understanding of fractions in real-world contexts. In many of these questions, you will be given a value for the part and will be asked to solve for the whole or vice versa. In these questions, it is essential to remember the following relationship: *part = fraction × whole*. As you are given information, track how that information fits into that formula. Look at the following example:

Of the 120 boys in a school, $\frac{3}{4}$ are taking chemistry. If $\frac{3}{5}$ of the students in the school are boys, the number of boys taking chemistry is what fraction of all the students at the school?

SOLUTION: You are being asked to solve for the number of boys taking chemistry as a fraction of all students at the school, so the numerator should be "number of boys taking chemistry" and the denominator should be "the number of students in the school." Now use the information from the question to solve for these values.

boys taking chemistry
students in the school

SOLUTION: In the first sentence, you are told that $\frac{3}{4}$ of all the boys are taking chemistry. Since there are 120 students in the school, the number of boys taking chemistry = $\frac{3}{4} \times 120 = 90$. Now figure out the number of students in the school. The whole is the number of students, the part is the number of boys, and $\frac{3}{5}$ is the fraction. Thus $120 = \frac{3}{5} \times n$, where n is the number of students in the school. Multiply both sides of the equation by $\frac{5}{3}$ to solve for n:

$$120 \times \frac{5}{3} = n$$

$$n = 200$$

SOLUTION: So the fraction you arrive at is $\frac{90}{200}$, which reduces to $\frac{9}{20}$.

Plugging in Numbers with Fractions

In many fraction questions, you will be given unspecified amounts and asked to solve for a relationship between these amounts. In these situations, the best strategy is to *choose values that satisfy the relationships in the question.* When plugging in numbers for fraction questions with no specified amounts, keep the following tips in mind:

- **When choosing a value, choose a value for the whole.** For example, if you are told that $\frac{1}{3}$ of the employees in a company are administrators and that $\frac{3}{4}$ of the administrators are men, then choose a value for the number of employees (the whole), and not the administrators or men.
- **Choose a value for the whole that will be divisible by the denominators of all the fractions in the question.** For example, if you are told that $\frac{1}{3}$ of the employees in a company are administrators and that $\frac{3}{4}$ of the administrators are men, then the value you choose for the number of employees should be divisible by 3 (the denominator of the first fraction) and 4 (the denominator of the second fraction). Good numbers here would be multiples of 12. Why is this strategy important? Because to the extent that it is possible, you want to work with integers. If the number that you choose is not divisible by 3 or 4, then the value for one of the parts will end up being a fraction, and the math will almost certainly be messier.

Let's look at an example:

Two-thirds of the cars in a lot are sedans, and the rest are trucks. If $\frac{9}{10}$ of the sedans are new and $\frac{3}{8}$ of the trucks are new, what fraction of the cars in the lot are used?

SOLUTION: Since the question does not provide any amounts, you should choose numbers to determine values for the total number of cars and the number of used cars. Based on the first tip provided earlier, you should choose a value for the whole, which in this case is the total number of cars. Based on the second tip, the value you choose should be divisible by 3, 8, and 10. The most obvious value here is $3 \times 8 \times 10 = 240$. If there are 240 cars, then $\frac{2}{3}(240) = 160$ are sedans, and the other 80 are trucks. Now determine how many sedans and how many trucks are used. If $\frac{9}{10}$ of the sedans are new, then the remaining $\frac{1}{10}$ are used. $\frac{1}{10}$ of 160 = 16, so there are 16 used sedans. If $\frac{3}{8}$ of the trucks are new, then $\frac{5}{8}$ are used. $\frac{5}{8}$ of 80 = 50, so 50 of the trucks are used. In total, there are 50 + 16 = 66 used cars. The final fraction of used cars/total cars = $\frac{66}{240}$. Divide the numerator and denominator by 6 and arrive at $\frac{11}{40}$.

Decimals

A decimal is another way of representing a fraction, for example, $\frac{1}{4} = 0.25$, $\frac{2}{5} = 0.4$, and so on.

Arithmetic with Decimals

Since the GRE provides you with a calculator, you should almost always use a calculator when adding and subtracting decimals. The calculator will also come in handy when multiplying or dividing decimals, but as illustrated later, there are shortcuts you should be alert to when working with powers of 10.

Place Values

Every **digit** in a number has a **place value**. For example, in the number 237.98, 2 is in the *hundreds place*, 3 is in the *tens place*, 7 is in the *units place*, 9 is in the *tenths place*, and 8 is in the *hundredths place*.

Place Values and Powers of 10

Look at what happens when you multiply the preceding value by 10:

$$237.98 \times 10 = 2,379.8$$

Note that the digits haven't changed, but their place values have! This illustrates an important point: *Whenever you multiply or divide a number by a power of 10, the decimal of the number shifts*:

If you multiply a number by a positive power of 10, the decimal will move to the right as many places as the value of the exponent.

$$2.79 \times 10^3 = 2,790$$

$$321.98 \times 10 = 3,219.8$$

If you divide a number by a positive power of 10, the decimal will move to the left as many places as the value of the exponent:

$$3,293 \div 10^2 = 32.93$$
$$1,203.79 \div 10^3 = 1.20379$$

QUANTITY A	QUANTITY B	
2.798×10^3	$2,798 \div 10^2$	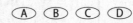

SOLUTION: Move the decimal three places to the right in Quantity A: 2,798. Move the decimal two places to the left in Quantity B: 27.98. Quantity A is greater.

The process also works in reverse. If you are doing calculations with a number that has a lot of zeros to the right or to the left of the decimal, you can use powers of 10 as shorthand for those values:

$2{,}400{,}000 = 24 \times 10^5$

$0.00037 = 37 \div 10^5 = 37 \times 10^{-5}$

Let's look at a GRE-style example:

$\frac{(1.9)(2 \times 10^6)}{190{,}000} = ?$

    (A) 0.02

    (B) 0.2

    (C) 2

    (D) 20

    (E) 200

SOLUTION: To make the calculations easier, express the denominator as 1.9×10^5. The fraction now reads:

$\frac{(1.9)(2 \times 10^6)}{1.9 \times 10^5}$

SOLUTION: Divide numerator and denominator by 1.9 to arrive at:

$\frac{2 \times 10^6}{10^5} = 2 \times 10^1 = 20$. The correct answer is D.

Common-Fraction-Decimal-Percent Equivalencies

$$\frac{1}{2} = .5 = 50\% \qquad \frac{1}{50} = .02 = 2\%$$

$$\frac{1}{3} = .33 = 33.33\% \qquad \frac{1}{100} = .01 = 1\%$$

$$\frac{1}{4} = .25 = 25\% \qquad \frac{1}{200} = .005 = .5\%$$

$$\frac{1}{5} = .2 = 20\% \qquad \frac{1}{1,000} = .001 = .1\%$$

$$\frac{1}{8} = .125 = 12.5\%$$

$$\frac{1}{10} = .10 = 10\%$$

$$\frac{1}{20} = .05 = 5\%$$

Exercise: Fractions and Decimals

Discrete Quantitative Questions

1. $\frac{1}{3}$ of the cookies in a jar are chocolate chip, $\frac{2}{3}$ of the remaining cookies are peanut butter, and the rest of the cookies are white chocolate. If 20 cookies are white chocolate, how many cookies are in the jar?

   Ⓐ 40
   Ⓑ 60
   Ⓒ 70
   Ⓓ 90
   Ⓔ 100

2. $\frac{1}{3}$ of the 120 marbles in a jar are red. If 20 red marbles are taken out and 40 black marbles are added, what fraction of the marbles in the jar will be red?

   Ⓐ $\frac{1}{8}$
   Ⓑ $\frac{1}{7}$
   Ⓒ $\frac{1}{6}$
   Ⓓ $\frac{1}{4}$
   Ⓔ $\frac{1}{3}$

For this question, write your answer in the box.

3. What is $\frac{3}{7}$ of $\frac{14}{5}$ of $\frac{15}{7}$?

4. $\frac{3}{8}$ of the students in a school are male, and $\frac{3}{5}$ of the male students take calculus. If $\frac{1}{4}$ of the female students take calculus, what fraction of the students at the school do <u>not</u> take calculus?

(A) $\frac{61}{160}$

(B) $\frac{99}{160}$

(C) $\frac{1}{2}$

(D) $\frac{3}{5}$

(E) $\frac{2}{5}$

5. Upon winning the lottery, John spent $\frac{1}{3}$ of his winnings on a home and $\frac{1}{4}$ of the remaining amount on a car. After these purchases, he had \$200,000 left. How much money did John win in the lottery?

(A) 400,000

(B) 480,000

(C) 600,000

(D) 800,000

(E) 2,400,000

6. Jar X is currently filled to $\frac{1}{3}$ of its capacity with water, and Jar Y is filled to $\frac{3}{4}$ of its capacity with water. If Jar Y has double the capacity of Jar X, what fraction of Jar Y would be filled when the contents of Jar X are poured into Jar Y?

(A) $\frac{10}{12}$

(B) $\frac{11}{12}$

(C) $\frac{12}{12}$

(D) $\frac{13}{12}$

(E) $\frac{17}{12}$

For this question, indicate all of the answer choices that apply.

7. If $\frac{1}{5^x} > \frac{1}{1,000}$, then x could equal which of the following values?

   - [A] 1
   - [B] 2
   - [C] 3
   - [D] 4
   - [E] 5
   - [F] 6

8. Which of the following fractions has the greatest value?

   - (A) $\dfrac{3^2}{7^5 \times 5^3}$
   - (B) $\dfrac{2^2}{7^5 \times 5^3}$
   - (C) $\dfrac{3^3}{7^6 \times 5^3}$
   - (D) $\dfrac{21}{7^5 \times 5^3}$
   - (E) $\dfrac{3^2 \times 2}{7^6 \times 5^3}$

9. A \$360,000 inheritance is split equally among three siblings. If one of the siblings splits her share equally among herself and her three children, how much of the inheritance does each of the three children get?

   - (A) 22,500
   - (B) 30,000
   - (C) 40,000
   - (D) 90,000
   - (E) 120,000

10. Each month, Janet saves $\frac{1}{3}$ of her paycheck and spends the rest. The amount of money Janet saves in a month is what fraction of the amount that she spends in a year?

   - (A) $\frac{1}{8}$
   - (B) $\frac{1}{12}$
   - (C) $\frac{1}{13}$
   - (D) $\frac{1}{24}$
   - (E) $\frac{1}{36}$

11. Bob, Peter, and Stan are going to combine all their savings to invest in a business. The amount of money in Bob's savings is $\frac{2}{3}$ of the amount in Stan's savings. The amount in Peter's savings is double the amount in Stan's savings. If Stan decides to invest only $\frac{3}{4}$ of his savings into the business, then the amount that Stan invests will be what fraction of the amount that Bob and Peter invest combined?

(A) $\frac{1}{8}$

(B) $\frac{9}{44}$

(C) $\frac{1}{4}$

(D) $\frac{9}{32}$

(E) $\frac{3}{8}$

12. All of the following fractions are greater than $\frac{2}{3}$ EXCEPT

(A) $\frac{4}{5}$

(B) $\frac{19}{27}$

(C) $\frac{11}{15}$

(D) $\frac{34}{50}$

(E) $\frac{3}{5}$

For this question, write your answer in the box.

13. If $(1.5 \times 10^4) \times 10^x = 150$, then what is the value of x?

14. After doing the last step of a certain calculation, Bob arrived at an answer of 387. Bob then realized that he had accidentally multiplied by 100 instead of dividing by 100. Had he done the calculations correctly, what would the result have been?

(A) 0.000387

(B) 0.00387

(C) 0.0387

(D) 0.387

(E) 3.87

Quantitative Comparison Questions

Each of the following questions consists of two quantities, Quantity A and Quantity B. You are to compare the two quantities. You may use additional information centered above the two quantities if additional information is given. Choose

- (A) if Quantity A is greater
- (B) if Quantity B is greater
- (C) if the two quantities are equal
- (D) if the relationship between the two quantities cannot be determined

	QUANTITY A	QUANTITY B	
1.	$\frac{1}{x} + \frac{1}{y}$	$\frac{(x+y)}{xy}$	(A) (B) (C) (D)

	QUANTITY A	QUANTITY B	
2.	$\frac{1}{3x}$	$\frac{1}{5x}$	(A) (B) (C) (D)

$$x > y > 0$$

	QUANTITY A	QUANTITY B	
3.	$\left(\frac{1}{3}\right)x$	$\left(\frac{1}{4}\right)y$	(A) (B) (C) (D)

	QUANTITY A	QUANTITY B	
4.	$\frac{1}{3} \times 75 \times \frac{3}{4} \times 200$	$1{,}200 \times 200 \times \frac{1}{15} \times \frac{1}{4}$	(A) (B) (C) (D)

	QUANTITY A	QUANTITY B	
5.	The number of thirds in 7	21	(A) (B) (C) (D)

	QUANTITY A	QUANTITY B	
6.	$\frac{7}{8}$ of $\frac{9}{11}$	$\frac{9}{10}$	(A) (B) (C) (D)

	QUANTITY A	QUANTITY B	
7.	$\frac{1}{3^{200}}$	$\frac{1}{2^{200}}$	(A) (B) (C) (D)

$$c > 0$$

	QUANTITY A	QUANTITY B	
8.	$\frac{7}{8}$	$\frac{7+c}{8+c}$	(A) (B) (C) (D)

Half of Kathy's salary is equivalent to $\frac{2}{3}$ of Bob's salary.

	QUANTITY A	QUANTITY B	
9.	$\frac{2}{3}$ of Kathy's salary	$\frac{1}{2}$ of Bob's salary	(A) (B) (C) (D)

	QUANTITY A	QUANTITY B	
10.	(0.0079)(23.2)	(0.79)(0.232)	Ⓐ Ⓑ Ⓒ Ⓓ

	QUANTITY A	QUANTITY B	
11.	$\frac{1}{\sqrt{2}} + \frac{1}{\sqrt{3}} + \frac{1}{\sqrt{4}} + \frac{1}{\sqrt{5}}$	$\frac{1}{2} + \frac{1}{3} + \frac{1}{4} + \frac{1}{5}$	Ⓐ Ⓑ Ⓒ Ⓓ

Exercise Answers

Skills Check: Improper Fractions

A. $\frac{11}{3}$

B. $\frac{36}{5}$

C. $\frac{-8}{3}$

Discrete Quantitative Questions

1. **D** Since you are not told how many cookies are in the jar, assign a variable: j. Now express the different quantities in terms of j. If $\frac{1}{3}$ of the cookies are chocolate chip, then chocolate chip cookies $= \frac{1}{3}j$. $\frac{2}{3}$ of the *remaining* cookies are peanut butter. The remaining cookies in the jar $= \frac{2}{3}j$, so the number of peanut butter cookies will be $\frac{2}{3}(\frac{2}{3})j = (\frac{4}{9})j$. Finally, you know that the remaining 20 cookies are white chocolate. What is the relationship between all these quantities? They must add up to the total: j. You should thus set up the following relationship: $\frac{1}{3}j + \frac{4}{9}j + 20 = j$. Combine like terms:

$$(\tfrac{3}{9})j + (\tfrac{4}{9})j + 20 = j$$

$$(\tfrac{7}{9})j + 20 = j$$

$$20 = (\tfrac{2}{9})j$$

Multiply both sides by $\frac{9}{2}$:

$$20(\tfrac{9}{2}) = j$$

$$j = 90$$

2. **B** To answer the question, you need a fraction where the numerator will be the number of red marbles left after 20 are removed, and the denominator will be the total number of marbles after 20 red marbles are removed and 40 black marbles are added. The denominator is easier to solve, so start there. After 20 red marbles are taken away, there are 100 total marbles. After 40 black marbles are added, there are 140 total marbles. The denominator of the fraction is 140. To determine a value for the numerator, first determine the number of red marbles before 20 are removed. Red marbles $= \frac{1}{3}(120) = 40$. There are originally 40 red marbles. After 20 are removed, there are 20. Thus the numerator of the fraction is 20. The fraction you are solving for will be $\frac{20}{140}$. Reduce and arrive at $\frac{1}{7}$.

3. $\frac{18}{7}$ Solution: First reduce, then multiply:

$$\frac{3}{\underset{1}{7}} \times \frac{\overset{2}{14}}{\underset{1}{8}} \times \frac{\overset{3}{15}}{7} = \frac{18}{7}$$

The correct answer is $\frac{18}{7}$.

4. B Since this is a fraction question with no amounts given, you should plug in values. Choose a value for the number of students that will divide evenly by 8, 4, and 5. The best number here is $8 \times 4 \times 5 = 160$. The denominator of the fraction will be 160, and the numerator will be the number of students who do not take calculus. First, determine how many males do not take calculus. The number of male students is $\frac{3}{8}(160) = 60$. If $\frac{3}{5}$ of these students take calculus, then $\frac{2}{5}$ of them do not. $\frac{2}{5}(60) = 24$. 24 male students do not take calculus. Now solve for the number of females who do not take calculus. If there are 160 students and $\frac{3}{8}$ are male, then $\frac{5}{8}$ are female. $\frac{5}{8}(160) = 100$. $\frac{1}{4}$ of these 100 females take calculus, so $\frac{3}{4}$ do not. $\frac{3}{4}(100) = 75$. So 75 female students do not take calculus. Add this to 24, which is the number of male students who do not take calculus. $24 + 75 = 99$. Thus $\frac{99}{160}$ of the students do not take calculus.

5. A Represent John's winnings as w:

the amount spent on his home $= \frac{1}{3}w$

The amount spent on his car is $\frac{1}{4}$ of what he did not spend on his home.

Since he spent $(\frac{1}{3})w$ on his home, he has $(\frac{2}{3})w$ remaining.

$\frac{1}{4}(\frac{2}{3})w = \frac{1}{6}w$

These two amounts + \$200,000 will equal the total winnings. Expressed algebraically, the equation is $\frac{1}{3}w + \frac{1}{6}w + 200,000 = w$. Now solve for w:

Multiply across the entire equation by 6:

$2w + w + 1,200,000 = 6w$

Combine like terms:

$1,200,000 = 3w$

Divide both sides by 3:

$400,000 = w$

6. B With so many relationships, this question can be confusing. Start by identifying the whole. The capacity of Jar Y is expressed in terms of the capacity of Jar X, so the capacity of Jar X is the whole. Next, plug in a value for the capacity of Jar X. Remember to choose a value that will be divisible by the denominators of the fractions in the question. In this case, 12 would be a good value for the capacity of Jar X since 12 is divisible by 3 and by 4. If the capacity of Jar X is 12, then the capacity of Jar Y is 24. Jar X is filled to $\frac{1}{3}$ of its capacity, so it has $\frac{1}{3}(12) = 4$ units of water. Jar Y is filled to $\frac{3}{4}$ of its capacity, so it has $\frac{3}{4}(24) = 18$ units of water. If the water in Jar X is poured into Jar Y, then Jar Y will have $4 + 18 = 22$ units of water. So the capacity of Jar Y is 24, and it will have 22 units of water. Thus the fraction of water in Jar Y $= \frac{22}{24} = \frac{11}{12}$.

7. **A, B, C, and D** The fractions in the given inequality have the same numerator. If two positive fractions have the same numerator, then the fraction with the smaller denominator will be the greater value. Thus 5^x must be *less* than 1,000. Now determine which values in the choices will satisfy the inequality: $5^x < 1,000$. $5^4 = 625$, so any integer value less than or equal to 4 will satisfy the constraints. However, $5^5 = 3,125$, so 5 and 6 are too large. The correct answers are A, B, C, and D.

8. **D** Though you can certainly calculate the value of each fraction, such an approach would be time-consuming. Since the question is asking you to compare fractions, identify any choices that have the same numerator or denominator. Notice that all of the fractions in Choices A, B, and D have the same denominator. Among those three choices, the fraction that has the greatest numerator will be the greatest: $21 > 3^2 > 2^2$. Thus Choice D is the greatest among those three fractions. Now compare C and E. Both fractions have the same denominator, so the fraction with the greater numerator will be larger. $3^3 > 3^2 \times 2$, so the fraction in Choice C is greater than the fraction in Choice E. Now compare C and D. To arrive at an equal denominator in both fractions, multiply the numerator and denominator of the fraction in Choice D by 7:

$$\frac{21 \times 7}{7^5 \times 5^3 \times 7} = \frac{21 \times 7}{7^6 \times 5^3}$$

Now that the fractions have the same denominator, compare their numerators:

Choice C: 3^3

Choice D: 21×7

$21 \times 7 > 3^3$. Thus the fraction in Choice D is greater.

9. **B** Since $360,000 is split equally among three siblings, each sibling receives $\frac{\$360,000}{3} = \$120,000$. The sibling will then split this $120,000 into 4 parts (herself and her three children), so each child receives $\frac{\$120,000}{4} = \$30,000$.

10. **D** Choose a value for Janet's monthly paycheck. Since the denominator of the fraction is 3, a multiple of 3 would be a smart number. Let's use 30. If Janet earns $30/month, then she saves $10/month and spends $20/month. If she spends $20 per month, then she spends $20 \times 12 = \$240$/year. The fraction you are solving for is $10/240 = \frac{1}{24}$.

11. **D** Since this question has only fractions and no given amounts, plug in numbers. Bob's and Peter's savings are given in terms of Stan's savings, so choose a value for Stan's savings. Since the fractions in the question have denominators of 3 and 4, choose a multiple of 3 and 4 for Stan's savings. Let's use $12. If Stan's savings is $12, then Bob's savings is $\frac{2}{3}(\$12) = \$8$ and Peter's savings is $2(\$12) = \$24$. Combined, Peter and Bob will invest $32. Originally, Stan was going to invest all $12, but now he will invest only $\frac{3}{4}$ of that amount. $\frac{3}{4}(12) = 9$, so Stan will invest $9. Stan's investment as a fraction of Bob's and Peter's investments is thus $\frac{9}{32}$.

12. **E** Recognize that $\frac{2}{3} = 0.66$

    Now compare the choices:

    Choice A: $\frac{4}{5} = 0.8 > 0.66 \rightarrow$ Eliminate A.

    Choice B: $\frac{18}{27} = \frac{2}{3}$, so $\frac{19}{27} > \frac{2}{3} \rightarrow$ Eliminate B.

    Choice C: $\frac{10}{15} = \frac{2}{3}$, so $\frac{11}{15} > \frac{2}{3} \rightarrow$ Eliminate C.

    Choice D: $\frac{34}{50} = \frac{68}{100} = 0.68 > 0.66 \rightarrow$ Eliminate D.

    Choice E: $\frac{3}{5} = 0.6 < 0.66 \rightarrow$ E is the answer.

13. **–2** Express 1.5×10^4 as 15,000. To go from 15,000 to 150, you must move the decimal two places to the left. Thus $x = -2$.

14. **C** Bob accidentally moved the decimal two places to the right instead of two places to the left. To correct the original error, he needs to first move the decimal two places to the left to arrive at 3.87. To do the correct calculation, he must move the decimal two places to the left again, to arrive at 0.0387.

Quantitative Comparison Questions

1. **C** Add the fractions in Quantity A by finding a common denominator of xy.

    $$\frac{1}{x} \times \frac{y}{x} = \frac{y}{xy}$$

    $$\frac{1}{y} \times \frac{x}{x} = \frac{x}{xy}$$

    Thus $\frac{1}{x} + \frac{1}{y} = \frac{y}{xy} + \frac{x}{xy} = \frac{y+x}{xy}$. The two quantities are equal.

2. **D** Choose values for x. The best numbers to consider are 0, 1, and –1. If $x = 1$, then Quantity A is greater. If $x = 0$, then the denominator of both quantities will equal 1 and the two fractions will therefore be equal. Since a relationship cannot be determined, the answer is Choice D.

3. **A** Since x is greater than y, and $\frac{1}{3}$ is greater than $\frac{1}{4}$, the value in Quantity A will be a bigger piece of a bigger whole than the value in Quantity B. Thus Quantity A is greater.

4. **B** To simplify the comparison, divide both quantities by 200. The new comparison is thus:

QUANTITY A	QUANTITY B	
$\frac{1}{3} \times 75 \times \frac{3}{4}$	$1{,}200 \times \left(\frac{1}{15}\right)\left(\frac{1}{4}\right)$	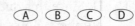

    Next, reduce both quantities:

    Quantity A: $\frac{1}{3} \times 75 = 25$, so Quantity A $= 25 \times \frac{3}{4}$

    Quantity B: $\frac{1}{4} \times 1{,}200 = 300$

    $300 \times \frac{1}{15} = \frac{15 \times 20}{15} = 20$

    $\frac{3}{4} \times 25 < 20$. Quantity B is greater.

5. **C** Determining the number of thirds in 7 is the same thing as determining how many times $\frac{1}{3}$ divides into 7. Written as a fraction, this becomes $\frac{7}{\frac{1}{3}} = ?$. Dividing by a fraction is equivalent to multiplying by the reciprocal of that fraction, so $\frac{7}{\frac{1}{3}} = 7 \times \frac{3}{1} = 21$. The values in the columns are equal.

6. **B** Instead of calculating a value for Quantity A, look at how the two columns compare. Both fractions in Quantity A are smaller than the fraction in Quantity B. Multiplying two positive fractions will yield only a smaller fraction, so the product of the fractions in Quantity A must be less than $\frac{9}{10}$.

7. **B** Since the two fractions have the same numerator, whichever fraction has the smaller denominator will be the greater fraction. 3^{200} is greater than 2^{200}, so the denominator in Quantity A is greater, meaning that the fraction in Quantity A is smaller.

8. **B** Choose values for c. Since you are given a range, choose extremes. First choose 1. In this case, the value in Quantity B will be $\frac{8}{9}$. $\frac{8}{9}$ is greater than $\frac{7}{8}$, so in this case, the value in Quantity B is greater. Now choose a larger value for c: 100. $\frac{7+100}{8+100} = \frac{107}{108}$, which is greater than $\frac{7}{8}$. Both values for c yielded a larger value in Quantity B than in Quantity A.

9. **A** Expressed algebraically, the prompt says that $\frac{1}{2}k = \frac{2}{3}b$, where k = Kathy's salary and b = Bob's salary. The quantities you are asked to compare are $\frac{2}{3}k$ and $\frac{1}{2}b$. $\frac{2}{3}k$ is greater than $\frac{1}{2}k$, and $\frac{1}{2}b$ is less than $\frac{2}{3}b$. Thus if $\frac{1}{2}k = \frac{2}{3}b$, then $\frac{2}{3}k$ must be greater than $\frac{1}{2}b$.

   This question can be done quickly if you identify what you are comparing and how those values relate to the given information. Since $\frac{2}{3}$ is greater than $\frac{1}{2}$, the value in Quantity A must be greater than half of Kathy's salary. Since $\frac{1}{2}$ is less than $\frac{2}{3}$, the value in Column B must be less than $\frac{2}{3}$ of Bob's salary. If half of Kathy's salary equals $\frac{2}{3}$ of Bob's salary, then $\frac{2}{3}$ of Kathy's salary must be more than $\frac{1}{2}$ of Bob's salary.

10. **C** You can use your calculator, but it is faster to express both quantities using powers of 10. In Quantity A, there are five digits total to the right of the decimal, so you can express Quantity A as $79 \times 232 \times 10^{-5}$. In Quantity B, there are five digits total to the right of the decimal, so you can express Quantity B as $79 \times 232 \times 10^{-5}$. The two quantities are equal.

11. **A** In each quantity, the same number of fractions is being added, and the numerators in Quantity A and Quantity B are the same. The difference is the denominators. The denominator of each of the values in Quantity B is greater than each corresponding denominator in Quantity A. If two positive fractions have the same numerator, the fraction with the smaller denominator is larger. Thus each fraction in Quantity A is greater than its corresponding fraction in Quantity B. Quantity A is greater.

Percentages

Part Versus Whole

A percent is another way to express a part-to-whole relationship. **Percent** literally means "per one hundred" and is used to determine the piece that a quantity represents when the whole is 100. For example, if Bob has 200 pies, and 75% of the pies are blueberry, then the number of blueberry pies is

$$75\% \times 200 = \frac{75}{100} \times 200 = 0.75 \times 200 = \frac{3}{4} \times 200 = 150$$

Note from the preceding example that to convert from a percent to a decimal, you should drop the percent and move the decimal two places to the left. For example:

$$40\% = 0.40 = \frac{4}{10} = \frac{2}{5}$$

The formula to calculate percent is

$\frac{\text{part}}{\text{whole}} = \frac{p}{100}$, where p = percent

62 is what percent of 1,000?

SOLUTION: Use the percent formula: 62 is the part and 100 is the whole, so:

$$\frac{62}{1,000} = \frac{p}{100}$$
$$p = \frac{62}{1,000} \times 100 = 6.2$$

Percent questions can be phrased in a few ways. Let's look at a few examples and how they fit into the preceding formula.

15 is what percent of 50?

SOLUTION: The part is 15 and the whole is 50. The solution is thus:

$$\frac{15}{50} = \frac{p}{100}$$
$$\frac{15}{50} \times 100 = p$$
$$p = 30$$

What percent of 200 is 350?

SOLUTION: The part is 350 and the whole is 200 (note that the part can be greater than the whole). The solution is thus:

$$\frac{350}{200} = \frac{p}{100}$$

$$\frac{350}{200} \times 100 = p$$

$$\frac{350}{2} = p$$

$$175 = p$$

60% of what number is 540?

SOLUTION: The part is 540, and the whole is unknown. Thus:

$$\frac{540}{p} = \frac{60}{100}$$

$$\frac{540}{p} = \frac{3}{5}$$

$$540(5) = 3p$$

$$p = 900$$

Percent Change

Some GRE questions will ask you to calculate the percent by which a certain value increases or decreases. For example:

> If the price of a shirt increased from $80 to $100, then by what percent did the price of the shirt increase?

Any time you are asked to solve for percent change, use the following formula:

$$\text{percent change} = \frac{\text{change}}{\text{original}} \times 100$$

When using this formula, make sure that the denominator is the original value and that the value in the numerator is positive. In the given example, the change is $100 - 80 = 20$. The original value is the price of the shirt *before* the increase, in this case, $80. Thus the percent change $= \frac{20}{80} \times 100 = 25\%$.

In the preceding example, you knew the original value and the new value, and you were asked to solve for the percent change. What if you are told the percent change and are asked to solve for the original or new value? Use the following formulas:

> If a quantity increases by p percent, the new quantity will equal $(100 + p)\% \times$ the original quantity.

> If the price of a $3,000 computer increased by 20%, what is the new price?

SOLUTION: Since the price increases by 20%, the new price will be $(100\% + 20\%) \times \$3,000 = 120\% \times 3,000 = 1.2 \times \$3,000 = \$3,600$.

After a 20% increase, the price of a computer is $3,000. What was the original price of the computer?

SOLUTION: Let o = the original price. Thus

$$(100\% + 20\%) \times o = \$3,000$$

$$120\% \times o = \$3,000$$

$$1.2o = \$3,000$$

$$o = \frac{\$3,000}{1.2} = \$2,500$$

In this example, many test-takers make the mistake of subtracting 20% from $3,000 to determine the original price. This approach is wrong because it confuses which whole the 20% is a piece of: *adding 20% to $2,500 is not the same as taking 20% away from $3,000.*

If a quantity decreases by p percent, the new quantity will equal $(100 - p)\% \times$ the original quantity.

After a 25% decrease, the price of a car was $24,000. What was the original price?

SOLUTION: Let p = the original price of the car. Thus

$$(100\% - 25\%) \times p = \$24,000$$

$$75\% \times p = \$24,000$$

$$0.75p = \$24,000$$

$$p = \frac{\$24,000}{0.75}$$

$$p = \$32,000$$

Consecutive Percentages

Certain GRE questions will involve more than one percent change to a value. For example:

On January 1, the price of a certain stock was $400. On January 2, the price of the stock was 20% greater than it was on January 1. On January 3, the price was 20% less than it was on January 2. What was the price of the stock on January 3?

SOLUTION: To answer these questions, you should use the preceding formulas, but keep the following point in mind: *Each successive percent change relates to the quantity that immediately precedes it, not to the starting quantity.*

It would be wrong to think that the 20% changes cancel each other out and yield a value equal to the original value. This is so because the value that goes up 20% from January 1 to January 2 is different from the value that goes down from January 2 to January 3. Since the percents are pieces of different wholes, they do not simply cancel out. So you should instead use the *percent change* formulas given in the previous section:

price on January 1 = $400

price on January 2 = $400(100% + 20%) = $400(120%) = $400(1.2) = $480

price on January 3 = 480(100% − 20%) = 480(80%) = 480(0.8) = $384

Percent Greater Versus Percent Of

If you don't read the following question carefully, you might fall for a trap:

150 is what percent greater than 50?

Many test-takers simply use the percent formula for this question:

$$\frac{150}{50} = \frac{p}{100} \rightarrow p = 300$$

But this is wrong. Why? Because the question is asking, 150 is what percent *greater* than 50, not what percent *of* 50. To calculate percent greater, use the following formula:

percent greater = % of − 100%

In the previous example, 150 is 300% *of* 50, so it is (300% − 100%) = 200% *greater* than 50.

Plugging in Numbers with Percentages

In the section on fractions and decimals, you read that plugging in numbers was a useful strategy in Discrete Quantitative questions that only give fractions and no specified amounts. The same applies to percent questions. If you see a Discrete Quantitative question with *only* percents and no actual amounts, plug in 100 for the total.

> 20% of the employees in a company are managers. 10% of these managers have been with the company for at least 10 years. The number of managers who have <u>not</u> been with the company for at least 10 years is what percent of all the employees?

> **SOLUTION:** Let the total number of employees = 100. Thus the number of managers is 20%(100) = 20. The percentage of managers who have *not* been with the company for 10 years is 100% − 10% = 90%. Thus the number of managers who have *not* been with the company for 10 years is 90%(20) = 18. Now the question is, 18 is what percent of 100? The answer is 18 (notice how simple the calculations are when you choose 100!).

Simple and Compound Interest

Though tested rarely, these topics are worthwhile to learn if you are aiming for a high score. The formula for simple interest is

principal × rate × time

If Bob invested $800 at 5% simple annual interest, how much interest did his investment earn after 5 years?

SOLUTION: the interest accrued = principal × rate × time = $800(0.05)5 = $200.

The formula for compound interest is

$$p(1 + \tfrac{r}{n})^{nt}$$

where p = principal, r = rate, n = number of times per year, and t = number of years.

If Bob invested $5,000 at 5% compound annual interest. What was the dollar amount of the investment after 3 years, rounded to the nearest dollar?

SOLUTION: $5,000 = p, 5% = r, n = 1, and t = 3. Thus the amount of the investment is $5,000(1.05)^3 = $5,788.125 \approx $5,788$

Quantitative Comparison Strategy: Percentages

Often percent questions in Quantitative Comparison questions will test your ability to differentiate between the original value and new values. When looking at successive percent changes, always keep in mind that each percent change occurs to the previous value, not the original one.

The price of a shirt increases by x%.
This price then decreases by x%.

QUANTITY A	QUANTITY B	
The original price of the shirt	The new price of the shirt	Ⓐ Ⓑ Ⓒ Ⓓ

SOLUTION: It may be tempting to assume that the percent changes will offset each other and that the answer is thus C. But the second percent change is on a bigger value than the original percent change. Thus the amount by which the second price decreases is greater than the amount by which the first price increased. Thus the final price must be less than the original price. The correct answer is A.

Exercise: Percentages

Discrete Quantitative Questions

1. 3.4 is what percent of 1,000?

    (A) 0.0034
    (B) 0.034
    (C) 0.34
    (D) 3.4
    (E) 34

For this question, write your answer in the box.

2. $\frac{y}{50} + \frac{y}{25}$ is what percent of $\frac{y}{75}$?

3. A shirt originally priced at x dollars is reduced by 20% percent. This new price is then reduced by 40%. The final price of the shirt is what percent of the original price?

    (A) 60%
    (B) 52%
    (C) 48%
    (D) 40%
    (E) 20%

4. If 10% of a equals 25% of b, then a is what percent of b?

    (A) 40
    (B) 50
    (C) 140
    (D) 150
    (E) 250

5. The price of a home in 1997 was 200% greater than the price in 1957. The price in 1957 was 300% greater than the price in 1927. The price of the home in 1997 is what percent greater than the price of the home in 1927?

    (A) 500
    (B) 600
    (C) 700
    (D) 1,100
    (E) 1,200

6. A 30% increase in the price of a shirt is equivalent to $60. If the price of the shirt were reduced by 20% instead of increased by 30%, what would be the price of the shirt?

   (A) 240
   (B) 200
   (C) 160
   (D) 120
   (E) 54

7. In 1980, a college had 4,000 students, of whom 30% were women. In 2010, the college had 12,000 students, of whom 60% were women. By what percent did the number of women students in the college increase from 1980 to 2010?

   (A) 100
   (B) 200
   (C) 400
   (D) 500
   (E) 600

8. The contents of a jar of jelly that is 40% full are poured into an empty 200-ounce vat, filling it to 25% of capacity. How many jars of jelly would be required to fill three of these vats?

   (A) 2
   (B) 3
   (C) 4
   (D) 5
   (E) 6

9. At a certain store, the retail price for a blouse is double the retail price for a T-shirt. If Beth buys a blouse at a 50% discount and a T-shirt at a 25% discount, the amount Beth pays is approximately what percent of the amount she would have paid had there been no discounts?

   (A) 58%
   (B) 50%
   (C) 38%
   (D) 30%
   (E) 25%

10. In a high school with 500 students, 15% of the students are freshmen. If 50 additional students enroll in the school, how many of those students would have to be freshmen for the number of freshmen to be 20% of the student body?

   Ⓐ 10

   Ⓑ 25

   Ⓒ 35

   Ⓓ 100

   Ⓔ 175

11. In a company of 800 employees, 25% hold administrative positions. How many administrative employees would have to be added for the number of administrative employees to be 40% of the total number of employees?

   Ⓐ 80

   Ⓑ 120

   Ⓒ 200

   Ⓓ 320

   Ⓔ 400

12. If Bob invests $10,000 at y percent simple annual interest for 5 years, which of the following represents the amount of interest he will have gained after 5 years?

   Ⓐ $10{,}000(1 + y)^5$

   Ⓑ $10{,}000(y)5$

   Ⓒ $10{,}000(\frac{y}{100})5$

   Ⓓ $10{,}000(y)^5$

   Ⓔ $10{,}000(\frac{y}{5})$

13. In Boronia, all purchases are taxed between 10% and 15%, depending on the type of item purchased. If Bob paid $30 tax for a certain item, which of the following could equal the pretax cost of the item? (Indicate all that apply.)

   Ⓐ 150

   Ⓑ 175

   Ⓒ 210

   Ⓓ 270

   Ⓔ 330

For this question, write your answer in the box.

14. Jack invests $5,000 at 4% compound annual interest. Rounded to the nearest units digit, what will be the value of Jack's investment in 3 years?

15. In 2007, there were 300 juniors and 200 seniors at a high school. In 2008, there were 400 juniors and 250 seniors at the same high school. What was the approximate percent increase in the ratio of juniors to seniors from 2007 to 2008?

   A) 6.5%
   B) 6.66%
   C) 24%
   D) 25%
   E) 30%

16. A shirt originally cost x dollars. After a y percent increase, the price of the shirt is z dollars. What is x, in terms of y and z?

   A) $\frac{z}{100 + y}$
   B) $100\frac{z}{y}$
   C) $\frac{100z}{100 + y}$
   D) $\frac{z}{y}$
   E) $\frac{100 + y}{z}$

17. Bob sold his car for $20,000. If Bob's profit was 25% of the purchase price of the car, what was the purchase price of the car?

   A) $4,000
   B) $8,000
   C) $12,000
   D) $16,000
   E) $18,000

For this question, write your answer in the box.

18. If y is 50% greater than x, then y is what percent of $2x$?

Quantitative Comparison Questions

Each of the following questions consists of two quantities, Quantity A and Quantity B. You are to compare the two quantities. You may use additional information centered above the two quantities if additional information is given. Choose

- Ⓐ if Quantity A is greater
- Ⓑ if Quantity B is greater
- Ⓒ if the two quantities are equal
- Ⓓ if the relationship between the two quantities cannot be determined

	QUANTITY A	QUANTITY B	
1.	90 as a percent of 50	The percent increase from 50 to 140	Ⓐ Ⓑ Ⓒ Ⓓ

The price of a stock is originally $x. After a y percent increase in 1992 and z percent decrease in 1993, the price returns to $x.

	QUANTITY A	QUANTITY B	
2.	y	z	Ⓐ Ⓑ Ⓒ Ⓓ

	QUANTITY A	QUANTITY B	
3.	73% of 29	0.29% of 7,300	Ⓐ Ⓑ Ⓒ Ⓓ

	QUANTITY A	QUANTITY B	
4.	30% of 400	65% of 200	Ⓐ Ⓑ Ⓒ Ⓓ

a is 25% of b

b is 75% of c

	QUANTITY A	QUANTITY B	
5.	c as a percentage of b	b as a percentage of a	Ⓐ Ⓑ Ⓒ Ⓓ

The price of a certain item is less than $200.

	QUANTITY A	QUANTITY B	
6.	A $40 reduction on the price of the item	A 20% reduction on the price of the item	Ⓐ Ⓑ Ⓒ Ⓓ

	QUANTITY A	QUANTITY B	
7.	The interest earned on $10,000 invested at 5% simple annual interest over 4 years	The interest earned on $10,000 invested at 10% compound annual interest over 2 years.	Ⓐ Ⓑ Ⓒ Ⓓ

The price of home *x* is 80% of the price of home *y*.

QUANTITY A	QUANTITY B	
8. The price of home *x* after a 20% increase	The price of home *y*	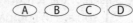

Exercise Answers

Discrete Quantitative Questions

1. **C** To calculate percent, use the following formula: (part/whole) = $\frac{p}{100}$. In this question, 3.4 is the part and 1,000 is the whole. Plug these values into the formula and arrive at 0.34.

2. **450** Since this question has variables in the choices, a good strategy is to plug in a value for *y*. To make the math simpler, choose a value for *y* that will divide evenly by 50, 25, and 75: 150. After plugging in 150 for *y*, the question is 3 + 6 is what percent of 2? Use the percent formula:

$$\frac{9}{2} = \frac{p}{100}$$

$$\frac{9}{2} \times 100 = p$$

$$450 = p$$

3. **C** Since this question gives only percents and no actual amounts, plugging in is a useful strategy. Choose a value for the original price of the shirt: 100. After a 20% reduction, the price of the shirt is 80. Taking 40% away from 80 is the same as keeping 60% of 80, so to calculate the price of the shirt after the second reduction, do 0.6(80) = 48. 48 is 48% of 100.

4. **E** Solution: Plug in values. Let *b* = 100. If *b* = 100, then

$$10\% \text{ of } a = 25\% \text{ of } 100 = 25$$

$$\downarrow$$

$$0.1a = 25$$

$$a = \frac{25}{0.1}$$

$$a = 250$$

Now use the percent formula: 250 is the part and 150 is the whole:

$$\frac{250}{100} = \frac{p}{100}$$

$$\frac{250}{100} \times 100 = p$$

$$p = 250$$

5. **D** Let the price of the home in 1927 = $100. The price of the home in 1957 is therefore $100 + 3($100) = $400. The price of the home in 1997 is therefore $400 + 2($400) = $1,200. Now, we need to determine 1,200 is what percent greater than 100. Use the percent greater formula: % greater = % of − 100% = $\left(\frac{1200}{100}\right) \times 100 - 100\% = 1,100\%$.

6. **C** You are asked to find the price of the shirt after a 20% decrease. In other words, you want to solve for 0.8 (original price). If a 30% increase represents $60, then $60 is 30% of the original price. Algebraically, you can represent this as $0.3x = 60$, where x = the original price. Solve for x:

$$0.3x = 60$$

$$x = 60/0.3$$

$$x = 200$$

Now reduce 200 by 20%: $200(100\% - 20\%) = 200(80\%) = 200(0.8) = 160$.

7. **D** To solve for percent increase, use the formula $\frac{change}{original} \times 100$. In this case, the new value is the number of women students at the college in 2010, and the old value is the number of women students at the college in 1980. The number of women students in 2010 is 60% of $12,000 = 0.6(12,000) = 7,200$. The number of women students in 1980 is 30% of $4,000 = 0.3(4,000) = 1,200$. Plug these values into the formula: $\frac{7,200 - 1,200}{1,200} \times 100 = 500\%$.

8. **D** First, identify what you're solving for. To fill three 200-ounce vats, you will need 600 ounces of jelly. To determine how many jars of jelly you need, you will need to determine how many ounces are in an individual jar of jelly. Use j to represent this value. You are told that 40% of j will fill a 200-ounce vat to 25% of its capacity. 25% of 200 is 50, so you know that 40% of $j = 50$. Now solve for j: $0.4j = 50 \rightarrow j = 125$. The number of jars you need will be $\frac{600}{125} = 4.8$. However, since you cannot have a fraction of a jar, you will need 5 jars to yield the necessary amount of jelly to fill the three vats.

9. **A** Since the question asks for a percent, use the formula $\frac{part}{whole} = \frac{p}{100}$. You must determine the part and the whole. This is a percent question with no actual amounts given, so the best approach is to plug in values. Let the original price of a T-shirt be $100 and the original price of a blouse be $200. After a 50% discount, the blouse will cost $100. After a 25% discount, the T-shirt will cost $75. In total, Beth pays $175. Before the discounts, Beth would have paid $300. Now find $175 as a percentage of $300:

$$\frac{175}{300} = \frac{p}{100}$$

$$175(100) = 300p$$

$$\frac{175}{3} = p$$

$$p \approx 58\%$$

10. **C** Since you are not told how many additional freshmen enroll in the school, assign a variable: x. You know that after x freshmen enroll in the school, the number of freshmen will be 20% of all students. Since you are given a relationship using percentages, use the formula:

$$\frac{part}{whole} = \frac{percent}{100}$$

In this case, the part is the number of freshmen after you add x. Of the 500 students, 15% were freshmen, so the original number of freshmen was $0.15(500) = 75$. After the change, the number of freshmen is $75 + x$. The whole is the total number of students in the school after you add 50: 550. The equation is $\frac{75+x}{550} = \frac{20}{100}$. Reduce $\frac{20}{100}$ and arrive at $75 + \frac{x}{550} = \frac{1}{5}$. Cross-multiply: $5(75 + x) = 550$. Divide both sides by 5. $75 + x = 110$. $x = 35$.

11. **C** If 25% of the original 800 employees are administrative, then there are $0.25(800) = 200$ administrative employees. Since you don't know how many administrative employees you are adding, assign a variable: x. After the increase, there will be $200 + x$ administrative employees. You know this number will be 40% of the total number of employees. How many total employees will there be? There were originally 800, but if you are adding x administrative employees, then there will be $800 + x$ total employees. You can therefore create the following equation:

$$\frac{200 + x}{800 + x} = \frac{40}{100}$$

$$\frac{200 + x}{800 + x} = \frac{2}{5}$$

$$1{,}000 + 5x = 1{,}600 + 2x$$

$$3x = 600$$

$$x = 200$$

12. **C** Plug in a value for y. Let $y = 5$. Now use the simple interest formula:

$$\text{interest accrued} = \text{principal} \times \text{rate} \times \text{time}$$

$$= 10{,}000(0.05)5$$

$$= 2{,}500$$

Substitute 5 for y into the choices and see which choice yields a value of 2,500.

13. **C and D** Since Bob paid $30 in tax, you know that $30 must be between 10% and 15% of the total cost. The cost for which $30 represents a 10% tax will be the higher bound of the price of the item, and the cost for which $30 represents a 15% tax will be the lower bound of the price of the item. Determine these bounds, and find which choices fall within the price range. Let the pretax cost be x. For the 10% tax, you can create the equation: $30 = 0.1x \rightarrow x = 300$. For the 15% tax, you can create the equation $30 = 0.15x \rightarrow x = 200$. Among the choices, the values between 200 and 300 are C and D.

14. **$5,624** Use the compound interest formula: $P(1 + r)^n = $ new. Thus you arrive at $5{,}000(1.04)^3 = \$5{,}624$.

15. **B** Use the percent change formula: $\frac{\text{new} - \text{old}}{\text{old}} \times 100$. Note that you are looking for the percent change in the ratios of the two groups, not in their actual values. The ratio of juniors to seniors in 2007 was $\frac{300}{200} = \frac{3}{2}$. The ratio of juniors to seniors in 2008 was $\frac{400}{250} = \frac{8}{5}$. Plug $\frac{8}{5}$ in for the new value and $\frac{3}{2}$ for the old value:

$$\frac{\frac{8}{5} - \frac{3}{2}}{\frac{3}{2}} \times 100 = 6.66\%$$

16. **C** When a Discrete Quantitative question has variables in the question and in the choices, consider plugging in numbers. In the question, the new price of the shirt, z, depends on the original price, x, and the percent increase, y, so choose values for x and y, and let those values determine z. Let $x = 100$ and $y = 25$. Thus the new price of the shirt is \$125. Plug the values you chose for x and y into the choices, and see which yields you \$125.

17. **D** The formula for calculating profit is $p = r - c$, where p = profit, r = revenue, and c = cost. The revenue for the car is \$20,000. You are told that the profit was 25% of the purchase price. You can express this algebraically as $r - c = 0.25c$. Now plug in \$20,000 for r: $20,000 - c = 0.25c$. Solve for c:

$$20,000 = 1.25c$$

$$\frac{20,000}{1.25} = c$$

$$c = 16,000$$

18. **75** Since you are dealing with a percent question with no amounts given, plug in values for the unknowns. Let $x = 100$. If y is 50% greater than x, then $y = 100 + 0.5(100) = 150$. You thus want to determine what percent 150 is of 200. Use the formula for calculating percents: $\frac{\text{part}}{\text{whole}} \times 100$. $(150/200) \times 100 = 75$.

Quantitative Comparison Questions

1. **C** To arrive at a value for Quantity A, use the percent formula: $\frac{\text{part}}{\text{whole}} = \frac{p}{100}$. In this case, 90 is the part and 50 is the whole, so Quantity A is equivalent to $\frac{90}{50} \times 100$. To arrive at a value for Quantity B, use the percent change formula (difference/original) $\times 100$. The difference between the two numbers is 90. The original number is 50. Plugging these values into the formula, you arrive at $\frac{90}{50} \times 100$. Column B and Column A have the same value.

2. **A** **Option 1: Solve it intuitively.**
   The price of the stock after a y percent increase is more than the original price of the stock. For a z percent decrease to bring the stock value back to its original price, z% of the price in 1993 must be the same as y% of the price in 1993. Since the value in 1993 is greater than the value in 1992, the whole that z% is taken from is bigger, which means a smaller piece of that whole is needed to arrive at y% of 1992. If you need a smaller piece, that means that z, as a percentage of 1993, is smaller than y, as a percentage of 1992. The answer is A.

   Option 2: Plug in numbers.
   Since you are dealing with percents, choose \$100 for x and 25 for y. Use these values to determine what value for z would bring the price back to \$100. If $y = 25$, then the price in 1992 will be 125. Now solve for z: 25 is what percent of 125? Use the percent formula: $\frac{\text{part}}{\text{whole}} \times 100 = \frac{25}{125} \times 100 = 20\%$. Thus when $y = 25$, $z = 20$. Column A is greater.

3. **C** Avoid calculating! Notice that the columns have very similar digits, but different place values. Write each column in decimal format and see how the

place values compare. Column A can be written as 0.73(29) and Column B can be written as 0.0029(7,300). 0.0029(7,300) = 0.73(29).

4. **B** 400 is double 200, but 65% is more than double 30%. Thus Quantity B is greater. Note that you can use your calculator here.

5. **B** Plug in the numbers! The prompt gives you a in terms of b and b in terms of c. Since you can express everything in terms of c, choose a value for c and work backward to get values for a and b. In this case, you should choose a value for c that will divide evenly by 4 twice. Why? Because $b = \frac{3}{4}(c)$ and $a = \frac{1}{4}(b)$. To get integer values for a and b, you will be dividing by 4 and then dividing by 4 again, so a good value for c would be 16. If $c = 16$, then $b = 12$. If $b = 12$, then $a = 3$. The value in Quantity A is thus $\frac{16}{12} \times 100 = 133.3\%$. The value in Quantity B is thus $\frac{12}{3} \times 100 = 400\%$. Quantity B is greater.

6. **A** Before doing any math, make sure to look at the columns. You are comparing a $40 reduction in the price of the item to a 20% reduction. So you need to determine how 20% of the price compares to $40. The difficulty here is that you only have a range for the price of the item, so you will only be able to arrive at a range for what 20% of the item would be. Let's see how that range compares to $40. First, assume that the item actually equaled $200. If that's the case, then a 20% reduction in the item would equal $40. But since the price of the item is less than $200, a 20% reduction in the item would be less than $40. Thus Quantity A is greater.

7. **B** Don't calculate! Instead, figure out how the columns relate to each other. First, notice that in both cases, the principal is the same ($10,000). In Column A, the interest earned will be 0.05(10,000)4, which is the same as 20% of 10,000. How does Column B relate to 20% of $10,000? Compound interest accrues on each successive period. For the first period, the interest is 10% of $10,000. For the second period, the interest is 10% of a value that is more than $10,000. The sum of these two quantities will be more than 20% of $10,000. Thus Quantity B is greater.

8. **B** The fastest way to do this question is to choose values. When choosing values for percent questions, always start by choosing a value for the whole, which in this case is y. Let $y = 100$, and let $x = 80$. Now the comparison is 20% more than 80 versus 100. 20% more than 80 is the same as 1.2(80), which equals 96. This value is less than 100. Thus Quantity B is greater.

Ratios

A ratio represents a relationship between two or more quantities. Examples of ratios are

> There are 3 boys for every 4 girls.

The preceding can be expressed as "The ratio of boys to girls is 3 to 4."

> A recipe requires 3 parts sugar, 2 parts salt, and 4 parts water.

The above can be expressed as: "The ratio of sugar to salt to water is 3 to 2 to 4."

Ratios can be represented in a few different ways:
- The word *to*   3 to 4
- Using a colon   3:4
- As a fraction $\frac{3}{4}$

The Elements of a Ratio

The relationship that a ratio specifies will be either **part-to-part** or **part-to-whole**. An example of a part-to-part ratio is "In a school, there are 7 boys for every 3 girls." An example of a part-to-whole ratio is "In a school, there are 7 boys for every 10 students."

It is important to note that you can derive a part-to-whole ratio from a part-to-part ratio, and vice versa. If the ratio of boys to girls in a school is 7:3, then the ratio of boys to all students is 7:10.

Ratios Do Not Specify Amounts!

It is important to remember that a ratio only provides a relationship between quantities, not the actual *amounts* of each quantity. If the ratio of boys to girls is 7:3, there can be any number of values for boys and girls, as long as those values satisfy the given ratio.

Expressing Ratios

As discussed previously, there are several ways of expressing ratios. For the purpose of the GRE, the best way to express a ratio between two quantities is as a fraction. But before doing so, you must label the units.

If you are told that the ratio of men to women is 1:3, then on your paper, you should label which quantity corresponds with the numerator of the fraction and which quantity corresponds with the denominator of the fraction:

$$\frac{m \text{ men}}{w \text{ women}} = \frac{1}{3}$$

To make the quantities easier to work with algebraically, it's even better to write:

$\frac{m}{w} = \frac{1}{3}$, where m = the number of men and w = the number of women

Proportions

The simplest types of ratio questions will give you a ratio and the value for one quantity and will ask you to find a value for the other quantity. *Whenever you have a ratio with the value for one quantity, set up a proportion.*

At a certain university, the ratio of doctoral students to master's students is 3 to 5. If there are 9,000 doctoral students, how many master's students are there?

Step 1: Set up a proportion. Remember to label your units!

$$\frac{3 \text{ doctoral students}}{5 \text{ master's students}} = \frac{9{,}000 \text{ doctoral students}}{m \text{ master's students}}$$

Step 2: Cross-multiply to solve for m:

$$\frac{\text{doctoral students}}{\text{master's students}} = \frac{3}{5} = 9{,}000/m$$

$$3m = 9{,}000(5)$$

$$m = 3{,}000(5) = 15{,}000$$

Representing Ratios Algebraically

Recall from the discussion of fractions that the denominator of a fraction specifies the number of slices a pie is cut into, and the numerator represents the number of slices of that pie. In a certain sense, ratios can be thought of in the same way.

If you are given a part:part ratio, such as "The ratio of boys to girls is 3 to 2," you can think of the number of boys as 3 slices of a pie and the number of girls as 2 slices of the same pie. Since you are not told the value of the slice of the pie, let x represent the quantity of 1 slice. Thus if the ratio of boys to girls is 3 to 2, then:

$$\frac{\text{boys}}{\text{girls}} = \frac{3}{2} = \frac{3x}{2x}$$

Representing ratios in this way is helpful in the following situations:

Situation 1: When you know values for the parts of a ratio and want to determine the whole, or vice versa.

In a certain business's budget, the dollar amounts allocated for marketing, product development, and administration are in the ratio 5:3:2. If the business's budget is $200,000, how much money is allocated for marketing?

Step 1: Since you are not given a value for any of the parts, use x to represent one part. Thus

$5x$ = dollars allocated for marketing

$3x$ = dollars allocated for product development

$2x$ = dollars allocated for administration

Step 2: Identify an algebraic relationship:

The $200,000 budget is split among the three segments, so the sum of the amounts for the three segments will equal $200,000:

$$5x + 3x + 2x = \$200{,}000$$

Step 3: Solve for the unknown: you are asked to solve for the amount of money allocated for marketing, so you must solve for $5x$. Using the preceding equation:

$$10x = 200,000$$

divide both sides by 2: $\qquad\downarrow$

$$5x = 100,000$$

Situation 2: When you do not have quantities for either part of a ratio, but have information about how the ratio changes.

In a certain school, the ratio of students to teachers is 20 to 1. If the school adds 1,000 students and 100 teachers, the new ratio of students to teachers will be 15 to 1. How many students are currently at the school?

Step 1: Set up the original ratio with x representing one slice of the pie

$$\frac{\text{original number of students}}{\text{original number of teachers}} = \frac{20x}{1x}$$

Step 2: Use the quantities from Step 1 to create a proportion

new number of students/new number of teachers $= \frac{15}{1} = \frac{20x + 1,000}{1x + 100}$.

Step 3: Cross-multiply and solve for $20x$ (the original number of students)

$$\frac{15}{1} = \frac{20x + 1,000}{1x + 100}$$

$$15(x + 100) = 20x + 1,000$$

$$15x + 1,500 = 20x + 1,000$$

$$5x = 500$$

$$x = 100$$

$$20x = 2,000$$

Multiple Ratios with a Common Element

On some GRE questions, you will be given two ratios that share a common part and be asked to solve for the ratio of the other parts. The most efficient way to answer these questions is to manipulate the two ratios so that the common element has the same value in both. How will you do this? By finding the least common multiple of the common element.

At a certain pet store, there are 3 dogs for every 2 cats and 5 cats for every 7 birds. What is the ratio of the number of dogs to the number of birds?

Step 1: Set up the given ratios:

$$\frac{d}{c} = \frac{3}{2}$$

$$\frac{c}{b} = \frac{5}{7}$$

Step 2: Manipulate the ratios so that the quantity for the overlapping element is the same in both ratios.

In the first ratio, there are 2 parts cats, and in the second ratio, there are 5 parts cats. To make the ratios comparable, manipulate the two fractions so that cats will be $5 \times 2 = 10$ in both fractions.

$$\frac{d}{c} = \frac{3 \times 5}{2 \times 5} = \frac{15}{10}$$

$$\frac{c}{b} = \frac{5 \times 2}{7 \times 2} = \frac{10}{14}$$

Now that both ratios are in terms of the same number of cats, the ratio of dogs to cats to birds is 15:10:14. The ratio of dogs to birds is thus 15:14.

Exercise: Ratios

Discrete Quantitative Questions

1. Which of the following equals the ratio of $3\frac{1}{3}$ to $2\frac{1}{2}$?

   (A) 1:3
   (B) 2:5
   (C) 5:2
   (D) 3:4
   (E) 4:3

For this question, write your answer in the box.

2. A certain exercise regimen suggests that an individual do 3 push-ups for every 2 sit-ups. If John follows this exercise regimen and does 30 sit-ups per day, how many push-ups would he have to do per day?

   ┌─────────────────────┐
   │   │
   │   │
   └─────────────────────┘

3. At a certain farm, the ratio of sheep to horses is 4:3. If the farm adds 5 sheep and 5 horses, what will the new ratio of sheep to horses be?

   (A) 9:8
   (B) 13:10
   (C) 19:18
   (D) 24:23
   (E) It cannot be determined from the given information.

4. If a zoo has 48 chimpanzees and 36 bonobos, then what is the ratio of chimpanzees to bonobos?

   (A) $\frac{3}{7}$
   (B) $\frac{4}{7}$
   (C) $\frac{3}{4}$
   (D) $\frac{4}{3}$
   (E) $\frac{7}{3}$

5. In a certain solution, the ratio of water to alcohol is 3:1. If water and alcohol combined make up half of the volume of the solution, what percentage of the solution is water?

(A) 12.5%
(B) 25%
(C) 37.5%
(D) 50%
(E) 75%

6. At Bridgewood High School, freshmen, sophomores, juniors, and seniors are in the ratio of 3:4:6:7, respectively. Which of the following CANNOT be the total number of students at the school?

(A) 40
(B) 80
(C) 90
(D) 100
(E) 140

7. A solution of alcohol and water contains alcohol and water in the ratio of 1:8. If the entire solution is 31.5 ounces, how many ounces of water are in the solution?

(A) 4.5
(B) 9
(C) 16
(D) 27
(E) 28

8. At a certain company, the ratio of managers to directors is 5:3. If 10 of the managers become directors, the new ratio will be 7:5. How many managers are currently at the company?

(A) 30
(B) 90
(C) 140
(D) 150
(E) 240

9. In a certain orchestra, the ratio of cello players to viola players is 4:5. If there are 2 more viola players than cello players, how many viola players are there?

(A) 8
(B) 9
(C) 10
(D) 11
(E) 12

10. In a certain company, the dollar amounts budgeted for advertising, product development, and administration are 4:3:1, respectively. If the company's entire budget is $200,000, how much did the company spend on product development?

  (A) 25,000
  (B) 50,000
  (C) 75,000
  (D) 80,000
  (E) 100,000

For this question, indicate all of the answer choices that apply.

11. A certain basket consists of white eggs and brown eggs. If the ratio of white eggs to brown eggs is 4:3, which of the following could be the total number of eggs in the basket?

  [A] 5
  [B] 15
  [C] 21
  [D] 70
  [E] 140
  [F] 161

12. In a stock portfolio of 80 shares, the ratio of shares invested in bonds to shares invested in mutual funds is 1:3. If the number of mutual funds remains the same, how many bonds would have to be added for the ratio of bonds to mutual funds to be 5:6?

  (A) 30
  (B) 40
  (C) 50
  (D) 70
  (E) 80

For this question, indicate all of the answer choices that apply.

13. In a certain organization, the ratio of managers to directors is 3:2, and the ratio of directors to administrators is 5:14. Which of the following could be the sum of managers, directors, and administrators in the organization?

   A 1,060
   B 1,300
   C 2,120
   D 5,300
   E 7,200

14. At a certain school, the ratio of students to teachers is greater than 3:1. If there are 500 students at the school, what is the maximum number of teachers that can be at the school?

   A 165
   B 166
   C 167
   D 168
   E 169

15. If $7a = 6b$ and $ab \neq 0$, what is the ratio of $\frac{1}{7}a$ to $\frac{1}{6}b$?

   A $\frac{13}{49}$
   B $\frac{13}{36}$
   C $\frac{36}{49}$
   D $\frac{6}{7}$
   E $\frac{7}{6}$

Quantitative Comparison Questions

Each of the following questions consists of two quantities, Quantity A and Quantity B. You are to compare the two quantities. You may use additional information centered above the two quantities if additional information is given. Choose

Ⓐ if Quantity A is greater
Ⓑ if Quantity B is greater
Ⓒ if the two quantities are equal
Ⓓ if the relationship between the two quantities cannot be determined

In a jar that contains only black and white marbles, the number of black marbles is more than double the number of white marbles.

QUANTITY A	QUANTITY B	
1. The ratio of white marbles to all the marbles in the jar	1 to 3	Ⓐ Ⓑ Ⓒ Ⓓ

There are more boys than girls at Brownwood School.

QUANTITY A	QUANTITY B	
2. The current ratio of boys to girls at Brownwood School	The ratio of boys to girls at Brownwood School if 10 additional girls and 20 additional boys enroll	Ⓐ Ⓑ Ⓒ Ⓓ

The ratio of 12 to x equals the ratio of x to 3.

QUANTITY A	QUANTITY B	
3. x	6	Ⓐ Ⓑ Ⓒ Ⓓ

The ratio of a company's revenues to its expenses is 5:4.

QUANTITY A	QUANTITY B	
4. The ratio of the company's profits to its expenses	$\frac{1}{4}$	Ⓐ Ⓑ Ⓒ Ⓓ

a, b, and c are integers, where $c < 25$. The ratio of a to b is 5 to 12, and the ratio of b to c is 4 to 7.

QUANTITY A	QUANTITY B	
5. a	5	Ⓐ Ⓑ Ⓒ Ⓓ

Exercise Answers

Discrete Quantitative Questions

1. **E** First, convert the fractions in the question to improper fractions: $3\frac{1}{3} = \frac{10}{3}$ and $2\frac{1}{2} = \frac{5}{2}$. Now express the ratio as a fraction: $\dfrac{\frac{10}{3}}{\frac{5}{2}}$. Multiply the numerator by the reciprocal of $\frac{5}{2}$: $\frac{10}{3} \times \frac{2}{5} = \frac{4}{3}$.

2. **45** First, express the ratio as a fraction: number of push-ups/number of sit-ups $= \frac{p}{s} = \frac{3}{2}$ (Note: p = number of push-ups and s = number of sit-ups). Next, set up a proportion: $\frac{p}{s} = \frac{3}{2} = \frac{p}{30}$. Now cross-multiply to solve for p:

$$90 = 2p$$

$$p = 45$$

3. **E** Remember that ratios specify relationships, not values. Let $4x$ = the original number of sheep and $3x$ = the original number of horses. The new ratio will be: number of sheep/number of horses $= \frac{4x+5}{3x+5}$. Without knowing how many horses or sheep there were originally, it is not possible to determine the new ratio. Another option is to plug in numbers. If the ratio of sheep to horses is 4:3, then there can be 4 sheep and 3 horses at the farm. In this case, the new ratio will be 9:8. However, the original number of sheep can be 8 and the original number of horses can be 6, in which case the new ratio would be $\frac{8+5}{6+5} = \frac{13}{10}$. Multiple answers are possible, meaning that a value cannot be determined.

4. **D** Express the ratio as a fraction: chimpanzees/bonobos $= \frac{48}{36}$. Reduce: $\frac{4(12)}{3(12)} = \frac{48}{36} = \frac{4}{3}$

5. **C** Let the amount of water $= 3x$ and the amount of alcohol $= 1x$. The sum of water and alcohol is thus $3x + 1x = 4x$. Since water and alcohol make up half of the volume of the solution, the volume of the entire solution will be $2(4x) = 8x$. To determine water as a percentage of the entire solution's volume, use the percent formula:

$$\frac{\text{part}}{\text{whole}} = \frac{\text{percent}}{100}$$

$$\downarrow$$

$$\frac{3x}{8x} = \frac{\text{percent}}{100}$$

$$\frac{3x}{8x} \times 100 = \text{percent}$$

$$\frac{3}{8} \times 100 = \text{percent}$$

$$\text{percent} = 37.5\%$$

6. **C** Represent the number of students algebraically:

   number of freshmen $= 3x$

   number of sophomores $= 4x$

   number of juniors $= 6x$

   number of seniors $= 7x$

   The total number of students will be the sum of these four groups: $3x + 4x + 6x + 7x = 20x$. Since the number of students in the school must be an integer (you can't have a fraction of a student!) and this integer $= 20x$, the number of students in the school must be a multiple of 20. Of the choices, the only value that is not a multiple of 20 is 90.

7. **E** Since you are not given a value for either part, represent the parts algebraically:

ounces of alcohol $= 1x$ and ounces of water $8x$

In terms of x, the volume of the solution is $1x + 8x = 9x$. Since the solution is 31.5 ounces,

$$9x = 31.5$$

$$x = 3.5$$

The number of ounces of water is $8x = 8(3.5$ ounces$) = 28$ ounces. The correct answer is Choice E.

8. **D** Since you are not given a value for either quantity, represent the values algebraically:

number of managers/number of directors $= \frac{5}{3} = \frac{5x}{3x}$

You are told that 10 managers will become directors. Thus after the change, the number of managers will be $5x - 10$, and the number of directors will be $3x + 10$. Use these values for the second ratio in the question:

new number of managers/new number of directors $= \frac{7}{5} = \frac{5x - 10}{3x + 10}$

Cross-multiply to solve:

$$\frac{7}{5} = \frac{5x - 10}{3x + 10}$$

$$7(3x + 10) = 5(5x - 10)$$

$$21x + 70 = 25x - 50$$

$$120 = 4x$$

$$x = 30$$

The original number of managers is $5x$. Plug in 30 for x: $5(30) = 150$.

9. **C** Since the question provides ratios with no actual values, represent the quantities algebraically:

$$\frac{\text{number of cello players}}{\text{number of viola players}} = \frac{4x}{5x}$$

Since the number of viola players $= 2 +$ number cello players, create the equation: $5x = 4x + 2$. Solve for x: $x = 2$. The number of viola players is $5x$. Plug in 2 for x. The answer is $5(2) = 10$.

10. **C** Since the question provides ratios with no actual values, represent each part of the budget algebraically:

$4x =$ amount budgeted for advertising

$3x =$ amount budgeted for product development

$x =$ amount budgeted for administration

The sum of these values is 200,000: $4x + 3x + x = 200,000$. Manipulate to solve for x:

$$8x = 200,000$$

$$x = 25,000$$

The amount budgeted for product development is $3x = 3(25,000) = 75,000$.

11. **C, D, E and F** Since the question provides ratios with no actual values, represent the parts algebraically: number of $\frac{\text{white eggs}}{\text{number of brown eggs}} = \frac{w}{b} = \frac{4x}{3x}$. The total number of eggs in the basket is thus $4x + 3x = 7x$. Since it is impossible to have a fraction of an egg, x must be an integer, and thus $7x$ must be a multiple of 7. The possible values must all be multiples of 7. Among the choices, 21, 70, 140, and 161 are the only multiples of 7.

12. **A** Let x be the total number of bonds and $3x$ be the total number of mutual funds. The sum of these quantities will be 80, the total number of shares. Thus:

$$3x + x = 80$$

$$4x = 80$$

$$x = 20 \text{ and } 3x = 60$$

Now that you know how many mutual funds and bonds there were originally, use these values to set up a proportion with the second ratio in the question. Let $y =$ the number of bonds that will be added:

$$\frac{\text{number of bonds}}{\text{number of mutual funds}} = \frac{5}{6} = \frac{20 + y}{60}.$$

Cross-multiply:

$$5(60) = 6(20 + y)$$

$$300 = 120 + 6y$$

$$180 = 6y$$

$$y = 30$$

13. **A, C, and D** Since the ratios share the common element of directors, your first step should be to manipulate the ratios so that the value for the number of directors is the same in both. (Note: In the following ratios, $m =$ the number of managers, $d =$ the number of directors, and $a =$ the number of administrators).

$$\frac{\text{number of managers}}{\text{number of directors}} = \frac{3 \times 5}{2 \times 5} = \frac{15}{10}$$

number of directors/number of administrators $= \frac{5 \times 2}{14 \times 2} = \frac{10}{28}$

Thus the ratio of managers to directors to administrators is 15:10:28. To determine the possible sum of the three, represent managers as $15x$, directors as $10x$, and administrators as $28x$. The sum of these values is $15x + 10x + 28x = 53x$. Since it is impossible to have a fraction of a person, x must be an integer, and thus $53x$ must be a multiple of 53. The possible values must all be multiples of 53.

14. **B** Your first step should be to set up a proportion, where s represents the number of students and t represents the number of teachers. However, note that the proportion will be an inequality since the ratio is *greater* than 3:1:

$$\frac{s}{t} > \frac{3}{1}$$

There are 500 students, so $\frac{500}{t} > \frac{3}{1}$. Cross-multiply to arrive at a range for t: $500 > 3t$. Solve for t: $\frac{500}{3} > t$. Since t must be an integer, the greatest value for t will be the greatest integer less than $\frac{500}{3}$. $\frac{500}{3} = 166.6$, so the greatest value for t is 166. The correct answer is B.

15. **C** The best approach here is to plug in values. Choose a value for a and let that value determine b. If $a = 6$, then $42 = 6b$, and $b = 7$. $\frac{1}{7}(a) = \frac{1}{7}(6) = \frac{6}{7}$, and $\frac{1}{6}(b) = (\frac{1}{6})(7) = \frac{7}{6}$. Now find the ratio of $\frac{6}{7}$ to $\frac{7}{6}$: $\frac{\frac{6}{7}}{\frac{7}{6}} = \frac{6}{7} \times \frac{6}{7} = \frac{36}{49}$. The correct answer is C.

Quantitative Comparison Questions

1. **B** Choose values that satisfy the constraints in the given information: let's say there are 3 white marbles and 7 black marbles. In this case, the ratio of white marbles to all marbles is $\frac{3}{10}$. $\frac{3}{10} < \frac{1}{3}$, so for the given values, Quantity B is greater. Choose a "weird" case: 7 is the smallest possible number of black marbles when there are 3 white marbles. Let's choose a larger value for the number of black marbles. Let there be 3 white marbles and 100 black marbles. In this case, the ratio of white marbles to all marbles is $\frac{3}{103}$. $\frac{3}{103} < \frac{1}{3}$, so Quantity B is still greater.

2. **D** Since there are more boys than girls, the current ratio of boys to girls must be greater than 1. The impact of adding 10 girls and 20 boys on the ratio will depend on the original ratio. For example, let's say there were originally 100 boys and 50 girls. In this case, the original ratio is $\frac{100}{50} = \frac{2}{1}$. When 20 boys and 10 girls are added, the new ratio is $\frac{120}{60} = 2$ to 1. In this case, the quantities are equal. Now let's say the original number of boys was 100 and the original number of girls was 90. In this case, the original ratio is $\frac{100}{90} = \frac{10}{9}$. The new ratio will be $\frac{120}{100} = \frac{6}{5}$. In this case, Quantity B is greater. Since there is more than one relationship between the quantities, the correct answer is Choice D.

3. **D** Set the ratios up as fractions: $\frac{12}{x} = \frac{x}{3}$. Next, cross-multiply: $x^2 = 36$. Since the exponent on x is even, $x = 6$ or -6. The relationship between the columns cannot be determined.

4. **C** Let the revenue = $5x$ and the expenses = $4x$. Use the profit formula: profit = revenue – expenses. Thus profit = $5x - 4x = x$. The ratio of profit to expenses is thus $\frac{x}{4x} = \frac{1}{4}$. The two quantities are equal.

5. **C** When you are given two ratios with a common element, you should manipulate the ratios so that the common element has the same value in both ratios. In this case, the common element is b. In the first ratio, $\frac{a}{b} = 5/12$, and in the second ratio, $\frac{b}{c} = \frac{4}{7}$. Manipulate the second ratio to make $b = 12$: $\frac{b}{c} = \frac{4 \times 3}{7 \times 3} = \frac{12}{21}$. Thus the ratio of $a:b:c = 5:12:21$. Since $c < 25$ and is an integer, c must equal 21. If $c = 21$, then $a = 5$.

CHAPTER 11

Algebra

Study this chapter to learn about:

- Linear equations
- Exponents and roots
- Quadratic equations
- Formulas, functions, and sequences
- Inequalities and absolute value

n broad terms, you can think of algebra as any situation where you manipulate an **equation** or **inequality** to solve for one or more unknown values. An unknown value is a **variable** (such as x or y) or an **expression** (such as $a + b$ or $\frac{c}{d}$). Before diving into manipulating equations and inequalities, you will first look at the basic mathematical operations.

Linear Equations

PEMDAS

PEMDAS is a helpful acronym for remembering the proper order of operations. When working with an expression that contains only values (no variables), you must perform the operations in the order dictated by PEMDAS. The following question would require proficiency with PEMDAS:

$(8 + 1)^2$ divided by $3 \times (5 + 2) = ?$

Before answering this question, let's review what each letter in *PEMDAS* stands for. The acronym **PEMDAS** represents **P**arentheses, **E**xponents, **M**ultiplication/**D**ivision, **A**ddition/**S**ubtraction.

When evaluating an expression, you must use the order as dictated by PEMDAS. However, note that there is no priority between multiplication and division, and no priority between addition and subtraction. When choosing between these operations, always move from left to right. The following list outlines what each operation represents:

- **Parentheses** ( ) or [ ]: parentheses are used to bracket off part of an expression from the rest of the expression. For example: $(3 + 5) \times 2$.
- **Exponents** 4^3, 3^5, and so on: exponents tell you how many times you multiply the base by itself. 4^3 is the same as $4 \times 4 \times 4$. 3^5 is the same as $3 \times 3 \times 3 \times 3 \times 3$.
- **Roots** $\sqrt{16}$, $\sqrt[3]{8}$, and so on: roots are the opposite of exponents. In terms of PEMDAS, roots take the same priority as exponents. *To get the square root of a number, you need to determine which value, when multiplied by itself, will yield the number under the square root.*

  For example, $\sqrt{16} = 4$, since $4 \times 4 = 16$.

- **Multiplication** 3×4; $(3)(4)$; xy: Note that multiplication is the opposite of division. If you multiply 3 times 4 and then divide that result by 4, the result is 3.
- **Division**, $\frac{6}{2}$: Next, you will evaluate any expressions that require multiplication or division. Note: *There is no hierarchy between multiplication and division!* When presented with these two operations, always work from left to right:

  6 divided by $3 \times 9 \rightarrow$ First do $6 \div 3 = 2$, then $2 \times 9 = 18$.

- **Addition/Subtraction** $4 + 7 + 11$; $8 - 3 = 5$: Next, you will evaluate any expressions that require addition or subtraction. Note: *Just as with multiplication and division, there is no priority between addition and subtraction!* When presented with these two operations, always work from left to right:

  $7 - 9 + 5 \rightarrow$ First, do $7 - 9 = -2$, then do $-2 + 5 = 3$.

Now that you've reviewed PEMDAS, let's work through the question at the beginning of this section:

  $(8 + 1)^2$ divided by $3 \times (5 + 2)$

You see two expressions within parentheses, so first evaluate those expressions:

  9^2 divided by 3×7

Next, you see a term raised to an exponent, so evaluate that term:

  81 divided by 3×7

Now you are left with division and multiplication. Remember, there's no priority between these two operations. Just work from left to right.

  81 divided by $3 = 27$

  $\downarrow$

  $27 \times 7 = 189$

Simplifying Expressions

Before you dive into the process for solving for a variable, let's review ways to simplify expressions. An **expression** is some combination of variables, values, or both. Examples of expressions are $3x + 7$, $\frac{2x}{y}$, $9z^3$.

When presented with an expression, either by itself or as part of an equation, your first step should always be to simplify the expression. Generally, there are three ways to do so:

Combine Like Terms

Simplify: $3x + 5z + 9x - 2z$.

SOLUTION: Combine the xs and arrive at $12x$. Combine the zs and arrive at $3z$. The expression simplifies to $12x + 3z$.

Simplify: $2(x+3) + 3(x + 3)$.

SOLUTION: Think of $(x +3)$ as a variable, such as z. $2z + 3z = 5z$. Therefore, $2(x + 3) + 3(x + 3) = 5(x + 3)$.

Find a Common Denominator

Simplify: $\frac{5a}{3} + \frac{2b}{5}$.

SOLUTION: Find a common denominator of 15 for both terms.

$$\frac{5a}{3} \times \frac{5}{5} = \frac{25a}{15}$$

$$\frac{2b}{5} \times \frac{3}{3} = \frac{6b}{15}$$

$$\downarrow$$

$$\frac{25a}{15} + \frac{6b}{15} = \frac{25a + 6b}{15}$$

Simplify: $\frac{7}{x} - \frac{3}{y}$.

SOLUTION: Find a common denominator of xy for both terms.

$$\frac{7}{x} \times \frac{y}{y} = \frac{7y}{xy}$$

$$\frac{3}{y} \times \frac{x}{x} = \frac{3x}{xy}$$

$$\downarrow$$

$$\frac{7y}{xy} - \frac{3x}{xy} = \frac{7y - 3x}{xy}$$

Factor

To factor an expression, take out the factors common to all terms in the expression.

Simplify: $6ab + 3a$

SOLUTION: Each term has $3a$ as a factor. To see this, rewrite the expression as $3a \times 2b + 3a \times 1$. Take $3a$ out of each term and arrive at $3a(2b + 1)$.

Simplify: $4x^2 + 3x$

SOLUTION: Each term shares a factor of x. Take x out of each term and arrive at $x(4x + 3)$

Basic Equations and Solving for a Variable

Whenever two expressions are set equal to each other, you have an equation:

$7 \times 6 = 14 \times 3$

The fundamental rule for all equations is the following: *you can perform any operation on an equation as long as you perform that operation on both sides.*

In the preceding example, if you divide both sides by 3, you will end up with $7 \times 2 = 14$. While the values on both sides of the equation changed, the equation itself is still true.

In algebra, equations will have variables, which are letters used to represent some unknown quantity in an equation.

If $3x + 2 = 14$, then $x = ?$

When asked to solve for a variable, your goal will be **isolate** the variable by undoing the operations done to that variable. To do so, you are going to use PEMDAS, but in reverse!

$3x + 2 = 14$ 1. Get rid of the addition by subtracting 2 from both sides.

$3x + 2 - 2 = 14 - 2$

$3x = 12$ 2. Get rid of the multiplication by dividing both sides by 3.

$\frac{3x}{3} = \frac{12}{3}$

$x = 4$

Let's look at another example:

If $\sqrt{x+2} - 3 = 4$, what is the value of x?

SOLUTION:

Step 1: Isolate $\sqrt{x+2}$ by adding 3 to both sides of the equation.

$$\sqrt{x+2} - 3 = 4$$
$$\underline{+\,3 = +\,3}$$
$$\sqrt{x+2} = 7$$

Step 2: $(x+2)$ is within parentheses, so you should manipulate the equation to isolate the expression within the parentheses. To do so, square both sides of the equation.

$$\sqrt{x+2} = 7$$
$$\underline{\sqrt{x+2}^{\,2} = 7^2}$$
$$x+2 = 49$$

Systems of Equations: Combination and Substitution

Often, the GRE will present you with two or more equations with multiple variables and will ask you to solve for the value of one or more of the variables in those equations. This is called a **system of equations**. When working with a system of equations, your ultimate goal is to arrive at a situation similar to what you saw in the previous section: *one equation with one variable.* To accomplish this, you can take two approaches: substitution or combination.

Substitution

Let's say you are given the following question:

$$3x + 2y = 18$$
$$2x + y = 9$$

What is x?

Step 1: Express one variable in terms of the other variable.

$$3x + 2y = 18$$
$$y = 9 - 2x$$

Step 2: Take the expression for y and substitute it for y in the first equation: $3x + 2(9 - 2x) = 18$.

Step 3: Solve for x.

$$3x + 18 - 4x = 18$$
$$-x + 18 = 18$$
$$-x = 0$$
$$x = 0$$

Combination

Most systems of equations on the GRE can be solved with substitution, but you will sometimes need to use combination. Let's look at an example:

$$3a + 2z = 12$$
$$4a + 3z = 18$$

Solve for a and z.

Step 1: When solving by combination, your ultimate goal is to arrive at the same coefficient for one of the variables. To do so, you will have to multiply each equation by a factor that will yield you a common coefficient for one of the variables. In this case, let's make the coefficients on z equal to 6:

$$3(3a + 2z = 12) \rightarrow 9a + 6z = 36$$
$$2(4a + 3z = 18) \rightarrow 8a + 6z = 36$$

Step 2: Multiply across one equation by negative 1.

$$-1(9a + 6z = 36) = -9a - 6z = -36$$
$$8a + 6z = 36$$

Step 3: Add the equations to arrive at one equation and one variable (your ultimate goal!).

$$-9a - 6z = -36$$
$$\underline{8a + 6z = 36}$$
$$-a = 0$$
$$a = 0$$

Substitute 0 for a into either equation to solve for x:

$$3(0) + 2z = 12$$
$$2z = 12$$
$$z = 6$$

Exercise: Linear Equations

Discrete Quantitative Questions

1. If $x + 7 = 14$, what is the value of $(x - 5)^2$?

   (A) 2
   (B) 4
   (C) 25
   (D) 49
   (E) 196

For this question, write your answer in the box.

2. If $\frac{1}{2}a + \frac{1}{3}a + \frac{1}{10}a = 28$, what is the value of a?

3. If $2x + 3y = 2y + 3$, what is y in terms of x?

   (A) $3 - 2x$
   (B) $3 + 2x$
   (C) $\frac{1}{x}$
   (D) x
   (E) $x + 6$

4. If $2a + 3b = 4$, and $x = 4a + 6b$, what is the value of x?

   (A) 4
   (B) 8
   (C) 12
   (D) 16
   (E) It cannot be determined from the given information.

5. If $\frac{9a}{2} + x = 3$ what is $\frac{a}{2}$, in terms of x?

   (A) $3 - x$
   (B) $\frac{3 - x}{2}$
   (C) $\frac{3 - x}{3}$
   (D) $\frac{3 - x}{9}$
   (E) $\frac{3 - x}{18}$

6. If $3p + 5q = 27$, and $p + 2q = 15$, then q equals.

   (A) -21
   (B) -3
   (C) 9
   (D) 12
   (E) 18

For this question, write your answer in the box.

7. If $1.5a + 3b = 20$ and $6a + 9b = 60$, what is the value of b?

8. If $x^2 + 5x + 6 = 32$, what is the value of $x^2 + 5x - 12$?

   (A) 14
   (B) 18
   (C) 20
   (D) 22
   (E) 24

For this question, write your answer in the box.

9. What is the value of $-2(3 - 5) \div 12^2$?

10. If $2a + 2b = 13$, $2b + 2c = 19$, and $2a + 2c = 8$, then $a + b + c =$

   (A) 5
   (B) 10
   (C) 15
   (D) 20
   (E) 40

11. If $3(x + b) + 5(x + b) = 72$, then $x + b =$

   (A) 8
   (B) 9
   (C) 15
   (D) 24
   (E) 36

12. If $a + 3b + 5c = 30$, and $6b + 10c = 20$, what is the value of $4a$?

    Ⓐ 10
    Ⓑ 20
    Ⓒ 40
    Ⓓ 60
    Ⓔ 80

13. If $\sqrt{\frac{y+3}{2}} = x$, what is y in terms of x?

    Ⓐ $x^2 + 3$

    Ⓑ $2x^2 + 3$

    Ⓒ $2x^2 - 3$

    Ⓓ $\frac{x^2 - 3}{2}$

    Ⓔ $\frac{x^2 + 3}{2}$

For this question, write your answer in the box.

14. If $3x = 12y - 7$, what is the value of $x - 4y$?

Quantitative Comparison Questions

Each of the following questions consists of two quantities, Quantity A and Quantity B. You are to compare the two quantities. You may use additional information centered above the two quantities if additional information is given. Choose

(A) if Quantity A is greater
(B) if Quantity B is greater
(C) if the two quantities are equal
(D) if the relationship between the two quantities cannot be determined

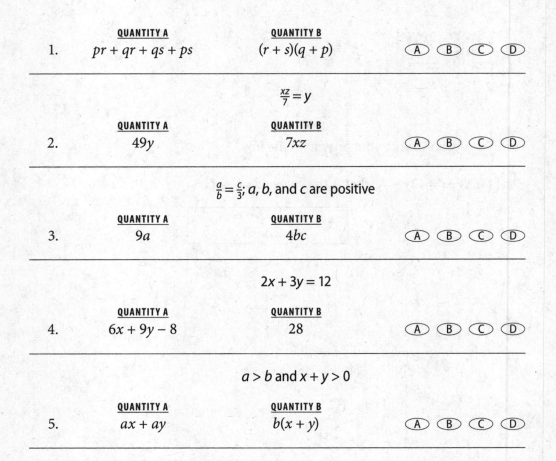

	QUANTITY A	QUANTITY B	
1.	$pr + qr + qs + ps$	$(r + s)(q + p)$	(A) (B) (C) (D)

$$\frac{xz}{7} = y$$

	QUANTITY A	QUANTITY B	
2.	$49y$	$7xz$	(A) (B) (C) (D)

$\frac{a}{b} = \frac{c}{3}$; a, b, and c are positive

	QUANTITY A	QUANTITY B	
3.	$9a$	$4bc$	(A) (B) (C) (D)

$$2x + 3y = 12$$

	QUANTITY A	QUANTITY B	
4.	$6x + 9y - 8$	28	(A) (B) (C) (D)

$a > b$ and $x + y > 0$

	QUANTITY A	QUANTITY B	
5.	$ax + ay$	$b(x + y)$	(A) (B) (C) (D)

Exercise Answers

Discrete Quantitative Questions

1. **B** To solve for $(x - 5)$, subtract 12 from both sides of the equation: $x - 5 = 2$. Substitute 2 for $(x - 5)$: $2^2 = 4$.

2. **30** To get rid of the denominators, multiply across the equation by 30 (which is a multiple of the values in all the denominators):

$$30(\tfrac{1}{2}a + \tfrac{1}{3}a + \tfrac{1}{10}a = 28)$$

$$15a + 10a + 3a = 840$$

Combine like terms:

$$28a = 840$$

$$a = 30$$

3. **A** To express y in terms of x, you need to isolate y. Subtract $2y$ and $2x$ from both sides of the equation and arrive at $y = 3 - 2x$.

4. **B** Notice that $4a + 6b = 2(2a + 3b)$. Therefore, to combine the equations, multiply the first equation by 2 and arrive at $4a + 6b = 8$. Substitute $4a + 6b$ into the second equation and arrive at $x = 8$.

5. **D** To express $\frac{a}{2}$ in terms of x, you need to isolate $\frac{a}{2}$. To do so, first subtract x from both sides: $\frac{9a}{2} = 3 - x$. To go from $\frac{9a}{2}$ to $\frac{a}{2}$, divide both sides by 9 and arrive at $\frac{a}{2} = \frac{3-x}{9}$.

6. **E** Since you have two linear equations, you have to decide between combination and substitution. Since the coefficient in front of p in the second equation is 1, substitution is the preferred method. Write p in terms of q: $p = 15 - 2q$. Substitute $(15 - 2q)$ for p in the first equation and arrive at $3(15 - 2q) + 5q = 27$. Distribute: $45 - 6q + 5q = 27$. Solve for q. $q = 18$.

7. $\frac{20}{3}$ Since none of the variables has a coefficient of 1, use combination. You want to solve for b, so multiply across the first equation by -4:

$$-4(1.5a + 3b = 20)$$

$$-6a - 12b = -80$$

Now the equations are:

$$-6a - 12b = -80$$

$$6a + 9b = 60$$

Add the equations and arrive at $-3b = -20$. Solve for b: $b = 20/3$.

8. **A** What is the relationship between $x^2 + 5x + 6$ and $x^2 + 5x - 12$? $x^2 + 5x + 6$ is 18 more than $x^2 + 5x - 12$. Since $x^2 + 5x + 6 = 32$, $x^2 + 5x - 12 = 32 - 18 = 14$.

9. $\frac{1}{36}$ Use PEMDAS: First evaluate the expression within the parentheses: $3 - 5 = -2$:

$$-2(-2) \div 12^2$$

Next, evaluate the exponential term: $12^2 = 144$

$$-2(-2) \div 144$$

Since multiplication is to the left of division, multiply $-2 \times -2 = 4$.

$$4 \div 144$$

Next, do the division: $\frac{4}{144} = \frac{1}{36}$.

10. **B** Solution: Add up the equations:

$$4a + 4b + 4c = 40$$

$$4(a + b + c) = 40$$

$$a + b + c = 10$$

11. **B** Solution: note that the two expressions share the common term of $(x + b)$. Combine like terms and arrive at $8(x + b) = 72$. Divide both sides of the equation by 8: $x + b = 9$.

12. **E** You should always attempt to simplify equations, if possible. In the second equation, you can factor 2 from all the terms: $2(3b + 5c) = 20$. Divide both sides by 2: $3b + 5c = 10$. Substitute 10 for $3b + 5c$ in the first equation: $a + 10 = 30$. Solve for a: $a = 20$. Therefore, $4a = 80$.

13. **C** To solve for y in terms of x, you must isolate y. First, get rid of the square root by squaring both sides of the equation: $\frac{y+3}{2} = x^2$. Next, multiply both sides by 2: $y + 3 = 2x^2$. Then subtract 3 from both sides: $y = 2x^2 - 3$. The correct answer is C.

14. $\frac{-7}{3}$ Since you are trying to solve for an expression that has y and x, manipulate the equation to get the xs and ys on the same side: $3x - 12y = -7$. Factor 3 from both terms on the right side of the equation: $3(x - 4y) = -7$. Solve for $x - 4y$: $x - 4y = \frac{-7}{3}$.

Quantitative Comparison Questions

1. **C**

   Step 1: To make the columns look similar, try to factor the expression in Quantity A:

   $$pr + qr = r(p + q) \text{ and } qs + ps = s(q + p).$$

   Step 2: Combine like terms: $r(p + q) + s(q + p) = (r + s)(p + q)$.

   The two quantities are equal.

2. **C**

   Step 1: To avoid working with a fraction, multiply both sides of the given equation by 7: $xz = 7y$

   Step 2: To make the columns look similar, substitute $7y$ for xz in Quantity B: $7(7y) = 49y$

   The two quantities are equal.

3. **B** To avoid working with fractions, cross-multiply and arrive at: $3a = bc$. To make the columns look similar, substitute $3a$ for bc in Quantity B: $4(3a) = 12a$. The comparison is $9a$ versus $12a$. Since you are told that a is positive, you can divide both quantities by a. The comparison is thus:

QUANTITY A	QUANTITY B	
9	12	Ⓐ Ⓑ Ⓒ Ⓓ

Quantity B is greater.

4. **C**

Step 1: To simplify the comparison, add 8 to both quantities: Quantity A = $6x + 9y$ and Quantity B = 36.

Step 2: To arrive at a value for Quantity A, manipulate the equation in the prompt to look similar to the expression in Quantity A:

$$3(2x + 3y = 12)$$

$$6x + 9y = 36$$

Step 3: Substitute 36 for $6x + 9y$ in Quantity A

The two quantities are equal.

5. **A**

Step 1: To make the two quantities look similar, factor the expression in Quantity A: $ax + ay = a(x + y)$.

Step 2: Divide both quantities by $(x + y)$. Quantity A = a and Quantity B = b. Since you are told that $a > b$, the value in Quantity A is greater.

Exponents and Roots

Exponent Basics

In the term 5^3, five is the **base** and 3 is the **exponent**. The exponent represents the number of times you multiply the base by itself. So 5^3 comes out to $5 \times 5 \times 5$. Both the exponent and base can be any real number (not just positive integers).

Most GRE questions dealing with exponents will require you to use a few simple rules and manipulate them in unorthodox situations. But before getting to these rules, let's look at some other properties of exponents:

> An even exponent always yields a positive result.

The base of an exponential expression can be positive or negative, but when the base is raised to an even exponent, the result will always be positive. Consider:

$$x^2 = 16$$

The most obvious solution to the preceding equation is 4. If you substitute 4 for x, you arrive at $4^2 = 16$, which is a true statement. But notice that -4 is also a solution for x! If you substitute -4 back into the equation, you arrive at $(-4)^2 = (-4)(-4) = 16$, which is also true.

The previous example illustrates the following general principle: An *even exponent will* hide *the sign of the base.*

In other words, whether the base is positive or negative, when it is raised to an even power, the result will be positive. This is because an even number of negative factors will always cancel out to create a positive product.

The flip-side of this fact concerns odd exponents. *An odd exponent will* preserve *the sign of the base.*

For example, if $x^3 = -8$, then there is just one solution for x: -2. Notice that 2 is not a solution for x because if you plug it back into the equation, you arrive at $(2)^3 = 8$, not -8.

Base of 0, 1, and −1

- When a base of zero is raised to any power, the result is zero: $0^2 = 0$
- When 1 is raised to any power, the result is 1: $1^{10} = 1$; $1^{-300} = 1$
- When -1 is raised to an even power, the result is 1. When -1 is raised to an odd power, the result will be -1: $-1^{10} = 1$; $-1^{-303} = -1$

Fractional Base

- When a positive proper fraction (a number between 0 and 1) is raised to a power, an interesting property results: the resulting value is less than the original base:

$$(\tfrac{1}{3})^2 = (\tfrac{1}{3})(\tfrac{1}{3}) = \tfrac{1}{9}$$

$$\tfrac{1}{9} < \tfrac{1}{3}$$

Compare the preceding to what happens when you raise an integer base to a power:

$$5^2 = (5)(5) = 25$$

$$25 > 5$$

- When a fraction is raised to a power, the exponent distributes to the numerator and denominator of that fraction: $(\tfrac{3}{2})^4 = \tfrac{3^4}{2^4} = \tfrac{81}{16}$.

Exponent Rules

Most situations with exponents will require knowledge of basic exponent rules. A good rule of thumb is that most exponent rules concern situations where *either the base or the exponent is the same and where you're either multiplying or dividing.*

Multiplying Exponents with the Same Base: Add the Exponents

- When multiplying exponential terms with the same base, keep the base and add the exponents: $(3^5)(3^3) = 3^{(5+3)}$. To understand why you are adding the exponents, write out 3^5 and 3^3. Notice that you arrive at: $(3 \times 3 \times 3 \times 3 \times 3)$ $(3 \times 3 \times 3)$. This leaves you with 3 multiplied by itself 8 times. Thus 3^8.

Dividing Exponents with the Same Base: Subtract the Exponents

- When dividing exponential terms with the same base, keep the base and subtract the exponents: $\frac{(5^7)}{(5^3)} = 5^{(7-3)} = 5^4$. To understand why you are subtracting the exponents, write out 5^7 and 5^3. Notice that you arrive at $\frac{(5 \times 5 \times 5 \times 5 \times 5 \times 5 \times 5)}{(5 \times 5 \times 5)}$. When you cancel out the common factors, you are left with four 5s in the numerator. Thus 5^4.

Raising a Power to a Power: Multiply the Exponents

- When raising an exponential term to a power, to simplify the term, you should multiply the exponents: $(5^4)^3 = 5^{(4 \times 3)} = 5^{12}$. Why? $(5^4)^3 = (5^4)(5^4)(5^4)$. This takes you back to the first scenario in which you were multiplying exponential terms with the same base. Recall that in such a situation, you should add the exponents. This will yield $5^{(4+4+4)} = 5^{12}$.

Multiplying and Dividing Exponents with Different Bases but the Same Exponent: Multiply or Divide the Bases

- When multiplying exponential terms with different bases but the same exponent, keep the exponent and multiply the bases. Thus far, you have looked only at situations in which the base is the same. What about when the bases are different? You can still manipulate the expression *if the exponents are the same!*

$$5^4 \times 3^4 = (5 \times 3)^4 = 15^4$$

Why are you allowed to combine the bases? Again, write them out.

$$5^4 = 5 \times 5 \times 5 \times 5$$

$$3^4 = 3 \times 3 \times 3 \times 3$$

Notice that when you multiply these two terms, you will end up with 4 combinations of (5×3), giving you $(5 \times 3)^4$.

It is also important to notice that this rule works in reverse. *If a product is raised to an exponent, then the exponent will distribute to all the factors in the product:*

$$(2^3 \times 3^5)^4 = (2^3)^4 \times (3^5)^4 = 2^{12} \times 3^{20}$$

When dividing exponential terms with different bases but the same exponent, keep the exponent and divide the bases: $\frac{12^3}{4^3} = (\frac{12}{4})^3 = 3^3$. To understand why, once again expand the numerator and denominator. You arrive at:

$$\frac{12}{4} \times \frac{12}{4} \times \frac{12}{4}$$

You thus have $(\frac{12}{4})$ three times, giving you $(\frac{12}{4})^3$.

Negative Exponents: Flip the Base

When raising a number to a negative exponent, to get rid of the negative exponent, you simply flip the base:

$$5^{-3} = (\tfrac{5}{1})^{-3} = (\tfrac{1}{5})^3 = \tfrac{1^3}{5^3} = \tfrac{1}{125}$$

$$(\tfrac{2}{3})^{-3} = (\tfrac{3}{2})^3 = \tfrac{3^3}{2^3} = \tfrac{27}{8}$$

Putting It All Together: Finding a Common Base

Knowing the preceding rules is essential for success on exponent questions, but the GRE will make such questions difficult by forcing you to evaluate expressions where it seems that none of these rules apply. To get past these difficulties, you should always be concerned with manipulating what's given to you to get to the *same base*. By doing so, you can then use the rules that were just covered. Look at the following:

$(8^4)(32^5) =$

- A 2^9
- B 2^{20}
- C 2^{37}
- D 8^{20}
- E 256^{20}

To simplify the expression, rewrite the exponential terms to have the same base. By doing so, you will be able to use the exponent rule that says you can add the exponents when multiplying exponential terms with the same base:

$8 = 2^3$, so $8^4 = (2^3)^4$. Using your exponent rules, you know this comes out to 2^{12}.

$32 = 2^5$, so $32^5 = (2^5)^5$. Using your exponent rules, you know this comes out to 2^{25}.

Now you can use your rules! The expression now reads: $(2^{12})(2^{25})$. Since you are multiplying exponential terms with the same base, you keep the base and add the exponents: $(2^{12})(2^{25}) = 2^{(12+25)} = 2^{37}$. The correct answer is C.

Let's look at another example:

$\dfrac{(8^6)(9^3)}{6^6} =$

- A 72^{12}
- B 12^3
- C 2^{12}
- D 92
- E 12^3

Again, your focus should be to manipulate the numerator and denominator so that all the terms are in their prime forms.

$8^6 = (2^3)^6 = 2^{18}$

$9^3 = (3^2)^3 = 3^6$

$6^6 = (3 \times 2)^6 = 3^6 \times 2^6$

So your new fraction is:

$\dfrac{(2^{18})(3^6)}{(2^6)(3^6)}$

Use your exponent rules for division and you get $2^{(18-6)} \times 3^0$. And this comes out to 2^{12}. The correct answer is C.

Table 1 lists the major exponent rules. You should commit these rules to memory and make sure that you understand the conceptual basis behind these rules, as outlined in this chapter.

Table 1 Exponent Rules Table

Rule	Example
$a^x \times a^y = a^{x+y}$	$3^2 \times 3^4 = 3^6$
$\dfrac{a^x}{a^y} = a^{x-y}$	$\dfrac{3^5}{3^2} = 3^3$
$(a^x)^y = a^{xy}$	$(3^2)^5 = 3^{10}$
$b^x \times a^x = (ba)^x$	$3^2 \times 5^2 = (3 \times 5)^2 = 15^2$
$\dfrac{b^x}{a^x} = \left(\dfrac{b}{a}\right)^x$	$\dfrac{15^2}{3^2} = \left(\dfrac{15}{3}\right)^2 = 5^2$

Table 2 lists common powers and roots that appear on the GRE. Committing these rules to memory will help you save precious time on the exam.

Table 2 Common Powers & Roots

$2^2 = 4$	$3^2 = 9$	$4^2 = 16$	$5^2 = 25$
$2^3 = 8$	$3^3 = 27$	$4^3 = 64$	$5^3 = 125$
$2^4 = 16$	$3^4 = 81$	$4^4 = 256$	$5^4 = 625$
$2^5 = 32$			
$2^6 = 64$			
$2^7 = 128$			

$\sqrt{4} = 2$	$\sqrt{36} = 6$	$\sqrt{121} = 11$
$\sqrt{9} = 3$	$\sqrt{49} = 7$	$\sqrt{144} = 12$
$\sqrt{16} = 4$	$\sqrt{64} = 8$	$\sqrt{169} = 13$
$\sqrt{25} = 5$	$\sqrt{81} = 9$	$\sqrt{400} = 20$
	$\sqrt{100} = 10$	$\sqrt{625} = 25$

Solving for an Unknown Exponent

So far, most of the questions that you have looked at have concerned shortcuts for evaluating exponential expressions. Sometimes, however, you will be asked to solve for a variable that is in the place of an exponent. Look at the following example:

If $2^x = 8$, then what is the value of x?

No exponent rule will work here. Instead, you must recognize the following property: *If two values are equal, then they must have the same prime factorization.* To solve for x, you should thus rewrite 8 as the product of its prime factors. $8 = 2^3$, so the equation now reads: $2^x = 2^3$. Now that the bases are equal, you know the exponents are equal, so $x = 3$.

If x and y are integers, and $(3^x)(2^y) = 324$, what is the value of $x + y$?

SOLUTION: Rewrite 324 as the product of its prime factors:

$324 = 9 \times 36 = 3 \times 3 \times 6 \times 6 = 3 \times 3 \times 3 \times 2 \times 3 \times 2 = (3^4)(2^2)$.

Thus $(3^x)(2^y) = (3^4)(2^2)$. Now that both sides of the equation are expressed in terms of the same bases, you know that $x = 4$ and $y = 2$.

Factoring Exponential Expressions

Sometimes you will be given an exponent question that concerns the addition or subtraction of exponential terms. Since exponent rules only apply to the multiplication or division of exponents, *you should almost always factor when two exponential terms are added or subtracted.* How will you do so? Look at the following example:

$2^{32} - 2^{30}$ is equivalent to which of the following?

    (A) 2^2
    (B) $2^2 3$
    (C) 2^{10}
    (D) 2^{30}
    (E) $2^{30} 3$

SOLUTION: 2^{32} can be rewritten as $(2^{30})(2^2)$. You can thus rewrite the expression as $(2^{30})(2^2) - (2^{30})(1)$. Since both terms share a factor of 2^{30}, the expression can be written as: $2^{30}(2^2 - 1) = 2^{30}(3)$. The correct answer is Choice E.

Roots

Roots are the opposite of exponents. Generally, a root will be denoted using the following symbol:

If $\sqrt{16} = x$, then what is x?

SOLUTION: x is the positive number that when squared yields 16. $4^2 = 16$, so the answer is 4.

Note that *when determining the square root of a number, the answer will always be positive.* Even though $(-4)^2 = 16$, -4 is not a solution for x in the question.

In the preceding example, 16 is a **perfect square.** A perfect square is any number whose square root is an integer. For example, 9 is a perfect square because its square root is 3, but 15 is not a perfect square, since its square root is 3.87. . . .

Multiplying and Dividing Roots

If you are asked to simply evaluate a square root, you can of course use your on-screen calculator. But many root questions will require you to instead manipulate the root. For example: $\sqrt{32} \times \sqrt{2} = ?$.

When multiplying square roots, you can combine all the terms underneath one square root. Thus

$$\sqrt{32} \times \sqrt{2} = \sqrt{32 \times 2} = \sqrt{64} = 8$$

When dividing square roots, you can combine all the terms underneath one square root:

$$\frac{\sqrt{32}}{\sqrt{2}} = \sqrt{\frac{32}{2}} = \sqrt{16} = 4$$

Note that these rules also work in reverse:

$$\sqrt{200} = \sqrt{100 \times 2} = \sqrt{100} \times \sqrt{2} = 10\sqrt{2}$$

Simplifying Roots

Simplifying a perfect square root is straightforward and can always be done on your calculator. But what if, after going through a question, you arrived at an answer of $\sqrt{32}$? If you looked at the choices, $\sqrt{32}$ would not appear in any of them. Why? Because $\sqrt{32}$ is not simplified. To simplify it, you have to take any perfect squares out of the radical. You would simplify $\sqrt{32}$ in the following way:

$$\sqrt{32} = \sqrt{16 \times 2} = \sqrt{16} \times \sqrt{2} = 4\sqrt{2}$$

$4\sqrt{2}$ is the simplified form of $\sqrt{32}$. Generally, when you are trying to simplify a square root, you should break it up into any known perfect squares and remove those perfect squares from the square root.

Simplify. $\sqrt{150}$

SOLUTION: First, rewrite 150 as 25×6. Thus $\sqrt{150} = \sqrt{25 \times 6}$. Now, break up the square root: $\sqrt{25 \times 6} = \sqrt{25} \times \sqrt{6}$. Finally, simplify any perfect squares. $\sqrt{25} = 5$, so the answer is $5\sqrt{6}$.

Quantitative Comparison Strategy: Exponents

When solving Quantitative Comparison questions that test exponents, it is essential to recall both the rules discussed previously, and *just as importantly*, the exceptions to these rules. Remember that success on Quantitative Comparison questions often requires testing for Choice D, which requires challenging your assumptions.

When solving a Quantitative Comparison question where either the exponent or the base is a variable, always test 0, 1, and –1. For example:

QUANTITY A	QUANTITY B
2^x	5^x

If x is positive, then Column B will always be greater. But remember that the exponents 0, 1, and –1 have interesting properties, so make sure to test those cases to see whether Column B is *always* greater.

- If $x = 0$, then the two quantities are equal.
- If $x = 1$, then Column B is greater.
- If $x = -1$, then Column A becomes $\frac{1}{2}$ and Column B becomes $\frac{1}{5}$, meaning that Column A is greater.

These different values give you contradictory relationships, and the answer is therefore D. When comparing numbers expressed as exponents, make sure to express each column using the same base:

QUANTITY A	QUANTITY B
$1{,}000^{600}$	$10^{1{,}800}$

Rewrite 1,000 using a base of 10: $1{,}000 = 10^3$. Substitute 10^3 for 1,000 in Column A, and compare the new expressions:

QUANTITY A	QUANTITY B
$(10^3)^{600}$	$10^{1{,}800}$

Use your exponent rules for Column A: $(10^3)^{600} = 10^{1{,}800}$. The two columns are equal, and the answer is therefore Choice C.

Exercise: Exponents and Roots

Discrete Quantitative Questions

1. $4^2 16^5 = 2^x$. What is x?

    (A) 7
    (B) 9
    (C) 10
    (D) 20
    (E) 24

For this question, write your answer in the box.

2. $\frac{21^{1,003}}{3^{1,002} 7^{1,001}}$ equals

    ┌─────────────────────┐
    │   │
    │   │
    └─────────────────────┘

3. If $5^x + 5^x + 5^x + 5^x + 5^x = 5^6$, then x equals

    (A) 1
    (B) $\frac{6}{5}$
    (C) 5
    (D) 6
    (E) 30

4. If $2^{x+2} \times 3^{y+3} = 576$, where x and y are integers, what is $x + y$?

    (A) 2
    (B) 3
    (C) 5
    (D) 6
    (E) 8

5. If $a = 0.729$, which of the following must be true?

    (A) $a > a^2 > \sqrt{a}$
    (B) $a > \sqrt{a} > a^2$
    (C) $a^2 > a > \sqrt{a}$
    (D) $\sqrt{a} > a^2 > a$
    (E) $\sqrt{a} > a > a^2$

6. $\frac{3^{30} + 3^{29}}{3^{29}}$ equals

    (A) 3

    (B) 4

    (C) 6

    (D) 15

    (E) 30

7. If $\frac{10^{2x}}{100^{3y}} < 1$, which of the following must be true?

    (A) $x < 3y$

    (B) $2x < 3y$

    (C) $2x < y$

    (D) $2x + 3y < 1$

    (E) $2x + 3y < 0$

8. $\sqrt{2}(12 - 4)9 =$

    (A) 3

    (B) 6

    (C) 9

    (D) 12

    (E) 18

9. If $\sqrt{a + b} = 8$ and $\sqrt{a} - \sqrt{b} = 0$, what is a?

    (A) 0

    (B) 2

    (C) 4

    (D) 8

    (E) 32

10. If $3^7 - 3^5 = (2^x)(3^y)$, where x and y are integers, what is $x + y$?

    (A) 2

    (B) 3

    (C) 8

    (D) 15

    (E) 243

11. $\sqrt{a^3} \times \sqrt{a} \times b^2$ is equivalent to which of the following?

    (A) ab

    (B) $ab\sqrt{a}$

    (C) $(a^2)(b)$

    (D) $(a^2)(b^2)$

    (E) $(a^4)(b^2)$

Quantitative Comparison Questions

Each of the following questions consists of two quantities, Quantity A and Quantity B. You are to compare the two quantities. You may use additional information centered above the two quantities if additional information is given. Choose

Ⓐ if Quantity A is greater
Ⓑ if Quantity B is greater
Ⓒ if the two quantities are equal
Ⓓ if the relationship between the two quantities cannot be determined

	QUANTITY A	QUANTITY B	
1.	5^{20}	25^8	Ⓐ Ⓑ Ⓒ Ⓓ

	QUANTITY A	QUANTITY B	
2.	$\dfrac{a^{-3}}{a^{-4}}$	a	Ⓐ Ⓑ Ⓒ Ⓓ

$$w = 2v$$

	QUANTITY A	QUANTITY B	
3.	$\dfrac{4^{-v}}{2^{-w}}$	1	Ⓐ Ⓑ Ⓒ Ⓓ

$$b > a > 0$$

	QUANTITY A	QUANTITY B	
4.	b^2	a^3	Ⓐ Ⓑ Ⓒ Ⓓ

a and b are integers
$$(2^a)(4^b) = 64$$

	QUANTITY A	QUANTITY B	
5.	$a + b$	3	Ⓐ Ⓑ Ⓒ Ⓓ

$$-1 < x < 0$$

	QUANTITY A	QUANTITY B	
6.	x^3	x^5	Ⓐ Ⓑ Ⓒ Ⓓ

	QUANTITY A	QUANTITY B	
7.	20^{40}	2^{120}	Ⓐ Ⓑ Ⓒ Ⓓ

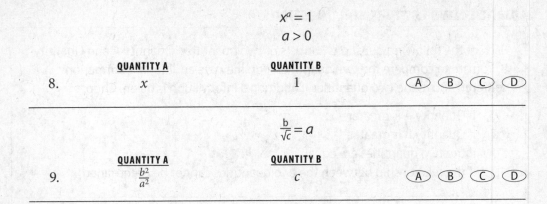

$$x^a = 1$$
$$a > 0$$

	QUANTITY A	QUANTITY B	
8.	x	1	Ⓐ Ⓑ Ⓒ Ⓓ

$$\frac{b}{\sqrt{c}} = a$$

	QUANTITY A	QUANTITY B	
9.	$\frac{b^2}{a^2}$	c	Ⓐ Ⓑ Ⓒ Ⓓ

Exercise Answers

Discrete Quantitative Questions

1. **E** To solve for x, you should express all the terms with a base of 2: $4^2 = (2^2)^2 = 2^4$. $16^5 = (2^4)^5 = 2^{20}$. Thus:

$$(2^4)(2^{20}) = 2^{24} = 2^x$$

$$\downarrow$$

$$x = 24$$

2. **5** When simplifying exponential expressions, you should express all bases in their prime forms. Express 21 in terms of base 7 and 3: $21^{1,003} = (7 \times 3)^{1,003} = (7^{1,003})(3^{1,003})$. The fraction now reads:

$$\frac{(7^{1,003})(3^{1,003})}{(3^{1,002})(7^{1,001})} = (7^2)3 = 147$$

3. **C** Note that you are adding the same term (5^x) five times. Thus:

$$5^x + 5^x + 5^x + 5^x + 5^x = 5(5^x) = (5^1)(5^x) = 5^{(x+1)} = 5^6$$

$$x + 1 = 6$$

$$x = 5$$

4. **B** Since the two sides of this equation are equal, they must have the same prime factorization. Thus the exponent on the 2 on the left side of the equation represents the number of times 2 appears in the prime factorization of 576, and the exponent on the 3 on the left side of the equation represents the number of times that 3 appears in the prime factorization of 576. To solve for these exponents, you should express 576 in terms of base 2 and 3:

$$576 = 2(288)$$

$$576 = (2)(2)(144)$$

$$576 = (2)(2)(12)(12)$$

$$576 = (2)(2)(4 \times 3)(4 \times 3)$$

$$576 = (2)(2)(2 \times 2 \times 3)(2 \times 2 \times 3)$$

$$576 = (2^6)(3^2)$$

Thus

$$(2^6)(3^2) = 2^{(x+2)} \times 3^{(y+3)}$$

$$6 = x + 2 \qquad 2 = y + 3$$

$$\downarrow$$

$$4 = x \qquad -1 = y$$

$$\downarrow$$

$$x + y = 3$$

5. **E** If the base of an exponential term is between 0 and 1, then as the exponent increases, the result decreases. Thus $a^2 < a$. Eliminate A, C, and D. Now compare B and E. What happens when you take the square root of a fraction? The opposite of when you square it! Squaring a positive fraction results in a value smaller than the original fraction, so taking the square root of a fraction results in a value larger than the original fraction. Thus the answer is E.

For illustration: $\sqrt{0.49} = 0.7$. Note that the result (0.7) is larger than the original value whose square root was taken.

6. **B** Split the numerator: $\frac{3^{30} + 3^{29}}{3^{29}} = \frac{3^{30}}{3^{29}} + \frac{3^{29}}{3^{29}}$. The first term can be reduced: $\frac{3^{30}}{3^{29}} = 3^1$. The second term can be reduced: $\frac{3^{29}}{3^{29}} = 1$. Thus the fraction reduces to $3 + 1 = 4$.

7. **A** To simplify exponential expressions, it is generally a good idea to make the bases similar. In this case, express the denominator as base 10: $100^{3y} = (10^2)^{3y} = 10^{6y}$.

The inequality now reads: $(10^{2x})/(10^{6y}) < 1$. Multiply both sides by 10^{6y}:

$$10^{2x} < 10^{6y}$$

$$2x < 6y$$

$$x < 3y$$

8. **D** First, simplify the values inside the radical: $12 - 4 = 8$. Next, multiply the terms underneath the radical: $2 \times 8 \times 9 = 144$. The square root of 144 is 12.

9. **E** A good rule of thumb is to eliminate radicals where possible. In the first equation, you can do so by squaring both sides: $\sqrt{a + b}^2 = 8^2 \rightarrow (a + b) = 64$. In the second equation, you should first add $\sqrt{b}$ to both sides: $\sqrt{a} = \sqrt{b}$. Now square both sides:

$$\sqrt{a}^2 = \sqrt{b}^2$$

$$a = b$$

Now substitute a for b in the first equation:

$$a + a = 64$$

$$2a = 64$$

$$a = 32$$

10. **C** When a question adds or subtracts exponential terms, a good rule of thumb is to factor out what the terms have in common. 3^7 and 3^5 share 3^5 as a factor, so the left side of the equation can be rewritten as $3^5(3^2 - 1) = 3^5(8) = (3^5)(2^3)$. Thus

$$(3^5)(2^3) = (2^x)(3^y)$$

$$x = 3 \qquad y = 5$$

$$\downarrow$$

$$x + y = 8$$

11. **C** When multiplying square roots, combine the terms underneath one radical. Thus $\sqrt{a^3} \times \sqrt{a \times b^2} = \sqrt{a^3 \times a \times b^2} = \sqrt{a^4 \times b^2} = \sqrt{a^4} \times \sqrt{b^2} = a^2 \times b$.

Quantitative Comparison Questions

1. **A** To make the columns comparable, rewrite 25^8 with a base of 5: $25^8 = (5^2)^8 = 5^{16}$. Now that both columns are expressed in base 5, the column with the larger exponent will have the greater value. The exponent in Quantity A is greater, so the answer is A.

2. **C** Simplify Quantity A: $\frac{a^{-3}}{a^{-4}} = a^{-3-(-4)} = a^{-3+4} = a^1 = a$. The two quantities are equal.

3. **C** Simplify Quantity A by expressing the numerator with base 2: $\frac{(2^2)^{-v}}{2^{-w}} = \frac{2^{-2v}}{2^{-w}} = 2^{-2v-(-w)} = 2^{-2v+w}$. Substitute $2v$ for w: $2^{-2v+2v} = 2^0 = 1$. The two quantities are equal.

4. **D** Although $b > a$, b is raised to a smaller exponent than a is. Thus a relationship cannot be determined. For illustration, plug in numbers: if $b = 2$ and $a = 1$, then $b^2 = 4$ and $a^3 = 1$. In this case, Quantity A is greater. But if $b = 4$ and $a = 3$, $b^2 = 16$, and $a^3 = 27$. In this case, Quantity B is greater. The relationship cannot be determined.

5. **D** First, rewrite all the terms in the given equation to have base 2: $(2^a)(2^{2b}) = 2^6$ => $a + 2b = 6$. Now you can plug in numbers: if $a = 0$, then $b = 3$. In this case, $a + b = 3$, and the two quantities are equal. If $b = 0$, then $a = 6$. In this case, $a + b = 6$, and Quantity A is greater. A relationship cannot be determined.

6. **B** When a fraction is raised to a power, the result gets closer to zero as the exponent increases. Since x is a negative fraction, the result will become less negative as the exponent increases. Thus when $-1 < x < 0$, x^5 is less negative than x^3, meaning that $x^5 > x^3$. Quantity B is greater.

7. **A** Your initial goal should be to manipulate the columns to make the bases comparable. However, it is not possible to express base 20 using base 2. Thus a different approach is required. Instead of making the bases comparable, make the exponents comparable. Note that $120 = (3)(40)$. Therefore, $2^{120} = 2^{(3 \times 40)} = (2^3)^{40} = 8^{40}$. Now the two quantities have the same exponent. The quantity with the greater base will have the greater value.

8. **D** If $x^a = 1$, it is possible that $a = 0$ and that x equals any number (since any number raised to the power of zero = 1). However, that possibility is eliminated by the information that $a > 0$. So what can x be? It would appear that x must equal 1, since 1 raised to any power equals 1. However, what if a is an even integer? In that case, x can equal −1, since a negative raised to an even power yields a positive result. If $x = 1$, the two quantities are equal. If $x = -1$, Quantity B is greater. Thus the relationship cannot be determined.

9. **C** Since the quantities compare c to an expression that contains a and b, you should manipulate the given equation to isolate c. First, cross-multiply: $\frac{b}{\sqrt{c}} = \frac{a}{1}$ $\rightarrow \frac{b}{a} = \sqrt{c}$. Next, square both sides: $\frac{b^2}{a} = \sqrt{c}^2 \rightarrow \frac{b^2}{a^2} = c$. The quantities are equal.

Quadratic Equations

So far, you have looked only at linear equations. In linear equations, there will always be one solution for a given variable. In contrast, in quadratic equations, *a variable will usually have more than one solution.* How do you know you have a quadratic equation?

> You have a **quadratic equation** whenever at least one of the variables in the equation is raised to an even exponent.

Let's say you are asked to evaluate $(-4)^2$. Using PEMDAS, you know that the result is $(-4) \times (-4) = 16$. Now let's say that you are asked to evaluate 4^2. You get $4 \times 4 = 16$. Note that both 4 and −4 gave the same result. Why? Because *raising a variable to an even exponent will always produce a positive result.*

Now let's flip it:

If $x^2 = 16$, what are the possible values of x?

You may be tempted to calculate the square root of 16 and say that $x = 4$. But watch out for the even exponent! Since the exponent on x is even, there will be a positive and a negative solution for x. Thus the two solutions are $x = 4$ or −4.

Other forms of quadratic equations are:

$$x^2 + 5x = -6 \qquad a^2 = a \qquad \frac{3}{x} = x$$

Common Templates of Quadratic Equations

On the GRE, quadratic equations will take a few common forms. The most common form is

$$ax^2 + bx + c = 0$$

When presented with a quadratic equation in the preceding form, you will usually be asked to find the solutions of that equation. To do so, you will need to factor. Let's look at an example:

If $x^2 + 7x + 5 = -7$, what are the possible values for x?

Step 1: Manipulate the equation to match the preceding template. In this example, you would need to set the equation equal to zero.

$$x^2 + 7x + 5 = -7$$

$$\underline{+7 = +7}$$

$$x^2 + 7x + 12 = 0$$

Step 2: Rewrite the equation in factored form: $x^2 + 7x + 12 = (x + \underline{})(x + \underline{})$.

Step 3: Determine the values for the slots. To get the factors of the equation, you need to find two integer values that add to yield your b and that multiply to yield your c. In the preceding equation, 7 is your b and 12 is your c. What two values multiply to 12 and add to 7? 3 and 4.

In the slots, you will put the two integer values that you arrived at in Step 2. Thus in its factored form, the equation is $(x + 3)(x + 4) = 0$.

Step 4: Solve for x. To solve for x, you must recognize an essential fact: *any time a product of two or more factors is zero, at least one of those factors must have a value of zero.*

In the preceding example, if $(x + 3)(x + 4) = 0$, then either:

$$(x + 3) = 0 \qquad \text{or} \qquad (x + 4) = 0$$

$$x = -3 \qquad\qquad\qquad x = -4$$

So the **roots** of this equation are −3 and −4. Note that if you plug either of these values into the original equation, you will arrive at a true statement.

Setting the Quadratic Equation Equal to Zero

Oftentimes, you will be presented with a quadratic equation that does not appear to match the preceding template.

For example, if $4x^2 = x$, then $x = ?$

Seeing x on both sides of the equation, many students are tempted to divide both sides of the equation by x to arrive at:

$$4x = 1$$

$$x = \tfrac{1}{4}$$

Though $\tfrac{1}{4}$ is certainly a solution to the equation, the hypothetical student committed an error here when dividing by x. Why? Because the student essentially eliminated one of the solutions for x! Instead of arriving at two solutions, the student arrived at only one.

So stick to the following rule: *Set quadratic equations equal to zero.* Let's redo the preceding example:

$$4x^2 = x$$

Step 1: Subtract x from both sides: $4x^2 - x = 0$.

Step 2: Factor x from both terms: $x(4x - 1) = 0$.

Step 3: Solve for x.

Since you have a product set equal to zero, either:

$$x = 0 \text{ or } 4x - 1 = 0$$
$$\downarrow$$
$$4x = 1$$
$$x = \tfrac{1}{4}$$

Expanding a Quadratic: FOIL

So far, you have looked at situations where you have taken quadratic equations in their expanded form and put them into factored form. Sometimes, you will be expected to go in the opposite direction: from factored form to expanded form. To do so, you will want to use an acronym that you may remember from high school: FOIL.

FOIL stands for:

First
Outer
Inner
Last

To expand the expression $(x + 3)(x - 5)$, do the following:

First: Multiply the first term in each parentheses together: $(x)(x) = x^2$

Outer: Multiply the first term in the first parentheses by the last term in the second parentheses: $x(-5) = -5x$

Inner: Multiply the inner terms of the product together: $3(x) = 3x$

Last: Multiply the last term in each set of parentheses together: $3(5) = -15$

Now you have an expression with four terms: $x^2 - 5x + 3x + 15$. Group like terms, and you will arrive at the quadratic: $x^2 - 2x + 15$.

When you have the opportunity to factor or use FOIL on the GRE, it's usually a good idea to do so!

Common Quadratics

Three quadratic expressions appear so frequently on the GRE that it is worth memorizing their structure instead of factoring or using FOIL each time you encounter them:

1. $(x + y)(x - y) = x^2 - y^2$
2. $(x + y)(x + y) = (x + y)^2 = x^2 + 2xy + y^2$
3. $(x - y)(x - y) = (x - y)^2 = x^2 - 2xy + y^2$

Memorizing the preceding formulas is useful for a couple of reasons:

- If you know the forms of these expressions after applying FOIL and after factoring, you will be able to save time when you encounter their general form on the GRE.
- Often, the GRE will put these expressions in an unorthodox form. In these cases, you will need to recognize that an unusual-seeming expression is actually one of the common quadratics.

For example, $(\sqrt{7} + \sqrt{3})(\sqrt{7} - \sqrt{3}) = ?$

Since you are multiplying two binomials, you might be tempted to distribute, but notice that $(\sqrt{7} + \sqrt{3})(\sqrt{7} - \sqrt{3})$ is in the same form as $(x + y)(x - y)$, where $\sqrt{7}$ is x and $\sqrt{3}$ is y. From the first special product, you know that $(x + y)(x - y) = (x^2 - y^2)$. Therefore,

$$(\sqrt{7} + \sqrt{3})(\sqrt{7} - \sqrt{3})$$

$$= \sqrt{7}^2 - \sqrt{3}^2$$

$$= 7 - 3$$

$$= 4$$

Exercise: Quadratic Equations

Discrete Quantitative Questions

1. If $2x^2 + 20x = -48$, then x could equal which of the following values?

   (A) -12
   (B) -8
   (C) -7
   (D) -4
   (E) 0

2. If $a - b = 4$, then $a^2 - 2ab + b^2 =$

   (A) 2
   (B) 8
   (C) 12
   (D) 16
   (E) 20

3. If $(x + 3)^2 = 81$, then x could equal which of the following?

   (A) -15
   (B) -12
   (C) -9
   (D) 3
   (E) 9

For this question, write your answer in the box.

4. If $x^2 - y^2 = 12$, and $x + y = 4$, then what is the value of x?

5. If $(a + b)^2 = 36$, and $ab = 4$, then $a^2 + b^2 =$

   (A) 3
   (B) 6
   (C) 9
   (D) 28
   (E) 32

6. If $2x + 2y = \frac{1}{2x - 2y}$, then $x^2 - y^2 =$

   (A) $\frac{1}{8}$

   (B) $\frac{1}{4}$

   (C) $\frac{1}{2}$

   (D) 1

   (E) 2

For this question, write your answer in the box.

7. If $a^2 + 8a + k = (a - 10)(a + 18)$, then what is the value of k?

8. If $y^2 + ky + b = (y - z)(y + q)$, then what is b, in terms of q and z?

   (A) $q + z$
   (B) $q - z$
   (C) qz
   (D) $-qz$
   (E) q/z

9. If $(\sqrt{a} - \sqrt{b})(\sqrt{a} + \sqrt{b}) = 12$, then what is a in terms of b?

   (A) $b + 12$
   (B) $b^2 + 12$
   (C) $\sqrt{b} + 12$
   (D) $\sqrt{b} + \sqrt{12}$
   (E) $\sqrt{b} - \sqrt{12}$

Quantitative Comparison Questions

Each of the following questions consists of two quantities, Quantity A and Quantity B. You are to compare the two quantities. You may use additional information centered above the two quantities if additional information is given. Choose

(A) if Quantity A is greater
(B) if Quantity B is greater
(C) if the two quantities are equal
(D) if the relationship between the two quantities cannot be determined

$$x^2 = 16$$

	QUANTITY A	QUANTITY B	
1.	x	4	Ⓐ Ⓑ Ⓒ Ⓓ

$$ab = 0$$
$$bc = 3$$

	QUANTITY A	QUANTITY B	
2.	a	0	Ⓐ Ⓑ Ⓒ Ⓓ

$$x + y = 9$$
$$x - y = 5$$

	QUANTITY A	QUANTITY B	
3.	$x^2 - y^2$	$y^2 - x^2$	Ⓐ Ⓑ Ⓒ Ⓓ

$$x^2 + 7x = -12$$

	QUANTITY A	QUANTITY B	
4.	x	$-x$	Ⓐ Ⓑ Ⓒ Ⓓ

$$x^2 - 5x = 6$$
$$-y^2 + 3y = 9y + 9$$

	QUANTITY A	QUANTITY B	
5.	x	y	Ⓐ Ⓑ Ⓒ Ⓓ

Exercise Answers

Discrete Quantitative Questions

1. **D** Simplify the equation by dividing both sides by 2: $x^2 + 10x = -24$. Since you have a quadratic, you should set it equal to zero: $x^2 + 10x + 24 = 0$. Now factor the quadratic: $(x + 6)(x + 4) = 0$. Either factor can equal zero, so:

$$(x + 6) = 0$$

$$x = -6 \text{ or } (x + 4) = 0$$

$$x = -4$$

2. **D** Notice that $a^2 - 2ab + b^2$ is one of the special products. The expression factors to $(a - b)^2$. If $(a - b) = 4$, then $(a - b)^2 = 16$.

3. **B** Note that the given equation is quadratic. There will thus be two solutions for $(x + 3)$: the positive square root of 81 and the negative square root of 81. Thus $(x + 3) = 9 \rightarrow x = 6$ or $(x + 3) = -9 \rightarrow x = -12$.

4. $\frac{7}{2}$ Since $x^2 - y^2$ is a difference of squares, you can factor the original equation to $(x + y)(x - y) = 12$. Substitute 4 for $(x + y)$ in the original equation: $4(x - y) = 12$. Divide both sides of the equation by 4: $(x - y) = 3$. So you know that $x - y = 3$ and that $x + y = 4$. To solve for x, you will add the equations:

$$x - y = 3$$

$$\underline{x + y = 4}$$

$$2x = 7$$

$$\downarrow$$

$$x = \frac{7}{2}$$

5. **D** Expand the expression on the left side of the first equation: $a^2 + 2ab + b^2 = 36$. Substitute 4 for ab: $a^2 + 8 + b^2 = 36$. Subtract 8 from both sides to solve for $(a^2 + b^2)$: $a^2 + b^2 = 28$.

6. **B** To isolate the variables, multiply both sides of the equation by $(2x - 2y)$: $(2x + 2y)(2x - 2y) = 1$. Notice that $(2x + 2y)(2x - 2y)$ is in the form of $(a + b)(a - b)$. Since $(a + b)(a - b)$ becomes $a^2 - b^2$ after applying FOIL, $(2x + 2y)(2x - 2y)$ becomes $(2x)^2 - (2y)^2 = 4x^2 - 4y^2$ after applying FOIL. The equation is now $4x^2 - 4y^2 = 1$. Factor 4 from both terms on the left side: $4(x^2 - y^2) = 1$. Divide by 4: $x^2 - y^2 = \frac{1}{4}$.

7. **−180** Notice that the right side of the equation is the factored form of the left side. How do you factor a common quadratic? Think of a simpler situation: $x^2 + 5x + 6 = (x + 3)(x + 2)$. Why? Because 3 and 2 multiply to yield 6 and add to yield 5. So in the original equation, −10 and 18 multiply to yield k. $k = -180$.

8. **D** Notice that the right side of the equation is the factored form of the left side. How do you factor a common quadratic? Think of a simpler situation: $x^2 + 5x + 6 = (x + 3)(x + 2)$. Why? Because 3 and 2 multiply to yield 6 and add to yield 5. So in the original equation, $-z$ and q multiply to yield b. Thus $b = -qz$.

9. **A** Note that the expression on the left side of the equation is the factored form of a difference of squares: $(x + y)(x - y) = x^2 - y^2$, so $(\sqrt{a} - \sqrt{b})(\sqrt{a} + \sqrt{b}) = \sqrt{a}^2 - \sqrt{b}^2 = a - b$. Thus $a - b = 12$. Isolate a: $a = b + 12$.

Quantitative Comparison Questions

1. **D** Since the exponent on the variable is even, $x = \sqrt{16} = 4$ or $x = -\sqrt{16} = -4$. The relationship cannot be determined. The correct answer is D.

2. **C** If $ab = 0$, then $a = 0$ and/or $b = 0$. If $bc = 3$, then neither b nor $c = 0$. Since b does not equal zero, a must equal zero. The two quantities are equal. The correct answer is C.

3. **A** Add the given equations to solve for x: $2x + 14 \rightarrow x = 7$. Substitute x for 7 in the first equation to solve for y:

    $$7 + y = 9$$

    $$y = 2$$

    The value of Quantity A is $7^2 - 2^2 = 45$. The value of Quantity B is $2^2 - 7^2 = 4 - 49 = -45$. Quantity A is greater.

4. **B** Set the quadratic equal to zero: $x^2 + 7x + 12 = 0$. Factor: $(x + 3)(x + 4) = 0$. There are two solutions:

    $$(x + 3) = 0$$

    $$x = -3 \text{ or } (x + 4) = 0$$

    $$x = -4$$

    Since both solutions are negative, $x < 0$ and $-x > 0$. Quantity B is greater.

5. **A** First, solve for x by setting the first equation equal to zero:

    $$x^2 - 5x - 6 = 0$$

    $$(x - 6)(x + 1) = 0$$

    $$x = 6 \text{ or } x = -1$$

    Next, solve for y by setting the second equation equal to zero:

    $$y^2 + 6y + 9 = 0$$

    $$(y + 3)(y + 3) = 0$$

    $$y = -3$$

    If $x = 6$, then Quantity A is greater. If $x = -1$, then Quantity A is greater.

Formulas, Functions, and Sequences

The next type of algebra question concerns situations where the question gives you a formula to determine some value.

Formulas

In formula questions, the question will define a formula for you and will ask you to substitute values or variables into the formula to arrive at an answer. A typical question would be:

A company estimates the number of potential customers, P, in a day by using the following formula: $P = \frac{8c^3}{z^4}$, where c = the number of customers the company had the previous day and z = the number of competitors for that month. If the company had 10 customers yesterday and has 2 competitors this month, how many customers will the company have today?

SOLUTION: Substitute the given values into the formula. Substitute 10 for c and 2 for z: $\frac{8(10)^3}{2^4} = \frac{8,000}{16} = 500$.

Formulas with Unknown Amounts

Sometimes, formula questions will not give you values for the variables. Instead, they will ask you to determine how changes in certain variables affect the output of the formula. In these cases, you should *always plug in numbers!* For example:

The formula for the volume of a sphere is $\frac{4}{3}\pi r^3$. If the radius of a sphere is doubled, the volume of the resulting sphere will be how many times the volume of the original sphere?

- Ⓐ 2
- Ⓑ 4
- Ⓒ 8
- Ⓓ 16
- Ⓔ 32

SOLUTION: Let the original radius = 2. The original volume is thus $(\frac{4}{3})\pi(2^3) = (\frac{4}{3})\pi(8)$. After the radius doubles, the new volume is $(\frac{4}{3})\pi(4^3) = (\frac{4}{3})\pi(64)$.

$\frac{(\frac{4}{3})\pi(64)}{(\frac{4}{3})\pi(8)} = 8$. The correct answer is C.

Functions

You can think of a function as a recipe. Recipes specify certain steps you need to take to achieve a desired dish; in the same way, functions specify certain operations you need to perform to achieve a given outcome. Because of their strange notation, functions tend to intimidate a lot of people, but it is important to remember that fundamentally *functions are just substitution!*

A simple function question would be the following:

If, for all numbers, x, $f(x)$ is defined by $f(x) = 3x + 5$, then $f(7) =$

It is important to note that "$f(x)$" does not mean $f \times x$. f is the name of the function, and the term in the parentheses represents the input of the function. Using the recipe analogy, this formula tells you that to get the value (also known as "output") of the function, f, you must multiply what is inside of the parentheses by 3 and then add 5. So in the preceding example, to get the value of $f(7)$, you must multiply 7 by 3 and then add 5. $3(7) + 5 = 26$.

Going from Output to Input

In the preceding example, you were given the formula for the function and its input, and you were asked to arrive at the output. Sometimes you will be given the formula for the function and its output, and you will be asked to arrive at the input. Look at the following example:

For all positive numbers, x, the function f is defined as $f(x) = (x + 3)^2 - 5$. If $f(a) = 59$, then $a = ?$

First, note that the function only applies to positive inputs, so you know your answer will be positive. To solve for a, you go through a similar substitution process as presented earlier.

Step 1: Plug a into the function and arrive at $f(a) = (a + 3)^2 - 5$

Step 2: Set the second expression equal to 59: $(a + 3)^2 - 5 = 59$

Step 3: Solve for a: $(a + 3)^2 = 64 \rightarrow (a + 3) = 8 \rightarrow a = 5$

Certain function questions will give you two functions and ask you to use the output of one function as the input for the other function. Look at the following example:

For all numbers, x, $f(x)$ is defined by $f(x) = x^2 + 12$, and $g(x)$ is defined by $g(x) = \sqrt{x} + 5$. What is the value of $f(g4)$?

This question wants you to use the output of $g(4)$ as your input for the function f. When working with a compound function, always go inside-out:

Step 1: Solve for $g(4)$: $g(4) = \sqrt{4} + 5 = 3$.

Step 2: Substitute the output of $g(4)$ into the function f: $f(3) = 3^2 + 12 = 21$.

Symbolism

A different type of function question will define a formula using symbols rather than the notation covered in the previous section. Such questions are often a source of intimidation for students, but the process for these questions is almost identical to the process for normal function questions.

If the operation * is defined for all numbers, a, by $a* = 2a^3$, and $(b + 3)* = 54$, then $b = ?$

Step 1: Understand the formula: you should substitute whatever is in front of the multiplication sign for a in the formula $2a^3$.

Step 2: Substitute $(b + 3)$ for a: $2(b + 3)^3 = 54$.

Step 3: Solve for b:

$$2(b + 3)^3 = 54$$

$$(b + 3)^3 = 27$$

$$b + 3 = 3$$

$$b = 0$$

Let's do another symbolism question with two symbols:

> If the operation # is defined for all numbers, a and b, by $a \# b = \sqrt{ab}$, then $60 \# (25 \# 9) = ?$
>
> **Step 1:** Understand the formula: multiply the terms before and after the symbol and then take their square root.
>
> **Step 2:** Since $60 \# (25 \# 9)$ is a compound function, you should first find the value of $(25 \# 9)$ and then input that value into the original function: $25 \# 9 = \sqrt{25 \times 9} = 15$.
>
> **Step 3:** Solve for $60 \# 15$: $\sqrt{60 \times 15} = \sqrt{900} = 30$.

Sequences

The last type of formula question you will see are **sequences**. A sequence is any group of numbers whose order is determined by a *rule*. Consecutive integers are an example of a sequence: for example, the rule for the set of consecutive integers 3, 4, 5, 6, 7 is that any given term in the set is one more than the term before it. Mathematically, the previous sequence would be defined in the following way:

$$a_n = a_{n-1} + 1, \text{ where } n > 1$$

The subnotation refers to the position of a term in the sequence. So a_1 is the first term of the sequence, a_2 is the second term, and so on. The rule tells you that *the nth term of the sequence equals the value of previous term plus 1.* Why does it specify "where $n > 1$"? Because this rule cannot apply to the first term, since there is no number preceding that term. Thus starting with the second term, any term will have a value one greater than the term before it.

Generally, sequence questions will ask you to determine one of three things:

1. The **rule** for a series of numbers
2. The value of a specific **term** in the sequence
3. The **sum or difference** of two or more terms in the sequence

> **Example 1:** The sequence $a_1, a_2, a_3, \ldots, a_n, \ldots$ is such that $a_n = 2a_{n-1}$ for all $n > 1$. If $a_2 = 7$, what is a_5?
>
> **SOLUTION:** The rule is that any given term is double the term before it. a_5 is 3 places after a_2, so
>
> $$a_5 = a_2 \times 2 \times 2 \times 2$$
>
> $$a_5 = 8a_2$$
>
> Since $a_2 = 7$, you know that $a_5 = 8 \times 7 = 56$.

Example 2: The sequence $a_1, a_2, a_3, \ldots, a_n, \ldots$ is such that $a_n = \frac{a_{n-1} - a_{n-2}}{2}$ for all $n > 2$. If $a_3 = 12$ and $a_4 = 5$, what is a_2?

SOLUTION: Substitute the value of a_4 for a_n, the value of a_3 for a_{n-1} and a_2 for a_{n-2}:

$$5 = \frac{12 - a_2}{2}$$

$$10 = 12 - a_2$$

$$a_2 = 2$$

Example 3: In the sequence S, $s_1 = 4$, $s_2 = 11$, and $s_3 = 18$. Which of the following could be the definition of the sequence?

    (A) $s_n = s_{n-1} + 4$
    (B) $s_n = 2s_{n-1} + 3$
    (C) $s_n = s_{n-1} + 7$
    (D) $s_n = 2s_{n-1} - 4$
    (E) $s_n = s_{n-1} - 7$

SOLUTION: Substitute the three values into each of the choices, and determine which choice maintains the values for all three terms:

A: $11 = 4 + 4$? No → Eliminate Choice A.

B: $11 = 2_4 + 3$? Yes

    $18 = 2_{11} + 3$? No

    → Eliminate Choice B.

C: $11 = 4 + 7$? Yes

    $18 = 11 + 7$? Yes

    → Keep Choice C.

D: $11 = 2_4 - 4$? No → Eliminate Choice D.

E: $11 = 4 - 7$ No → Eliminate Choice E.

Exercise: Formulas, Functions, and Sequences

Discrete Quantitative Questions

For this question, write your answer in the box.

1. If all the edges of a cube are doubled, the new volume of the cube will be how many times the original volume? (Volume of a cube = e^3)

2. A student's efficiency, E, is measured by the following formula: $E = \frac{3t^3}{d^2}$, where t = hours spent studying and d = hours spent browsing the Internet. Yesterday, Gerald and Harry spent the same amount of time studying, but Gerald spent twice as much time browsing the Internet. Yesterday, Harry's efficiency was how many times greater than Gerald's efficiency?

   (A) 2
   (B) 3
   (C) 4
   (D) 7
   (E) 8

For this question, write your answer in the box.

3. For all numbers, a and b, if the operation * is defined by $a * b = 3a + 2b$, then $5 * 3 =$

4. For all numbers x where $x \neq 0$, if $f(x)$ is defined by $f(x) = \frac{1}{x}$ and $g(x)$ is defined by $g(x) = \frac{1}{1+x}$, then $f(g(2)) =$

   (A) $\frac{1}{3}$
   (B) $\frac{1}{2}$
   (C) 1
   (D) 2
   (E) 3

5. For all numbers, x, the function f is defined by $f(x) = \frac{ax^3}{3}$, where a is a constant. If $f(3) = 45$, then $a =$

 Ⓐ 3
 Ⓑ 5
 Ⓒ 15
 Ⓓ 30
 Ⓔ 35

6. For all numbers a and b, if the operation $ is defined by $a \$ b = \frac{ab}{2}$, then $3 \$ (5 \$ 8) =$

 Ⓐ 10
 Ⓑ 20
 Ⓒ 30
 Ⓓ 40
 Ⓔ 60

7. For all numbers, x, if $f(x)$ is defined by $f(x) = 3x^2$, and $f(x - 3) = 12$, then x could equal which of the following?

 Ⓐ 2
 Ⓑ 4
 Ⓒ 5
 Ⓓ 7
 Ⓔ 8

For this question, indicate all of the answer choices that apply.

8. For which of the following does $a \star b = b \star a$?

 Ⓐ $a \star b = b(a - b)$
 Ⓑ $a \star b = 3(a + b)$
 Ⓒ $a \star b = (ab)^3$

9. The sequence $a_1, a_2, a_3, \ldots, a_n, \ldots$ is such that $a_n = 3a_{n-1} + 2a_{n-2}$ for all $n > 2$. If $a_3 = 7$ and $a_4 = 35$, what is a_2?

 Ⓐ 7
 Ⓑ 14
 Ⓒ 17
 Ⓓ 19
 Ⓔ 21

10. In a certain sequence, each term is 7 greater than the term before it. If the third term of the sequence is 39, what is the 13th term?

    Ⓐ 102
    Ⓑ 109
    Ⓒ 116
    Ⓓ 123
    Ⓔ 130

Quantitative Comparison Questions

Each of the following questions consists of two quantities, Quantity A and Quantity B. You are to compare the two quantities. You may use additional information centered above the two quantities if additional information is given. Choose

Ⓐ if Quantity A is greater
Ⓑ if Quantity B is greater
Ⓒ if the two quantities are equal
Ⓓ if the relationship between the two quantities cannot be determined

$$a \,\&\, b = \frac{1}{a} + \frac{1}{b}$$

	QUANTITY A	QUANTITY B	
1.	2 & 3	3 & 2	Ⓐ Ⓑ Ⓒ Ⓓ

$$f(x) = 7 + 2(x - 3)^2$$

	QUANTITY A	QUANTITY B	
2.	The minimum value of $f(x)$	7	Ⓐ Ⓑ Ⓒ Ⓓ

In a certain body fat measurement, a 1-unit increase represents a 5-pound increase in body fat

	QUANTITY A	QUANTITY B	
3.	The difference in body fat, in pounds, between a 5-unit measurement and an 8-unit measurement	30 pounds	Ⓐ Ⓑ Ⓒ Ⓓ

The sequence $a_1, a_2, a_3, \ldots, a_n, \ldots$ is such that $a_n = 2a_{n-1}$, for all $n > 1$.

	QUANTITY A	QUANTITY B	
4.	a_4	4	Ⓐ Ⓑ Ⓒ Ⓓ

The sequence $a_1, a_2, a_3, \ldots, a_n, \ldots$ is such that $a_n = a_{n-1} + 7$, for all $n > 1$.

	QUANTITY A	QUANTITY B	
5.	a_3	$a_1 + 15$	Ⓐ Ⓑ Ⓒ Ⓓ

Exercise Answers

Discrete Quantitative Questions

1. **8** Plug in values: Let the original edge of the cube = 2. The original volume of the cube is thus $2^3 = 8$. If the original edge = 2, then the new edge = 4. The new volume of the cube is thus $(4^3) = 64$. The new volume is thus 8 times the original volume.

2. **C** Plug in values: Let $t = 1$ for Gerald and Harry. Let $d = 2$ for Harry and let $d = 4$ for Gerald. Harry's efficiency is thus $\frac{3(1^3)}{2^2} = \frac{3}{4}$. Gerald's efficiency is $\frac{3(1^3)}{4^2} = \frac{3}{16}$. $\frac{3}{4}$ is 4 times greater than $\frac{3}{16}$.

3. **21** The formula specifies to triple the value in front of the star, double the value after the star, and then add the resulting terms. Substitute 5 for a in the original formula and substitute 3 for b to arrive at $3(5) + 2(3) = 21$.

4. **E** Solution: When working with compound functions, solve for the inside value first: $g(2) = \frac{1}{1+2} = \frac{1}{3}$. $f(g(2)) = f(\frac{1}{3}) = \frac{1}{\frac{1}{3}} = 3$.

5. **B** Substitute 3 for x in the original function:

$$\frac{a(3^3)}{3} = \frac{27a}{3}$$

$$9a = 45$$

$$a = 5$$

6. **C** When working with compound functions, first obtain the value of the function within the parentheses. $5 \$ 8 = \frac{(5)(8)}{2} = 20$. Substitute 20 for $(5 \$ 8)$ and arrive at a value for: $3 \$ 20$. Repeat the formula: $\frac{(3)(20)}{2} = 30$.

7. **C** Substitute $(x - 3)$ for x:

$$3(x - 3)^2 = 12$$

$$(x - 3)^2 = 4$$

$$(x - 3) = +2 \text{ or } -2$$

If $(x - 3) = 2$, then $x = 5$. If $(x - 3) = -2$, then $x = 1$. Only 5 appears in the choices.

8. **B and C** Substitute values for a and b. Let $a = 2$ and $b = 3$. Now identify for which of the choices $2 \star 3 = 3 \star 2$.

   A: $3 \star 2 = 2(3 - 2) = 2$; $2 \star 3 = 3(2 - 3) = -3$. → Eliminate Choice A.

   B: $3 \star 2 = 3(3 + 2) = 3(5) = 15$; $2 \star 3 = 3(2 + 3) = 3(5) = 15$. The outputs are equal. → B is an answer.

   C: $3 \star 2 = (3 \times 2)^3 = 6^3 = 216$; $2 \star 3 = (2 \times 3)^3 = 6^3 = 216$. The outputs are equal. → C is an answer.

9. **A** Solution: $a_4 = 3a_3 + 2a_2$. Thus:

$$35 = 3(7) + 2a_2$$

$$14 = 2a_2$$

$$7 = a_2$$

10. **B** To determine the 13th term, you will have to add 7 a certain number of times to the third term. How many times? To go from the 3rd to the 4th term, you add 7 once. To go from the 3rd to the 5th term, you add 7 twice. Thus to go from the 3rd to the 13th term, you should add 7 ten times. The 13th term thus equals 3rd term $+ 7(10) = 39 + 7(10) = 109$.

Quantitative Comparison Questions

1. **C** Substitute the values in the quantities into the given formula: $\frac{1}{2} + \frac{1}{3} = \frac{1}{3} + \frac{1}{2}$. The two quantities are equal.
2. **C** Because of the even exponent, $(x - 3)^2 \geq 0$. Thus the minimum value for $2(x - 3)^2 = 0$. The value of the function will be minimized when $2(x - 3)^2 = 0$. $7 + 0 = 7$. The two quantities are equal.
3. **B** Since each unit represents a 5-pound increase, the difference in pounds between three units is $3(5) = 15$.
4. **D** Without knowing the value of any of the terms in the sequence, you cannot determine anything about the value of a_4.
5. **B** $a_3 = a_2 + 7$. $a_2 = a_1 + 7$. Substitute $a_1 + 7$ for a_2 in the first equation: $a_3 = (a_1 + 7) + 7 = a_1 + 14$. Quantity B is greater.

Inequalities and Absolute Value

Inequalities look like the following:

$$5 > -2 \qquad y > 7 \qquad ab \leq 15 \qquad 3 < z < 9$$

Any time you see $<, >, \leq, \geq$, you are dealing with an inequality.

The following list translates inequalities:

Types of Inequalities

- $a > b$ means "a is greater than b"
- $a < b$ means "a is less than b"
- $a \geq b$ means "the value of a is at least equal to the value of b"
- $a \leq b$ means "the value of a is at most equal to the value of b"
- $3 < a < 5$ means "the value of a is between 3 and 5" (This is called a compound inequality.)

Inequalities Versus Equations

The fundamental difference between equations and inequalities is the following: Whereas an equation will give you a concrete value for a variable, an inequality will only give you a range.

Compare:

$$x = 7 \qquad \text{and} \qquad x > 7$$

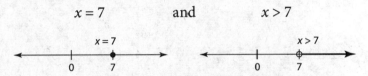

If you plot these on the number line, you will see that the equation $x = 7$ provides one and only one value for x. On the other hand, the inequality $x > 7$ does not provide a specific value; instead, it restricts the possible values that x can be. Since $x > 7$, it can only be any number to the right of 7 on the number line.

Manipulating Inequalities

As is the case with equations, your initial goal with inequalities will usually be to simplify what's given to you. Fortunately, most of the rules you have learned for manipulating equations will also apply to inequalities.

Addition and Subtraction with Inequalities

$x + 3 > 12$. Solve for x.

SOLUTION:

$$x + 3 > 12$$
$$\underline{-3 \quad -3}$$
$$x > 9$$

Here is another example:

If $-x + 2y > y - 2x$, then which of the following must be true? (Indicate all that apply.)

A $x > 0$
B $y > 0$
C $x + y > 0$

SOLUTION: Combine like terms:

$$-x + 2y > y - 2x$$

$$\underline{+\ 2x \qquad\quad +\ 2x}$$

$$x + 2y > y$$

$$\downarrow$$

$$\underline{-\ y - y}$$

$$x + y > 0$$

The correct answer is C.

Multiplication and Division with Inequalities

When multiplying or dividing across an inequality, keep in mind the following rules:

> If you multiply or divide across an inequality by a positive value,
> the inequality arrow does not change.

If $2x > 6$, what is the range for x?

SOLUTION: To isolate x, divide both sides of the inequality by 2.

$$2x > 6$$

$$x > 3$$

Note that the sign does not change, since you are dividing by a positive.

> If you multiply or divide across an inequality by a negative value,
> the inequality arrow flips.

$-2x < 6$. Solve for x.

SOLUTION: Divide both sides by -2:

$$-2x < 6$$

$$\frac{-2x}{-2} < \frac{6}{-2}$$

$$x < -3$$

But remember to flip the sign: $x > -3$.

> You cannot multiply or divide across an inequality by an unknown.

For example, if you are told that $\frac{x}{y} > 1$, you may be tempted to multiply both sides by y and arrive at $x > y$. However, this would be incorrect. Why? Because you do not know the sign of y. Since you don't know the sign of y, you do not know whether the inequality arrow will flip when you multiply. Thus you need to keep the inequality in its original form.

Manipulating Compound Inequalities

From the introduction to this section, recall that a compound inequality looks like the following: $-7 < a + 3 < 12$.

The rules for manipulating compound inequalities are the exact same ones as those for normal inequalities. Just make sure that you perform the same operation on all three parts of the inequality.

Let's solve for a in the preceding example:

$$-7 < a + 3 < 12$$
$$\underline{-3} \quad \underline{-3} \quad \underline{-3}$$
$$-10 < a \quad < 9$$

Extremes with Inequalities

In some inequality questions, you will be presented with multiple inequalities, or with an inequality and an equation, and will be asked to draw inferences about their products. In these examples, *choosing extreme values for the variables is often the optimal approach.*

> If $a = 3$ and $-6 < b < 12$, which of the following can equal ab? (Indicate all that apply.)
>
> A -18
> B 0
> C 18
> D 24
> E 36

SOLUTION: Since you are trying to figure out possible values of ab, you should consider the greatest value that ab could be and the smallest value that ab could be. Since you know $a = 3$, the product will be smallest when b is smallest. So choose the extreme value for b: in this case, -6. If $b = -6$, then $ab = -18$. However, you know $b > -6$. Therefore, $ab > -18$. Now try the upper bound. If $b = 12$, then $ab = 36$. However, you know that $b < 12$, meaning that $ab < 36$. You arrive at the compound inequality: $-18 < ab < 36$. The answer is B, C, and D.

Maximization and Minimization with Inequalities

Another common type of inequality question will give you two inequalities and ask you for the maximum or minimum value of their product. In these cases, *it is essential to consider the extremes for all variables.*

If $-7 \le a \le 12$ and $-11 \le b \le 5$, what is the maximum value of ab?

SOLUTION: The trap here is to multiply the maximum value for a and the maximum value for b and arrive at 60. However, note that *if a and b are both negative, their product will be positive!* Thus it is possible that the product of the smallest values of a and b will yield a larger value than the product of the largest values of a and b. And that is exactly what happens here: take the minimum value for a, -7; and the minimum value for b, -11; and the product is 77, which is greater than 60.

Let's look at an example with minimization:

If $-12 \le q \le 9$ and $8 \le r \le 12$, then the minimum value of $qr = ?$

SOLUTION: As in the preceding example, it might be tempting to multiply the smallest value for q and r and arrive at -96. However, note that when you multiply a negative and positive value, the result becomes smaller as the positive number becomes larger—for example, $-3(9) < -3(7)$. Thus you will minimize qr when you multiply the minimum value of q by the maximum value of r: $-12 \times 12 = -144$.

Absolute Value

In its simplest form, **absolute value** refers to the distance between a number, variable, or expression and zero. Absolute value is denoted using brackets, for example, $|x + y|$ or $|-3|$.

Since absolute value refers to distance, the absolute value of a number or expression will always be positive. For example, $|-8| = 8$ since -8 is 8 units away from zero.

Absolute Value with Unknowns

When an unknown term or expression is within an absolute value, there will be two possible values for the unknown. For example, if $|x| = 2$, then $x = 2$ or $x = -2$. Why are there two values for x? Because absolute value refers to distance! Both 2 and -2 are two units away from zero, so x can equal either of those values. When solving for an unknown within an absolute value, use the following process:

If $9 + |x + 4| = 28$, what are the possible values for x?

Step 1: Isolate the absolute value:

$$9 + |x + 4| = 28$$
$$\underline{-9} \qquad\qquad \underline{-9}$$
$$|x + 4| = 19$$

Step 2: Create two equations. In one equation, the expression inside the absolute value will equal the positive value on the right. In the other equation, the expression inside the absolute value will equal the negative version of the value on the right:

Equation 1   **Equation 2**
$x + 4 = +(19)$ or $x + 4 = -(19)$

Step 3: Solve for the unknown in both equations:

Equation 1   **Equation 2**
$x = 15$ $x = -23$

Absolute Values and Inequalities

In tougher absolute value questions, you will be given a range for the absolute value instead of a concrete value. For example:

$$|x| < 3 \qquad\qquad |x - 3| \geq 6 \qquad\qquad |z + y| < 2$$

To solve these questions, take the following approach:

If $|x + 3| < 7$, what of the following describes the range for x?

Step 1: Set up two solutions:

$$(x + 3) < 7 \quad \text{and} \quad -(x + 3) < 7$$
$$\underline{-3}$$
$$x < \qquad 4$$

Step 2: Multiply by -1 (flip the sign!):

$$-(x + 3) < 7$$
$$\downarrow$$
$$(x + 3) > -7$$
$$\underline{-3} \quad \underline{-3}$$
$$x > \qquad -10$$

Step 3: Combine the inequalities:

$$x < 4 \quad \text{and} \quad x > -10$$

$$\downarrow$$

$$-10 < x < 4$$

Test Positives and Negatives

When answering a "must be true" question or Quantitative Comparison question with absolute values, it is helpful to test positive and negative cases.

For this question, indicate all of the answer choices that apply.

If $x \neq 0$, then which of the following must be true? (Indicate all that apply).

- A $|x| = x$
- B $\sqrt{x^2} = |x|$
- C $\frac{|x|}{x} = 1$
- D $\frac{|x|^2}{|x|} = x$
- E $|x| \times |x| = x^2$

SOLUTION: Choose a positive and a negative value for x, and see which choices are true for both cases. Let's use -2 and 2 for x. Note that you will start with the *negative* case, since this is the case most likely to contradict the given equations.

A: $|-2| = 2.$ $2 \neq -2$ → Eliminate Choice A.

B: $\sqrt{(-2)^2} = \sqrt{4} = 2.$ $|-2| = 2.$ The equation is true when $x = -2$.
Now try 2: $\sqrt{2^2} = \sqrt{4} = 2.$ $|2| = 2.$ The equation is true when $x = -2$.
→ Keep Choice B.

C: $\frac{|2|}{-2} = \frac{2}{-2} = -1.$ $-1 \neq 1$ → Eliminate Choice C.

D: $\frac{|-2|^2}{|-2|} = \frac{2^2}{2} = \frac{4}{2} = 2.$ $2 \neq -2$ → Eliminate Choice D.

E: $|-2| \times |-2| = 2 \times 2 = 4.$ $(-2)^2 = 4.$ The equation is true when $x = -2$.
Now try 2: $|2| \times |2| = 2 \times 2 = 4.$ $(2)^2 = 4.$ The equation is true when $x = 2$.
→ Keep Choice E.

The correct answer is B and E.

Exercise: Inequalities and Absolute Value

Discrete Quantitative Questions

1. If $-x + y > y + 2x$, which of the following must be true?

   - (A) $x < 0$
   - (B) $y > 0$
   - (C) $x + y > 0$
   - (D) $x + y < 0$
   - (E) $xy > 0$

2. If $|x + 3| = 12$ and $|y + 2| = 9$, the maximum value of $xy =$

   - (A) 63
   - (B) 84
   - (C) 99
   - (D) 132
   - (E) 165

For this question, indicate all of the answer choices that apply.

3. If $3 + 9|x + 3| = 48$, then x could equal which of the following?

   - ☐A −8
   - ☐B −5
   - ☐C 2
   - ☐D 3
   - ☐E 5

4. If $x^2 > 16$, then x could equal which of the following?

   - (A) −3
   - (B) −2
   - (C) 0
   - (D) 3
   - (E) 5

5. If a, b, and c are positive integers, $a > b > c$, and $a + b + c < 27$, what is the maximum value for a?

    Ⓐ 23
    Ⓑ 24
    Ⓒ 25
    Ⓓ 26
    Ⓔ 27

For this question, indicate all of the answer choices that apply.

6. If $x < y < 0$, which of the following *must* be true?

    Ⓐ $xy < y$

    Ⓑ $x + y < 0$

    Ⓒ $\frac{x}{y} > 0$

    Ⓓ $|x| > |y|$

    Ⓔ $\frac{x}{y} > 1$

7. If $x > 8$, $y > 2x$, and $z > x$, then $y + z$ can equal all of the following EXCEPT

    Ⓐ 56
    Ⓑ 48
    Ⓒ 40
    Ⓓ 32
    Ⓔ 24

For this question, write your answer in the box.

8. If $|a + 3| \leq 6$ and $|b + 4| \leq 12$, what is the maximum value of ab?

9. If b, c, x, and y are positive and $\left(\frac{x}{y}\right)\left(\frac{b}{c}\right) > \frac{x}{c}$, which of the following must be true?

    Ⓐ $x > b$
    Ⓑ $x > c$
    Ⓒ $b > y$
    Ⓓ $b < y$
    Ⓔ $b > c$

10. For how many integers, a, is it true that $2 < |a| < 9$?

    Ⓐ 4
    Ⓑ 5
    Ⓒ 6
    Ⓓ 10
    Ⓔ 12

Quantitative Comparison Questions

Each of the following questions consists of two quantities, Quantity A and Quantity B. You are to compare the two quantities. You may use additional information centered above the two quantities if additional information is given. Choose

    Ⓐ if Quantity A is greater
    Ⓑ if Quantity B is greater
    Ⓒ if the two quantities are equal
    Ⓓ if the relationship between the two quantities cannot be determined

$$x \geq \tfrac{7}{8} \text{ and } y \geq \tfrac{1}{7}$$

	QUANTITY A	QUANTITY B	
1.	$x + y$	1	Ⓐ Ⓑ Ⓒ Ⓓ

$$x > y$$

	QUANTITY A	QUANTITY B	
2.	$|x|$	$|y|$	Ⓐ Ⓑ Ⓒ Ⓓ

$$-2 \leq a \leq 6 \text{ and } 3 \leq b \leq 5$$

	QUANTITY A	QUANTITY B	
3.	the minimum value of ab	-6	Ⓐ Ⓑ Ⓒ Ⓓ

$$3a > -3b$$

	QUANTITY A	QUANTITY B	
4.	$a + b$	0	Ⓐ Ⓑ Ⓒ Ⓓ

$$2x + 12 > 3y$$

	QUANTITY A	QUANTITY B	
5.	$6y - 4x$	24	Ⓐ Ⓑ Ⓒ Ⓓ

Exercise Answers

Discrete Quantitative Questions

1. **A** To simplify the inequality, combine like terms. Add x to both sides: $y > y + 3x$. Subtract y from both sides: $0 > 3x$. Divide both sides by 3: $0 > x$.

2. **E** To determine the maximum value of xy, you should first find the solutions for x and y. Solve for x:

$$(x + 3) = 12 \quad \text{or} \quad (x + 3) = -12$$
$$x = 9 \qquad\qquad x = -15$$

Solve for y:

$$(y + 2) = 9 \quad \text{or} \quad (y + 2) = -9$$
$$y = 7 \qquad\qquad y = -11$$

The maximum value for xy will be $(-15)(-11) = 165$.

3. **A and C** When solving for an absolute value, you must isolate the term or expression inside the absolute value. Here, subtract 3 from both sides: $9|x + 3| = 45$. Divide both sides by 9: $|x + 3| = 5$. Thus

$$(x + 3) = 5 \quad \text{or} \quad (x + 3) = -5$$
$$x = 2 \qquad\qquad x = -8$$

4. **E** Back-solving is a good approach here. Start with B: $(-2)^2 = 4$. 4 is not greater than 16, so eliminate B. Since B is too small, any choice with an absolute value smaller than 2 will be too small. Thus C is also too small. Now look at 3: $3^2 = 9$. $9 < 16$. So you can eliminate D. 3^2 and $(-3)^2$ have the same value, so A is also out.

5. **A** To maximize the value of a, you should first maximize the value of $a + b + c$. Since $a + b + c < 27$ and all the variables are integers, the maximum value of $a + b + c = 26$. Next, you should minimize the values of b and c. Since they are both positive integers and $b > c$, the minimum value for $c = 1$ and the minimum value for $b = 2$. Plug these values into the equation: $a + 2 + 1 = 26$. Solve for a: $a = 23$.

6. **B, C, D, and E** Use properties of positives and negatives to manipulate the choices:

   A: Divide both sides by y: $x > 1$ (remember to flip the sign!). You know that $x < 0$, so x cannot be greater than 1. → Eliminate Choice A.

   B: The sum of two negatives is negative. → Choice B is true.

   C: negative/negative > 0. → Choice C is true.

   D: If x is more negative than y, then x is further from zero than y is. → Choice D is true.

   E: Multiply both sides by y: $x < y$ (remember to flip the sign!). → Choice E is true.

7. **E** You have a range for x, and you have ranges for y and z in terms of x. Manipulate to get ranges for y and z. If $x > 8$, then $2x > 16$. If $y > 2x$, then $y > 16$. If $z > x$ and $x > 8$, then $z > 8$. Choosing extremes, you know that if $y > 16$ and $z > 8$, then $y + z > 24$. All of the values in the choices are greater than 24 except for E.

8. **144** To solve for the maximum value of ab, first get the ranges of a and b individually. If $|a + 3| \le 6$, then $a + 3$ must be at most 6 units away from zero. Expressed algebraically, this means that $-6 \le a + 3 \le 6$. Solve for a: $-9 \le a \le 3$. Go through the same process to determine a range for b. Using this reasoning, you can determine that $-12 \le b + 4 \le 12$. Solve for b: $-16 \le b \le 8$. It might be tempting to choose 24 as the maximum value of ab, but notice that $(-16)(-9)$ will yield 144.

9. **C** Solution: Rewrite the inequality as $(x/c)(b/y) > x/c$. Divide both sides by (x/c): $b/y > 1$. Multiply both sides by y: $b > y$. Note that you were able to divide by these variables because you are told that all the variables are positive.

10. **E** Think of absolute value as distance from zero. If $|a|$ is between 2 and 9, then a is between 2 and 9 units away from zero. Looking to the right of zero, this means that a can be any integer from 3 through 8, inclusive. Looking to the left of zero, this means that a can be any integer from -8 through -3, inclusive. There are 6 integers from 3 through 8, inclusive, and 6 integers from -8 through -3, inclusive. Thus there are 12 possible values for a. The correct answer is E.

Quantitative Comparison Questions

1. **A** Since you are comparing an unknown to a value, let's determine how the possible values of that unknown relate to 1. You have ranges for x and y, so choose extremes. If $x = \frac{7}{8}$ and $y = \frac{1}{7}$, then sum will be $\frac{57}{56}$, which is greater than 1. If you choose larger values for x and y, the sum will only get larger. Therefore, $x + y$ will always be greater than 1.

2. **D** The best approach here is to choose values. Since the columns deal with absolute values, you should consider positive and negative cases that satisfy $x > y$.

   Case 1: $x = 3$ and $y = 2$. In this case, $|3|$ is greater than $|2|$ and Column A is greater.

   Case 2: $x = 3$ and $y = -5$. In this case, $|3|$ is less than $|-5|$, and Column B is greater. A relationship cannot be determined.

3. **B** It might be tempting to multiply the minimum value for a and the minimum value for b to arrive at -6. However, note that when you multiply a negative by a positive, the larger the positive number is, the more negative the product is. Thus to minimize ab, you should multiply -2 by the largest value for b: 5. $-2(5) = -10$, which is less than -6.

4. **A** When comparing an unknown to zero, your concern should be the sign of that unknown. You want to know the sign of $a + b$, so you should manipulate the given information to isolate $a + b$. Add $3b$ to both sides and arrive at $3a + 3b > 0$. Factor: $3(a + b) > 0$. Divide both sides by 3: $a + b > 0$.

5. **B** Since you want to compare $6y - 4x$ to a value, you should manipulate the given information to see if you can arrive at a range for $6y - 4x$. First, isolate the terms with y and x by subtracting $2x$ from both sides of the given inequality: $12 > 3y - 2x$. Since $6y - 4x$ is double $3y - 2x$, you should multiply both sides of the inequality by 2:

$$2(12 > 3y - 2x)$$

$$24 > 6y - 4x$$

CHAPTER 12

From Words to Algebra

Study this chapter to learn about:

- Word problems
- Statistics
- Rates
- Probability

Students of math at almost every level experience some intimidation when confronted with lengthy word problems. The words in the situation often seem to conceal the math necessary to get to the answer. This whole chapter is devoted to ways to get past this difficulty. Word problems fall into several predictable categories, and this chapter exploits this predictability by providing you with a framework to implement each time the GRE throws a certain type of word problem at you. This point will be reiterated throughout the chapter, but it is worth mentioning now: your ultimate goal is to convert the words into algebra. This is the most difficult and most important component of these questions. Be sure to give yourself sufficient time to convert the words into algebra. Once you have done so, it is simply a matter of implementing the algebraic concepts that have been covered thus far in the book.

Word Problems

Word problems tend to be intimidating for many test-takers. One of the most common sentiments students express is concern over where to start. You are given a sentence or several sentences and expected to somehow develop mathematical relationships from these sentences. In the following pages, you will see step-by-step approaches for dealing with these situations. Keep in mind that your ultimate goal should always be the following:

Create algebraic relationships!

Once you've created relationships, you can then use your algebra skills to solve the problem. Let's look at a typical word problem and a step-by-step methodology for creating these algebraic relationships.

The sum of the lengths of two pipes is 70 feet. The length of the longer piece is 20 feet more than the length of the shorter piece. What is the length of the shorter piece?

Step 1: Identify your unknowns. *An unknown is any quantity with an unspecified value.* An unknown can be something like Bob's age, Jack's height, the number of people in a room, and so on. In the preceding question, there are two unknowns: the length of the shorter pipe and the length of the longer pipe.

Step 2: Assign variables to the unknowns. Since your ultimate goal is to derive algebraic relationships, you should express your unknowns as variables: Let l = the length of the longer pipe and let s = the length of the shorter pipe. You can use other letters as well, but it is helpful to use letters that help you remember which unknown the variable refers to (in this case, you can use l for "longer" and s for "shorter").

Step 3: Identify relationships among the unknowns. This is the final step in going from words to algebra. Once you identify a relationship, you can create an equation or inequality and start solving for your variables. Words such as *is*, *equals*, *is greater*, and *is less* are helpful indicators of relationships. In the previous example, there are two relationships among the variables:

> **Relationship 1: The sum of the lengths of two pipes is 70 feet.** Since *sum* means addition, you should interpret this information to mean *the length of the shorter pipe + length of the longer pipe = 70*

Using variables: ↓   ↓

$$l \ + \ s = 70$$

> **Relationship 2: The length of the longer piece is 20 feet greater than the length of the shorter piece.** The word *is* indicates a relationship between l and s. On your paper, write down:

$$l = s$$

Now translate the wording "20 feet greater." Since the longer piece is 20 feet more than the shorter piece, it must be true that s alone is not enough to equal l. Thus to make the two sides of the equation equal, you must add 20 to s:

$$l = s + 20$$

Step 4: Solve for the unknown. At this point, you have two algebraic relationships:

$$l + s = 70$$

$$l = s + 20$$

Since the question asked for the length of the shorter piece, the final step is to use substitution to solve for s. Substitute $(s + 20)$ for l in the first equation: $(s + 20) + s = 70$. Solve for s:

$$2s + 20 = 70$$

$$2s = 50$$

$$s = 25$$

Price and Quantity Relationships

Some word problems will require you to recognize the following relationship:

(price/unit) × (number of units) = total price

Though it might be intimidating, this is a translation that most people use every day. To illustrate this, look at the following example:

If Bob purchased 15 $30 shirts, how much money did he pay for all the shirts?

SOLUTION: Plug the values into the given formula. The price per shirt is $30, and the number of shirts is 15. Thus the total price is $30 × 15 = $450.

Now look at a more GRE-like example:

Bob spends a total of $140 at a certain shop, where he purchases a total of 20 shirts and ties. If the price of each shirt is $10, and the price of each tie is $5, how many shirts does he buy?

Step 1: Assign variables. Since you are not given a value for the number of shirts or the number of ties, let s = the number of shirts and t = the number of ties.

Step 2: Identify relationships. There are two relationships in the question:

Relationship 1: Bob purchases a total of 20 shirts and ties. Thus $t + s = 20$.

Relationship 2: The total amount Bob pays for the shirts and ties is $140. This amount will be the sum of the amount he paid for the shirts and the amount he paid for the ties. If each shirt costs $10, then he paid $10s$ for all the shirts. If each tie costs $5, then he paid $5t$ for all the ties. The algebraic relationship will be $10s + 5t = 140$.

Step 3: Combine the equations to solve.

$$t + s = 20$$

$$10s + 5t = 140$$

Since you are asked to solve for s, you should use the first equation to write t in terms of s: $t = 20 - s$. Next, substitute $(20 - s)$ for t in the second equation:

$$10s + 5(20 - s) = 140$$

Solve for s:

$$10s + 5(20 - s) = 140$$

$$10s + 100 - 5s = 140$$

$$5s = 40$$

$$s = 8$$

Age Questions

A common type of word problem that gives many students difficulty concerns age. The approach toward these questions is very similar to what you have looked at so far, though you will need to keep a couple key facts in mind. Let's look at an example:

Bob is 13 years older than Jack. In 3 years Bob will be twice as old as Jack. How old is Jack?

Step 1: Assign variables. Let j = Jack's *current* age and let b = Bob's *current* age.

Before moving on, it is important to understand the emphasis on *current* age. In most age questions, you will be given information about the people's ages at some earlier or later point. By assigning variables for the current age, you will be able to express these new ages in terms of the current ages instead of introducing new variables.

Step 2: Identify relationships.

Relationship 1: Bob is 13 years older than Jack

$$b = j + 13$$

Relationship 2: In 3 years Bob will be twice as old as Jack. Bob's age in 3 years will be $b + 3$. Jack's age in 3 years will be $j + 3$. Thus you can construct the following equation: $b + 3 = 2(j + 3)$

Step 3: Combine the equations to solve.

$$b = j + 13$$

$$b + 3 = 2(j + 3)$$

Since the question asks to solve for j, you should substitute $(j + 13)$ for b in the second equation.

$$(j + 13) + 3 = 2(j + 3)$$

$$j + 16 = 2j + 6$$

$$10 = j$$

Common Translations for Word Problems		
	CORRECT	INCORRECT
x is 5 greater than y	$x = 5 + y$	$x + 5 = y$
x is 5 less than y	$x = y - 5$	$x = 5 - y$
x is half of y	$x = \frac{1}{2}y$	$x = 2y$
x is twice y	$x = 2y$	$x = \frac{1}{2}y$
x is greater than y	$x > y$	$x < y$

Exercise: Word Problems

Discrete Quantitative Questions

1. The sum of Kathy's salary and Janet's salary is $200,000. If Kathy's salary is $20,000 less than Janet's salary, what is Janet's salary?

   Ⓐ $50,000
   Ⓑ $110,000
   Ⓒ $125,000
   Ⓓ $140,000
   Ⓔ $175,000

2. Bob breaks up a 220-mile trip into three parts. If the first part of the trip is 20 miles longer than the second part of the trip, and the third part of the trip is 50 miles longer than the second part of the trip, how many miles was the second part of the trip?

   Ⓐ 50
   Ⓑ 60
   Ⓒ 70
   Ⓓ 80
   Ⓔ 100

3. A certain store sells only shirts and ties. The price of a shirt is $40 and the price of a tie is $20. If Bob pays $340 for 10 items from this store, how many shirts did he purchase?

   Ⓐ 3
   Ⓑ 4
   Ⓒ 5
   Ⓓ 6
   Ⓔ 7

4. A manufacturer purchased three equally priced computers and five equally priced monitors for a total of $4,000. If the price of each computer was 5 times the price of each monitor, how much did each monitor cost?

   Ⓐ 200
   Ⓑ 400
   Ⓒ 600
   Ⓓ 800
   Ⓔ 1,000

5. An $800 bill is to be split equally among 10 friends. If x of the friends do not pay their share and the remaining friends split the bill evenly, how much will each of the remaining friends pay, in terms of x?

(A) $\frac{800}{x}$

(B) $\frac{80}{x}$

(C) $\frac{800}{x-10}$

(D) $\frac{800}{10-x}$

(E) $\frac{800}{x-10}$

6. Bob is 10 years older than Jack. In 2 years, Bob will be double Jack's age. How old will Bob be in 5 years?

(A) 8

(B) 18

(C) 22

(D) 23

(E) 27

7. Telecharge charges $0.75 for the first minute of a call and $0.25 for each minute thereafter. If total cost for a Telecharge call is $5.75, how many minutes long was the call?

(A) 18

(B) 19

(C) 20

(D) 21

(E) 22

8. The price of Stock A is $5 greater than the price of Stock B. If the price of Stock A increases by $10, the new price will be double the price of Stock B. What is the price of Stock B?

(A) 10

(B) 15

(C) 20

(D) 25

(E) 30

9. Bob can spend a maximum of $56 on hamburgers and shakes. Hamburgers cost $5 apiece, and shakes cost $4 apiece. If Bob purchases both hamburgers and shakes, what is the maximum number of hamburgers he can purchase?

Ⓐ 7
Ⓑ 8
Ⓒ 9
Ⓓ 10
Ⓔ 11

10. The height of a tree increases by x feet each year. At the start of a certain year, the height of the tree is 10 feet. If the height of the tree is 60 feet after 8 years, what is the value of x?

Ⓐ 6.25
Ⓑ 7.75
Ⓒ 8
Ⓓ 8.25
Ⓔ 9

11. In an auditorium with 300 students, the number of boys is more than double the number of girls. What is the maximum number of girls who can be in the auditorium?

Ⓐ 97
Ⓑ 98
Ⓒ 99
Ⓓ 100
Ⓔ 101

For this question, write your answer in the box.

12. Were Jack 6 years older, he would be double Bob's age. Jack is currently 1 year older than Bob. How old is Bob?

13. A group of marbles is arranged into x rows and y columns. If the number of columns is 7 times the number of rows, and there are 343 total marbles, how many rows are there?

Ⓐ 7
Ⓑ 14
Ⓒ 49
Ⓓ 62
Ⓔ 74

Quantitative Comparison Questions

Each of the following questions consists of two quantities, Quantity A and Quantity B. You are to compare the two quantities. You may use additional information centered above the two quantities if additional information is given. Choose

Ⓐ if Quantity A is greater
Ⓑ if Quantity B is greater
Ⓒ if the two quantities are equal
Ⓓ if the relationship between the two quantities cannot be determined

Kate is 3 years older than Sara.

	QUANTITY A	QUANTITY B	
1.	Kate's age 4 years ago	Sara's age 1 year ago	Ⓐ Ⓑ Ⓒ Ⓓ

An auditorium has x rows and $x - 1$ chairs per row.

	QUANTITY A	QUANTITY B	
2.	The number of chairs in the auditorium	x^2	Ⓐ Ⓑ Ⓒ Ⓓ

The sum of Bob's weight and Jack's weight is 50 pounds. Bob weighs more than Jack.

	QUANTITY A	QUANTITY B	
3	Bob's weight	25	Ⓐ Ⓑ Ⓒ Ⓓ

A candy retailer charges $2 for Jupiter bars and $1 for Big Slugger bars. In a certain day, the retailer sells both bars and earns a total of $30 for her sale of Jupiter bars and Big Slugger bars.

	QUANTITY A	QUANTITY B	
4.	The maximum number of Big Slugger bars that the retailer could have sold	29	Ⓐ Ⓑ Ⓒ Ⓓ

In 5 years, Jack will be 8 years older than Bob. In 5 years, Tanya will be 8 years older than Sam.

	QUANTITY A	QUANTITY B	
5.	Jack's age	Tanya's age	Ⓐ Ⓑ Ⓒ Ⓓ

If a dealership increased the price of its sedans by $3,000, then the price of a sedan would be double the price of a truck.

	QUANTITY A	**QUANTITY B**	
6.	The price of a sedan	The price of a truck	Ⓐ Ⓑ Ⓒ Ⓓ

The total price of 3 equally priced stereos is equivalent to the total price of 2 equally priced MP3 players.

	QUANTITY A	**QUANTITY B**	
7.	The ratio of the price of a stereo to the price of an MP3 player	$\frac{2}{3}$	Ⓐ Ⓑ Ⓒ Ⓓ

Exercise Answers

Discrete Quantitative Questions

1. **B** Let k = Kathy's salary and j = Janet's salary. The first relationship is that $k + j = 200,000$. The next relationship is that Kathy's salary is $20,000 less than Janet's salary. Expressed algebraically, this relationship is: $k = j - 20,000$. Next, combine the equations to solve for j. To do so, substitute $(j - 20,000)$ for k in the first equation: $(j - 20,000) + j = 200,000$. Solve for j:

    $$2j - 20,000 = 200,000$$

    $$2j = 220,000$$

    $$j = 110,000$$

2. **A** Let f = the number of miles of the first part of the trip. Let s = the number of miles of the second part of the trip. Let t = the number of miles of the third part of the trip. The sum of the three parts is 220 miles, so $f + s + t = 220$. The first part of the trip is 20 miles longer than the second part, so $f = s + 20$. The second part of the trip is 50 miles longer than the first part, so $t = s + 50$. To solve for s, substitute $(s + 20)$ for f and $(s + 50)$ for t in the original equation: $(s + 20) + s + (s + 50) = 220$. Solve for s:

    $$3s + 70 = 220$$

    $$3s = 150$$

    $$s = 50$$

3. **E** Let s = the number of shirts Bob purchases. Let t = the number of ties Bob purchases. If Bob purchases 10 items, then $s + t = 10$. The next relationship is the more difficult one. The $340 that Bob pays is the sum of the amount he pays for shirts and the amount he pays for ties.

    The amount he pays for the shirts is ($/shirt) × (number of shirts) = $40s$.

    The amount he pays for the ties is ($/tie) × (number of ties) = $20t$.
    So $40s + 20t = 340$. You now have two equations:

$$s + t = 10$$

$$40s + 20t = 340$$

To solve for s, use substitution. First, manipulate the first equation to express t in terms of s: $t = 10 - s$. Next, substitute that expression for t in the second equation: $40s + 20(10 - s) = 340$. Solve for s:

$$40s + 20(10 - s) = 340$$

$$40s + 200 - 20s = 340$$

$$20s = 140$$

$$s = 7$$

4. **A** Let c = the price of each computer and m = the price of each monitor.

   The manufacturer thus paid a total of $3c$ for the computers and $5m$ for the monitors. The sum of these values equals \$4,000: $3c + 5m = 4,000$. The other algebraic relationship you can create from the information is $c = 5m$. There are now two equations:

   $$3c + 5m = 4,000$$

   $$c = 5m$$

   To solve for m, substitute $5m$ in for c in the first equation: $3(5m) + 5m = 4,000$. Distribute and combine like terms: $20m = 4,000$. Solve for m: $m = 200$.

5. **D** The question asks you to determine the amount paid per friend. This can be expressed as the following ratio: total bill/number of people paying. The numerator of this ratio will be 800. The denominator will be the total number of friends splitting the bill after x do not pay. If there were 10 friends originally, and x do not pay, the number of people paying is $10 - x$. Thus the ratio will be $\frac{800}{10 - x}$.

6. **D** Let b = Bob's current age and j = Jack's current age. You are asked to solve for $b + 5$. Use the assigned variables to construct algebraic relationships. The first sentence provides a relationship between Bob's current age and Jack's current age: $b = j + 10$. The second sentence provides a relationship between their ages in 2 years: $b + 2 = 2(j + 2)$. Use substitution to solve for b:

   Step 1: Manipulate the first equation to write j in terms of b: $b - 10 = j$

   Step 2: Substitute $b - 10$ for j in the second equation:

   $$b + 2 = 2(b - 10 + 2)$$

   $$b + 2 = 2(b - 8)$$

   $$b + 2 = 2b - 16$$

   $$18 = b$$

   In 5 years, Bob will be 23.

7. **D** Since you are asked to solve for the length of the call, you should assign a variable: l = length of the call. The total charge of \$5.75 consists of two parts: the charge for the first minute and the charge for all subsequent minutes. The

charge for the first minute is \$0.75. The charge for all subsequent minutes will be cost/minute × number of minutes. You are told that cost/minute is \$0.25. If l is the length of the entire phone call, then the number of minutes charged at \$0.25 will be $l - 1$. Thus you can construct the following equation: $0.75 + 0.25(l - 1) = 5.75$. Solve for x:

$$0.75 + 0.25(l - 1) = 5.75$$

$$0.75 + 0.25l - 0.25 = 5.75$$

$$0.5 + 0.25l = 5.75$$

$$0.25l = 5.25$$

$$l = 21$$

8. **B** Assign variables: Let a = the price of stock A, and let b = the price of stock B. The information in the problem provides two relationships:

"The price of stock A is \$5 greater than the price of stock B": expressed algebraically: $a = b + 5$

"If the price of stock A increases by \$10, the new price will be double the price of stock B.": $a + 10 = 2b$

Now use substitution to solve for b:

$$a = b + 5$$

$$a + 10 = 2b$$

Substitute $b + 5$ for a in the second equation: $(b + 5) + 10 = 2b$. Solve for b:

$$(b + 5) + 10 = 2b$$

$$b + 15 = 2b$$

$$15 = b$$

9. **D** Let h = the number of hamburgers Bob purchases, and let s = the number of shakes Bob purchases. The amount Bob spends on hamburgers is $5h$, and the amount he spends on shakes is $4s$. Since the maximum that he can spend is \$56, the sum of these two quantities must be less than or equal to 56: $5h + 4s \le 56$. Since the question asks for the maximum number of hamburgers that Bob can purchase, you should minimize the number of shakes that he purchases by letting $s = 1$:

$$5h + 4(1) \le 56$$

$$5h \le 52$$

$$h \le \tfrac{52}{5}$$

Since h must be an integer, the maximum value for h will be the greatest integer less than $\tfrac{52}{5}$. $\tfrac{52}{5} = 10.4$. Thus the greatest value for h will be 10.

10. **A** The final height of the tree will be the sum of the original height and the increase after 8 years. If the height of the tree increases by x feet each year, then the tree will have increased by $8x$ feet after 8 years. Thus you can create the following equation: $10 + 8x = 60$. Solve for x:

$$8x = 50$$

$$x = \frac{50}{8} = 6.25$$

11. **C** Let b = the number of boys and g = the number of girls.

    Relationship 1: $b + g = 300$

    Relationship 2: $b > 2g$

    Substitution with inequalities can be difficult. Think of what would be the case if $b = 2g$. Substitute $2g$ for b in the first equation and arrive at $2g + g = 300 \rightarrow 3g = 300 \rightarrow g = 100$. Since $2g < b$ instead of $2g = b$, the number of girls must be less than 100. The greatest integer less than 100 is 99 (you only consider integers since the number of girls must be a whole number).

12. **7** Let j = Jack's current age and b = Bob's current age.

    Relationship 1: $j + 6 = 2b$

    Relationship 2: $j = b + 1$

    To solve for b, substitute $b + 1$ for j in the first equation:

    $$(b + 1) + 6 = 2b$$

    $$b + 7 = 2b$$

    $$7 = b$$

13. **A** Rows × columns = total marbles. Thus $xy = 343$. You also know that $y = 7x$. To solve for x, substitute $7x$ for y in the first equation:

    $$x(7x) = 343$$

    $$7x^2 = 343$$

    $$x^2 = 49$$

    $$x = 7$$

Quantitative Comparison Questions

1. **C** Let k = Kate's current age, and let s = Sara's current age. Based on the prompt, you can create the following relationship: $k = s + 3$. Since the quantities compare Kate's age and Sara's age, make them comparable by substituting $(s + 3)$ for k in Quantity A. The value for Quantity A will be $(s + 3) - 4 = s - 1$. The value for Quantity B will be $s - 1$. Thus the two quantities are equal.

2. **B** Since the columns ask you to compare the number of chairs in the auditorium to x^2, you should attempt to express the number of chairs in terms of x. To determine the total number of chairs, do $\frac{chairs}{row}$ × number of rows. Thus the number of chairs = $x(x-1) = x^2 - x$. Quantity A is thus $x^2 - x$ and Quantity B is x^2. Since x must be positive (there can't be a negative number of chairs or rows), x^2 must be greater than $x^2 - x$.

3. **A** Let b = Bob's weight and j = Jack's weight. Use these variables to create the equation $b + j = 50$. If Bob weighs more than Jack, then Bob's weight must account for more than half of their sum. Algebraically,

$$b > \frac{50}{2}$$

$$b > 25$$

Thus Quantity A is greater.

4. **B** Let j = the number of Jupiter bars sold and b = the number of Big Slugger bars sold. The revenue for the Jupiter bars is $2j$ and the revenue for the Big Slugger bars is $1b$. Since the total revenue on the two bars is $30, it follows that $2j + b = 30$. To maximize b, minimize j. Since the retailer sold both candy bars, the minimum value for j is 1. Thus $2(1) + b = 30 \rightarrow b = 28$. The maximum for b is 28. Quantity B is greater.

5. **D** The given information provides no relationship between Jack's age and Tanya's age.

6. **D** Let s = the price of a sedan and t = the price of a truck. Thus $s + 3,000 = 2t$. You are given one relationship between two variables. Without additional information, you cannot determine the relationship between the variables.

7. **C** Let s = the price of each stereo and m = the price of each MP3 player. The total price of the three stereos is thus $3s$, and the total price of each MP3 player is thus $2m$. Since the total prices are equal, $3s = 2m$. Manipulate to solve for s/m:

$$3s = 2m$$

Divide both sides by 3: $\downarrow$

$$s = \left(\tfrac{2}{3}\right)m$$

Divide both sides by m: $\downarrow$

$$\tfrac{s}{m} = \left(\tfrac{2}{3}\right)$$

The two quantities are equal.

Statistics

Statistics refers to the properties of a set of **data.** For the purposes of the GRE, you can think of **data** as numerical pieces of information. For example, the number of students in a class is a data point, as is the average grade for a class, or the range of scores in a class. Though statistics is a broad field within mathematics, on the GRE, you will be expected to understand the following statistical concepts:

- Mean
- Median
- Mode
- Range
- Standard deviation

Let's look at a set of data to understand these concepts:

The test scores for seven students in a class are 72, 90, 72, 83, 81, 63, and 94. The **median** refers to the data point that has an equal number of data points greater than it and less than it. In other words, the median is the middle value in a set when the data points are listed in increasing order.

To determine the median, list the data points from least to greatest.

Listed in increasing order, the data points in the preceding list will read: 63, 72, 72, 81, 83, 90, 94. Since there are seven data points, the median is the fourth data point.

Median
↓
63, 72, 72, 81, 83, 90, 94
Bottom 3   Top 3

In this case, the middle value is 81.

When the number of terms in a set is even, the median will be the average of the two middle terms.

What is the median of 2, 8, 10, 11, 12, and 14?

SOLUTION: Since there are six data points, the median will be the average of the middle two values. In this case, the middle two values are 10 and 11.

To determine the median, find the average of 10 and 11. $\frac{10 + 11}{2} = \frac{21}{2} = 10.5$.

- The **range** refers to the positive difference between the largest and smallest value in a set. In the earlier example, the range is $94 - 63 = 31$.

- The **mode** is the data point that appears most frequently in a set. In the earlier example, the mode is 72.

- The **average** of a set is the sum of the data points/the number of data points. Put more simply:

  $A = \frac{S}{N}$

  where A = average of the set, S = sum of the set, and N = number of data points in the set.

The average of the set in the earlier example is $\frac{72 + 90 + 72 + 83 + 81 + 63 + 94}{7} = \frac{555}{7} = 79.28$.

Averages

Of all statistical topics, averages are tested most frequently. Unfortunately, most average questions will not be as simple as the preceding one. Usually, the GRE will give you the average for a set and expect you to solve for the values of one or more data points in a set or the number of items in a set. Regardless of how the question is framed, you will always use the average formula: $A = \frac{S}{N}$.

If the word "average" appears on the GRE, it will always be followed by "(arithmetic mean)." For example, a question might ask: "What is the average (arithmetic mean) of 6 and 8?" Don't be swayed by the term *arithmetic mean*—it's just a fancy term for *average*.

If a company's average yearly revenue over a 10-year period was $550,000, what was the company's total revenue during that period?

SOLUTION: Since you want to solve for the sum, manipulate the average formula to isolate the sum:

$$A = \frac{S}{N}$$

$$A \times N = S$$

Substitute the given values for A and N: $550,000 \times 10 = \$5,500,000$.

Sometimes you will have to use the average formula multiple times in a question:

The average height of eight students is 64 inches. If the average height of seven of the students is 62, how tall is the eighth student?

SOLUTION: Use the average formula to determine the sum of the heights of all eight students:

$$A \times N = S$$

$$64 \times 8 = 512$$

Next, use the average formula to determine the sum of the heights of seven of the students:

$$A \times N = S$$

$$62 \times 7 = 434$$

Let the height of the eighth student = h. You know that h + (the sum of the heights of the seven other students) = (the sum of the heights of the eight students). Thus $h + 432 = 512 \rightarrow h = 80$.

An even more difficult example will use three averages in the question:

A company's average daily revenue over a 10-day period was $40,000. If the average daily revenue for the first 4 days was $25,000, what was the average daily revenue for the last 6 days?

SOLUTION: revenue for the first 4 days + revenue for the last 6 days = total revenue

Total revenue = $A \times N$ = \$40,000 × 10 = \$400,000

Revenue for the first four days = $A \times N$ = \$25,000 × 4 = \$100,000

Revenue for the last 6 days = $A \times 6$ = $6A$, where A is the average daily revenue for the last 6 days.

Thus:

$$\$100,000 + 6A = \$400,000$$

$$6A = \$300,000$$

$$A = \frac{\$300,000}{6} = \$50,000$$

Weighted Averages

When determining the average of two data points, the average will always fall in the middle of the two data points. For example, the average of 30 and 40 = $\frac{30 + 40}{2} = \frac{70}{2} = 35$.

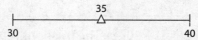

But what if one of the data points appears more often than the other data point? For example: What is the average of 30, 30, and 40? In this case, the average = $\frac{30 + 30 + 40}{3} = \frac{100}{3} = 33.33$. Now that you have added an additional data point of 30 to the set, the average is *weighted* closer to 30 than it is to 40.

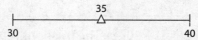

The preceding example represents a **weighted average.** You will have a weighted average any time the frequency of a data point pulls the average closer to that data point than to the other data point. In the preceding example, the fact that there were more 30s than 40s meant that the average was skewed more toward 30 than toward 40.

Quantitative Comparison Strategy

Weighted averages are tested most frequently in Quantitative Comparison questions. For these questions, it is important to keep in mind the mandate that you must *minimize calculations*! Oftentimes, one of the quantities will be the average of the set if the number of data points were equal. Think about which data point the average is skewed toward, and you will cut back on time spent calculating.

A student took 10 exams for his biology course. His average on 6 of the exams was 80. His average on the other 4 exams was 90.

Quantity A	Quantity B
His average for the course	85

Solution: Look at the columns! Notice that 85 is the average of 80 and 90. If 80 and 90 appeared with equal frequency, then the student's average for the course would be 85. However, six of the data points correspond with the average of 80 and four of the data points correspond with the average of 90. The average for the course will thus be closer to 80 than to 90 and therefore less than 85. The correct answer is B.

Though it is tested less commonly, you should also know how to calculate a weighted average. Let's use the preceding example:

A student took 10 exams for his biology course. His average on 6 of the exams was 80. His average on the other 4 exams was 90. What was his average for the 10 exams?

- **Approach 1: Use the average formula.** For the 4 courses in which he averaged 90, the sum is 90(4). For the 6 courses in which he averaged 80, the sum is 80(6). The average for all 10 courses is thus $\frac{80(6) + 90(4)}{10} = \frac{840}{10} = 84$.
- **Approach 2: Use the weights.**

Note that $\frac{80(6) + 90(4)}{10} = 80(\frac{6}{10}) + 90(\frac{4}{10})$. The fractions represent the weight of each data point as a piece of the total weights of the set. From this, you can extrapolate the following formula:

$$\text{weighted average} = \frac{\text{frequency of data point 1}}{\text{total number of data points}} \times \text{data point 1} +$$
$$\frac{\text{frequency of data point}}{\text{total number of data points}} \times \text{average of data point 2}$$

Note that this approach works when the number of data points is represented as a ratio or percent as well!

For the first 10 days of a 30-day period, a stock's average return was $6.00. For the last 20 days of the 30-day period, the stock's average return was $12.00. What was the stock's average return for the 30-day period?

SOLUTION: The two data points are $6.00 and $12.00. The frequency of the $6.00 data point is $\frac{10}{30} = \frac{1}{3}$. The frequency of the $12.00 data point is $\frac{20}{30} = \frac{2}{3}$. The weighted average is thus $(\frac{1}{3})6 + (\frac{2}{3})12 = 2 + 8 = 10$.

More on the Median

Earlier, the section defined the median as *the middle data point when the data points are in increasing order.* Though calculating the median for small sets simply requires that you put the data points in increasing order and find the middle value, it becomes trickier when the set has a large number of data points. For example, if you want the median of 51 data points, it would be too time-consuming to list all of them. Instead, you should recognize that the median will be the 26th data point.

Why? Because there will be 25 data points below this value and 25 data points above this value.

> A certain test was administered to 29 students. 6 students scored 60, 8 students scored 73, and 15 students scored 79. What was the median score for the 29 students?

> **SOLUTION:** The median is the 15th-largest (or smallest) score. The smallest 6 data points have a value of 60. The next 8 data points have a value of 73. These two groups account for the first 14 data points. The next data point will thus equal the median. That data point occurs in the last set. Since all the data points in the last set are 79, the median is 79.

Standard Deviation

Standard deviation refers to how far from the mean the numbers in a set typically fall. Two sets can have the same mean and the same number of items, but completely different spreads from the mean. The concept of standard deviation is employed to represent this spread. The greater the average spread of the data, the greater the standard deviation. Look at the following three sets, all of which have the same mean:

> 2, 2, 2, 2, 2
> 0, 1, 2, 3, 4
> –2, 0, 2, 4, 6

In the first set, all the data points are equal, so there is no spread from the mean. The standard deviation is thus zero. In the second set, the distance between successive numbers is one, so the standard deviation is greater than in the first set. In the third set, the distance between successive numbers is two, so the standard deviation is even greater than in the second set.

You might be wondering what the standard deviations of the first and second sets are. Fortunately, *the GRE almost never tests the exact formula for standard deviation*. It does, however, expect you to understand the concept and to be able to *compare* the standard deviation of different sets of numbers.

> Which of the following sets has the greatest standard deviation?

> (A) {4, 4, 4, 4, 4}
> (B) {3, 4, 4, 4, 5}
> (C) {3, 4, 4, 4, 8}
> (D) {0, 2, 4, 4, 12}
> (E) {1, 4, 4, 4, 7}

> **SOLUTION:** Look at how the choices compare to A, which has a spread of zero. The further the values in a set move away from 4, the greater the standard deviation. The values in Choice D spread the most from 4. Thus the correct answer is D.

Exercise: Statistics

Discrete Quantitative Questions

1. Bob's average for three tests was 83. If he scored 72 and 94 on the first two tests, what was his score on the third test?

   (A) 81
   (B) 82
   (C) 83
   (D) 84
   (E) 85

2. Janet's average for four tests was 75. If she scored 63 and 83 on the first two tests, what was her average for the last two tests?

   (A) 73
   (B) 75
   (C) 77
   (D) 79
   (E) 81

3. The average of a and b is 70. The average of a and c is 100. What is $b - c$?

   (A) −60
   (B) −30
   (C) 15
   (D) 30
   (E) 60

4. The set of numbers 2, 3, 5, 9, 11, x is in increasing order. If the average of the set equals the median, what is x?

   (A) 12
   (B) 14
   (C) 15
   (D) 30
   (E) 42

5. In 2012, a store's average monthly revenue was $20,000. For the first 10 months of the year, the store's average monthly revenue was $18,000. If the revenue in December was 50% greater than the revenue in November, what was the store's revenue in November?

   Ⓐ 24,000
   Ⓑ 30,000
   Ⓒ 36,000
   Ⓓ 48,000
   Ⓔ 56,000

For this question, write your answer in the box.

6. Three crates have an average weight of 70 pounds and a median weight of 90 pounds. What is the maximum possible weight, in pounds, of the lightest box?

                              ☐

For this question, indicate all of the answer choices that apply.

7. A real estate agent is selling 5 homes priced at $200,000, $240,000, $300,000, $320,000, and $350,000. If the price of the $200,000 home increases by $20,000, which of the following must be true?

   Ⓐ The median price will increase.
   Ⓑ The median price will decrease.
   Ⓒ The average price will increase.
   Ⓓ The standard deviation will decrease.
   Ⓔ The range of the prices will decrease.

Amount spent per day	$100	$120	$130	$170	$200
Number of days	5	4	3	7	6

8. The preceding table shows a business's spending over a 25-day period, in thousands of dollars. For each number amount spent in the first row, the second row gives the number of days that the business spent that amount. What was the median amount of money that the business spent during the 25-day period?

   Ⓐ $100,000
   Ⓑ $120,000
   Ⓒ $130,000
   Ⓓ $170,000
   Ⓔ $200,000

9. If a is the standard deviation of b, c, and d, what is the standard deviation of $b + 3$, $c + 3$, and $d + 3$, in terms of a?

  (A) a
  (B) $a + 3$
  (C) $a + 6$
  (D) $a + 9$
  (E) $3a$

10. A certain company has only directors and managers. The company has 300 directors and 200 managers. If the average age of the directors is 42 and the average age of the managers is 38, what is the average age of all the company's employees?

  (A) 39.8
  (B) 40
  (C) 40.2
  (D) 40.4
  (E) 41

11. A student's average score for 10 tests was x. The grader then discovered that there was an error on two of the tests. On one of the tests, the student's score should have been 10 points lower. On another test, the student's score should have been 20 points higher. After the grader corrects these mistakes, what is the student's new average, in terms of x?

  (A) $x - 1$
  (B) x
  (C) $x + 1$
  (D) $x + 10$
  (E) $x + 20$

12. What is the average of n, $n + 1$, $n + 7$, $n + 9$, and $n + 13$, in terms of n?

  (A) $n + 2$
  (B) $n + 3$
  (C) $n + 6$
  (D) $n + 8$
  (E) $n + 15$

Quantitative Comparison Questions

Each of the following questions consists of two quantities, Quantity A and Quantity B. You are to compare the two quantities. You may use additional information centered above the two quantities if additional information is given. Choose

- Ⓐ   if Quantity A is greater
- Ⓑ   if Quantity B is greater
- Ⓒ   if the two quantities are equal
- Ⓓ   if the relationship between the two quantities cannot be determined

At a certain company, the average annual salary of the college graduates is $73,000, and the average annual salary of the people who did not graduate from college is $52,000.

QUANTITY A	QUANTITY B	
1. The average annual salary for all the employees of the company	$52,000	Ⓐ Ⓑ Ⓒ Ⓓ

QUANTITY A	QUANTITY B	
2. The average of 6, 6, 7, 7, 7, 7, 8, and 10	7	Ⓐ Ⓑ Ⓒ Ⓓ

The average age of the boys at a certain school is 16.3.
The average age of the girls at the same school is 16.8.

QUANTITY A	QUANTITY B	
3. The ratio of boys to girls at the school	$\frac{1}{2}$	Ⓐ Ⓑ Ⓒ Ⓓ

$$a > b$$

QUANTITY A	QUANTITY B	
4. The average of a, a, and b	The average of a, a, a, b, and b	Ⓐ Ⓑ Ⓒ Ⓓ

The average of five positive integers is 20.

QUANTITY A	QUANTITY B	
5. The greatest possible range of the five integers	99	Ⓐ Ⓑ Ⓒ Ⓓ

	QUANTITY A	QUANTITY B	
6.	The average of 2, 19, 34, and 60	The average of 0, 2, 19, 34, and 60	Ⓐ Ⓑ Ⓒ Ⓓ

$$b > a > 0$$

	QUANTITY A	QUANTITY B	
7.	The average of the reciprocals of a and b	$(b + a)/ab$	Ⓐ Ⓑ Ⓒ Ⓓ

$a, b,$ and c are positive integers

	QUANTITY A	QUANTITY B	
8.	The standard deviation of a, b, and c	The standard deviation of $2a$, $2b$, and $2c$	Ⓐ Ⓑ Ⓒ Ⓓ

Exercise Answers

Discrete Quantitative Questions

1. **C** The sum of Bob's three test scores $= A \times N = 83 \times 3 = 249$. His score for the two given tests $= 166$. His score for the third test is thus $249 - 166 = 83$.

2. **C** The sum of Janet's four test scores $= A \times N = 75 \times 4 = 300$. The sum of her first two test scores $= 63 + 83 = 146$. The sum of her last two test scores thus equals $300 - 146 = 154$. Her average for these last two tests $= \frac{S}{N} = \frac{154}{2} = 77$.

3. **A** Use the average formula for both sets.

$$A = \frac{S}{N}$$
$$\frac{a+b}{2} = 70$$
$$a + b = 140$$
$$A = \frac{S}{N}$$
$$\frac{a+c}{2} = 100$$
$$a + c = 200$$

Now set up a system of equations to solve for $b - c$:

$$a + b = 140$$
$$-(a + c = 200)$$
$$\downarrow$$
$$a + b = 140$$
$$-a - c = -200$$
$$\downarrow$$
$$b - c = -60$$

4. **A** Since the set has an even number of items, the median is the average of the two middle terms: $\frac{5+9}{2} = 7$. The average of the set is $\frac{2+3+5+9+11+x}{6} = \frac{30+x}{6}$. You are told that the average equals the median, so:

$$\frac{30+x}{6} = 7$$

$$30 + x = 42$$

$$x = 12$$

5. **A** the revenue for the entire year = average monthly revenue × number of months = $20,000 × 12 = $240,000. The revenue for the first 10 months = average monthly revenue × number of months = $18,000 × 10 = $180,000. The revenue for the last two months is thus $240,000 – $180,000 = $60,000. Let n = the revenue in November. Since the revenue in December was 50% greater than the revenue in November, the revenue in December = $1.5n = \frac{3}{2}n$. Solve for n:

$$n + \tfrac{3}{2}n = 60,000$$

$$\tfrac{5}{2}n = 60,000$$

$$n = 24,000$$

6. **30** The sum of the weights of the crates = $A \times N = 70 \times 3 = 210$. Let the weight of the lightest box = l and the weight of the heaviest box = h. Thus

$$l + 90 + h = 210$$

$$l + h = 120$$

To maximize the weight of the lightest box, you must minimize the weight of the heaviest box. Since the heaviest box is to the right of the median, its weight can be no less than the median weight. Thus the least weight for the heaviest box = the median = 90. Substitute 90 for h:

$$l + 90 = 120$$

$$l = 30$$

7. **C, D, and E** The median value of the original set is $300,000. The increase in the price of the smallest home is too small to affect the median. Eliminate Choices A and B. The $20,000 increase means that the sum of the set will increase. If the sum of a set increases and the number of items stay the same, then the average must increase. Choice C is true. The increase in the smallest price decreases the spread of all the data points. Thus the standard deviation will decrease. Choice D is true. The increase in the smallest price will decrease the distance between the smallest and greatest values in the set. The range will thus decrease. Choice E is true.

8. **D** The median refers to the middle data point when all the data points are in increasing order. Since there are 25 data points, the median will be the 13th largest data point (since there are 12 data points below this value and 12 above it). The bottom 12 data points are in the $100,000; $120,000; and $130,000 columns. The 13th data point is thus in the next column: $170,000.

9. **A** Standard deviation is a measure of the typical spread of the data points from the mean. If all of the data points in a set are increased by the same

value, the spread between the data points will not change. Thus the standard deviation will not change. Since the standard deviation of the original set was a, the standard deviation of the new set is also a.

10. **D** Since the frequency of the data points differs, this is a weighted average. Let's use this formula: weighted average = (frequency of data point 1/total number of data points) × data point 1 + (frequency of data point 2/total number of data points) × data point 2. In the question, the data points are the average ages for the two groups. Let the average age for the directors be data point 1 and the average age for the managers be data point 2. Thus the weighted average = $(\frac{300}{500})42 + (\frac{200}{500})38 = (\frac{3}{5})42 + (\frac{2}{5})38 = 25.2 + 15.2 = 40.4$.

11. **C** Since the choices have variables, you can plug in numbers.

    Step 1: Let $x = 100$.

    Step 2: Answer the question when $x = 100$. Originally, the sum of the scores is thus $A \times N = 100 \times 10 = 1,000$. After the corrections, one of the scores will decrease by 10 points, and one of the scores will increase by 20 points. The net change is thus $(20 - 10) = 10$. The new sum is 1,010. The new average is thus $\frac{S}{N} = 1,010/10 = 101$. The goal is 101.

    Step 3: Substitute 100 for x in the choices, and identify which choice matches the target of 101.

12. **C** The sum of the terms is $n + (n + 1) + (n + 7) + (n + 9) + (n + 13) = 5n + 30$. Since there are 5 terms, the average of the set is $\frac{5n + 30}{5} = n + 6$.

Quantitative Comparison Questions

1. **A** The average for a set must fall between the average of each subset. Thus the average annual salary must be greater than $52,000.

2. **A** Don't calculate! Look at how the average of 6, 6, 8, and 10 compares to 7. The average of those numbers is $\frac{6 + 6 + 8 + 10}{4} = \frac{30}{4} > 7$. Quantity A has four numbers with an average of 7 (7, 7, 7, and 7) and four numbers with an average greater than 7. Its average must therefore be greater than 7.

3. **D** Without knowing where the average age for the entire school falls in relation to 16.3 and 16.8, it is not possible to determine the ratio of boys to girls.

4. **A** Express Quantities A and B algebraically:

    Quantity A → $A = \frac{S}{N} = \frac{2a + b}{3}$

    Quantity B → $A = \frac{S}{N} = \frac{3a + 2b}{5}$

The comparison is now:

	Quantity A	Quantity B
	$\frac{2a + b}{3}$	$\frac{3a + 2b}{5}$
Cross-multiply:	↓	
	$5(2a + b)$	$3(3a + 2b)$
Distribute:	↓	
	$10a + 5b$	$9a + 6b$
Subtract $9a$ from both columns:	↓	
	$a + 5b$	$6b$
Subtract $5b$ from both columns:	↓	
	a	b

Since you are told that $a > b$, Quantity A is greater.

5. **B** To maximize the range, minimize the smallest value and maximize the greatest value. Since the terms are positive integers, the minimum value for an item in the set is 1. To maximize the greatest value, minimize the rest of the terms. In this case, that would mean making them all equal to 1. Therefore:

$$1 + 1 + 1 + 1 + x = \text{the sum of the set} = 100$$

$$4 + x = 100$$

$$x = 96$$

The maximum possible range is $96 - 1 = 95$. Quantity B is greater.

6. **A** The difference between the two sets is the 0 in the second set. Since 0 is less than the average of 2, 19, 34, and 60, the average of the second set must be smaller than the average of the first set. Quantity A is greater.

7. **B** Express Quantity A algebraically:

$$\frac{\frac{1}{a} + \frac{1}{b}}{2} = \frac{\frac{b + a}{ab}}{2} = \frac{b + a}{2ab}$$

The numerators of the two quantities are the same. Since the denominator of Quantity B is smaller, that fraction is larger.

8. **B** In Quantity B, each term in Quantity A is doubled. The spread of the set will thus be doubled. Since the spread in Quantity B is greater, the standard deviation of Quantity B is greater.

Rates

Rate questions always come in one of two forms: distance or work. In both cases, there will be a constant relationship between the rate, time, and work or distance:

rate × time = distance

or

rate × time = work

The primary difference in the two equations is the following:

For distance questions, rate represents **distance per unit of time** and the result represents some distance traveled. For work questions, rate represents **output per unit of time** and the result represents the number of units produced (such as widgets, lawns mowed, papers, etc.).

Distance Problems: Rate × Time = Distance

The rate × time = distance formula is almost always the best way to solve distance equations. In simpler questions, you will be given two components of the formula and asked to solve for the third.

If a car travels at a constant rate of 50 miles per hour, in how many hours will the car have traveled 325 miles?

Step 1: Set up the rate × time = distance chart:

rate (mi/hr) × time (hr) = distance (miles)

   ↓   ↓   ↓

   50   × t = 325

Step 2: Solve for t:

$$50t = 325$$

$$t = 6.5 \text{ hours}$$

Unit Conversions

When solving rate questions, be sure that you use the same unit throughout the question. If the rate is expressed per minute, then you must express time in minutes, not seconds or hours.

Running at a constant rate, Bob travels 5 miles in 1 hour. If Bob travels for 20 minutes, how many miles does he travel?

Step 1: Set up the $r \times t = d$ chart:

rate (mi/hr) × time (hr) = distance (miles)

Bob's rate is distance/time = 5 miles/1 hour, and his time is 20 minutes. It might be tempting to simply substitute these values into the original formula, but this would be incorrect. Why? Because the units do not match up. The rate is expressed per hour, whereas the time is expressed in minutes. Before plugging the values into the formula, you should convert the time from 20 minutes to $\frac{1}{3}$ hour.

Step 2: Once you have done so, you can plug the values into the formula:

$$\text{rate (mi/hr)} \times \text{time (hr)} = \text{distance (miles)}$$

$$\downarrow \qquad\qquad \downarrow \qquad\qquad \downarrow$$

$$5 \qquad \times \qquad \tfrac{1}{3} \qquad = \qquad \tfrac{5}{3}$$

Multiple Rates

For distance questions, the $r \times t = d$ table is particularly useful for problems that involve multiple rates or multiple travelers. In these situations, you will generally want to create two rows on the $r \times t = d$ table, fill them in with the appropriate values or variables, and use the resulting expressions to identify a relationship between the distances.

Bob and Jack start at opposite ends of a 200-mile track. Bob travels at a constant rate of 50 miles per hour and Jack travels at a constant rate of 75 miles per hour. If they start traveling toward each other at the same time, in how many hours will they meet?

Step 1: Put the given information into the $r \times t = d$ table:

$$\text{rate (mi/hr)} \times \text{time (hr)} = \text{distance (miles)}$$

$$\downarrow \qquad\qquad \downarrow \qquad\qquad \downarrow$$

Bob: $50 \quad \times \quad t \quad = \quad 50t$

Jack: $75 \quad \times \quad t \quad = \quad 75t$

Note that there are two rows—one for Jack and one for Bob. You are asked to solve for the amount of time they travel, so let t represent time. Since Bob and Jack start and end at the same time, they will each have traveled for t hours. In terms of t, Bob travels $50t$ miles and Jack travels $75t$ miles.

Now you must identify the relationship between these distances. Since they are traveling toward each other, Bob will travel some of the 200 miles and Jack will travel the remaining distance. Thus the distances the two travel must add up to 200. Algebraically, you can represent this relationship as:

Bob's distance + Jack's distance = 200

$$\downarrow \qquad\qquad \downarrow \qquad\qquad \downarrow$$

$$50t \qquad + \qquad 75t \qquad = 200$$

Step 2: Solve for t:

$$125t = 200$$

$$t = \tfrac{8}{5} \text{ hour}$$

Train A and train B start at the same point and travel in opposite directions. Train A travels at a constant rate of 80 miles per hour, and train B travels at a constant rate of 60 miles per hour. If train A starts traveling 2 hours before train B, how many miles will train A have traveled when the two trains are 720 miles apart?

Step 1: Put the given information into the $r \times t = d$ table. The rate for trains A and B are given as 80 miles per hour and 60 miles per hour, respectively. To solve for the number of miles Train A will have traveled, you need to determine how many hours Train A traveled. Let t = the number of hours Train A travels. Since Train A started 2 hours before Train B, and the two trains stop traveling at the same time, Train B must have traveled $t - 2$ hours. Thus in terms of t, Train A's distance is $80t$ and Train B's distance is $60(t - 2)$.

rate (mi/hr) × time (hr) = distance (miles)

↓   ↓   ↓

Train A: 80   × t = $80t$

Train B: 60   × $t - 2$ = $60(t - 2)$

As in the previous example, it is essential to identify the relationship between the two trains' distances. For the two trains to end up 720 miles apart, Train A must cover some portion of the 720 miles and Train B must cover the rest. Thus the sum of their distances is 720. Expressed algebraically, the equation is:

Train A's distance + Train B's distance = 720

↓   ↓   ↓

$80t$ + $60(t - 2)$ = 720

Step 2: Now solve for t:

$$80t + 60t - 120 = 720$$
$$140t = 840$$
$$t = 6$$

You are asked to solve for the number of miles Train A traveled, so plug 6 in for Train A's time:

rate (mi/hr) × time (hr) = distance (miles)

↓   ↓   ↓

80   ×   6   = 80(6)

Train A's distance is $80 \times 6 = 480$.

Don't Average Rates!

Look at the following question:

> Sarah goes on a 600-mile trip. She travels at a constant rate of 50 miles per hour for the first 300 miles of the trip, and at a constant rate of 100 miles per hour for the last 300 miles of the trip. What is Sarah's average speed in miles per hour for the entire trip?
>
> (A) $\frac{200}{3}$
> (B) 70
> (C) 75
> (D) 80
> (E) 85

Solution: Many test-takers are tempted to average the rate of 50 and 100 to arrive at an average speed of 75. Though perhaps intuitive, this would be incorrect. Why? Because Sarah spent more time traveling at a rate of 50 miles per hour than at a rate of 100 miles per hour. Her overall rate will thus be closer to 50 than to 100. Based on this logic alone, you can immediately eliminate C, D, and E.

To actually calculate her average speed, you should use the rate formula: rate $= \frac{distance}{time}$. The total distance is 600 miles, so you need to calculate the total time. To determine the total time, you should determine the time for each part of the trip, and then add these up. Use the $r \times t = d$ formula to determine the time for each part of the trip:

$$\text{rate (mi/hr)} \times \text{time (hr)} = \text{distance (miles)}$$
$$\downarrow \qquad \downarrow \qquad \downarrow$$

Part 1: $50 \times x = 300$
Part 2: $100 \times y = 300$

Solve for x:

$50x = 300$
$x = 6$

Solve for y:

$100y = 300$
$y = 3$

The total time is $x + y = 6 + 3 = 9$. The average speed for the trip is thus $\frac{600}{9} = \frac{200}{3}$.

The correct answer is Choice A.

Work Problems: Rate × Time = Work

The second type of rate problem involves work. In contrast to distance problems, work problems are concerned with some output per unit of time. An output can be something produced (such as widgets, cups, cars, etc.) or a job done (such as mowing a lawn, cooking a meal, writing a paper, etc.). In both cases, you want to use the work formula, though as you will see, the way you express work will differ. Let's look at a simple work question:

> If a machine produces pencils at a constant rate of 1,500 pencils per hour, in how many hours will the machine have produced 6,750 pencils?

SOLUTION: Put the given values into the rate × time = work (RTW) table. The machine's rate is 1,500 pencils/hour, and its output (work) is 6,750 pencils. Since you are trying to solve for time, assign a variable: t

rate (pencils/hr) × time (hr) = work (pencils)

$\downarrow$ $\quad\quad$ $\downarrow$ $\quad$ $\downarrow$

$1{,}500 \quad \times \quad t \quad = 6{,}750$

Solve for t:

$$1{,}500t = 6{,}750$$

$$t = \frac{6{,}750}{1{,}500} = 4.5$$

Let's look at another example, this time with work represented as some job done instead of units produced:

> Working at a constant rate, Bob can mow 3 same-sized lawns in 5 hours. How many hours will it take Bob to mow 2 same-sized lawns?

SOLUTION: Set up the RTW table. Remember that rate $= \frac{\text{work}}{\text{time}}$, so Bob's rate will be $\frac{\text{lawns}}{\text{hour}} = \frac{3}{5}$.

rate (lawns/hr) × time (hr) = work (lawns)

$\downarrow$ $\quad\quad$ $\downarrow$ $\quad$ $\downarrow$

$\frac{3}{5} \quad \times \quad t \quad = 2$

Solve for t:

$$\frac{3}{5}t = 2$$

$$t = 2\left(\frac{5}{3}\right) = \frac{10}{3} \text{ hours}$$

Combining Rates

In certain work questions, you will be given the individual rates of two or more elements and will be asked about what happens when they work together.

> Working alone at a constant rate, Bob can mow 1 lawn in 3 hours. Working alone at a constant rate, Jack can mow 1 same-sized lawn in 8 hours. If Bob and Jack work together but independently at their respective constant rates, how many hours will it take them to mow half a same-sized lawn?

SOLUTION: Bob's rate is $\frac{\text{work}}{\text{time}} = \frac{1}{3}$. Jack's rate is $\frac{\text{work}}{\text{time}} = \frac{1}{8}$. To determine how long it takes them to mow the lawn when they work together, you need their combined rate. *The combined rate is the sum of their individual rates.* In this case, their combined rate is $\frac{1}{8} + \frac{1}{3} = \frac{11}{24}$. This means that, when they work together, Bob and Jack can mow $\frac{11}{24}$ of a lawn in 1 hour. Now input this rate into the $r \times t = w$ formula:

$$\text{rate (lawns/hr)} \times \text{time (hr)} = \text{work (lawns)}$$
$$\downarrow \qquad\qquad \downarrow \qquad \downarrow$$
$$\frac{11}{24} \qquad \times \qquad t \qquad = \frac{1}{2}$$

Note that you input $\frac{1}{2}$ for the total work done, since the question is asking for the time necessary for them to mow *half* the lawn.

Solve for t:

$$(\tfrac{11}{24})t = \tfrac{1}{2}$$
$$t = (\tfrac{1}{2})(\tfrac{24}{11}) = \tfrac{12}{11} \text{ hours}$$

Exercise: Rates

Discrete Quantitative Questions

For this question, write your answer in the box.

1. Susan takes a 45-mile trip. She travels the first 15 miles in 40 minutes. She travels the remaining 30 miles at double the rate at which she traveled the first 15 miles. What is her average speed for the entire trip in miles per minute?

   ┌─────────────────────────────┐
   │   │
   └─────────────────────────────┘

2. Boris ran the first 12 miles of a 24-mile race in 1.8 hours. If his rate for the entire race was 6 miles per hour, how many hours did it take him to run the last 12 miles?

   (A) $\frac{5}{3}$

   (B) $\frac{9}{5}$

   (C) 2

   (D) 2.2

   (E) 6

3. Working at a constant rate, a certain hose can fill a pool in 10 minutes. Working at a different constant rate, another hose can fill the same pool in 15 minutes. If the two hoses work together but independently to fill the pool after it is half full, how many minutes will it take the hoses to fill the pool?

   (A) 3

   (B) 4.5

   (C) 5

   (D) 6

   (E) 12.5

4. Four machines, working independently at the same constant rate, can fill a production lot in 3 hours. How many of these machines would be needed to fill the lot in 30 minutes?

   (A) 12

   (B) 24

   (C) 36

   (D) 40

   (E) 48

5. Working at a constant rate, a cook can create a batch of pasta in 20 minutes. Another cook, working at a constant rate, can create the same batch of pasta in 10 minutes. If the two cooks work together but independently, how many hours will it take them to create 3 batches of pasta?

   (A) $\frac{1}{4}$

   (B) $\frac{1}{3}$

   (C) $\frac{1}{2}$

   (D) $\frac{3}{5}$

   (E) 2

6. A hose fills an empty tank with water at a rate of 15 liters/second. At the same time, water drains from the tank at a rate of 10 liters/second. If the tank has a capacity of 200 liters, in how many seconds will the tank be half full?

   (A) 4

   (B) 8

   (C) 20

   (D) 25

   (E) 40

7. Working together at their respective constant rates, Bob and Sam can mow a lawn in 12 hours. If Bob's rate is twice Sam's rate, how many hours would it take Bob, working alone, to mow the lawn?

   (A) 15

   (B) 18

   (C) 24

   (D) 32

   (E) 36

8. Working alone at a constant rate, Machine A can produce 15 widgets in 2 minutes. Working alone at a constant rate, Machine B can produce 20 widgets in 3 minutes. If the two machines start working at the same time, after how many minutes will Machine A have produced 40 more widgets than Machine B?

Ⓐ 12
Ⓑ 24
Ⓒ 36
Ⓓ 48
Ⓔ 60

9. The birthrate of a certain species is approximately 500 organisms per day. The death rate of the species is approximately 300 organisms per day. If the population has 50,000 organisms at the beginning of a certain year, approximately how many organisms will be in the population at the end of the year?

Ⓐ 73,000
Ⓑ 123,000
Ⓒ 159,500
Ⓓ 232,500
Ⓔ 293,000

For Questions 10 and 11, write your answer in the box.

10. Bob and Jack start traveling at the same time at constant rates and in the same direction. If Bob's rate is 2 miles per hour greater than Jack's, after how many hours will Bob and Jack be $\frac{1}{5}$ of a mile apart?

11. Two scientists, working at the same constant rate, can fill 8 equally sized beakers in 10 minutes. How many scientists would be needed to fill 24 of these beakers in 5 minutes?

Quantitative Comparison Questions

Each of the following questions consists of two quantities, Quantity A and Quantity B. You are to compare the two quantities. You may use additional information centered above the two quantities if additional information is given. Choose

- Ⓐ if Quantity A is greater
- Ⓑ if Quantity B is greater
- Ⓒ if the two quantities are equal
- Ⓓ if the relationship between the two quantities cannot be determined

---

Sally travels the first 30 miles of a 60-mile trip at 50 miles per hour and the last 30 miles of the trip at 40 miles per hour.

QUANTITY A	QUANTITY B	
1. Sally's average speed for the trip, in miles per hour	45	Ⓐ Ⓑ Ⓒ Ⓓ

Dennis can cook x cakes in 3 hours, and he can cook y pies in 0.5 hours, where $x > y$.

QUANTITY A	QUANTITY B	
2. The number of cakes that Dennis can cook in 6 hours	The number of pies that Dennis can cook in 3 hours	Ⓐ Ⓑ Ⓒ Ⓓ

Traveling at a constant rate, Jake ran a lap in x minutes.

QUANTITY A	QUANTITY B	
3. The number of minutes it would take Jake to run the lap if he doubled his rate	$\frac{x}{2}$	Ⓐ Ⓑ Ⓒ Ⓓ

Car A and Car B start at opposite ends of a 200-mile track and begin driving toward each other at the same time. When the cars meet, Car A is 80 miles from its starting point.

QUANTITY A	QUANTITY B	
4. The rate of car A	The rate of car B	Ⓐ Ⓑ Ⓒ Ⓓ

Car A starts a race 10 miles behind Car B and ends the race 15 miles ahead of Car B.

QUANTITY A	QUANTITY B	
5. The distance that Car A traveled	30 miles	Ⓐ Ⓑ Ⓒ Ⓓ

A tank that is half full is filled with gas at a constant rate of 3 liters per minute.

	QUANTITY A	QUANTITY B	
6.	The number of minutes it will take to fill the tank completely.	30	Ⓐ Ⓑ Ⓒ Ⓓ

Working at the same constant rate, 8 machines can produce 7 computers in 6 hours.

	QUANTITY A	QUANTITY B	
7.	The number of machines needed to produce 21 computers in 18 hours	8	Ⓐ Ⓑ Ⓒ Ⓓ

Exercise Answers

Discrete Quantitative Questions

1. $\frac{9}{16}$ To determine average speed, use the rate formula: $r = \frac{d}{t}$. You are told that the distance for the trip is 45 miles, so the formula now reads $r = \frac{45}{t}$. You must determine the time spent on the trip. To do so, determine the time for the first part of the trip and for the second part, and add up these quantities. You are told that the time for the first part of the trip is 40 minutes. For the second part of the trip, use the formula: $t = \frac{d}{r}$. The distance for the second part of the trip is 30 miles. The rate for the second part of the trip is twice the rate for the first part. The rate for the first part is $\frac{15}{40} = \frac{3}{8}$, so the rate for the second part of the trip is $2 \times \frac{3}{8} = \frac{3}{4}$. Plug these values into the formula for time and arrive at $t = 30/(\frac{3}{4}) = 40$. The time for the second part of the trip is also 40 minutes, so the time for the entire trip is 80 minutes. Now you can plug this value into the rate formula: $r = \frac{d}{t} = \frac{45}{80}$. Reduce and arrive at $\frac{9}{16}$.

2. **D** Boris's rate for the entire 24-mile race is 6 miles per hour. Plugging these values into the $r \times t = d$ formula, you arrive at

$$6t = 24$$

$$t = 4$$

Thus the whole race took him 4 hours. If it took him 1.8 hours to run the first part of the race, then the second part of the race took him $4 - 1.8 = 2.2$ hours.

3. **A** To get the combined rate of the two hoses, you should add up their rates. Rate = $\frac{work}{time}$, so the rate of the first hose is $\frac{1}{10}$ and the rate of the second hose is $\frac{1}{15}$. Add up these rates: $\frac{1}{10} + \frac{1}{15} = \frac{5}{30} = \frac{1}{6}$. Since the pool is already half full, the work that the two hoses need to do is only $\frac{1}{2}$. Now plug these values into the $r \times t = w$ formula.

$$r \times t = w$$

$$\tfrac{1}{6}t = \tfrac{1}{2}$$

Solve for t: $t = \dfrac{\frac{1}{2}}{\frac{1}{6}} = \tfrac{1}{2} \times 6 = 3$.

4. **B** Let r be the rate of each machine. If 4 work together, their combined rate is $4r$. You are told that these 4 machines will fill the production lot in 3 hours. Plug these values into the $r \times t = w$ formula:

$$r \times t = w$$
$$\downarrow$$
$$4r \times 3 = 1$$
$$12r = 1$$
$$r = \tfrac{1}{12}$$

The rate of each machine, in production lots/hour, is $\tfrac{1}{12}$. Now plug this value into the $r \times t = w$ formula to determine how many machines, y, would be necessary to fill the lot in 30 minutes. Since your rate is in lots/hour, express 30 minutes as 0.5 hours.

$$r \times t = w$$
$$\downarrow$$
$$y\left(\tfrac{1}{12}\right) \times 0.5 = 1$$

Solve for y:

$$\tfrac{y}{12} \times \tfrac{1}{2} = 1$$
$$\tfrac{y}{24} = 1$$
$$y = 24$$

5. **B** Rate $= \dfrac{\text{work}}{\text{time}}$, so the rate of the first cook, in batches per minute, is $\tfrac{1}{20}$, and the rate of the second cook, in batches per minute, is $\tfrac{1}{10}$. To get their combined rate, add up these rates: $\tfrac{1}{10} + \tfrac{1}{20} = \tfrac{3}{20}$. To determine how long it will take the cooks to produce 3 batches, use the $r \times t = w$ formula:

$$r \times t = w$$
$$\downarrow$$
$$\tfrac{3t}{20} = 3$$

Solve for t: $t = 20$ minutes. The question asks for how many *hours* it will take, so convert minutes to hours. 20 minutes is $\tfrac{1}{3}$ of an hour.

6. **C** The rate at which the tank fills will be the difference between the rate of the hose filling the tank and the rate at which the tank empties: 15 liters/second – 10 liters/second = 5 liters/second. Since the question asks for the time at which the tank will be half full, the work is 100 liters. Now use the $r \times t = w$ formula to solve the problem:

$$r \times t = w$$

$$\downarrow$$

$$5 \times t = 100$$

Solve for t: $t = 20$ seconds.

7. **B** Let s = Sam's rate. Bob's rate is thus $2s$, and their combined rate is $s + 2s = 3s$. Now use the $r \times t = w$ formula to find the value for s.

$$r \times t = w$$

$$\downarrow$$

$$3s \times 12 = 1$$

$$36s = 1$$

$$s = \tfrac{1}{36}$$

Bob's rate is twice Sam's rate, so Bob's rate is $2(\tfrac{1}{36}) = \tfrac{1}{18}$. Now plug this rate into the $r \times t = w$ formula.

$$r \times t = w$$

$$\downarrow$$

$$\tfrac{1}{18} \times t = 1$$

$$t = 18$$

8. **D** Use the $r \times t = w$ table to determine the number of minutes it will take Machine A to produce 40 more widgets than machine B. Machine A's rate is widgets/minute $= \tfrac{15}{2}$, and Machine B's rate is widgets/minute $= \tfrac{20}{3}$. Since the machines start at the same time, use t to represent each of their times. Plug these values into the table.

$$r \times t = w$$

$$\downarrow$$

Machine A $\tfrac{15}{2} t = \tfrac{15t}{2}$

Machine B $\tfrac{20}{3} t = \tfrac{20t}{3}$

Represented algebraically, Machine A's work is thus $\tfrac{15t}{2}$ and Machine B's work is $\tfrac{20t}{3}$. You know that Machine A produces 40 more widgets, so $\tfrac{15t}{2} = 40 + \tfrac{20t}{3}$. Now solve for t:

Bring t to one side: $\tfrac{15t}{2} - \tfrac{20t}{3} = 40$

$$\downarrow$$

Get a common denominator: $\tfrac{45t}{6} - \tfrac{40t}{6} = 40$

$$\downarrow$$

Combine like terms: $\frac{5t}{6} = 40$

$\downarrow$

Multiply both sides by $\frac{6}{5}$ to solve for t: $t = 40 \times \left(\frac{6}{5}\right) = 48$

9. **B** To answer this question, you need to determine the net increase in the population during the year. If 500 organisms were born each day and 300 organisms died each day, then the population increased at a constant rate of 200 organisms/day. For the entire year, the population increase will be 200 organisms/day × 365 days = 73,000. The approximate total population will thus be 50,000 + 73,000 = 123,000.

10. $\frac{1}{10}$ Use the $r \times t = d$ table. Let j = Jack's rate and $j + 2$ = Bob's rate:

rate (mi/hr) × time (hr) = distance (miles)

$\downarrow$ $\downarrow$ $\downarrow$

Jack: j × t $= jt$

Bob: $(j + 2)$ × t $= (j + 2)(t)$

If they end up $\frac{1}{5}$ of a mile apart, then Bob's distance must be $\frac{1}{5}$ mile more than Jack's. Expressed algebraically, you arrive at $(j + 2)(t) = \frac{1}{5} + jt$. Solve for t:

$$(j + 2)(t) = \frac{1}{5} + jt$$

$$jt + 2t = \frac{1}{5} + jt$$

$$2t = \frac{1}{5}$$

$$t = \frac{1}{10}$$

11. **12** Use the $r \times t = w$ formula, where x is the rate of each scientist:

rate (beakers/min) × time (min) = work (beakers)

$\downarrow$ $\downarrow$ $\downarrow$

$2x$ ×   10 $= 8$

Thus

$$(2x)10 = 8$$

$$2x = \frac{8}{10}$$

$$x = \frac{8}{20}$$

$$x = \frac{2}{5}$$

Now that you know the rate of each scientist, you need to determine how many scientists are needed to fill 24 beakers in 5 minutes. Let y = the number of scientists. Substitute the given information into the $r \times t = w$ table:

rate (beakers/min) × time (min) = work (beakers)

$\downarrow$ $\downarrow$ $\downarrow$

$\left(\frac{2}{5}\right)y$ ×   5 $= 24$

Thus

$$\frac{2}{5}y \times 5 = 24$$

$$2y = 24$$

$$y = 12$$

Quantitative Comparison Questions

1. **B** Since Sally spends half of the distance of the trip traveling 50 miles per hour, and the other half of the distance of the trip traveling 40 miles per hour, she must spend more time traveling 40 miles per hour than 50 miles per hour. Her average speed must therefore be closer to 40 than to 50. Since 45 is the midpoint of 40 and 50, her average speed must be less than 45.

2. **D** Dennis cooks cakes at a rate of $\frac{\text{cakes}}{\text{hours}} = \frac{x}{3}$. He cooks pies at a rate of $\frac{\text{pies}}{\text{hours}} = \frac{y}{0.5}$. $\frac{y}{0.5} = \frac{y}{\frac{1}{2}} = \frac{2y}{1}$. Use the $r \times t = w$ table to arrive at a value for each of the quantities.

   Quantity 1: $r \times t = w$

   $\downarrow$

   $$\frac{x}{3} \times 6 = 2x$$

   Quantity 2: $r \times t = w$

   $\downarrow$

   $$2y \times 3 = 6y$$

   If $x = 6$ and $y = 2$, then the two quantities are equal. If $x = 6$ and $y = 1$, then Quantity A is greater. A relationship cannot be determined.

3. **C** Jake's rate is $\frac{\text{lap}}{\text{minutes}} = \frac{1}{x}$. Double that rate would be $\frac{2}{x}$. To solve for how long it would take him to run a lap at this rate, use the $r \times t = d$ table:

   $$\frac{2}{x} \times t = 1$$

   $$t = \frac{x}{2}$$

   The two quantities are equal.

4. **B** If Car A is 80 miles from its starting point when the cars meet, then Car B is 120 miles from its starting point. Since the cars traveled for the same time and Car B traveled a greater distance, Car B's rate must have been greater.

5. **D** From the given information, you can infer that Car A traveled 25 more miles than Car B. However, Car A could have traveled a total of 26 miles or a total of 31 miles. Thus the relationship between the quantities cannot be determined.

6. **D** Without knowing the capacity of the tank, you cannot determine the amount of time it will take to fill the tank.

7. **C** The combined rate of the eight machines is computers/hours $= \frac{7}{6}$. Note that a rate of $\frac{21 \text{ computers}}{18 \text{ hours}}$ reduces to $\frac{7 \text{ computers}}{6 \text{ hours}}$. Thus the number of machines necessary to produce 21 computers in 18 hours equals the number of computers necessary to produce 7 computers in 6 hours.

Probability

Probability refers to the likelihood that a given event will occur. To calculate the probability of a single event, use the following formula:

$$\text{probability} = \frac{\text{desired outcomes}}{\text{total outcomes}}$$

The formula is illustrated in the following example.

A certain jar has 3 red marbles, 5 black marbles, and 7 white marbles. If a marble is to be selected at random from the jar, what is the probability that a black marble will be selected?

(A) $\frac{1}{5}$

(B) $\frac{1}{3}$

(C) $\frac{7}{15}$

(D) $\frac{8}{15}$

(E) $\frac{4}{5}$

SOLUTION: In the example, an "outcome" is considered the event of selecting a marble. Since there are 15 marbles to select, there are 15 total outcomes. The "desired outcomes" refers to the number of events that satisfy the outcome you want. Since there are 5 black marbles, there are five "desired outcomes." Using the formula, the probability of selecting a black marble is thus: desired outcomes/total outcomes = $\frac{5}{15} = \frac{1}{3}$.

Mutually Exclusive Events

Imagine hearing that there is a 0.6 chance of rain. What would be the chance that it will not rain? 0.4. Why? Because the two events are mutually exclusive. Either it will rain or it won't, so the probability of the events must add up to 1. This example highlights the following rule: *when events are mutually exclusive, the sum of their probabilities is 1.*

For this question, write your answer in the box.

A certain event has two possible outcomes, a and b. If the probability of a is $\frac{p}{3}$, and the probability of b is $\frac{p}{5}$, what is the value of p?

SOLUTION: Since the event has only two outcomes, the probability of a and the probability of b must add to 1. Thus $\frac{p}{3} + \frac{p}{5} = 1$. To solve for p, multiply across the equation by 15:

$$5p + 3p = 15$$

$$8p = 15$$

$$p = \frac{15}{8}$$

Probability of Multiple Events

In the previous example, you looked at the probability of a single event occurring (selecting a black marble). Tougher probability questions will concern the probability that multiple events will occur. These questions will take two forms: *probability questions with "and" and probability questions with "or."*

Probability with "or": Add Them Up

If a probability question concerns the likelihood that one event *or* another event will happen, add up the probabilities of each event. For example:

In a certain bookcase, 10 books are about science, 8 are about literature, 5 are about history, and 2 are about psychology. If a book is selected at random, what is the probability that the book is about science or history?

    Ⓐ 0.08
    Ⓑ 0.2
    Ⓒ 0.3
    Ⓓ 0.4
    Ⓔ 0.6

SOLUTION: Two different events, a science book or history book, would satisfy the desired outcome. Thus to determine the number of desired outcomes, you should add the number of science books and the number of history books: $10 + 5 = 15$. The total number of outcomes is the sum of the books: $10 + 8 + 5 + 2 = 25$. The probability of selecting a science book or history book is thus $\frac{15}{25} = \frac{3}{5} = 0.6$. The correct answer is E.

Probability with "and": Multiply Them

If a question concerns the probability that an event occur multiple times, multiply the probabilities of each event.

> If a fair-sided coin is flipped three times, what is the probability the coin will land on heads all three times?
>
> A 0.125
> B 0.25
> C 0.5
> D 0.75
> E 1.5

SOLUTION: On any given flip, the probability that the coin will land on heads is 0.5. Since the question concerns the probability that the coin will land on heads all three times it is flipped, you should multiply these probabilities. $0.5 \times 0.5 \times 0.5 = 0.125$. The correct answer is A.

Counting

Fundamental Counting Principle

To calculate the number of ways to combine groups, calculate the product of the number of elements in each group.

> Bob's wardrobe contains 5 shirts, 7 pairs of pants, and 4 ties. If he wants to select an outfit that consists of 1 shirt, 1 pair of pants, and 1 tie, how many different outfits can he select?
>
> A 16
> B 20
> C 28
> D 35
> E 140

SOLUTION: Since the question concerns the combination of different groups, find the product of the number of elements in each group. $5 \times 7 \times 4 = 140$. The correct answer is E.

Permutations

One application of the fundamental counting principle concerns questions that ask you for the number of ways the items in a set can be ordered. These are called *permutation* questions and usually use the words *orderings* or *arrangements*. To answer such questions, you should use the **slot method**. Let's use the following example to illustrate how the slot method works:

For this question, write your answer in the box.

How many five-digit locker codes can be created from the digits 0–9, inclusive, if no digit can repeat?

SOLUTION: The order of the digits is relevant to the question, so consider it a permutation and use the slot method.

Step 1: Set up a number of slots corresponding to the number of items that are being selected. Since the code is five digits, you will set up five slots:

___ ___ ___ ___ ___

Step 2: Starting with the first slot, put in the number of possible choices for each slot. Since you are selecting from 10 digits, there are 10 possibilities for the first slot. Since the digits cannot repeat, whichever number occupies the first slot cannot occupy the second slot. Thus there are 9 possibilities for the second slot. By the same reasoning, there are 8 possibilities for the third slot, 7 possibilities for the fourth slot, and 6 possibilities for the fifth slot.

The slots should thus look like the following:

$$\underline{10} \ \underline{9} \ \underline{8} \ \underline{7} \ \underline{6}$$

Step 3: Multiply across.

$$\underline{10} \times \underline{9} \times \underline{8} \times \underline{7} \times \underline{6} = 30{,}240$$

Exercise: Probability

Discrete Quantitative Questions

1. A restaurant offers a special that consists of an entrée, a main course, and a dessert. If customers can choose from 4 entrées, 5 main courses, and 3 desserts, how many different meals can be chosen?

   (A) 3
   (B) 12
   (C) 20
   (D) 40
   (E) 60

For this question, write your answer in the box.

2. *S* is the set of all positive integers from 1–100, inclusive. If a number is to be randomly drawn from *S*, what is the probability that the number chosen will be a multiple of 4?

3. Next week, the probability of rain on each day will be 0.6. What is the probability that it will rain on Monday, but not on Tuesday?

   (A) 0.1
   (B) 0.16
   (C) 0.24
   (D) 0.36
   (E) 0.42

4. A fair, six-sided die is to be rolled 3 times. What is the probability that the die will land on a prime number each time?

   (A) 0.125
   (B) 0.25
   (C) 0.5
   (D) 0.75
   (E) 0.9

5. 20 of the 80 employees at a certain organization are doctors. If two employees are to be selected at random, which of the following is closest to the probability that neither employee selected is a doctor?

   (A) 0.2
   (B) 0.4
   (C) 0.6
   (D) 0.7
   (E) 0.8

6. A certain jar contains 21 marbles, 7 of which are red. If two marbles are to be selected, with replacement, what is the probability that both marbles will be red?

   (A) $\frac{1}{9}$
   (B) $\frac{1}{6}$
   (C) $\frac{1}{3}$
   (D) $\frac{2}{3}$
   (E) $\frac{3}{4}$

7. How many three-letter arrangements can be selected from the letters ABCDE?

   (A) 15
   (B) 20
   (C) 60
   (D) 120
   (E) 240

8. 10 people enter a competition in which the winner earns a gold medal, the second-place finisher earns a silver medal, the third-place finisher earns a bronze medal, and no other awards are given. In how many different ways can the medals be awarded?

   (A) 512
   (B) 720
   (C) 729
   (D) 800
   (E) 1,000

9. Set A consists of the integers 2, 3, 5, 7, and 9. Set B consists of the integers 1, 4, 6, 8, and 10. If a number in Set A is to be multiplied by a number in Set B, how many different products are possible?

(A) 5
(B) 10
(C) 15
(D) 20
(E) 25

Quantitative Comparison Questions

Each of the following questions consists of two quantities, Quantity A and Quantity B. You are to compare the two quantities. You may use additional information centered above the two quantities if additional information is given. Choose

(A) if Quantity A is greater
(B) if Quantity B is greater
(C) if the two quantities are equal
(D) if the relationship between the two quantities cannot be determined

---

The probability that a certain event will occur is x.
The probability that the event will not occur is y.

	QUANTITY A	QUANTITY B	
1.	xy	$x + y$	(A) (B) (C) (D)

Y is the set of all integers from 1–10,000 inclusive.
A number is to be randomly selected from Y.

	QUANTITY A	QUANTITY B	
2.	The probability that the number will be a multiple of 3	The probability that the number will be a multiple of 5	(A) (B) (C) (D)

A fair-sided coin is to be flipped 5 times.

	QUANTITY A	QUANTITY B	
3.	The probability that the coin will land on heads at least once	The probability that the coin will not land on tails each time	(A) (B) (C) (D)

If a coin is flipped three times, the probability that it
will land on heads all three times is 0.064.

QUANTITY A	QUANTITY B	
4. The probability that the coin will land on tails on any given flip	0.5	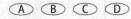

Exercise Answers

Discrete Quantitative Questions

1. **E** Use the fundamental counting principle: $4 \times 5 \times 3 = 60$.

2. $\frac{1}{4}$ First, calculate how many multiples of 4 there are from 1–100, inclusive. Recall that the formula to calculate the number of items in an evenly spaced set is:

    $$\frac{last - first}{spacing} + 1$$

    Thus the number of multiples of 4 from 1–100, inclusive, is $\frac{100 - 4}{4} + 1 = 25$. There are thus 25 desired outcomes. Since there are 100 total outcomes, the probability of selecting a multiple of 4 is $\frac{25}{100} = \frac{1}{4}$.

3. **C** Since the question concerns the probability that multiple events will occur, multiply the probabilities of each desired event. The probability of rain on Monday is 0.6. The probability that it won't rain on Tuesday is $1 - 0.6 = 0.4$. Thus the probability that it will rain on Monday, but not on Tuesday, is $0.4 \times 0.6 = 0.24$.

4. **A** Since the question concerns the probability that multiple events will occur, multiply the probabilities of each event. Since there are three prime numbers from 1–6 (2, 3, and 5), the probability that the die will land on a prime number on a single roll is $\frac{3}{6} = 0.5$. The probability that the die will land on a prime number on all three rolls is thus $0.5 \times 0.5 \times 0.5 = 0.125$.

5. **C** Since the question concerns the probability that multiple events will occur, multiply the probabilities of each event. The probability that the first employee selected is not a doctor is $\frac{60}{80} = \frac{3}{4}$. After the first employee is chosen, there are 79 total employees and 59 total nondoctors left. Thus the probability that the second employee selected will also be a doctor is $\frac{59}{79}$. Since the question says "closest to," you can estimate $\frac{59}{79}$ as roughly $\frac{60}{80} = \frac{3}{4}$. The approximate probability that neither employee is a doctor is thus $\frac{3}{4} \times \frac{3}{4} = 0.75 \times 0.75 = 0.5625$. The closest answer is C.

6. **A** Since multiple events must be satisfied to yield a desired outcome, you should multiply the individual probabilities of each desired event. The probability that the first marble chosen is red is $\frac{7}{21} = \frac{1}{3}$. The probability that the second marble chosen is red is also $\frac{7}{21} = \frac{1}{3} \cdot \frac{1}{3} \times \frac{1}{3} = \frac{1}{9}$.

7. **C** The word *arrangement* indicates that this is a permutation question and that you should thus use the slot method. You should set up three slots. There are five possibilities for the first slot, four possibilities for the second slot, and three possibilities for the third slot:

$\underline{5} \times \underline{4} \times \underline{3}$

Finally, multiply across: $5 \times 4 \times 3 = 60$.

8. **B** The order in which the awards are given yields different outcomes, so this is a permutation question. Since three awards will be given, set up three slots. There are 10 possibilities for the first slot, 9 possibilities for the second slot, and 8 possibilities for the third slot:

$\underline{10}\,\underline{9}\,\underline{8}$

Finally, multiply across: $10 \times 9 \times 8 = 720$.

9. **E** Use the fundamental counting principle. Multiply the number of items in Set A by the number of items in Set B. $5 \times 5 = 25$.

Quantitative Comparison Questions

1. **B** Since x and y are mutually exclusive events, their sum = 1. Since x and y are fractions, their product is less than 1. Thus Quantity B is greater.

2. **A** Remember to *compare* instead of calculating. Since there are more multiples of 3 than there are multiples of 5, the probability of selecting a multiple of 3 is greater than the probability of selecting a multiple of 5. Quantity A is greater.

3. **C** Although you may be tempted to figure the math out here, you can solve it much more quickly by recognizing a key point. For at least one coin flip to land on heads, it must be the case that not *all* of the coin flips land on tails. The values in the two quantities are thus equal.

4. **A** If x is the probability that the coin will land on heads on one flip, then $x^3 = 0.064 \rightarrow x = 0.4$. If there is a 0.4 chance the coin will land on heads on a given flip, then there is a 0.6 chance that the coin will land on tails on a given flip. Quantity A is greater.

CHAPTER 13

Geometry

- Lines and angles
- Triangles
- Polygons
- Circles
- Solids and cylinders
- The coordinate plane

About 20 percent of the questions on the GRE will deal with geometry. These questions will address your knowledge of geometric properties and formulas and your ability to use these formulas to construct algebraic relationships. When answering geometry questions, you should generally follow these steps:

1. Draw the diagram and input all given information.
2. Infer all properties and relationships implied by the diagram.
3. Use these relationships to create algebraic relationships.
4. Solve for what the question is asking for.

Notice that the approach for geometry questions is in many ways similar to the approach for word problems. In both cases, your ultimate goal is to use the information given to construct algebraic relationships. The distinguishing element of geometry questions is that you will use geometric principles instead of words to create these algebraic relationships. This chapter focuses on these principles and how they are tested on the exam.

Note that if a figure says "Not Drawn to Scale," then the relationships between the sides and angles in the diagram do not match their visual appearance. However, the opposite is also true: if the figure does *not* say "Not Drawn to Scale," then you can assume that the diagram is accurate. Nonetheless, you must be careful about making assumptions.

Lines and Angles

An **angle** is formed at the intersection of two **rays** or **lines**. The measurement of an angle can be between 0 degrees and 360 degrees. The angle below has a measure of 45 degrees.

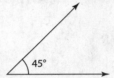

One type of angle that occurs throughout geometry questions is a **right angle**. A right angle has a measure of 90 degrees and is denoted by the square at the intersection of the two lines or rays. When two lines intersect to form a right angle, those lines are said to be **perpendicular**.

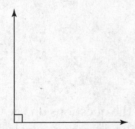

A straight line will always have an angle measure of 180 degrees. From this, you can infer Property 1: *the angles on a line must add up to 180*. Angles whose measures sum to 180 are termed **supplementary angles**.

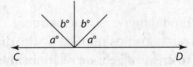

What is the value of $(a + b)$ in the figure above?

SOLUTION: Since these four angles lie on line CD:

$$a + a + b + b = 180$$

$$2a + 2b = 180$$

$$a + b = 90$$

Intersecting Lines and Vertical Angles

The intersection of two lines will always create four angles.

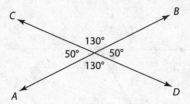

These angles have two properties:

1. They will add up to 360.
2. The angles opposite each other will be equal. These angles are termed **vertical angles**.

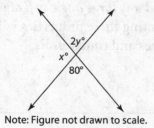

Note: Figure not drawn to scale.

What is the value of x in the figure above?

SOLUTION: Since x and $2y$ lie on the same line, $x + 2y = 180$. The angle vertical to $2y = 80$, so you can substitute 80 for $2y$ in the equation and solve: $x + 80 = 180 \rightarrow x = 100$.

Note that the two preceding properties can apply to situations in which more than two lines intersect. Here is the more general form of Property 1: *the angles around a point must add up to 360.*

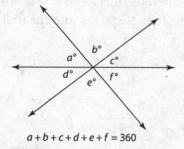

$$a + b + c + d + e + f = 360$$

Since these angles are all around a point, $a + b + c + d + e + f = 360$. In addition, $a = f$, $b = e$, $c = d$. Finally, a, b, and c are supplementary, and d, e, and f are supplementary.

Parallel Lines and Transversals

Parallel lines by definition will never intersect. On the GRE, you will be expected to understand the relationships among the angles of parallel lines cut by a **transversal.**

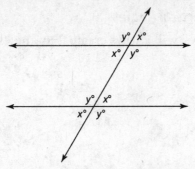

The best way to think about the relationship among the angles is in terms of the small angles and the large angles. All of the smaller angles will be **acute** (less than 90 degrees), and all of the larger angles will be **obtuse** (greater than 90 degrees). *All the smaller angles will have the same measure, and all of the larger angles will have the same measure.* Thus in the preceding diagram, $x < 90$, and $y > 90$. Finally, *the sum of any small angle and any large angle will always be 180.* Thus $x + y = 180$. Understanding and implementing these properties will equip you well on most questions that test parallel lines and transversals.

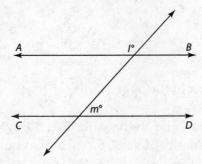

In the diagram above, lines AB and CD are parallel. If the ratio of l to m is 3 to 2, what is l?

SOLUTION: When two parallel lines are cut by a transversal, the sum of the small and large angles is 180. Thus $l + m = 180$. Since $\frac{l}{m} = \frac{3}{2}$, you can let $l = 3x$ and let $m = 2x$. Substitute these terms into the first equation:

$$l + m = 180$$

$$\downarrow$$

$$3x + 2x = 180$$

$$5x = 180$$

$$x = 36 \text{ and } l = 3x, \text{ so } l = 3(36) = 108.$$

Exercise: Lines and Angles

Discrete Quantitative Questions

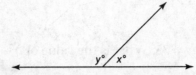

1. If $y = 3x$ in the diagram above, then what is x?

   Ⓐ 45
   Ⓑ 60
   Ⓒ 90
   Ⓓ 115
   Ⓔ 135

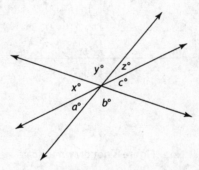

Note: Figure not drawn to scale

Questions 2–3 refer to the figure above.

2. If $a + b = 100$, what is $y + z$?

   Ⓐ 60
   Ⓑ 80
   Ⓒ 100
   Ⓓ 140
   Ⓔ It cannot be determined from the given information.

3. If $a > b > c$, then which of the following must be true?

   Ⓐ $a > 60$
   Ⓑ $b < 60$
   Ⓒ $z < 60$
   Ⓓ $x = a$
   Ⓔ $x + a > 120$

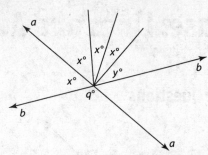

4. In this figure, $x + y = 75$. What is the value of $q - y$?

    (A) 95

    (B) 100

    (C) 105

    (D) 110

    (E) 145

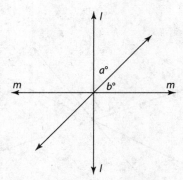

Note: Figure is not drawn to scale

5. In the figure, lines l and m are perpendicular. If $a = 3b$, then $a - b = ?$

    (A) 22.5

    (B) 35

    (C) 45

    (D) 67.5

    (E) 75

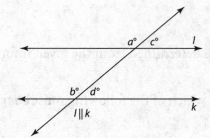

Questions 6–8 refer to the figure above.

6. If $b = 100$, then $c = ?$

    (A) 50

    (B) 60

    (C) 70

    (D) 80

    (E) 100

7. If $a = d + 30$, then $d = ?$

  (A) 75
  (B) 80
  (C) 85
  (D) 90
  (E) 95

8. If $a - c = 20$, then what is the value of b?

  (A) 60
  (B) 80
  (C) 100
  (D) 110
  (E) 120

For this question, write your answer in the box.

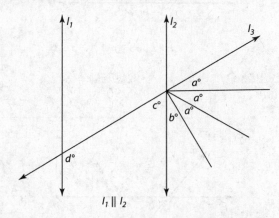

$l_1 \parallel l_2$

9. In the figure above, $d = 100$.   If $a + b = 40$, then $a = ?$

Quantitative Comparison Questions

Each of the following questions consists of two quantities, Quantity A and Quantity B. You are to compare the two quantities. You may use additional information centered above the two quantities if additional information is given. Choose

- (A) if Quantity A is greater
- (B) if Quantity B is greater
- (C) if the two quantities are equal
- (D) if the relationship between the two quantities cannot be determined

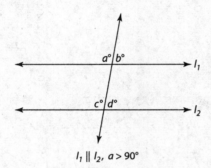

$l_1 \parallel l_2$, $a > 90°$

	QUANTITY A	QUANTITY B	
1.	d	90	Ⓐ Ⓑ Ⓒ Ⓓ

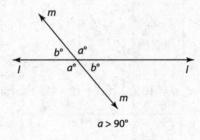

$a > 90°$

	QUANTITY A	QUANTITY B	
2.	b	90	Ⓐ Ⓑ Ⓒ Ⓓ

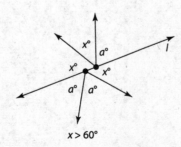

$x > 60°$

Note: Figure is not drawn to scale

	QUANTITY A	QUANTITY B	
3.	x	a	Ⓐ Ⓑ Ⓒ Ⓓ

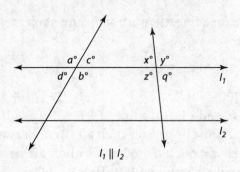

$l_1 \parallel l_2$

	QUANTITY A	QUANTITY B	
4.	a	z	(A) (B) (C) (D)

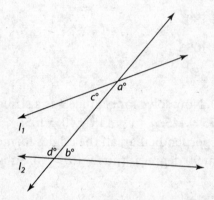

l1 and *l2* intersect to the left of the diagram

	QUANTITY A	QUANTITY B	
5.	$a + b$	180	(A) (B) (C) (D)

Exercise Answers

Discrete Quantitative Questions

1. **A** Since y and x form the angles on a line, they must be supplementary. Thus $y + x = 180$. Substitute $3x$ for y:

$$3x + x = 180$$

$$4x = 180$$

$$x = 45$$

2. **C** Angles a, b, and x lie on a line, so $a + b + x = 180$. Substitute 100 for $(a + b)$:

$$100 + x = 180$$

$$x = 80$$

Since x, y, and z lie on a line, they are supplementary: $x + y + z = 180$. Substitute 80 for x:

$$80 + y + z = 180$$

$$y + z = 100$$

3. **A** Since angles a, b, and c lie on a line, $a + b + c = 180$. If a is the largest of the three values, then a must be greater than 60. To understand why, think of what would happen when $a = 60$. If $a = 60$ and b and c are smaller than a, then the sum of the three angles cannot be 180. Thus $a > 60$.

4. **C** Since b is a straight line, the five angles above a must add to 180: $4x + y = 180$. Since $x + y = 75$, you can use substitution to solve for x: $y = 75 - x$. Substitute $(75 - x)$ for y in the first equation:

$$4x + (75 - x) = 180$$

$$3x = 105$$

$$x = 35$$

If $x = 35$, then $y = 40$. Now solve for q. Since a is a straight line, $x + q = 180$. $x = 35$, so $q = 180 - 35 = 145$. $q - y = 145 - 40 = 105$.

5. **C** Since l and m are perpendicular, all the angles formed at the intersection of l and m must equal 90 degrees. Thus $a + b = 90$. Substitute $3b$ for a to solve for b:

$$3b + b = 90$$

$$4b = 90$$

$$b = 22.5$$

$$\downarrow$$

$$a = 90 - 22.5 = 67.5$$

Thus $a - b = 67.5 - 22.5 = 45$.

6. **D** Since b is a large angle created by the transversal and c is the small angle created by the transversal, $b + c = 180$. Substitute 100 for b:

$$100 + c = 180$$

$$c = 80$$

7. **A** Since l and k are parallel lines cut by a transversal, the sum of the smaller and larger angles must equal 180. Thus $a + d = 180$. Substitute $d + 30$ for a:

$$(d + 30) + d = 180$$

$$2d + 30 = 180$$

$$2d = 150$$

$$d = 75$$

8. **C** Since a and c are the two angles above l, their sum must equal 180: $a + c = 180$. Add the two equations to solve for a:

$$a - c = 20$$
$$+$$
$$\underline{a + c = 180}$$
$$2a = 200 \rightarrow a = 100$$

Since a and b are the larger angles formed by the transversal, they must be equal. Thus $b = 100$.

9. **30** Since $(3a + b)$ and d are the larger angles formed by the transversal, $3a + b = 100$. Combine this equation with $a + b = 40$:

$$3a + b = 100$$
$$a + b = 40$$

To solve for a, express b in terms of a: $b = 40 - a$. Substitute $40 - a$ for b in the first equation:

$$3a + (40 - a) = 100$$
$$2a + 40 = 100$$
$$2a = 60$$
$$a = 30$$

Quantitative Comparison Questions

1. **B** Since $a > 90$, a must be the larger angle created by the transversal. Thus b and d must be the smaller angles created by the transversal. The smaller angles created by the transversal are always less than 90 degrees. Thus Quantity B is greater.

2. **B** Since a and b create line l, they must be supplementary. If $a > 90$, then $b < 90$.

3. **A** The angles above line l must add to 180. Thus $2x + a = 180$. The angles below line l must add to 180. Thus $2a + x = 180$. Add these equations:

$$2x + a = 180$$
$$+$$
$$\underline{x + 2a = 180}$$
$$3x + 3a = 360$$

Divide both sides by 3: $x + a = 120$. Since $x > 60$, $a < 60$.

4. **D** Although a and z are the larger angles formed by a transversal, the transversals forming these angles are different. Thus you can only infer that a and x are each greater than 90. No information can be deduced about their relationship. The correct answer is D.

5. **A** Since lines 1 and 2 intersect to the left of the diagram, they are not parallel. As they converge, the angles closer to them become smaller. Thus $a > c$, and $b > d$. Since a and c are supplementary and b and d are supplementary, a and c must each be greater than 90. Thus their sum must be greater than 180.

Triangles

Triangles are the GRE's favorite shape. They appear not only in questions that explicitly ask you about triangles, but also in disguised form on questions addressing other polygons, such as squares or rectangles. As you may recall from high school, there are numerous properties associated with triangles. Let's look below at the properties you need to master for the GRE.

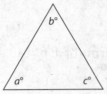

Basic Properties of Triangles

Basic Property 1: The sum of the internal angles in a triangle equals 180. Thus in the preceding diagram, $a + b + c = 180$.

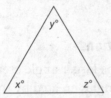

In the figure above, $x = y = 2z$. What is x?

SOLUTION: Since x, y, and z are the interior angles of a triangle, $x + y + z = 180$. Use the given information to express all variables in terms of z:

$$2z + 2z + z = 180$$

$$5z = 180$$

$$z = 36$$

Since $x = 2z$, $x = 2(36) = 72$.

Basic Property 2: The length of any given side of a triangle must be greater than the difference of the other two side lengths and less than the sum of the other two side lengths.

For this question, indicate all the answer choices that apply.

If a triangle has side lengths of 4 and 7, which of the following could be the length of the third side of the triangle?

- [A] 3
- [B] 4
- [C] 5
- [D] 9
- [E] 11
- [F] 13

SOLUTION: The third side of the triangle must be greater than (7 – 4) and less than (7 + 4). Thus the length of the third side must be between 3 and 11. Of the choices, the length could be 4, 5, or 9.

Basic Property 3: *The greater the measurement of a triangle's angle, the greater the length of the corresponding side.*

An angle's *corresponding side* is the side opposite that angle. In the following triangle, each angle's corresponding side is indicated by the arrows. Note that this relationship also works in reverse: the greater the length of a side, the greater the measurement of the corresponding angle. It is also important to note that this information only provides a relationship between the corresponding sides and angles of a triangle. *Without additional information, you cannot infer how much greater one side or angle is than another side or angle.*

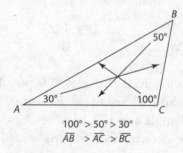

$$100° > 50° > 30°$$
$$\overline{AB} > \overline{AC} > \overline{BC}$$

Isosceles Triangles

An **isosceles triangle** is any triangle that has two equal angles. Since the two angles are equal, the corresponding sides will also be equal. Thus as you saw with the Basic Property 3, the relationship works in reverse. *If a triangle has two equal sides, it will be isosceles, and the angles opposite those sides will be equal.*

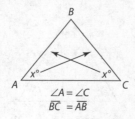

$$\angle A = \angle C$$
$$\overline{BC} = \overline{AB}$$

This information is helpful because when you are working with an isosceles triangle, you can assign the same variable to different angles or sides.

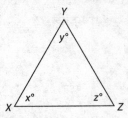

In the figure above, side YZ = side XY. If $x = 2y$, then $y = ?$

SOLUTION: Since YZ and XY are equal, their corresponding angles must be equal. Thus $x = z$. The sum of the interior angles of a triangle is 180, so $x + x + y = 180$. Substitute $2y$ for x:

$$2y + 2y + y = 180$$

$$5y = 180$$

$$y = 36$$

However, from the fact that a triangle is isosceles, you cannot necessarily infer which sides or angles are equal.

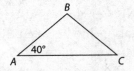

triangle ABC is isosceles

QUANTITY A	QUANTITY B
The measure of angle C	40

SOLUTION: Since triangle ABC is isosceles, it is possible that angle $C = 40$, in which case the two quantities are equal. However, it can also be the case that angle $B = 40$ and angle $C = 100$, in which case angle $C > 40$. Thus, the relationship cannot be determined. The answer is D.

Equilateral Triangles

An **equilateral triangle** is a triangle in which all angles are equal and all sides are equal. Since the angle measurements are the same and their sum is 180, *each angle in an equilateral triangle measures 60 degrees.*

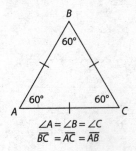

Perimeter of a Triangle

The **perimeter** of a triangle is the sum of all the side lengths.

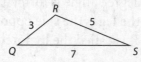

The perimeter of the preceding triangle is 3 + 5 + 7 = 15.

Area of a Triangle

The area of a triangle refers to the amount of space within the triangle. Area is expressed in square units, such as cm² (square centimeters), in.² (square inches), and so on. The formula for the **area of a triangle** is $(\frac{1}{2}) \times b \times h$.

Note that the base (b) and height (h) *must* be perpendicular to each other. Look at the following figure:

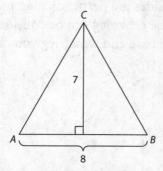

In this example, the base is 8 and the height is 7. You know that the height is 7 because the line segment drawn from angle C creates a perpendicular angle when it intersects the base, AB. The area of this triangle will thus be $\frac{1}{2} \times 8 \times 7 = 28$.

In the example, AB was the base of the triangle. However, any side can be the base of a triangle. The height will be defined as the perpendicular line from the angle opposite the base. Next, you will see the same triangle as earlier, but now BC is the base.

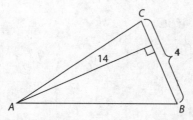

Now, to calculate the area: $\frac{1}{2} \times 4 \times 14 = 28$.

Sometimes you will have to extend the base to determine the corresponding height:

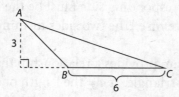

In this example, the base is 6. To draw the height, it was necessary to extend base BC until it intersected the height. The area of this triangle is $\frac{1}{2} \times 6 \times 3 = 9$.

Right Triangles

The GRE's favorite shape is a right triangle. A right triangle is any triangle that has a 90-degree angle. The 90-degree angle is formed at the intersection of the two shorter sides, which are called the **legs**. The side opposite the 90-degree angle is the longest side of a right triangle. It is called the **hypotenuse**.

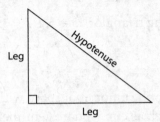

The formula for the area of any triangle applies to right triangles, but in right triangles, determining the area is easier than with other triangles. Why? Because the base and height will simply be the two sides that form the 90-degree angle. This is so because these two sides are perpendicular, meaning that one leg can be considered the base and the other leg can be considered the height (it doesn't matter which leg you call the base and which leg you call the height).

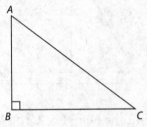

The area of the preceding triangle is 48. If the length of $AB = 8$, then what is the length of BC?

SOLUTION: The area of a right triangle is $\frac{1}{2} \times$ (leg 1) $\times$ (leg 2). Substitute 8 for (leg 1) and BC for leg 2:

$$48 = \tfrac{1}{2} \times (8) \times (BC)$$

$$48 = 4(BC)$$

$$12 = BC$$

The Pythagorean Theorem

Recall from Basic Property 3 that the greater the angle of a triangle, the longer the corresponding side. Since the 90 degree angle in a triangle must be the largest angle of the triangle, its corresponding side must be the longest side of the triangle. This side is called the **hypotenuse**. The two sides forming the 90 degree angle are called the **legs**.

The **Pythagorean theorem** provides a relationship that always holds true between the sides of a right triangle. If a = the length of one leg, b = the length of the other leg, and c = the length of the hypotenuse, then:

$$a^2 + b^2 = c^2$$

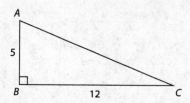

What is the perimeter of the triangle above?

    Ⓐ 13
    Ⓑ 17
    Ⓒ 25
    Ⓓ 30
    Ⓔ 42

SOLUTION: To determine the perimeter, solve for side *BC*, which is the hypotenuse. You can use the Pythagorean theorem to solve for the hypotenuse:

$$5^2 + 12^2 = c^2$$

$$169 = c^2$$

$$13 = c$$

Thus the perimeter is $5 + 12 + 13 = 30$.

Pythagorean Triplets

There are certain combinations of right-triangle side lengths that occur throughout the GRE. Though you can always use the Pythagorean theorem in these situations, you will save precious time by memorizing these triplets and their multiples:

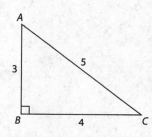

COMBINATIONS	TRIPLETS
3-4-5	6-8-10
$3^2 + 4^2 = 5^2$	9-12-15
$9 + 16 = 25$	12-16-20

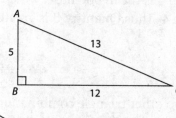

COMBINATIONS	TRIPLETS
5-12-13	10-24-26
$5^2 + 12^2 = 13^2$	
$25 + 144 = 169$	

COMBINATIONS	TRIPLETS
8-15-17	None
$8^2 + 15^2 = 17^2$	
$64 + 225 = 289$	

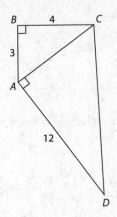

What is the perimeter of the figure above?

SOLUTION: To determine the perimeter, you need to add up all the sides. You know all the side-lengths except *CD*. To solve for *CD*, first solve for *AC*. The legs of right triangle *ABC* have lengths of 3 and 4, so *AC* = 5. If *AC* = 5 and *AD* = 12, then *CD* = 13. The perimeter of the figure is thus 3 + 4 + 12 + 13 = 32.

However, be careful about assuming that any right triangle with two side lengths from the Pythagorean triplets will necessarily conform to the preceding list. The triplets only apply in situations where the largest value of the triplet is the length of the hypotenuse:

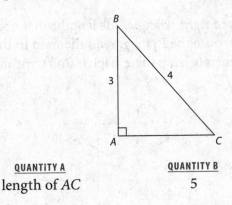

QUANTITY A	QUANTITY B
length of *AC*	5

SOLUTION: Even though *ABC* is a right triangle with two sides of 3 and 4, it is not a Pythagorean triplet. The side with length 4 is the hypotenuse, which means that the length of *AC* must be less than 4. Thus Quantity B is greater.

Isosceles Right Triangles and the Diagonal of a Square

In addition to the Pythagorean triplets, there are two other triangle combinations that you will need to know for the GRE: *isosceles right triangles* and *30-60-90 triangles*.

An **isosceles right triangle** is any right triangle in which the lengths of the legs are equal. Since the lengths of the legs are equal, their corresponding angles will also be equal, with each having a measurement of 45 degrees. Thus another term for an isosceles right triangle is a **45-45-90 triangle**.

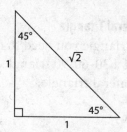

The legs of every isosceles right triangle will have a specific ratio that you should memorize:

leg opposite 45 : leg opposite 45 : side opposite 90

↓   ↓   ↓

1 1 $\sqrt{2}$

x x $x\sqrt{2}$

It is important to note that the preceding combination only specifies a *ratio*, and not actual values. For example, if you are told that the leg length of an isosceles triangle is 5, then the hypotenuse is $5\sqrt{2}$. Or if the leg length is 7, then the hypotenuse is $7\sqrt{2}$. *The best way to think about the relationships of the leg lengths is that the hypotenuse will be $\sqrt{2} \times$ the leg.*

One commonly tested fact about 45-45-90 triangles is that **the diagonal of a square will form two 45-45-90 triangles**. This is helpful because you can use the diagonal of the square to solve for the side lengths of the square and vice versa.

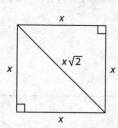

What is the area of a square with a diagonal of length 20?

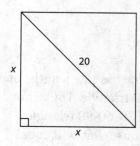

SOLUTION: To solve for the area, you need the length of a side. The length of the side will be the leg of an isosceles right triangle with a hypotenuse of 20. Let x = leg length:

$$x\sqrt{2} = 20$$

$$x = \frac{20}{\sqrt{2}}$$

$$\text{area} = x^2 = \frac{20^2}{\sqrt{2}^2} = \frac{400}{2} = 200$$

30-60-90 Triangles and the Equilateral Triangle

The other type of special right triangle you need to master is the 30-60-90 triangle. To understand the properties of a 30-60-90 triangle, look at what happens when you draw the height of an equilateral triangle:

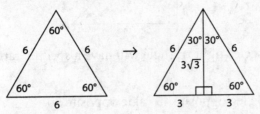

Fact 1: The height of an equilateral triangle will cut the base in half.

Fact 2: The resulting smaller triangles will have degree measurements of 30-60-90.

Fact 3: The sides of the 30-60-90 triangle will be in the following ratio, which you must memorize:

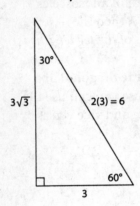

30:60:90

$1:\sqrt{3}:2$

$x:x\sqrt{3}:2x$

Finally, as was the case with 45-45-90 triangles, with 30-60-90 triangles, the side relationships only specify ratios, not values.

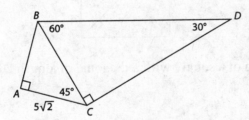

What is the perimeter of triangle *BCD* in the figure above?

SOLUTION: To determine the perimeter, you must determine the side lengths of *BCD*. Note that side *BC* is the hypotenuse of the 45-45-90 triangle *ABC*. Thus $BC = 5\sqrt{2} \times \sqrt{2} = 5 \times 2 = 10$. Since *BC* is the shorter leg of 30-60-90 triangle *BCD*, the longer leg, *CD*, will equal $10\sqrt{3}$, and the hypotenuse, *BD*, will equal $10 \times 2 = 20$. The perimeter of *BCD* is thus $10 + 20 + 10\sqrt{3} = 30 + 10\sqrt{3}$.

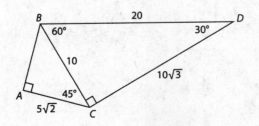

Exercise: Triangles

Discrete Quantitative Questions

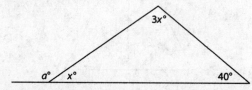

1. In the figure above, what is the value of *a*?

   Ⓐ 30
   Ⓑ 35
   Ⓒ 140
   Ⓓ 145
   Ⓔ 150

2. In triangle *ABC*, side *AB* = 3 and side *BC* = 8. Which of the following CANNOT be the perimeter of triangle *ABC*?

   Ⓐ 18
   Ⓑ 19
   Ⓒ 20
   Ⓓ 21
   Ⓔ 22

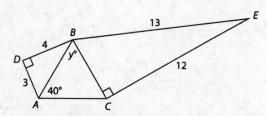

Note: Diagram not drawn to scale

3. What is the value of *y* in the figure above?

   Ⓐ 30
   Ⓑ 40
   Ⓒ 45
   Ⓓ 60
   Ⓔ 100

For this question, write your answer in the box.

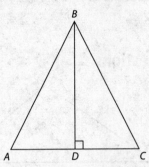

4. In the figure shown, the length of altitude BD is $3\sqrt{3}$. What is the area of equilateral triangle ABC?

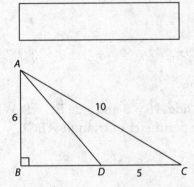

5. What is the length of AD in the figure above?

(A) $3\sqrt{5}$

(B) $3\sqrt{3}$

(C) 8

(D) $8\sqrt{3}$

(E) $9\sqrt{2}$

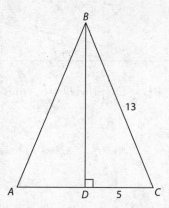

6. In the figure above, angle *BAD* = angle *ABD*. What is the area of triangle *ABD*?

   (A) 30
   (B) 60
   (C) 72
   (D) 102
   (E) 144

7. The base of a 20-foot rope is 8 feet above the ground. If the rope is extended at a 60-degree angle, the top of the rope will be how many feet above the ground?

   (A) 18
   (B) 28
   (C) $10\sqrt{3}$
   (D) $10\sqrt{2} + 8$
   (E) $10\sqrt{3} + 8$

For this question, write your answer in the box.

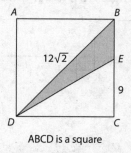

ABCD is a square

8. In the figure above, what is the area of triangle *BDE*?

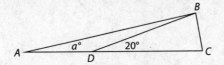

9. In the figure above, BD = DC. If AD = 6, what is BD?

(A) 4
(B) 6
(C) 8
(D) 10
(E) 12

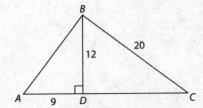

10. What is the perimeter of triangle ABC?

(A) 44
(B) 45
(C) 54
(D) 60
(E) 96

For this question, write your answer in the box.

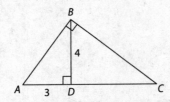

11. If the perimeter of triangle ABC is 20, what is the length of DC?

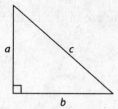

12. The area of the triangle above is 24. If *a* is 2 more than *b*, what is *c*?

    Ⓐ 6
    Ⓑ 8
    Ⓒ 10
    Ⓓ $\sqrt{13}$
    Ⓔ $2\sqrt{13}$

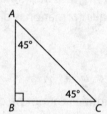 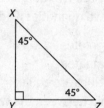

13. If *XZ* is double *AC*, then the area of triangle *XYZ* is how many times greater than the area of triangle *ABC*?

    Ⓐ $\sqrt{2}$
    Ⓑ 2
    Ⓒ 4
    Ⓓ 8
    Ⓔ 16

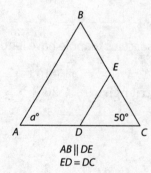

$AB \parallel DE$
$ED = DC$

14. What is the value of *a*?

    Ⓐ 30
    Ⓑ 50
    Ⓒ 80
    Ⓓ 130
    Ⓔ 150

15. If the angles of a triangle are in the ratio 3:4:5, what is the measurement of the smallest angle?

   Ⓐ 45
   Ⓑ 60
   Ⓒ 75
   Ⓓ 90
   Ⓔ 100

Quantitative Comparison Questions

Each of the following questions consists of two quantities, Quantity A and Quantity B. You are to compare the two quantities. You may use additional information centered above the two quantities if additional information is given. Choose

   Ⓐ if Quantity A is greater
   Ⓑ if Quantity B is greater
   Ⓒ if the two quantities are equal
   Ⓓ if the relationship between the two quantities cannot be determined

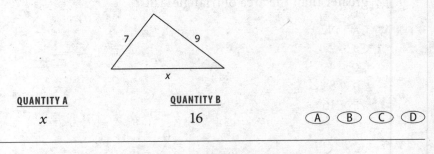

QUANTITY A	QUANTITY B	
1. x	16	Ⓐ Ⓑ Ⓒ Ⓓ

Two sides of an isosceles triangle have lengths of 7 and 12.

QUANTITY A	QUANTITY B	
2. The perimeter of the triangle	26	Ⓐ Ⓑ Ⓒ Ⓓ

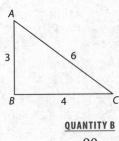

QUANTITY A	QUANTITY B	
3. The degree measure of angle ABC	90	Ⓐ Ⓑ Ⓒ Ⓓ

QUANTITY A	QUANTITY B	

4. The area of an equilateral triangle with an altitude of 8 | The area of an equilateral triangle with a side length of 8

Ⓐ Ⓑ Ⓒ Ⓓ

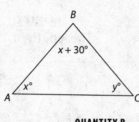

QUANTITY A	QUANTITY B	

5. x y

Ⓐ Ⓑ Ⓒ Ⓓ

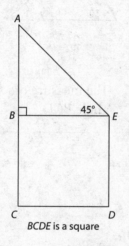

BCDE is a square

QUANTITY A	QUANTITY B	

6. $\frac{1}{2} \times$ the area of *BCDE*   The area of triangle *ABE*

Ⓐ Ⓑ Ⓒ Ⓓ

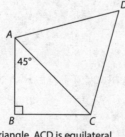

Triangle *ACD* is equilateral

QUANTITY A	QUANTITY B	

7. The perimeter of triangle *ABC* | The perimeter of triangle *ACD*

Ⓐ Ⓑ Ⓒ Ⓓ

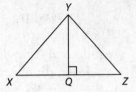

The area of triangle *XYQ* < the area of triangle *YQZ*

	QUANTITY A	QUANTITY B	
8.	The length of *XY*	The length of *YZ*	

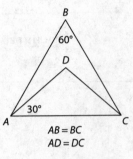

AB = BC
AD = DC

	QUANTITY A	QUANTITY B	
9.	The measure of angle *BAD*	The measure of angle *BCD*	

Exercise Answers

Discrete Quantitative Questions

1. **D** Since the interior angles of a triangle add up to 180,

$$(x + 3x + 40) = 180$$

$$4x + 40 = 180$$

$$4x = 140$$

$$x = 35$$

Since *a* and *x* are supplementary, $a + x = 180$. Substitute 35 for *x*:

$$a + 35 = 180$$

$$a = 145$$

2. **E** The length of *AC* must be greater than $(8 - 3)$ and less than $(8 + 3)$. Thus $5 < AC < 11$. The perimeter of the triangle will be $AB + BC + AC = 8 + 3 + AC = 11 + AC$. Since $5 < AC < 11$, the perimeter must be less than $(11 + 11) = 22$ and greater than $(5 + 11) = 16$. The only value in the choices that is not between 16 and 22 is E.

3. **E** Triangle *ABD* is a 3-4-5 triangle, so $AB = 5$. Triangle *BCE* is a 5-12-13 triangle, so $BC = 5$. Since *AB* and *BC* are equal, their corresponding angles

must be equal: angle *BAC* = angle *BCA*. You are told that angle *BAC* = 40, so you can infer that angle *BCA* = 40. Since the interior angles of a triangle sum to 180, $y + 40 + 40 = 180 \rightarrow y = 100$.

4. **$9\sqrt{3}$** To get the area of *ABC*, you will need to determine the length of the base. Since *BD* is the altitude of an equilateral triangle, *BCD* is a 30-60-90 triangle. The altitude is opposite the 60-degree angle, and *DC* is opposite the 30-degree angle. Since $BD = 3\sqrt{3}$, $DC = \frac{3\sqrt{30}}{\sqrt{3}} = 3$. If $DC = 3$, then $AC = 3$ (since triangles *ABD* and *BDC* are identical). Thus $AC = 6$. The area of triangle *ABC* is:

$$\frac{1}{2} \times b \times h$$
$$= \frac{1}{2} \times 6 \times 3\sqrt{3}$$
$$= \frac{1}{2} \times 18\sqrt{3}$$
$$= 9\sqrt{3}$$

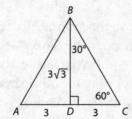

5. **A** Since triangle *ABC* has a leg of 6 and a hypotenuse of 10, side *BC* = 8 (this is a 6-8-10 triangle). If *BC* = 8, then *BD* = 8 − 5 = 3. $AB^2 + BD^2 = AD^2$. Substitute:

$$6^2 + 3^2 = AD^2$$
$$36 + 9 = AD^2$$
$$45 = AD^2$$
$$\sqrt{45} = AD^2$$
$$3\sqrt{5} = AD$$

6. **C** Since angle *BAD* = angle *ABD*, triangle *ABD* is an isosceles right triangle. Let x = the length of each leg of triangle *ABD*. The area will be $\frac{(x)(x)}{2}$. Solve for x. Triangle *BDC* is a right triangle with a leg of 5 and hypotenuse of 13. It is thus a 5-12-13 triangle. Side *BD* = 12. Substitute 12 for x to solve for the area of triangle *ABD*: $\frac{(12)(12)}{2} = 72$.

7. **E** First, draw the diagram:

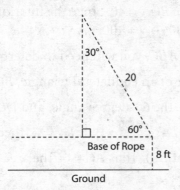

The rope starts off 8 feet above the ground. To determine its total height from the ground, solve for the side opposite the 60-degree angle and add 8. Since the triangle in the diagram is a 30-60-90 triangle, the side opposite the 60-degree angle will be $\sqrt{3}$ × the side opposite the 30-degree angle. The side opposite the 30-degree angle is half of the hypotenuse: $\frac{20}{2} = 10$. The side opposite the 60-degree angle is thus $10\sqrt{3}$. The rope is thus $8 + 10\sqrt{3}$ feet off the ground.

8. **18** Since triangles *BDC* and *EDC* are right triangles, calculate the area of triangle *BDC* and subtract that from the area of triangle *EDC*. Calculate the area of triangle *BDC*: since *ABCD* is a square, the diagonal is times the base. Thus *DC* = 12. If *DC* = 12, the area of triangle *BDC* = $12 \times 12 \times \frac{1}{2} = 72$.

Calculate the area of triangle *EDC*: Since *ABCD* is a square, the diagonal is $\sqrt{2}$ times the base. Thus *DC* = 12. If *DC* = 12, the area of triangle *EDC* = $12 \times 9 \times \frac{1}{2} = 54$. The difference of the areas of triangles BDC and EDC is 72 − 54 = 18.

9. **B** Since ∠*BDC* is the exterior angle of triangle *BAD*,

$$\angle BDC = \angle BAD + \angle DBA$$

$$2a = a + \angle DBA$$

$$\angle DBA = a$$

If ∠*DBA* = *a*, then triangle *BAD* is isosceles, and *BD* = *AD*. Since *AD* = 6, *BD* = 6. Since *BD* = *DC*, *DC* = 6.

10. **D** To solve for the perimeter, you need to solve for *AB* and *DC*. Triangle *ABD* is a 9-12-15 triangle (one of the multiples of a 3-4-5 triangle), so *AB* = 15. Triangle *BDC* is a 12-16-20 triangle (one of the multiples of a 3-4-5 triangle), so *DC* = 16. The perimeter is thus 15 + 20 + 9 + 16 = 60.

11. $\frac{16}{3}$ *This is a challenging question!* First, identify that *AB* = 5, since *AB* is the hypotenuse of a 3-4-5 triangle. Next, let *DC* = *x*. Since triangle *BDC* is a right triangle, you can use the Pythagorean theorem to express *BC* in terms of *x*:

$$x^2 + 16 = (BC)^2$$

$$\sqrt{x^2 + 16} = BC$$

Thus $5 + 3 + x + \sqrt{x^2 + 16} = 20$. Solve for x:

$$8 + x + \sqrt{x^2 + 16} = 20$$

$$x + \sqrt{x^2 + 16} = 12$$

$$\sqrt{x^2 + 16} = 12 - x$$

Square both sides:

$$\sqrt{x^2 + 16}^2 = (12 - x)^2$$

$$x^2 + 16 = 144 - 24x + x^2$$

$$\underline{- x^2 \qquad\qquad\qquad - x^2}$$

$$16 = 144 - 24x$$

$$\downarrow$$

$$-128 = -24x$$

$$\tfrac{16}{3} = x$$

12. **C** Since c is the hypotenuse of the right triangle, solve for a and b, and use the Pythagorean theorem to solve for c. Since the area is 24,

$$a \times b \times \tfrac{1}{2} = 24$$

$$ab = 48$$

Substitute $(b + 2)$ for a:

$$(b + 2)b = 48$$

$$b^2 + 2b = 48$$

$$b^2 + 2b - 48 = 0$$

$$(b + 8)(b - 6) = 0$$

$$b = -8 \text{ or } b = 6$$

Since b represents the length of a side, it must be positive. Thus $b = 6$. If $b = 6$, then $a = 8$. The triangle is thus a 6-8-10 triangle. $c = 10$.

13. **C** Plug in values: Let $XZ = 2\sqrt{2}$. In this case, XY and XZ will each equal 2. The area of triangle XYZ will be $2 \times 2 \times \tfrac{1}{2} = 2$. If $XZ = 2\sqrt{2}$, then $AC = \sqrt{2}$. If $AC = \sqrt{2}$, then AB and $BC = 1$. The area of triangle ABC is thus $1 \times 1 \times \tfrac{1}{2} = \tfrac{1}{2}$. 2 is 4 times as great as $\tfrac{1}{2}$.

14. **C** Since AB and ED are parallel lines cut by a transversal, the measure of angle BAD = the measure of angle EDC. Solve for EDC. Since $ED = DC$, angle ECD = angle DEC. Thus angle $DEC = 50$. Thus $50 + 50 + EDC = 180 \rightarrow EDC = 80$. Since $EDC = 80$, $BAD = 80$.

15. **A** Use the unknown multiplier:

$$3x = \text{smallest angle}$$

$$4x = \text{middle angle}$$

$$5x = \text{largest angle}$$

Thus

$$3x + 4x + 5x = 180$$

$$12x = 180$$

$$x = 15$$

The measurement of the smallest angle is $3(15) = 45$.

Quantitative Comparison Questions

1. **B** Based on the triangle inequality theorem,

    $$(9 - 7) < x < (7 + 9)$$

    $$2 < x < 16$$

    Since $x < 16$, Quantity B is greater. The correct answer is B.

2. **D** Since the triangle is isosceles, the third side can have a length of 7 or 12. If the length of the third side is 7, then the perimeter is $7 + 7 + 12 = 26$. In this case, the two quantities are equal. If the third side is 12, then the perimeter is $7 + 12 + 12 = 31$. In this case, Quantity A is greater. The relationship cannot be determined.

3. **A** Recall that the relationship of the sides in an obtuse triangle is $a^2 + b^2 < c^2$. In the triangle, this inequality is satisfied: $3^2 + 4^2 < 6^2$. Thus triangle ABC is obtuse and the measure of angle ABC > 90.

4. **A** To determine a relationship between the areas, determine the relationship between the side lengths. If the altitude in the triangle in Quantity A is 8, then the side length must be more than 8. To understand why, see the following figure.

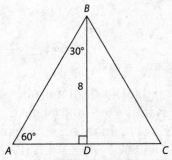

    Side AB is the hypotenuse of triangle ABD, which means that $AB > 8$. Thus the side length of the triangle in Quantity A is greater than the side length of the triangle in Quantity B. Therefore, the area of the triangle in Quantity A is greater.

5. **D** From the diagram, you can infer that

    $$x + (x + 30) + y = 180$$

    $$2x + y = 150$$

    However, without any other relationships, the relationship between x and y cannot be determined.

6. **C** Recall that the diagonal of a square splits the square into two right triangles. Since leg BC of 45-45-90 triangle ABE = the side of $BCDE$, the hypotenuse of ABE = the diagonal of $BCDE$. Thus $ABE = \frac{1}{2}$ of $BCDE$. The two quantities are equal.

7. **B** The shared side of the two triangles is AC. The perimeter of triangle $ACD = 3(AC)$. Since AC is the hypotenuse of a right triangle, the legs must be less than AC. Thus the perimeter of ABC will be less than $3(AC)$ and therefore less than the perimeter of ACD.

8. **B** The area of $XYQ = \frac{1}{2} \times XQ \times YQ$. The area of $YQZ = \frac{1}{2} \times QZ \times YQ$. Thus

$$\tfrac{1}{2} \times XQ \times YQ < \tfrac{1}{2} \times QZ \times YQ \rightarrow XQ < QZ$$

To solve for XY, use the Pythagorean theorem: $(XQ)^2 + (YQ)^2 = (XY)^2$. To solve for YZ, use the Pythagorean theorem: $(QZ)^2 + (YQ)^2 = (YZ)^2$. Since both triangles share side YQ and $XQ < QZ$, XY must be less than YZ.

9. **C** Since $AB = BC$, angle BAC = angle BCA.

$$BAC + BCA = 110$$

$$BAC = 55 \text{ and } BCA = 55$$

If $\angle BAC = 55$, then $\angle BAD = 55 - 30 = 25$. Since $AD = DC$, angle $\angle DCA = 30$. If $\angle DCA = 30$ and $\angle BCA = 55$, then $\angle BCD = 55 - 30 = 25$. The two quantities are equal.

Polygons

A **polygon** is any two-dimensional shape. Familiar examples of polygons are squares, triangles, and rectangles. Here are some definitions that you will find useful in working with polygons:

- **The Sum of the Angles:** The sum of the angles of any polygon can be determined by using the following formula: sum of the angles = $(n - 2)180$, where n = the number of sides.
- **The Perimeter of a Polygon:** The perimeter of any polygon will be the sum of its side lengths.
- **Quadrilaterals:** A quadrilateral is any four-sided polygon. *The sum of the angles of any quadrilateral is 360.* The quadrilaterals most commonly tested on the GRE are parallelograms.
- **Parallelograms:** A parallelogram is a quadrilateral in which opposite sides are parallel.

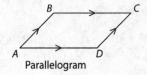

Parallelogram

A parallelogram has the following properties:

1. Opposite sides are equal.
2. Opposite angles are equal.
3. The area = base × height.
4. The diagonal of a parallelogram creates two equivalent triangles.
5. Adjacent angles add up to 180.

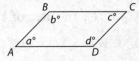

In the parallelogram above, $a = 2b$. What is c?

SOLUTION: From Property 4, you know that $a + b = 180$. Substitute $2b$ for a:

$$2b + b = 180$$

$$3b = 180$$

$$b = 60$$

$$a = 120$$

From Property 2, you know that $a = c$. Thus $c = 120$.

Rectangles and Squares

A **rectangle** is a special type of parallelogram in which all angles equal 90 degrees. The area of a rectangle is $l \times w$. The perimeter of a rectangle is $2(l + w)$.

A **square** is a special type of rectangle in which all sides are equal. The area of a square $= s^2$ (where $s =$ the length of a side). The perimeter of a square is $4s$ (where $s =$ the length of a side).

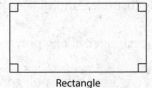

Rectangle   Square

What is the area of a square that has a perimeter of 20?

SOLUTION: Let $s =$ the length of a side of the square. Thus

$$4s = 20$$

$$s = 5$$

The area of the square is $5^2 = 25$.

In a certain rectangle, the length is double the width. If the area of the rectangle is 72, what is the length of the rectangle?

SOLUTION: Let w = the width of the rectangle. The length therefore equals $2w$. The area of the rectangle is $lw = 2w \times w = 2w^2 = 72$. Thus

$$w^2 = 36$$

$$w = 6$$

$$2w = 2(6) = 12$$

Maximizing the Area of a Polygon

Some tougher GRE questions will give you the perimeter of a parallelogram or triangle and ask you for the maximum area. *Given a fixed perimeter, the maximum area of any polygon will be reached when all sides are equal.*

Maximum Area of a Rectangle

To maximize the area of a rectangle, you should make the side lengths equal. Notice that when you do so, you create a square!

What is the maximum area of a rectangle with a perimeter of 28?

SOLUTION: To maximize the area of the rectangle, make all the sides equal. Let x = the length of one side. The perimeter is thus

$$4x = 28$$

$$x = 7$$

If $x = 7$, the area is $7^2 = 49$.

Maximizing Area with Given Side Lengths

In the preceding examples, you used the perimeter of the shapes to determine the side lengths that would maximize the area. Sometimes you will be given the lengths of the two sides of a parallelogram or triangle and asked to determine the maximum area from this information. In these situations, use the following rule: *Given the lengths of two sides of a triangle or parallelogram, you can maximize the area by making the two sides perpendicular.* In the case of a parallelogram, this means creating a rectangle. In the case of a triangle, this means creating a right triangle.

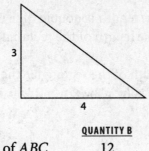

QUANTITY A	QUANTITY B
The maximum area of ABC	12

SOLUTION: To maximize the area of the triangle, make it a right triangle. Assume that the legs are AB and BC. In this case, the area of the triangle is $\frac{1}{2} \times 3 \times 4 = 6$. Quantity B is greater.

Exercise: Polygons

Discrete Quantitative Questions

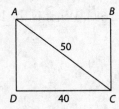
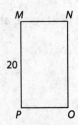

1. The area of rectangle *ABCD* is equal to the area of rectangle *MNOP*. What is the length of *MN*?

   (A) 30
   (B) 40
   (C) 50
   (D) 60
   (E) 70

For this question, write your answer in the box.

2. The angles in a six-sided polygon are in the ratio 2:3:4:4:5:6. What is the measure of the smallest angle?

3. A certain rectangle has an area of 36 and a perimeter of 26. If the length of the rectangle is greater than the width, what is the rectangle's length?

   (A) 4
   (B) 6
   (C) 9
   (D) 10
   (E) 13

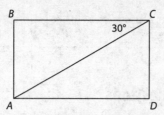

4. The area of the rectangle above is $36\sqrt{3}$. What is the length of diagonal *AC*?

   Ⓐ 6
   Ⓑ 12
   Ⓒ 18
   Ⓓ 24
   Ⓔ 30

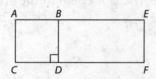

Note: Figure not drawn to scale

5. In the figure above, the area of square *ABCD* is half the area of rectangle *AEFC*. What is the ratio of *AC* to *BE*?

   Ⓐ $\frac{1}{4}$
   Ⓑ $\frac{1}{3}$
   Ⓒ $\frac{1}{2}$
   Ⓓ $\frac{1}{1}$
   Ⓔ $\frac{2}{1}$

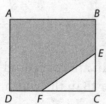

6. In the figure above, *ABCD* is a square with an area of 64. If *E* is the midpoint of *BC* and *F* is the midpoint of *DC*, what is the area of the shaded region?

   Ⓐ 24
   Ⓑ 32
   Ⓒ 48
   Ⓓ 56
   Ⓔ 60

For this question, write your answer in the box.

7. What is the maximum possible area of a rectangle with a perimeter of 24?

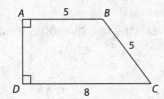

8. What is the area of the figure above?

    Ⓐ 18
    Ⓑ 24
    Ⓒ 26
    Ⓓ 32
    Ⓔ 40

For Questions 9 and 10, write your answer in the box.

9. What is the maximum possible area of a triangle with a side of length 7 and another side of length 10?

10. A rectangle has an area of 48 and a diagonal of 10. What is the perimeter of the rectangle?

Quantitative Comparison Questions

Each of the following questions consists of two quantities, Quantity A and Quantity B. You are to compare the two quantities. You may use additional information centered above the two quantities if additional information is given. Choose

- (A) if Quantity A is greater
- (B) if Quantity B is greater
- (C) if the two quantities are equal
- (D) if the relationship between the two quantities cannot be determined

The area of square *A* is double the area of square *B*

	QUANTITY A	QUANTITY B	
1.	The ratio of the length of a side of square *A* to the length of a side of square *B*	2	(A) (B) (C) (D)

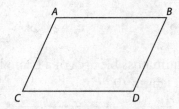

Quadrilateral *ABCD* is a parallelogram
Angle *ACD* is less than 60

	QUANTITY A	QUANTITY B	
2.	The measure of angle *CAB*	120	(A) (B) (C) (D)

	QUANTITY A	QUANTITY B	
3.	The measure of each interior angle in a regular octagon	130	(A) (B) (C) (D)

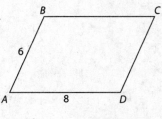

	QUANTITY A	QUANTITY B	
4.	The area of parallelogram ABCD	48	(A) (B) (C) (D)

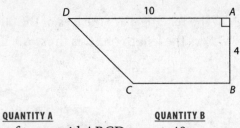

QUANTITY A	QUANTITY B	
5. The area of trapezoid ABCD	40	Ⓐ Ⓑ Ⓒ Ⓓ

Exercise Answers

Discrete Quantitative Questions

1. **D** *ADC* is a right triangle with sides 30, 40, and 50 (this is a multiple of the 3-4-5 triangle). Thus *AD* = 30. If *AD* = 30, the area of *ABCD* = *lw* = 30(40) = 1,200. Since the area of *MNOP* = 1,200:

$$0 \times (MN) = 1{,}200$$

$$MN = 60$$

2. **60** Recall that *the sum of the angles of a polygon* = $(n - 2)180$, where n = number of sides. Thus the sum of the angles in a six-sided polygon is $(6 - 2)180$ = 4(180) = 720. Use the unknown multiplier to represent the quantities of the angles as $2x$, $3x$, $4x$, $4x$, $5x$, and $6x$. The sum of these quantities = 720:

$$2x + 3x + 4x + 4x + 5x + 6x = 720$$

$$24x = 720$$

$$x = 30$$

The smallest angle = $2x$ = 2(30) = 60.

3. **C** Let l = length of the rectangle and w = width of the rectangle:

$$\text{Area} = lw = 36$$

$$\text{Perimeter} = 2(l + w) = 26$$

$$l + w = 13$$

Use substitution to solve for l: $w = 13 - l$. Substitute $(13 - l)$ for w in the first equation:

$$l(13 - l) = 36$$

$$13l - l^2 = 36$$

$$l^2 - 13l + 36 = 0$$

$$(l - 4)(l - 9) = 0$$

$$l = 4 \text{ or } l = 9$$

If l = 4, then w = 9. If l = 9, then w = 4. Since you are told that $l > w$, l = 9. The correct answer is C.

4. **B** The length and width of the rectangle are the legs of the 30-60-90 triangle ABC. Let the length of $AB = x$. The length of BC is thus $x\sqrt{3}$. Thus:

$$x \times x\sqrt{3} = 36\sqrt{3}$$

$$x^2 = 36$$

$$x = 6$$

The hypotenuse of a 30-60-90 triangle is double the shorter leg. Thus $AC = 12$.

5. **D** Since this question only provides relationships and no values, plugging in is a good strategy. First, choose a value for the area of the square. If $AB = 2$, then the area of the square $= 2^2 = 4$. If the area of the square is 4, then the area of the rectangle must be 8. Since $lw = AC \times AE = 8$, $AE = 4$. If $AB = 2$, then $BE = 2$. The ratio of AC to BE is $\frac{2}{2} = \frac{1}{1}$.

6. **D** To determine the area of the shaded region, subtract the area of the triangle from the area of the square. You are told that the area of the square is 64, so you must solve for the area of the triangle. Since the area of the square is 64, the length of each side must be 8. If the length of each side is 8, then $FC = 4$ and $EC = 4$. Since ECF is a right triangle, its area is $\frac{1}{2} \times 4 \times 4 = 8$. The area of the shaded region is thus $64 - 8 = 56$.

7. **36** To maximize the area of a rectangle, make the length and width as close as possible. You are told that

$$2(l + w) = 24$$

$$l + w = 12$$

Let $l = w = 6$. The resulting shape will be a square. The area of the square is $6^2 = 36$.

8. **C** Identify shapes within the figure that you are familiar with. The shape can be redrawn as a rectangle and right triangle, as indicated in the figure below:

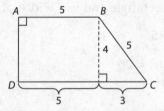

To find the area of the figure, add the area of the resulting rectangle and triangle. The area of the rectangle is $l \times w = 5 \times 4 = 20$. The area of the triangle is $\frac{1}{2} \times b \times h = \frac{1}{2} \times 3 \times 4 = 6$. The area of the figure is $20 + 6 = 26$. The correct answer is C.

9. **35** To maximize the area of a triangle, make the given sides perpendicular. When you do so, you will have a right triangle. Since 7 and 10 are the leg lengths of this right triangle, the area of the triangle is $\frac{1}{2} \times 7 \times 10 = 35$.

10. **28** You are asked to solve for $2(l + w)$, where $l = $ length of the rectangle and $w = $ width of the rectangle: area $= lw = 48$.

The formula for the perimeter of a rectangle is $2(l + w)$, where $l = $ the rectangle's length and $w = $ the rectangle's width. Thus, our goal in this question is to solve for $l + w$.

Since the area of the rectangle is 48, we know that $lw = 48$. Next, note that the diagonal of a rectangle is equivalent to the hypotenuse of a right triangle whose legs are the length and width of the rectangle. We can thus create the formula: $l^2 + w^2 = 10^2 = 100$.

Now, let's combine these two equations to solve for $l + w$.

Note that $(l + w)^2 = l^2 + 2lw + w^2$. Substitute 100 for $l^2 + w^2$, and 48 for lw to arrive at:

$$(l + w)^2 = 100 + 2(48) = 196.$$

Square-root both sides:

$$l + w = 14$$

Finally, substitute 14 for $(l + w)$ in the perimeter formula and arrive at:

$$2(l + w) = 2(14) = 28.$$

Quantitative Comparison Questions

1. **B** Plug in numbers. Let the area of square $A = 16$. In this case, the area of square $B = 8$. Each side of square A has a length of $\sqrt{16} = 4$. Each side of square B has a length of $\sqrt{8} = 2\sqrt{2}$. The ratio of 4 to $2\sqrt{2}$ is less than 2.

2. **A** Interior angles of a parallelogram must add up to 180. Thus the sum of the measures of angles ACD and CAB is 180. If the measure of angle ACD is less than 60, then the measure of angle CAB must be greater than 120.

3. **A** Recall that the sum of the interior angles of a regular polygon can be arrived at with the following formula: $(n - 2)180$, where n = number of sides. Since an octagon has 8 sides, the sum of its angles is $(8 - 2)180 = 1,080$. The measure of each angle is $\frac{1,080}{8} = 135$. Quantity A is greater.

4. **B** The area of a parallelogram can be determined by using the formula base × height. The base of the parallelogram is 8. To determine the relationship between the quantities, you must determine the relationship between the height and 6. Note that when you drop the height, a right triangle is formed in which the height of the parallelogram is one of the legs, and side AB is the hypotenuse.

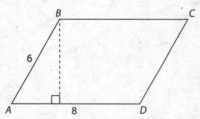

Since each leg of a right triangle must be smaller than the hypotenuse, the height of the parallelogram must be less than 6. The area of the parallelogram is thus less than 48.

5. **B** Instead of calculating, recognize that if BC were extended to have a length of 10, the area of the resulting rectangle would be 40. Since BC is less than 10, the area of the trapezoid must be less than 40.

Circles

A **circle** is a group of points that are all equidistant from a central point, known as the **center**. Any line segment that connects the center to a point on the circle is called the **radius**. Any circle has infinite radii, and all radii for a given circle are equal.

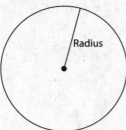

A **chord** is any line that connects two points on a circle. The **diameter** of a circle is any chord that passes through the center of the circle. The diameter is the longest possible chord.

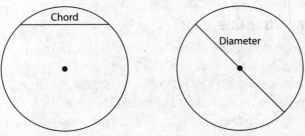

Note that *for any given circle, the diameter is twice the radius.* Thus when you are provided with the diameter of a circle, you can determine its radius and vice versa. A diameter is one type of **chord**.

Circumference and Area

Let's now look at calculations that involve the diameter and radius. The **circumference** of a circle is the perimeter of the circle. Think of it in the following way: If you flattened the circle to be a straight line, the length of that straight line would be the circle's circumference.

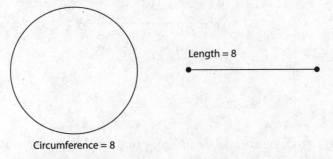

There is a constant relationship between circumference and diameter:

$$\frac{\text{circumference}}{\text{diameter}} = \pi$$

From this, you can derive the formula for circumference:

$$\text{circumference} = \pi \times \text{diameter} \ (d)$$

Pi (π) might appear intimidating, but it's simply a constant. Its value is roughly 3.14. For the GRE, though, almost any question that involves π will expect you to represent your answer using π instead of a decimal. For example, if you are asked to solve for the circumference of a circle with a diameter of 8, the answer would be 8π instead of $8 \times 3.14 = 25.12$.

What is the radius of a circle whose circumference is 24π?

(A) 6
(B) 12
(C) 18
(D) 24
(E) 30

SOLUTION: Use the circumference formula:

$$\pi(d) = 24\pi$$

$$24 = d$$

Since the radius is half of the diameter, the radius of the circle is 12. The correct answer is B.

The next element of a circle that you can calculate using radius and diameter is the **area**. The area of a circle represents the amount of space within that circle.

The formula for area of a circle is πr^2.

If a circle has a circumference of 16π, what is its area?

(A) 4π
(B) 8π
(C) 16π
(D) 64π
(E) 256π

SOLUTION: To solve for the circle's area, you need to determine the radius. Use the formula for circumference to determine the radius:

$$16\pi = \pi d$$

$$d = 16$$

Since $d = 2r$, $r = 8$. Substitute 8 for r in the area formula: area $= \pi 8^2 = 64\pi$. The answer is D.

Sector Area and Arc Length

Sector area represents the area of a piece of a circle. **Arc length** represents the length of a piece of a circle's circumference.

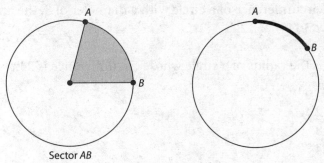

Sector *AB*

Keep in mind the following:

- **To determine sector area,** you will need to know the area of the circle and what fraction the given piece is of the entire circle's area.
- **To determine arc length,** you will need to know the circumference of the circle and what fraction the arc length is of the entire circumference.

If you are told what fraction the arc length or sector area is of a given circle, the question is pretty straightforward. Let's say a circle has an area of 16π. If you are asked to determine the area of $\frac{1}{4}$ of this circle, just divide the area by 4 and arrive at 4π. Likewise, let's say a circle has a circumference of 8π. If you are asked to calculate $\frac{1}{4}$ of the circumference, just divide the circumference by 4, and arrive at 2π.

Unfortunately, a real GRE question will not make things so simple. Instead of telling you what fraction the sector is of the entire circle, a typical question will expect you to infer this information from the **central angle** of the sector or arc. The central angle is simply the angle formed by two intersecting radii. For example, when you formed a quarter circle in the preceding example, the central angle was 90 degrees:

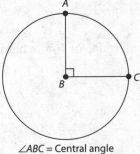

∠*ABC* = Central angle

From the preceding example, you can infer the following two relationships:

$$\frac{\text{central angle}}{360} = \frac{\text{sector area}}{\text{circle area}}$$

$$\frac{\text{central angle}}{360} = \frac{\text{arc length}}{\text{circumference}}$$

Why do these relationships hold? *Because the central angle is simply a fraction of the entire circle's angle measurement.* Since the angles around a circle's center measure 360, a central angle of 60 degrees means the sector area is $\frac{60}{360} = \frac{1}{6}$ of the circle's area. Similarly, if the central angle is 40, then the arc length is simply $\frac{40}{360} = \frac{1}{9}$ of the circumference. So how will you use the central angle to determine sector area? Let's look at an example.

If a circle has an area of 90π, what is the area of a sector with a central angle of 60 degrees?

1. Determine what fraction the sector is of the entire circle. Use the formula:

$$\frac{\text{central angle}}{360} = \frac{\text{sector area}}{\text{circle area}}$$

In this case, $\frac{60}{360} = \frac{1}{6}$. Thus the sector area is $\frac{1}{6}$ of the circle's entire area.

2. Multiply the area of the circle by $\frac{1}{6}$: $90\pi \times \frac{1}{6} = 15\pi$.

In the example, you used the central angle to determine the sector area, but you can also use sector area or arc length to determine the central angle.

A sector has an arc length of 9π and an area of 100π. What is the central angle of the sector?

SOLUTION: Use the formula central angle/360 = arc length/circumference. You know the arc length, so to determine the central angle, you need to determine the circumference, and then solve the proportion. You can use the area to determine the radius: $100\pi = \pi r^2$. Thus $r = 10$. If $r = 10$, then the diameter = 20, and the circumference = 20π. Now you can plug these values into the original formula: substitute 20π for the circumference and 9π for the arc-length:

$$\frac{\text{central angle}}{360} = \frac{\text{arc length}}{\text{circumference}}$$

$$\downarrow$$

$$\frac{\text{central angle}}{360} = \frac{9\pi}{20\pi}$$

$$\frac{\text{central angle}}{360} = \frac{9}{20}$$

$$\text{central angle} \times 20 = 360 \times 9$$

$$\text{central angle} = 162$$

Triangle in a Semicircle

If a triangle is inscribed in a semicircle, two properties follow:

1. The triangle is a right triangle.
2. The diameter of the circle = the triangle's hypotenuse.

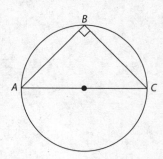

Exercise: Circles

Discrete Quantitative Questions

1. What is the circumference of a circle whose area is 49π?

    (A) 7π
    (B) 14π
    (C) 24.5π
    (D) 35π
    (E) 49π

2. What is the area of a circle whose circumference is π?

    (A) $\frac{\pi}{4}$

    (B) $\frac{\pi}{2}$

    (C) π

    (D) 2π

    (E) 4π

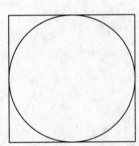

3. In the figure above, a circle is inscribed in a square with an area of 16. What is the area of the circle?

    (A) π
    (B) 2π
    (C) 4π
    (D) 8π
    (E) 16π

For the following question, write your answer in the box.

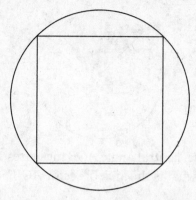

4. In the figure above, a square is inscribed in a circle whose area is 200π. What is the area of the square?

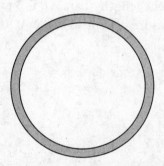

5. In the figure above, a circular pond is bordered by a garden with a uniform width of 2, represented by the shaded region. If the area of the circular pond is 81π, what is the area of the shaded region?

(A) 16π

(B) 20π

(C) 36π

(D) 40π

(E) 169π

Questions 6 and 7 refer to the figure below.

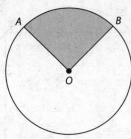

6. In the circle above, central angle *AOB* measures 120 degrees. If the radius of the circle is 3, what is the area of sector *AOB*?

   (A) $\frac{3}{2}\pi$
   (B) 3π
   (C) 6π
   (D) 9π
   (E) 18π

7. In the circle above, the length of arc *AB* is 3π. If the circle has an area of 16π, what is the measure of central angle *AOB*?

   (A) 45
   (B) 67.5
   (C) 95
   (D) 115
   (E) 135

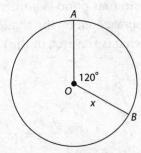

8. In the figure above, the measure of angle *AOB* is 120 degrees. If the radius of *OB* is *x*, then arc *AB* is what fraction of the area of sector *AOB*, in terms of *x*?

   (A) $\frac{\pi}{x}$
   (B) $\frac{\sqrt{3}}{x}$
   (C) $\frac{2}{x}$
   (D) $\frac{3}{x}$
   (E) $\frac{4}{x}$

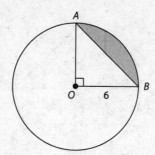

9. If the radius of the circle above is 6, then what is the area of the shaded region?

     Ⓐ 18
     Ⓑ 36
     Ⓒ $9\pi - 18$
     Ⓓ $18\pi - 18$
     Ⓔ $18\pi - 36$

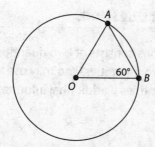

10. If the radius of the circle above is 4, what is the length of side AB?

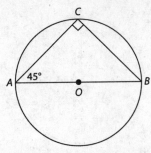

11. In the figure above, radius OB has a length of 4. What is the area of triangle *ABC*?

   (A) 4
   (B) 8
   (C) 12
   (D) 16
   (E) 20

Quantitative Comparison Questions

Each of the following questions consists of two quantities, Quantity A and Quantity B. You are to compare the two quantities. You may use additional information centered above the two quantities if additional information is given. Choose

   (A) if Quantity A is greater
   (B) if Quantity B is greater
   (C) if the two quantities are equal
   (D) if the relationship between the two quantities cannot be determined

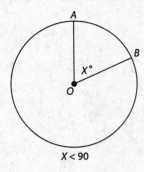

X < 90

QUANTITY A	QUANTITY B	
1. The area of sector AOB as a percentage of the circle's area	25%	(A) (B) (C) (D)

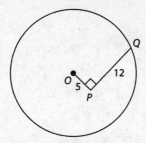

Point O is the center of the circle above.

QUANTITY A	QUANTITY B	
2. The radius of the circle	13	Ⓐ Ⓑ Ⓒ Ⓓ

The circumference of a certain circle is less than 40π

QUANTITY A	QUANTITY B	
3. The radius of the circle	19	Ⓐ Ⓑ Ⓒ Ⓓ

QUANTITY A	QUANTITY B	
4. The ratio of a circle's circumference to its diameter	3	Ⓐ Ⓑ Ⓒ Ⓓ

A circular wheel with a diameter of 3 feet rotates at a
constant speed of 2 revolutions per second.

QUANTITY A	QUANTITY B	
5. The distance the wheel travels in 1 minute	360 feet	Ⓐ Ⓑ Ⓒ Ⓓ

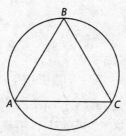

Equilateral triangle *ABC* is inscribed in the circle
above. The length of arc *ABC* is 36.

QUANTITY A	QUANTITY B	
6. The circumference of the circle	60	Ⓐ Ⓑ Ⓒ Ⓓ

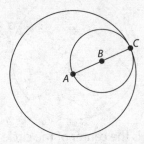

Point A is the center of the larger circle above. Point
B is the center of the smaller circle above.

QUANTITY A	QUANTITY B	
7. The ratio of the area of the smaller circle to the area of the larger circle	$\frac{1}{2}$	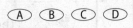

Exercise Answers

Discrete Quantitative Questions

1. **B** Use the area formula:

$$49\pi = \pi(r^2)$$

$$49 = r^2$$

$$r = 7$$

The diameter is thus 14. The circumference = 14π

2. **A** Use the circumference formula:

$$\pi d = \pi$$

$$d = 1$$

$$r = \frac{1}{2}$$

Now substitute $\frac{1}{2}$ for r in the area formula: area = $\pi(\frac{1}{2})^2 = \frac{\pi}{4}$.

3. **C** If the area of the square is 16, then each of its sides = $\sqrt{16}$ = 4. The side of the square represents the diameter of the circle, so the circle's diameter is also 4. Thus the radius of the circle is 2. Substitute 2 for the radius in the area formula: area = $\pi(r^2) = \pi(2^2) = 4\pi$.

4. **400** The key to solving this question is to recognize that the diameter of the circle is the diagonal of the square:

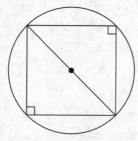

To solve for the area of the square, first solve for the diagonal: if area of the circle = 200π, then

$$200\pi = \pi(r^2)$$

$$200 = r^2$$

$$10\sqrt{2} = r$$

If $r = 10\sqrt{2}$, then the diameter = $20\sqrt{2}$. The diagonal of the square is thus $20\sqrt{2}$. Recall that the diagonal of a square forms two 45-45-90 triangles. The side length of the square will be the leg of one of the 45-45-90 triangles. Since the hypotenuse of one of the resulting 45-45-90 triangles is $20\sqrt{2}$, the length of the leg will be 20. Thus the side of the square = 20. The area of the square is $20^2 = 400$.

5. **D** The area of the shaded region = area of the larger circle – area of the pond. You are told that the area of the pond is 81π, so solve for the area of the larger circle. The radius of the larger circle = the radius of the pond + width of the garden. Use the area formula to solve for the radius of the pond:

$$81\pi = \pi r^2$$

$$81 = r^2$$

$$9 = r$$

Add 9 to the width of the garden: 9 + 2 = 11. The radius of the larger circle is thus 11, and its area is $\pi(11^2) = 121\pi$. The area of the shaded region is thus: $121\pi - 81\pi = 40\pi$.

6. **B** Since the central angle measures 120, the sector area = $\frac{120}{360}$ × the circle area = $\frac{120}{360} \times \pi 3^2 = \frac{1}{3}(9\pi) = 3\pi$.

7. **E** Use the formula: central angle/360 = arc length/circumference. Plug in what you are told: $\frac{\text{central angle}}{360} = \frac{3\pi}{\text{circumference}}$. To solve for the central angle, you must solve for the circumference.

$$\text{area} = \pi r^2 = 16\pi$$

$$r^2 = 16$$

$$r = 4$$

The diameter = $2r$ = 8. The circumference = 8π. Substitute 8π for the circumference in the preceding proportion:

$$\frac{\text{central angle}}{360} = \frac{3\pi}{8\pi}$$

$$\frac{\text{central angle}}{360} = \frac{3}{8}$$

$$\text{central angle} = (\tfrac{3}{8})360 = 135$$

8. **C** Since the central angle is 120 degrees, the arc length = $\frac{120}{360} \times 2\pi x$, and the sector area = $\frac{120}{360} \times \pi x^2$. Thus

$$\frac{\text{length of arc AB}}{\text{area of sector AOB}} = \frac{\frac{120}{360} \times 2\pi x}{\frac{120}{360} \times \pi x^2}$$

$$= \frac{1}{3} \times \frac{2\pi x}{\frac{1}{3} \times \pi x^2}$$

$$= \frac{2\pi x}{\pi x^2}$$

$$= \frac{2x}{x^2}$$

$$= \frac{2}{x}$$

9. **C** To determine the area of the shaded region, calculate the area of sector *AOB* and subtract the area of triangle *AOB*. Since the central angle of sector *AOB* is 90, the area of sector AOB = $\frac{90}{360} \times \pi r^2 = \frac{90}{360} \times \pi 6^2 = \frac{1}{4}(36\pi) = 9\pi$. The area of right triangle AOB = $\frac{1}{2} \times \text{leg}_1 \times \text{leg}_2 = \frac{1}{2} \times 6 \times 6 = 18$. The area of the shaded region is thus $9\pi - 18$.

10. **4** Since *AO* and *AB* are radii of the circle, they must be equal. Thus, corresponding angles *BAO* and *ABO* must be equal. Since angle *ABO* = 60, angle *BO* = 60. Thus angle *AOB* + 60 + 60 = 180 → angle *AOB* = 60. All three angles of the triangle are equal, which means all three sides are equal. Thus the length of *AB* is 4.

11. **D** When a right angle is inscribed in a semicircle, its hypotenuse = the diameter of the circle. Thus *AB* = 8. Since *ABC* is a 45-45-90 triangle, each of the legs = $\frac{8}{\sqrt{2}}$. The area of triangle *ABC* is thus $\frac{1}{2} \times (\frac{8}{\sqrt{2}})^2 = \frac{1}{2} \times \frac{64}{2} = \frac{1}{2} \times 32 = 16$.

Quantitative Comparison Questions

1. **B** Since $x < 90$, the sector area will be less than $\frac{90}{360} \times$ the area of the circle. Thus the sector area will be less than 25% of the area of the circle.

2. **C** Since point Q is on the circle, the circle's radius is equivalent to *OQ*. Note that *OQ* is the hypotenuse of right triangle *OPQ*. Since the legs of the right

triangle are 5 and 12, the hypotenuse *OPQ* and thus the radius of the circle must be 13.

3. **D** Test Choice B against the conditions in the prompt. If the radius of the circle is 19, then the circumference of the circle is 38π. Since you are told that the circumference is less than 40π, a radius greater than 19 or smaller than 19 would satisfy the given conditions. Thus the relationship between the two quantities cannot be determined.

4. **A** Since circumference $= \pi \times$ diameter, Quantity A can be expressed as $\frac{\pi \times \text{diameter}}{\text{diameter}} = \pi$. π is approximately 3.14, which is greater than 3. Thus Quantity A is greater.

5. **A** Each time the wheel revolves, it travels the equivalent of its circumference. Thus the wheel travels $3\pi \times 2 = 6\pi$ feet per second. Set up a proportion: $\frac{\text{distance}}{\text{time}} = \frac{6\pi \text{ feet}}{\text{second}} = \frac{x \text{ feet}}{60 \text{ seconds}} \rightarrow x = 360\pi$. Quantity A is greater.

6. **B** Since triangle *ABC* is equilateral, the rays of each angle intersect $\frac{1}{3}$ of the circle's circumference. Thus, arc *ABC* represents $\frac{2}{3}$ of the circle's circumference. If arc *ABC* is $\frac{2}{3}$ of the circle's circumference, it follows that $36 = \frac{2}{3} \times y$, where $y = $ the circle's circumference. Thus $y = 36 \times \frac{3}{2} = 54$. Quantity B is greater.

7. **B** Since *AC* is the radius of the larger circle and the diameter of the smaller circle, it follows that the diameter of the larger circle is double the diameter of the smaller circle. To determine the ratio, plug in numbers. Let $AC = 4$ and $BC = 2$. If $AC = 4$, the area of the larger circle is $\pi 4^2 = 16\pi$ and the area of the smaller circle is $\pi 2^2 = 4\pi$. The ratio of the area of the smaller circle to the area of the larger circle is thus $\frac{4\pi}{16\pi} = \frac{4}{16} = \frac{1}{4}$. Quantity B is greater.

Solids and Cylinders

So far, you have only looked at two-dimensional shapes. The GRE will occasionally test your knowledge of three-dimensional shapes. You will need to know how to calculate the surface area and volume of rectangular solids, cubes, and cylinders. A **cube** is a type of rectangular solid, so let's consider cubes and rectangular solids together.

If your test date is very close, you should focus on memorizing the formulas in bold.

Surface Area of a Rectangular Solid and a Cube

The following figure is a rectangular solid:

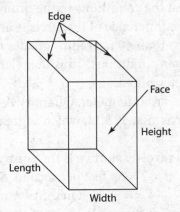

The **edge** of a rectangular solid refers to any line that joins two vertices, and the **face** of a rectangular solid refers to any of the rectangles formed by four edges. All rectangular solids have six faces, and *opposite faces have the same dimensions.*

The surface area of any three-dimensional shape refers to the total area covered by the shape's surface.

It may seem tedious to calculate surface area of a rectangular solid, since you would presumably need to calculate the area of each face. But remember that opposite faces have the same dimensions. So instead of calculating the area of each face, just calculate the area of each unique face and double that.

The formula for calculating surface area of a rectangular solid is therefore:

$$SA_{\text{rectangular solid}} = 2lw + 2lh + 2wh$$

What is the surface area of a rectangular solid with dimensions $3 \times 4 \times 5$?

SOLUTION: Use the preceding formula. Let $l = 3$, $w = 4$, and $h = 5$. Substitute: $2(3)(4) + 2(3)(5) + 2(4)(5) = 94$.

A cube is a type of rectangular solid in which all **edges** are equal. Since all edges of a cube are equal, all faces will have an equal area.

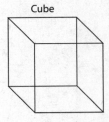

Thus *to calculate the surface area of a cube, just calculate the area of one face and multiply that by six* (since the cube has six sides). The formula for the surface area of a cube is

$$SA_{cube} = 6e^2, \text{ where } e = \text{the length of an edge}$$

If the area of one face of a cube is 81, what is the surface area of the cube?

SOLUTION: Since all faces have the same area, the surface area of the cube = $81 \times 6 = 486$.

Volume of a Rectangular Solid and Cube

The volume of a rectangular solid refers to the amount of space within that shape. Volume is measured in cubic units, such as 2 cubic meters or 3.7 cubic inches. To calculate the *volume of a rectangular solid*, just multiply all the dimensions:

$$V_{rectangular\ solid} = l \times w \times h$$

The same rule applies to a cube. But since all the edges of a cube are equal, you just need one side of the cube to calculate a *cube's volume*:

$$V_{cube} = e^3$$

If the volume of a rectangular solid with a length of 4, a width of 2, and a height of x equals the volume of a cube with an edge of 4, what is x?

(A) 1
(B) 2
(C) 4
(D) 8
(E) 16

SOLUTION: Since the volumes are equal,

$$4 \times 2 \times x = 4^3$$

$$8x = 64$$

$$x = 8$$

The correct answer is D.

Diagonal of a Rectangular Solid

The **diagonal** of a rectangular solid is the straight line distance from one vertex to the opposite vertex.

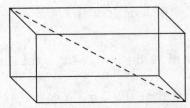

To determine the *diagonal of a rectangular solid,* use the following formula:

$$\text{diagonal}_{\text{rectangular solid}} = \sqrt{l^2 + w^2 + h^2}$$

If a rectangular solid has dimensions of 5, 5, and 10, what is the greatest straight-line distance from one vertex to another vertex?

- Ⓐ 10
- Ⓑ 20
- Ⓒ 25
- Ⓓ $5\sqrt{2}$
- Ⓔ $5\sqrt{6}$

SOLUTION: Use the formula: Let $l = 5$, $w = 5$, and $h = 10$. The diagonal = $\sqrt{5^2 + 5^2 + 10^2} = \sqrt{150} = 5\sqrt{6}$. The correct answer is E.

The diagonal of a cube = $e\sqrt{3}$.

Cylinders

A **cylinder** is rectangular solid whose base is a circle.

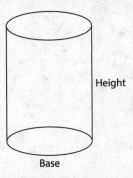

Height

Base

To determine the volume of a cylinder, multiply the area of the base by the height. In the case of a cylinder, the area of the base is πr^2 since the base is a circle. The formula for the *volume of a cylinder* is

$$V_{\text{cylinder}} = \pi r^2 h$$

For this question, write your answer in the box.

How many cubic feet of water are needed to fill a cylinder with a radius of 10 feet and a height of 6 feet?

$$\boxed{}$$

SOLUTION: Use the volume formula: volume $= \pi r^2 h = \pi 10^2(6) = 600\pi$

The formula for the surface area of a cylinder is:

$$SA_{cylinder} = 2\pi rh + 2\pi r^2$$

This formula, however, is rarely tested.

Exercise: Solids and Cylinders

Discrete Quantitative Questions

1. If the volume of a cube equals its surface area, what is the length of an edge of the cube?

   (A) 3
   (B) 6
   (C) 9
   (D) 12
   (E) 18

2. What is the surface area of a cube whose volume is 125?

   (A) 100
   (B) 125
   (C) 150
   (D) 175
   (E) 200

For this question, write your answer in the box.

3. What is the volume, in cubic inches, of a cube whose edges each measure 2 feet?

   +-------------------------+
   | |
   +-------------------------+

4. A certain cylinder with radius, r, and height, h, has the same volume as a cube with edge, e. If the radius of the cylinder equals the edge of the cube, what is h, in terms of e?

   (A) $e\pi$
   (B) $e^2\pi$
   (C) $e^5\pi$
   (D) e/π
   (E) e^2/π

5. What is the length of the diagonal of a cube whose surface area is 216?

   Ⓐ 6

   Ⓑ 9

   Ⓒ 12

   Ⓓ $6\sqrt{3}$

   Ⓔ $9\sqrt{3}$

6. An empty cylindrical tank with a radius of 5 inches and a height of 10 inches is filled with water at a rate of 75 cubic feet per second. Approximately how many seconds will it take for the tank to be full?

   Ⓐ 8

   Ⓑ 9

   Ⓒ 11

   Ⓓ 13

   Ⓔ 15

For this question, write your answer in the box.

7. The edge of Cube X is half the length of the edge of Cube Y. What is the ratio of the volume of Cube X to the volume of Cube Y?

   $$\boxed{} \atop \boxed{}$$

8. The length of a certain rectangular solid is doubled, its width is tripled, and its height is quadrupled. The volume of the resulting rectangular solid will be what percent greater than the volume of the original rectangular solid?

   Ⓐ 1,100%

   Ⓑ 1,200%

   Ⓒ 2,200%

   Ⓓ 2,300%

   Ⓔ 2,400%

For this question, write your answer in the box.

9. What is the maximum number of cubes with an edge of length 5 that can fit into a box whose dimensions are $10 \times 15 \times 20$?

$$\boxed{}$$

10. Three metal cubes with edges of two will be dropped into an empty cylindrical tank with a base radius of 3 and a height of 8. The three cubes will take up what fraction of the volume of the tank?

(A) $\frac{1}{3}$

(B) $\frac{1}{\pi}$

(C) $\frac{3}{\pi}$

(D) $\frac{1}{3}\pi$

(E) $\frac{2}{3}\pi$

Quantitative Comparison Questions

Each of the following questions consists of two quantities, Quantity A and Quantity B. You are to compare the two quantities. You may use additional information centered above the two quantities if additional information is given. Choose

(A) if Quantity A is greater
(B) if Quantity B is greater
(C) if the two quantities are equal
(D) if the relationship between the two quantities cannot be determined

	QUANTITY A	QUANTITY B	
1.	The diagonal of a cube whose edges have a length of 3	The diagonal of a rectangular solid whose dimensions are $2 \times 3 \times 4$	(A) (B) (C) (D)

	QUANTITY A	QUANTITY B	
2.	The volume of a rectangular solid whose dimensions are $4 \times 5 \times 6$	The volume of a cylinder with a base radius of e and a height of 6	(A) (B) (C) (D)

The edge of a certain cube is greater than 6.

	QUANTITY A	QUANTITY B	
3.	The volume of the cube	The surface area of the cube	(A) (B) (C) (D)

Exercise Answers

Discrete Quantitative Questions

1. **B** Let e = the edge of the cube. Using the formulas for surface area and volume, divide both sides by e^2: $\frac{e^3}{e^2} = \frac{6e^2}{e^2} \rightarrow e = 6$

$$e^3 = 6e^2$$

$$e = 6$$

2. **C** To solve for surface area, use the formula surface area of a cube = $6e^2$, where e = edge length. If the volume is 125, then

$$e^3 = 125$$

$$e = 5$$

   Substitute e into the formula for surface area: $6(5)^2 = 150$.

3. **13,824 cubic inches** First, convert from feet to inches. 2 feet = 24 inches. The volume of the cube, in cubic inches, is thus $24^3 = 13{,}824$ cubic inches.

4. **D** Let e = the length of the cube's edge. Thus the radius of the cylinder also = e. Now create an equation: $\pi(e^2)h = e^3$. Isolate h: $h = \frac{e}{\pi}$.

5. **D** Recall that the length of the diagonal of a cube = $e\sqrt{3}$, where e = length of an edge of the cube. To solve for the edge of the cube, we'll use the fact that the surface area of the cube = 216.

   Use the formula for surface area to solve for the edge:

$$6e^2 = 216$$

$$e^2 = 36$$

$$e = 6$$

   Now, substitute 6 for e into the formula for the diagonal of a cube to arrive at $6\sqrt{3}$.

6. **C** The volume of the tank is $\pi(r^2)h = \pi(5^2)10 = 250\pi$. To solve for time, use the $r \times t = w$ formula, where the rate is 75 cubic feet/second, and the work is 250π:

$$r \times t = w$$

$$75t = 250\pi$$

$$T = 250\pi/75 \approx 10.5 \text{ seconds}$$

   The closest answer is C.

7. $\frac{1}{8}$ Plug in numbers. Let the edge of cube $y = 4$. The edge of Cube X is thus 2. In this case, the volume of Cube Y is $4^3 = 64$, and the volume of Cube X is $2^3 = 8$. $\frac{\text{Volume of X}}{\text{Volume of Y}} = \frac{8}{64} = \frac{1}{8}$.

8. **D** Plug in numbers. Let the original length = 2, the original width = 3, and the original height = 4. The original volume is thus $2 \times 3 \times 4 = 24$. The new length will be $2 \times 2 = 4$. The new width will be $3 \times 3 = 9$. The new height will be $4 \times 4 = 16$. The new volume is thus $4 \times 9 \times 16 = 576$. Now use the percent greater formula: Percent of – 100%: $(\frac{576}{24} \times 100) - 100 = 2{,}300\%$.

9. **24** The volume of the box is $10 \times 15 \times 20 = 3{,}000$. Each of the small cubes being placed into the box has a volume of $5^3 = 125$. The number of cubes that can fit into the box $= \frac{3{,}000}{125} = 24$.

10. **D** Each metal cube has a volume of $2^3 = 8$. Since there are three metal cubes, their combined volume is $8 \times 3 = 24$. The volume of the cylinder is $\pi(r^2)h = \pi(3^2)(8) = 72\pi$. $\frac{24}{72\pi} = \frac{1}{3}\pi$.

Quantitative Comparison Questions

1. **B** The formula for the diagonal of a cube is $e\sqrt{3}$. The value in Quantity A is thus $3\sqrt{3}$. The formula for the diagonal of a rectangular solid is $\sqrt{l^2 + w^2 + h^2}$. The value in Quantity B is thus $\sqrt{4 + 9 + 16} = \sqrt{29}$. $\sqrt{29} > 3\sqrt{3}$. Thus Quantity B is greater because squaring both sides of the equation will show that $29 > 9 \times 3$.

2. **B** The value in Quantity A is $4 \times 5 \times 6 = 120$. The value in Quantity B is $\pi(3^2)6 = 54\pi$. $54\pi > 120$. Quantity B is greater.

3. **A** Let $e =$ the edge of the cube. You are thus comparing e^3 to $6e^2$. To simplify the comparison, divide both sides by e^2 (you can do this since e^2 is positive). The new comparison is thus:

QUANTITY A	QUANTITY B
e	6

Since you are told that $e > 6$, Quantity A is greater.

The Coordinate Plane

The **coordinate plane** is used to designate points in a two-dimensional plane. It is created by two perpendicular lines that meet at the **origin**. The horizontal line is called the **x-axis** and the vertical line is called the **y-axis**. These lines split the plane into four **quadrants**: I, II, III, and IV.

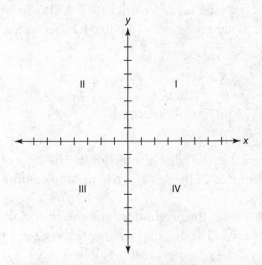

Points on the coordinate plane are designated by assigning two numbers: an **x-coordinate** and a **y-coordinate**. A point is written in the form (**x,y**).

The x-coordinate designates the horizontal position of a point. If a point is to the right of the origin, then its x-coordinate is positive. If a point is to the left of the origin, then its x-coordinate is negative. If a point is on the y-axis, then its x-coordinate is zero.

The y-coordinate designates the vertical position of a point. If a point is above the origin, then its y-coordinate is positive. If a point is below the origin, then its y-coordinate is negative. If a point is on the x-axis, then its y-coordinate is zero.

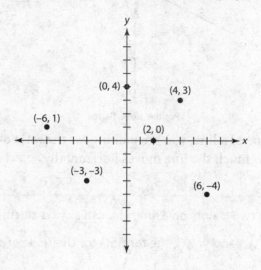

Properties of a Line

On the coordinate plane, a line is formed by joining two points. Any line on the coordinate plane will be defined by the following equation:

$y = mx + b$

x and y can refer to any point on the line, but m and b are constants—they define properties of a line.

Slope

In the equation $y = mx + b$, m refers to the slope of the line. The **slope** of a line indicates its steepness and whether it is rising or falling.

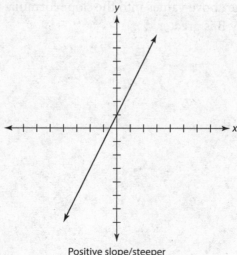

Positive slope/steeper

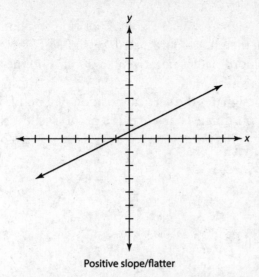

Positive slope/flatter

To determine the slope of a line, you are looking for the ratio of how much the line rises vertically to how much the line moves horizontally.

If you are given two points on a line, you can always calculate the slope.

Given points (x_1, y_1) and (x_2, y_2), the formula for the *slope of a line* is:

$$m = \frac{y_2 - y_1}{x_2 - x_1}$$

What is the slope of a line that contains the points (2,3) and (5,7)?

SOLUTION: Use the preceding formula: $\frac{y_2 - y_1}{x_2 - x_1} = \frac{7 - 3}{5 - 2} = \frac{4}{3}$.

Line k passes through the points (2,3) and (4,6).

QUANTITY A	QUANTITY B
The slope of line k	2

SOLUTION: Plug the above values into the slope formula: $\frac{y_2 - y_1}{x_2 - x_1} = \frac{6 - 3}{4 - 2} = \frac{3}{2}$. $2 > \frac{3}{2}$, so Quantity B is greater.

Y-intercept

In the equation $y = mx + b$, b refers to the **y-intercept** of the line. The y-intercept of a line refers to where a line crosses the y-axis. Since this point is on the y-axis, the x-coordinate will always be zero.

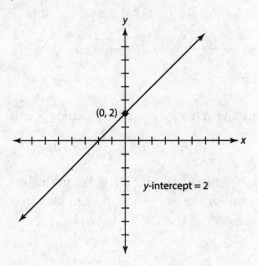

Points and the Equation for a Line

Once you know the slope and y-intercept of a line, you can substitute those values into the equation for the line. For example, if you are told that a line has a y-intercept of 3 and a slope of 7, plug in 3 for b and 7 for m: $y = 7x + 3$.

Sometimes, the GRE will define a line using a different form than the previous one. *Always manipulate the equation to be in* $y = mx + b$ *form.*

If the equation for line k is $2x + 3y = 6$, what is the slope of line k?

SOLUTION: Isolate y so that the equation is in $y = mx + b$ form. Subtract $2x$:

$$2x + 3y = 6$$

$$\underline{-2x \qquad -2x}$$

$$3y = -2x + 6$$

Divide both sides by 3:

$$\frac{3y}{3} = \frac{-2x + 6}{3}$$

$$y = -\frac{2}{3}x + 2$$

The slope of the line is $-\frac{2}{3}$.

Using Two Points to Determine a Line

Generally, if the GRE asks you to determine the equation for a line, it will do so by providing you with two points. Let's look at how to do so:

What is the equation for the line that passes through (2,11) and (5,20)?

Step 1: Use the slope formula to determine m:

$$\frac{y_2 - y_1}{x_2 - x_1} = \frac{20 - 11}{5 - 2} = \frac{9}{3} = 3$$

Step 2: Substitute the value for m in the equation for the line:

$$y = 3x + b$$

Step 3: Solve for b: Since (2,11) and (5,20) lie on the line, both points will satisfy the equation for the line. Thus you can plug in the coordinates for either point to solve for b. Use the point (2,11):

$$11 = 3(2) + b$$

$$b = 5$$

Step 4: Substitute b into the equation:

$$y = 3x + 5$$

Using a Line to Determine a Point

In the previous example, you used two points on a line to determine its equation. In other situations, you will be given the equation for a line and will be asked to find a point that lies on the line. Let's look at an example:

If line k is defined by the equation $y = 7x + 3$, then which of the following points must lie on the line?

- Ⓐ (3,7)
- Ⓑ (7,3)
- Ⓒ (3,0)
- Ⓓ (2,17)
- Ⓔ (17,2)

SOLUTION: Plug each point into the equation. Whichever point keeps the equation true will be your answer.

$$\textbf{A: } 7 = 7(3) + 3? \qquad \rightarrow \text{False}$$

$$\textbf{B: } 3 = 7(7) + 3? \qquad \rightarrow \text{False}$$

$$\textbf{C: } 0 = 7(3) + 3? \qquad \rightarrow \text{False}$$

$$\textbf{D: } 17 = 7(2) + 3? \qquad \rightarrow \text{True}$$

$$\textbf{E: } 2 = 7(17) + 3? \qquad \rightarrow \text{False}$$

The correct answer is D.

Horizontal and Vertical Lines

Any horizontal line will have a slope of zero. Because such lines have no slope, they will always be written in the form: $y = b$. For example, the equation for the line below is $y = 7$.

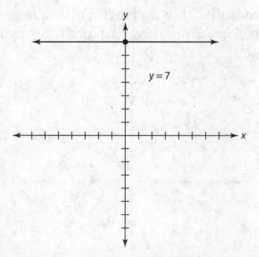

Any vertical line will have an undefined slope. Such lines will be written in the form: $x = a$, where a represents the **x-intercept** of the line. For example, the equation for the line below is $x = 4$.

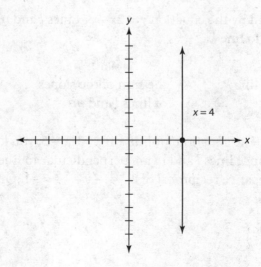

Parallel and Perpendicular Lines

If two lines are **parallel**, then their slopes are equal and the lines *never* intersect. (See figure.)

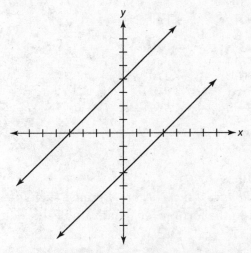

If two lines are **perpendicular**, then the product of their slopes is −1. Another way to say this is that their slopes are negative reciprocals. (See figure.)

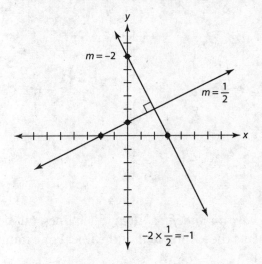

Line k is defined by the equation $y = 2x - 3$. Lines l and m are each perpendicular to line k.

<u>QUANTITY A</u>
the slope of line k

<u>QUANTITY B</u>
the sum of the slopes
of lines l and m

SOLUTION: Since the equation for line k is $y = 2x - 3$, you know that the slope of line k is 2. Since lines l and m are perpendicular to line k, each of their slopes is the negative reciprocal of 2: $-\frac{1}{2}$. $-\frac{1}{2} + -\frac{1}{2} = -1$. Quantity A is greater.

Distance Between Two Points

You can use the Pythagorean theorem to calculate the distance between two points on the coordinate plane. For example:

What is the distance between (1,3) and (4,7)?

Step 1: Plot the two points.

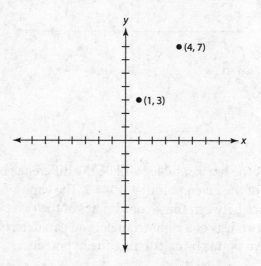

Step 2: Connect the two points to create a right triangle.

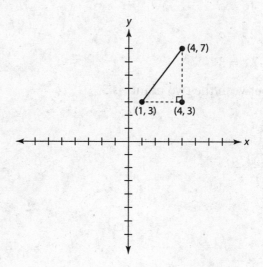

Step 3: Calculate the lengths of each side of the resulting triangle:

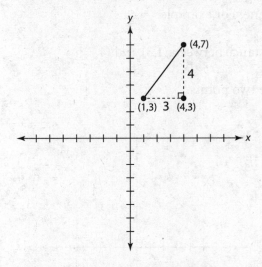

The length of the horizontal leg will be the difference between the
x-coordinates of the given points: $4 - 1 = 3$. The length of the vertical leg will
be the difference between the y-coordinates of the two points: $7 - 3 = 4$. Now
that you have two legs of a right triangle, you can determine the distance
between the two points by calculating the hypotenuse:

$$3^2 + 4^2 = c^2$$

$$9 + 16 = c^2$$

$$25 = c^2$$

$$c = 5$$

The distance between the two points is 5.

Exercise: The Coordinate Plane

Discrete Quantitative Questions

For this question, write your answer in the box.

1. What is the slope of a line whose equation is $2x + 5y - 3 = 12$?

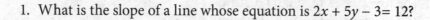

2. If line p is defined by the equation $3x - 2y = -12$, then which of the following points must lie on line p?

   (A) (0,12)
   (B) (12,18)
   (C) (12,24)
   (D) (2,3)
   (E) (3,2)

3. What is the x-intercept of line k, if line k has a slope of $\frac{2}{3}$ and contains the point (6,14)?

   (A) -15
   (B) -14
   (C) 0
   (D) 10
   (E) 15

4. In the xy-plane, the center of circle C is at point (0,0). If the point $(-5,5)$ is on the circumference of the circle, what is the radius of the circle?

   (A) 5
   (B) 10
   (C) 7.5
   (D) $5\sqrt{2}$
   (E) $10\sqrt{2}$

For this question, indicate all answers that apply.

5. If the slope of a line on the coordinate plane is negative, which of the following must be true?

   ☐A The line passes through Quadrant I.
   ☐B The line passes through Quadrant II.
   ☐C The line passes through Quadrant III.
   ☐D The line passes through Quadrant IV.
   ☐E The line passes through the origin.

6. If line l is perpendicular to line k, which of the following must be true?

   Ⓐ The slopes of l and k are equal.
   Ⓑ The product of the slopes of l and k is 1.
   Ⓒ The product of the slopes of l and k is −1.
   Ⓓ The y-intercepts l and k are equal.
   Ⓔ The x-intercepts of l and k are equal.

7. Point (2,3) is the vertex of a square, and point (−2,7) is the opposite vertex of the same square. What is the area of the square?

   Ⓐ 8
   Ⓑ 9
   Ⓒ 16
   Ⓓ 25
   Ⓔ $16\sqrt{2}$

8. Line k is defined by the equation $y = 4x - b$. If the x-intercept of line k is 3, what is b?

   Ⓐ 0
   Ⓑ $\frac{3}{4}$
   Ⓒ $\frac{4}{3}$
   Ⓓ 4
   Ⓔ 12

9. Line l is defined by the equation $y = 3x + 10$. If lines l and k intersect to form a right angle at the point (3,4), which of the following is the equation of line k?

   Ⓐ $y = -3x + 6$
   Ⓑ $y = -3x + 10$
   Ⓒ $y = 3x + 10$
   Ⓓ $y = -\frac{1}{3}x + 5$
   Ⓔ $y = -\frac{1}{3}x + 6$

10. Line k is defined by the equation $ax + by = c$. If the slope of line k is positive, which of the following must be true?

Ⓐ $\frac{a}{b} > 0$

Ⓑ $\frac{a}{b} < 0$

Ⓒ $a > 0$

Ⓓ $b > 0$

Ⓔ $a + b > 0$

Quantitative Comparison Questions

Each of the following questions consists of two quantities, Quantity A and Quantity B. You are to compare the two quantities. You may use additional information centered above the two quantities if additional information is given. Choose

Ⓐ if Quantity A is greater
Ⓑ if Quantity B is greater
Ⓒ if the two quantities are equal
Ⓓ if the relationship between the two quantities cannot be determined

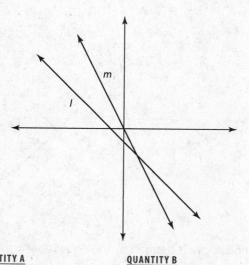

	QUANTITY A	QUANTITY B	
1.	The slope of line l	The slope of line m	Ⓐ Ⓑ Ⓒ Ⓓ

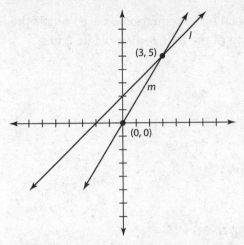

Lines *l* and *m* intersect at the point (3,5)

	QUANTITY A	**QUANTITY B**	
2.	The slope of line *l*	2	Ⓐ Ⓑ Ⓒ Ⓓ

Line *q* passes through the origin and contains the point (*a*,*b*).

	QUANTITY A	**QUANTITY B**	
3.	The slope of line *q*	*b/a*	Ⓐ Ⓑ Ⓒ Ⓓ

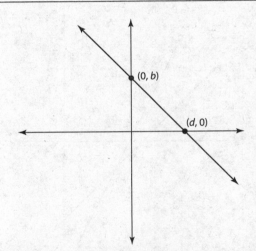

The line above is defined by the equation $y = mx + b$.

	QUANTITY A	**QUANTITY B**	
4.	*m*	*b/d*	Ⓐ Ⓑ Ⓒ Ⓓ

Line *p* is defined by the equation $2y - 3x + 7 = 12$.

	QUANTITY A	**QUANTITY B**	
5.	The slope of line *p*	The *y*-intercept of line *p*	Ⓐ Ⓑ Ⓒ Ⓓ

In the *xy*-plane, the circumference of Circle *C*
contains the points (*x*,0) and (0,*y*).

QUANTITY A	QUANTITY B	
6. The diameter of the circle	$|x| + |y|$	Ⓐ Ⓑ Ⓒ Ⓓ

Line *l* is defined by the equation $y = 3x - 7$.
Line *l* intersects line *k* at the point (5,8).

QUANTITY A	QUANTITY B	
7. The slope of line *k*	0	Ⓐ Ⓑ Ⓒ Ⓓ

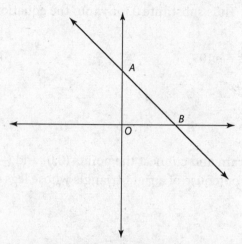

The equation of the line graphed above is $y = -\frac{2}{3}x + 3$.

QUANTITY A	QUANTITY B	
8. *OA*	*OB*	Ⓐ Ⓑ Ⓒ Ⓓ

Exercise Answers

Discrete Quantitative Questions

1. $-\frac{2}{5}$ Isolate *y* to put the equation into slope-intercept form:

   $$2x + 5y - 3 = 12$$
   $$2x + 5y = 15$$
   $$5y = -2x + 15$$
   $$y = \frac{-2x + 15}{5}$$
   $$y = -\frac{2}{5}x + 3$$

   The slope is $-\frac{2}{5}$.

2. **C** Substitute the coordinates into the equation for the line. The coordinates that satisfy the equation will be the answer. Of the choices, only (12, 24) satisfies the equation. For illustration: $3(12) - 2(24) = 36 - 48 = -12$.

3. **A** First, determine the equation for the line. Since the slope is $\frac{2}{3}$, the equation initially reads: $y = \frac{2}{3}x + b$. To solve for b, substitute the coordinates (6,14) into the equation:

$$y = \frac{2}{3}x + b$$

$$14 = \frac{2}{3}(6) + b$$

$$14 = 4 + b$$

$$b = 10$$

The equation for the line is thus $y = \frac{2}{3}x + 10$. Since the x-intercept represents the point at which the line intersects the x-axis, the y-coordinate of that point will be zero. Thus substitute 0 for y into the equation to determine the x-intercept:

$$0 = \frac{2}{3}x + 10$$

$$-10 = \frac{2}{3}x$$

$$-10\left(\frac{3}{2}\right) = x$$

$$-15 = x$$

4. **D** Draw the diagram and connect the points (0,0) and (–5,5). The resulting line will be the hypotenuse of a right triangle whose legs each have a length of 5.

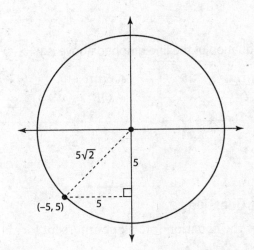

Since this is an isosceles right triangle, the hypotenuse will be $5\sqrt{2}$.

5. **B and D** Any line with a negative slope will intercept quadrants II and IV. Whether the line intercepts Quadrant I or III depends on the line's y-intercept. Since you are not given information about the line's y-intercept, you cannot determine whether it will pass through the other quadrants or the origin. The correct answer is II and IV. For illustration, see the following figure:

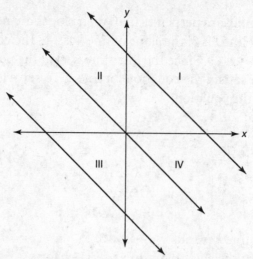

All three lines have negative slopes and pass through Quadrants II and IV. Whether the lines pass through the other quadrants depends on their *y*-intercepts.

6. **C** If two lines are perpendicular, then the slope of one line is the negative reciprocal of the slope of the other line. The product of reciprocals is 1. The product of negative reciprocals is thus –1.

7. **C** To determine the area, you need to determine the length of a side. To determine the length of a side, connect the two points to create a right angle:

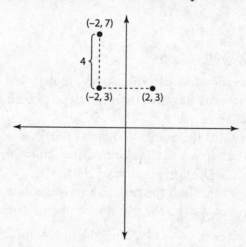

The right angle is formed at the point (–2,3). To determine the length of a side of the square, subtract the *y*-coordinate of the upper point from the *y*-coordinate of the point below it: $7 - 3 = 4$. The length of a side of the square is 4. The area is thus $4^2 = 16$.

8. **E** Since the *x*-intercept represents the point at which the line intersects the *x*-axis, the coordinates of the *x*-intercept are (3,0). Substitute 3 for *x* and 0 for *y* to solve for *b*: $0 = 4(3) - b \rightarrow 0 = 12 - b \rightarrow 12 = b$.

9. **D** Since lines l and k are perpendicular, their slopes are negative reciprocals. Since the slope of line l is 3, the slope of line k is $-\frac{1}{3}$. The equation for line k now reads: $y = -\frac{1}{3}x + b$. Since the lines intersect at the point (3,4), those coordinates must satisfy the equation for line k. To solve for b, plug those coordinates into the equation:

$$y = -\tfrac{1}{3}x + b$$

$$4 = -\tfrac{1}{3}3 + b$$

$$4 = -1 + b$$

$$5 = b$$

The equation for line k is thus $y = -\frac{1}{3}x + 5$.

10. **B** Isolate y so that the equation is in $y = mx + b$ form:

$$ax + by = c$$

$$by = -ax + c$$

$$y = \tfrac{-ax + c}{b}$$

$$y = \tfrac{-a}{b}x + \tfrac{c}{b}$$

The slope of the line is thus $-\frac{a}{b}$. Since the slope of the line is negative, $\frac{-a}{b} < 0$. Thus $\frac{a}{b} > 0$.

Quantitative Comparison Questions

1. **A** Since the lines go downward, both slopes are negative. Line m is steeper, meaning its slope is more negative than the slope of l. Thus the slope of l is greater. The correct answer is A.

2. **B** Since line m contains the points (0,0) and (3,5), its slope is $(5 - 0)/(3 - 0) = \frac{5}{3}$. Line m is steeper than line l, so the slope of line l must be less than $\frac{5}{3}$, meaning its slope is less than 2. The correct answer is B.

3. **C** Since line q passes through the origin, it must contain the point (0,0). The slope of line q is thus $\frac{b-0}{a-0} = \frac{b}{a}$. The two quantities are equal. The answer is C.

4. **B** The slope of the line is $\frac{b-0}{0-d} = \frac{b}{-d}$. Since the line points downward, its slope must be negative. Thus $\frac{b}{-d} < 0$. Multiply both sides by -1 (remember to flip the inequality!): $\frac{b}{d} > 0$. Since $m < 0$ and $\frac{b}{d} > 0$, Quantity B is greater.

5. **B** Manipulate the equation to be in $y = mx + b$ form:

$$2y - 3x + 7 = 12$$

$$2y - 3x = 5$$

$$2y = 3x + 5$$

$$y = \tfrac{3}{2}x + \tfrac{5}{2}$$

The slope is $\frac{3}{2}$ and the y-intercept is $\frac{5}{2}$. Quantity B is greater.

6. **C** Since the circle touches the axes at these points, the distance between the center of the circle and $(0,y)$ must equal the distance between the center of the circle and $(x,0)$.

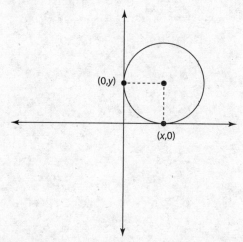

Thus $|y|$ = the radius of the circle, as does $|x|$. Thus the sum of $|x|$ and $|y|$ = the circle's diameter. The two quantities are equal.

7. **D** The only information given about line k is that it contains the point $(5,8)$. One point on a line is not sufficient to infer any information about that line's slope.

8. **B** OA is the distance between the origin and the y-intercept of the line. Since the y-intercept of the line is 3, OA is 3. OB is the distance between the origin and the x-intercept of the line. To determine the x-intercept of the line, set y equal to zero:

$$0 = (\tfrac{-2}{3})x + 3$$

$$-3 = (\tfrac{-2}{3})x$$

$$3 = (\tfrac{2}{3})x$$

$$4.5 = x$$

OB is thus 4.5. Quantity B is greater.

Data Interpretation

Data Interpretation questions present you with one or more tables, charts, or graphs, and ask you to make calculations and inferences based on this information. Most of the time, the questions will appear in graphs in one of three forms: bar graphs, circle graphs, or line graphs. Each Quantitative Reasoning section will have three Data Interpretation questions. The tables, charts, and graphs will appear either at the top or to the left of every corresponding question.

The math on these questions is fairly straightforward; the difficult part is fully comprehending the information in the charts and answering the questions quickly and efficiently. Most of the questions will test concepts that you should be familiar with from the previous chapters: fractions, decimals, percentages, ratios, averages, probability, and, occasionally, geometry. Since these topics are already known to you, the key to doing well on these questions is to *fully understand the data so that you use the proper information to answer the questions.* Though your calculator will certainly come in handy on many of these questions, Data Interpretation questions are designed to test your estimation and approximation abilities, so you would be well-served to practice these questions with and without a calculator.

The two graphs and three multiple-choice questions following them illustrate a typical Data Interpretation question group and will form the basis of this overview of Data Interpretation strategies and methodology:

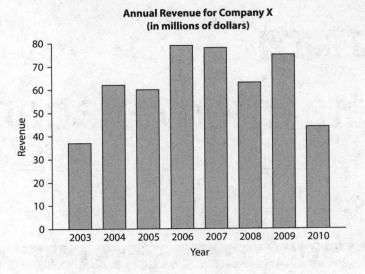

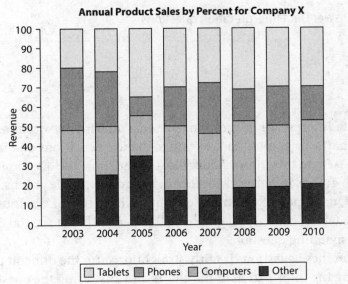

1. For which year was the percentage change in revenue from the previous year the greatest?

   (A) 2003
   (B) 2004
   (C) 2008
   (D) 2009
   (E) 2010

For this question, indicate all of the answer choices that apply.

2. For which of the following years was the revenue from computers greater than in the previous year?

   Ⓐ 2004
   Ⓑ 2005
   Ⓒ 2006
   Ⓓ 2008
   Ⓔ 2010

For this question, write your answer in the box.

3. During the period from 2006–2008, what was the average annual revenue from phones? Round your answer to the nearest $100,000.

```
┌─────────────────┐
│                 │
│                 │
└─────────────────┘
```

The first step to understanding the data is to note the title of the given graph. The first graph provides you with the annual revenue for a company from 2003–2010. Notice that the title tells you that the data is in *millions of dollars*. Thus the numbers on the *y*-axis represent millions of each labeled quantity.

The second graph provides you with the breakdown of the company's annual revenue by product sales. Make sure to understand the legend and to understand how to read each bar. For example, you should note that even though the top bar of the *Computers* component of 2003 ends at ≈45, computers did *not* account for 45% of that year's revenue since the bottom bar ends at ≈22. Thus computers accounted for ≈(45 – 22) = ≈23% of that year's revenue.

How to Answer Data Interpretation Questions

When answering Data Interpretation questions, you will want to keep a few principles in mind.

- **Principle 1: When possible, you should estimate.** Many of the questions you see in Data Interpretation will use words such as *approximately* or *closest to*. When you see these words, the test-makers are essentially *telling* you that you are not expected to arrive at a precise value. Instead, make sure that you stay roughly within the range of the given information, and the answer you arrive at will almost always be near only one of the choices. This strategy is particularly helpful in situations with bar graphs, where it might not be quite clear whether, for example, the review in 2003 is $38 million or $39 million. The short answer is that it does not matter. Stay within reasonable estimates, and the correct choice will still be obvious.

- **Principle 2: Don't confuse percentages, averages, and numbers.** Question 1 asks you to determine which year had the greatest percent change from the previous year. You should first recognize that the years with the greatest *absolute* change from the previous year were 2003 and 2010. You may then be tempted to select 2010 since the *absolute* difference between 2009 and 2010 is greater than the *absolute* difference between 2003 and 2004. But recall from the percentages chapter that percent change depends on the original value. Since the revenue in 2003 is so much less than the revenue in 2009, the percent change from 2003 might be greater than from 2009, even though the absolute change is less. Thus you should calculate the percent change for those two periods (*keeping in mind the importance of estimating!*):

  Percent change from 2003 to 2004: The revenue in 2003 is roughly $37 million and the revenue in 2004 is roughly $64 million. The percent change is thus: $\frac{62-37}{37} = \approx 0.68 = 68\%$.

  Percent change from 2009 to 2010: The revenue in 2009 is roughly $75 million and the revenue in 2010 is roughly $44 million. The percent change is thus $\frac{75-44}{75} = \approx 0.41 = 41\%$. Thus the correct answer for Question 1 is B.

- **Principle 3: Use your eye.** Unless noted otherwise, the diagrams are drawn to scale. This is helpful since you can minimize calculations when you are comparing choices or elements of a graph. For example, in Question 2, you can determine all of the correct answers by eyeballing instead of by doing calculations:

  Choice A: In the second graph, the percentage revenue from computers in 2004 is about equal to the percentage revenue from computers in 2003. From the first graph, you know the total revenue in 2004 was greater than in 2003. Thus the revenue from computers in 2004 is an equal slice of a larger whole (relative to 2003). → Keep Choice A.

  Choice B: In the second graph, the percentage revenue from computers in 2005 is slightly less than the percentage revenue from computers in 2004. From the first graph, you know the total revenue in 2005 was less than in 2004. Thus the revenue from computers in 2005 is a smaller slice of a smaller whole (relative to 2004). → Eliminate Choice B.

  Choice C: In the second graph, the percentage revenue from computers in 2006 is greater than the percentage revenue from computers in 2005. From the first graph, you know the total revenue in 2006 was greater than in 2005. Thus the revenue from computers in 2006 is a larger slice of a larger whole (relative to 2005). → Keep Choice C.

  Choice D: In the second graph, the percentage revenue from computers in 2008 is roughly equal to the percentage revenue from computers in 2007. From the first graph, you know the total revenue in 2008 was less than in 2007. Thus the revenue from computers in 2008 is an equal slice of a smaller whole (relative to 2007). → Eliminate Choice D.

Choice E: In the second chart, the percentage revenue from computers in 2010 is roughly equal to the percentage revenue from computers in 2009. In the first chart, you know the total revenue in 2010 was less than in 2009. Thus the revenue from computers in 2010 is an equal slice of a smaller whole (relative to 2009). Eliminate Choice E. The correct answer for Question 2, therefore, is choices A and C.

- **Principle 4: Link to what you know.** Since these questions test mathematical skills covered in previous chapters, you should recall the relevant properties that a question is addressing. For example, Question 3 requires you to use the average formula twice. Since the total revenues for 2006 and 2007 are roughly equal ($78 million), and the percentage revenues from phones during those two years are roughly equal (30%), the total for those two years is approximately $78 million × 30% × 2 = $46.8 million. The other data point is the revenue from phones in 2008. The percentage revenue from phones in 2008 is roughly 32%, and the total revenue is roughly $63 million. Thus the revenue from phones in 2008 is approximately $63 million × 32% = $20.16 million. The total average is approximately $\frac{\$46.8 \text{ million} + \$20.16 \text{ million}}{3}$ = $22,320,000. Rounding off to the nearest $100,000 gives an answer of $22,300,000.

Exercise: Data Interpretation

Questions 1–6 refer to the following diagrams:

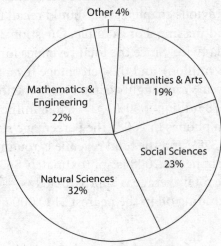

Approximate Percentage of 2007 Graduates in Each Concentration

Total 2007 Graduates = 4, 792

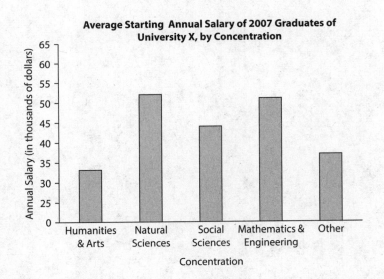

1. The average starting annual salary of 2007 graduates concentrating in mathematics and engineering was approximately what percent greater than that of graduates concentrating in the humanities and arts?

   (A) 33.3%
   (B) 50%
   (C) 83.3%
   (D) 133.3%
   (E) 150%

2. If 10% of the graduates concentrating in the social sciences were psychology majors, approximately how many 2007 graduates were psychology majors?

    (A) 50

    (B) 110

    (C) 230

    (D) 470

    (E) 1,200

3. What is the approximate average combined annual salary for students concentrating in the humanities and arts and in the natural sciences?

    (A) $38,000

    (B) $39,000

    (C) $42,000

    (D) $44,000

    (E) $46,000

4. If the areas of the sectors in the circle graph are proportionate to the percentages shown, then what is the approximate measure, in degrees, of the sector representing the percentage of students concentrating in the humanities and arts?

    (A) 19

    (B) 34

    (C) 42

    (D) 68

    (E) 136

For this question, indicate all of the answer choices that apply.

5. Which of the following can be inferred from the data above?

    [A] The average starting annual salary for all 2007 graduates of University X was above $40,000.

    [B] The range of starting salaries for all 2007 graduates of University X was less than $30,000.

    [C] The median starting salary of 2007 graduates concentrating in Other was less than the median starting salary of 2007 graduates concentrating in natural sciences.

6. Approximately how many students concentrating in the natural sciences would have needed to switch concentrations to mathematics and engineering for the percentage of students concentrating in the natural sciences to equal the percentage of students concentrating in mathematics and engineering?

Ⓐ 120

Ⓑ 180

Ⓒ 240

Ⓓ 300

Ⓔ 360

Questions 7 to 10 refer to the following diagrams:

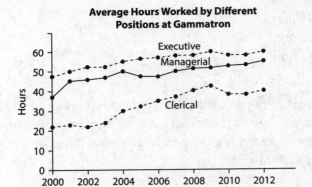

Average Hours Worked by Different Positions at Gammatron

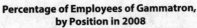

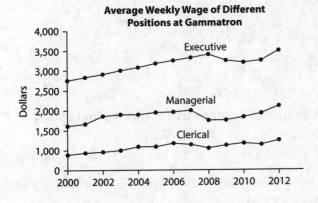

Average Weekly Wage of Different Positions at Gammatron

Percentage of Employees of Gammatron, by Position in 2008

Total Employees = 2,000

7. From 2009 to 2012, by approximately what percent did the average hourly wage of an executive at Gammatron increase?

    Ⓐ 4%

    Ⓑ 5%

    Ⓒ 6%

    Ⓓ 7%

    Ⓔ 8%

8. If a is the total amount of money paid to managerial employees in 2008, and b is the total amount of money paid to executive employees in 2008, then the average of a and b is closest to

    Ⓐ $72,000

    Ⓑ $85,000

    Ⓒ $100,000

    Ⓓ $120,000

    Ⓔ $140,000

For this question, indicate all of the answer choices that apply.

9. If an employee from Gammatron in 2008 were picked at random, which of the following could be the probability that this employee would have an average weekly wage above $1,500?

    ☐A $\frac{11}{50}$

    ☐B $\frac{6}{25}$

    ☐C $\frac{34}{100}$

    ☐D $\frac{29}{50}$

    ☐E $\frac{17}{25}$

10. The total salary paid to clerical employees in 2008 is closest to

    Ⓐ $15 million

    Ⓑ $18 million

    Ⓒ $20 million

    Ⓓ $23 million

    Ⓔ $25 million

Questions 11 to 14 refer to the following diagram:

Percentage of the 500 Freshmen and 600 Sophomores Who Take Certain Classes at University X

Class	Percent of Freshmen Who Take Class	Percent of Sophomores Who Take Class
Molecular Biology	3%	6%
American Literature	8%	5%
Statistics	14%	10%
Political Science	7%	5%
Psychology	12%	9%
Economics	8%	6%
Sociology	3%	7%

11. The number of freshmen who take American literature is how much greater than the number of sophomores who take American literature?

   (A) 3
   (B) 10
   (C) 30
   (D) 40
   (E) 70

12. The number of freshmen who take statistics is approximately what percent greater than the number of sophomores who take statistics?

   (A) 10%
   (B) 14.3%
   (C) 16.7%
   (D) 28.6%
   (E) 40%

For this question, write your answer in the box.

13. What is the ratio of the number of freshmen <u>not</u> taking any of the listed classes to the total number of freshmen and sophomores?

$$\frac{\boxed{}}{\boxed{}}$$

For this question, indicate all of the answer choices that apply.

14. Based on the table above, which of the following is true?

    A The range of the number of freshmen in each of the listed courses is greater than the range of sophomores in each of the listed courses.

    B The standard deviation of the number of freshmen in each of the listed courses is greater than the standard deviation of the number of sophomores in each of the listed courses.

    C The median of the number of freshmen in each of the listed courses is greater than the median of the number of sophomores in each of the listed courses.

Exercise Answers

1. **B** The average salary for mathematics and engineering majors is ≈$51,000, and the average salary for humanities and arts majors is ≈$34,000. The percent greater formula is % of – 100% = % GREATER. Plug in the values to get the salary of mathematics and engineering students as a percentage of the salary of humanities and arts students: $51,000/$34,000 = 150%. Subtract 100%. The answer is 50%.

2. **B** The approximate number of students concentrating in the social sciences was 23% × 4,792 ≈ 1,102. 10% of 1,102 is approximately 110.

3. **E** The total salary for graduates of the humanities and arts = average × number of students. The average is approximately $34,000. The number of students is approximately 0.19(4,792) ≈ 910. The total salary for these students is approximately $34,000(910). The total salary for graduates of the natural sciences = average × number of students. The average is approximately $53,000. The number of students is approximately 0.32(4,792) ≈ 1,533. The total salary for these students is approximately $53,000(1,533). The average salary for both concentrations combined equals:

$$\frac{\text{Total salary}}{\text{number of students}}$$

$$\downarrow$$

$$\frac{\$34{,}000(910) + \$53{,}000(1{,}533)}{910 + 1{,}533}$$

$$= \frac{112{,}189{,}000}{2{,}433}$$

$$= \$46{,}111$$

The closest answer is E.

4. **D** The sector area for humanities and arts represents 19% of the total circle. Thus the central angle = 19% (360) = 68.4.

5. **A** Before doing the calculations, try to eyeball the figure.

   Choice A: Other than the humanities and arts, all of the average salaries are near or above $40,000. Since humanities and arts graduates make up only 19% of the entire population of graduates, their relative weight is not enough to bring the total average below $40,000.   → Choice A is true.

   Choice B: Each of the bars provides an *average*. Since numerical values cannot be inferred from an average, the actual range for the starting salary of any of the concentrations cannot be determined.   → Eliminate Choice B.

   Choice C: The same reasoning that applied to Choice B applies to Choice C. Since you do not know the actual salaries in either set, you cannot determine the median of either set or how the medians compare.

                                                                    → Eliminate Choice C.

6. **C** To make the number of students in each concentration equal, their percentages must be equal. Let x represent the percentage of students that leave the Natural Science concentration and enroll in the mathematics and engineering concentration. Thus

   $$32 - x = 22 + x$$

   $$10 = 2x$$

   $$5 = x$$

   Thus 5% of the total students would have to switch. 5% of 4,792 ≈ 240.

7. **D** To solve for percent increase, use the percent change formula: $\frac{\text{new} - \text{original}}{\text{original}} \times 100$. To determine the average hourly wage for executives in 2009, divide the weekly wage by the number of hours worked each week: $3,250/60. To determine the average hourly wage for executives in 2012, divide the weekly wage by the number of hours worked each week: $3,500/60. Substitute these values into the percent change formula:

   $$\frac{\frac{3{,}500}{60} - \frac{3{,}250}{60}}{\frac{3{,}250}{60}} \times 100 \approx 7\%$$

8. **D** In 2008, executive employees made approximately $3,300 per week. In 2008, managerial employees made approximately $1,750 per week. However, there were more managerial employees than executive employees in 2008. To solve for the average weekly wage of the two groups combined, set up a weighted average, where the weight of managerial employees is approximately $\frac{3}{5}$ and the weight of executive employees is approximately $\frac{2}{5}$.

managerial + executive

$$\downarrow \qquad\qquad \downarrow$$

$$\$1,750(\tfrac{3}{5}) + \$3,300(\tfrac{2}{5})$$

$$\downarrow$$

$$\$2,370$$

Finally, to get the yearly average, multiply this value by 52: $(2,370)(52) =$ $123,240.

9. **D and E** In 2008, managerial and executive employees had average weekly wages above $1,500. Thus the probability of choosing an employee with such a weekly wage is at least $\frac{34+24}{100} = \frac{58}{100} = \frac{29}{50}$. Eliminate choices A, B, and C. However, it is possible that some of the employees in the "Other" category also had weekly wages above $1,500. Thus it is possible for the probability to be above $\frac{29}{50}$. Since $\frac{17}{25} > \frac{29}{50}$, E is an answer as well.

10. **D** If 22% of the 2,000 employees in 2008 were clerical, then there were $0.22(2,000) = 440$ clerical employees. The average weekly wage for each of these employees was approximately $1,000. Thus, the average yearly wage for each of these employees was approximately $\$1,000 \times 52 = \$52,000$. The total yearly wage for all such employees was thus:

$$A \times N = S$$

$$\$52,000 \times 440 = \$22,800,000$$

11. **B** Since there are 500 freshmen, the number of freshmen who take American literature = 8%(500) = 0.08(500) = 40. Since there are 600 sophomores, the number of sophomores who take American literature = 5%(600) = 0.05(600) = 30. 40 − 30 = 10.

12. **C** The number of freshmen who take statistics is 14% of 500 = 0.14(500) = 70. The number of sophomores who take statistics is 10% of 600 = 0.1(600) = 60. Now solve for the following question: 70 is what percent greater than 60? Use the percent greater formula:

percent greater = percent of − 100%

Solve for percent of: (70/60) × 100 = 116.66%. Thus percent greater = 116.66% − 100% = 16.66%. The closest answer is C.

13. $\frac{9}{44}$ 55% of the freshmen *are* taking the listed classes, so 100% − 55% of the freshmen are *not* taking the listed classes. Since there are 500 freshmen at the school, the number of freshmen *not* taking the listed classes is 45%(500) = 0.45(500) = 225. The total number of freshmen and sophomores in the school is 500 + 600 = 1,100. Thus, the desired ratio is $\frac{225}{1,100} = \frac{9}{44}$.

14. **A, B, and C**

   Choice A: Solve for the maximum and minimum within each of the columns. The greatest number of freshmen taking a listed course is $0.14(500) = 70$. The least number of freshmen taking a listed course is $0.03(500) = 15$. The range for the number of freshmen in a listed course is thus $70 - 15 = 55$. The greatest number of sophomores taking a listed course is $0.1(600) = 60$. The least number of sophomores taking a listed course is $0.05(600) = 30$. The range for the number of sophomores in a listed course is thus $60 - 30 = 30$. The range for the freshmen is thus greater than the range for the sophomores. $\rightarrow$ Choice A is true.

   Choice B: Compare the spreads of the two sets. Though you can calculate the standard deviation of each set, you should instead pay attention to how dispersed the numbers are. For freshmen, the numbers in increasing order are $(0.03)500, (0.03)500, (0.07)500, (0.08)500, (0.08)500, (0.12)500, (0.14)500 = 15, 15, 35, 40, 40, 60, 70$. For sophomores, the percentages in increasing order are $(0.05)600, (0.05)600, (0.06)600, (0.06)600, (0.07)600, (0.09)600, (0.10)600 = 30, 30, 36, 36, 42, 54, 60$. The spread for the number of freshmen is greater. $\rightarrow$ Choice B is true.

   Choice C: Calculate the median for each set. To calculate the median number of students in a listed course for freshmen, first list the percentages in increasing order: 3, 3, 7, 8, 8, 12, 14. The median is thus 8% of 500 = 40. To calculate the median number of students in a listed course for sophomores, first list the percentages in increasing order: 5, 5, 6, 6, 7, 9, 10. The median is thus 6% of 600 = 36. $40 > 36$. $\rightarrow$ Choice C is true.

PART 5

GRE Practice Tests

The following practice tests recreate the range of questions you are likely to encounter when you take the GRE. Working through these practice tests under test-like conditions will help you gain the knowledge and confidence you will need to achieve your goals on the GRE. Each of the practice tests is composed of three parts:

1. Analytical Writing	Issue Task	30 minutes
	Argument Task	30 minutes
2. Verbal (2 sections)	20 questions per section	30 minutes per section
3. Quantitative (2 sections)	20 questions per section	35 minutes per section

In order to maximize the benefits you gain from these practice tests, you should make your practice experience as similar as possible to the conditions you will experience on the actual test:

■ Find a quiet and comfortable place where you will not be interrupted.

■ Take an entire test in one sitting if you can find the time. If not, try to clear time to complete at least an entire section in one sitting.

■ Time yourself and stick to the time limit. If you run short on time, force yourself to make educated guesses; you may need to make guesses on the real test.

■ Have your testing materials—answer sheet, scratch paper, and pencils—in hand before you begin the test. Remember, you can use a calculator only on the Integrated Reasoning section.

■ Answer the questions in order. You cannot skip around on the GRE, so make sure not to get into the habit of doing so.

■ Write on scratch paper, not the test itself. You will not be able to write on the computer screen (!), so get into the habit of using scratch paper.

■ Be sure to type your responses to the Analytical Writing questions.

You can also take these practice tests on your tablet or smartphone as well as your laptop or home computer. See page 2A in the Welcome section for details.

Don't forget that there are **three additional practice tests** available online or on the app.

CHAPTER 15

Practice Test 1

SECTION 1

Analytical Writing

Analyze an Issue

30 minutes

For this task, you will be given a brief quotation that states or implies an issue of general interest. You will also be given instructions on how to respond to that issue. You will then have 30 minutes to plan and write a response.

Be sure to follow the instructions that you are given. In writing your response, support your ideas with reasons and examples drawn from your reading, your studies, and/or your personal experiences. Your response will be evaluated based on how well you organize and express your ideas, how well you support your opinions with reasons and examples, and how well you follow the rules of standard English grammar and usage.

Take a few minutes to plan your response. When you are finished writing, make sure to review your work and make any necessary revisions.

ISSUE TOPIC

Most of the money devoted to basic scientific research should instead be diverted to applied scientific research.

Respond to the above topic by composing an essay that states how much you agree or disagree with the given claim. Be sure to use evidence to support your stance and to consider evidence that would challenge your stance.

GO ON TO NEXT PAGE ➤

STOP.
This is the end of Section 1.

SECTION 2

Analytical Writing

Analyze an Argument

30 Minutes

For this task, you will be given a brief passage that presents an argument. You will also be given instructions on how to respond to the passage. You will then have 30 minutes to plan and write a response in which you evaluate the argument according to the instructions that you are given. Be aware that you are **not** being asked to present your own personal views on the topic.

In writing your response, be sure to support your ideas with reasons and examples. Your response will be evaluated based on how well you analyze the argument presented in the prompt, how well you organize and express your ideas, and how well you follow the rules of standard English grammar and usage.

Take a few minutes to plan your response. When you are finished writing, make sure to review your work and make any necessary revisions.

ARGUMENT TOPIC

In 2010, the Elmrose Corporation housed all of its operations and employees in one office. Since then, the company has expanded to multiple locations and has seen profits decline steadily each year. Clearly, if Elmrose wants to boost profits, it should relocate all of its operations and employees to one office.

Write a response in which you discuss the evidence that would be necessary to establish the argument's validity. Make sure to explain how that evidence would strengthen or weaken the argument.

_____

_____

_____

_____

_____

_____

_____

_____

_____

_____

_____

_____

_____

_____

_____

_____

STOP.
This is the end of Section 2.

SECTION 3

Verbal Reasoning

20 questions—30 minutes

This section includes three types of questions; Reading Comprehension, Text Completion, and Sentence Equivalence. Read the following directions before you begin the section.

Directions

Reading Comprehension Questions
- *Multiple-Choice Questions—Select One Answer Choice*: Select one answer choice from a list of five choices.
- *Multiple-Choice Questions—Select One or More Answer Choices:* From a list of three answer choices, select all that are correct.
- *Select-in-Passage*: Select the sentence in the passage that meets a certain description.

Text Completion Questions
- For each blank, select one choice from the corresponding list of choices. Fill all blanks in the way that best completes the text.

Sentence Equivalence Questions
- Select the <u>two</u> answer choices that (1) complete the sentence in a way that makes sense and (2) produce sentences that are similar in meaning.

GO ON TO NEXT PAGE ➤

In Questions 1 to 6, for each blank, select the choice that best completes the text.

1. In prioritizing efficiency, modern society downplays (i) _____ in favor of an all-consuming (ii) _____.

Blank (i)	Blank (ii)
Ⓐ idealism	Ⓓ putrefaction
Ⓑ ambition	Ⓔ adamancy
Ⓒ evenhandedness	Ⓕ pragmatism

2. Despite the _____ of evidence supporting his theory, Wasselman used his charisma to attract a legion of followers.

Ⓐ confluence
Ⓑ dearth
Ⓒ nadir
Ⓓ elision
Ⓔ consumption

3. A trademark characteristic of postmodernism is the turn from self-seriousness to (i) _____: Because everything has been explained and already done, the only remaining recourse is (ii) _____.

Blank (i)	Blank (ii)
Ⓐ pathos	Ⓓ amused detachment
Ⓑ sentimentality	Ⓔ heightened awareness
Ⓒ irony	Ⓕ cautious investigation

4. Humor is a central component of her plays, not a (i) _____ one. This fact, however, has been lost on critics who interpret her attempts at comedy as either (ii) _____ or, even when it's intended, as (iii) _____, eliciting mild laughter, but outside of the scope of what the play is attempting to accomplish.

Blank (i)	Blank (ii)	Blank (iii)
Ⓐ pivotal	Ⓓ incidental	Ⓖ derivative
Ⓑ undermining	Ⓔ overrated	Ⓗ irrelevant
Ⓒ superficial	Ⓕ sophomoric	Ⓘ detrimental

5. To state that the writer is a (i) _____ is to fundamentally misunderstand his main themes. Though wariness of human motives does characterize his writings, this (ii) _____ is explored within a context that repeatedly emphasizes the human capacity for, and tendency toward, (iii) _____.

Blank (i)	Blank (ii)	Blank (iii)
Ⓐ hedonist	Ⓓ belligerence	Ⓖ deliverance
Ⓑ misanthrope	Ⓔ self-absorption	Ⓗ benevolence
Ⓒ miser	Ⓕ cynicism	Ⓘ determinism

6. The (i) _____ of medieval thinkers to explain the workings of the universe has led some critics to question the (ii) _____ of human rationality.

Blank (i)	Blank (ii)
Ⓐ ambiguity	Ⓓ legitimacy
Ⓑ meaning	Ⓔ effectiveness
Ⓒ inability	Ⓕ nuances

GO ON TO NEXT PAGE ➤

Question 7 is based on the passage below. Select <u>one</u> answer choice.

On a certain examination, more students in class A scored above 80 percent than did the students in any other class. On the same examination, more students in class B scored above 90 percent than did the students in any other class.

7. The previous statements best support which of the following conclusions?

    Ⓐ Students in class B had a higher average score on the examination than did the students in class A.

    Ⓑ More students in class A scored between 80 percent and 90 percent than in class B.

    Ⓒ Class A has more students than class B.

    Ⓓ More students in class A scored above 95 percent than in class B.

    Ⓔ The median score for class A is above 80 percent

Questions 8 to 10 refer to the passage below. For each question, select <u>one</u> answer choice, unless the instructions state otherwise.

Traditionally viewed as the mindless defamations of mutinous teenagers, graffiti has rarely been the subject of serious scholarly inquiry. Fortunately, the discovery of graffiti on the walls at the archeological site of Pompeii has been the impetus for a wholescale
5 reconsideration of the relevance of graffiti to archeological and historical studies. Yes, graffiti is (and probably always was) mostly done by hormone-addled teenagers, and yes, the concise nature of graffiti does not lend itself to the type of exegesis to which most academics are inclined. But graffiti, especially graffiti on the walls at a cherished
10 historical site, can lend insight into the powerless voices that would otherwise have been censored by most ancient societies. By examining a culture's graffiti, we can understand the discontents of that culture in a more organic context—one free of the posturing that is all too pervasive in preserved historical documents. Perhaps graffiti will
15 not tell us the purpose of a law or the mischievous family dramas of ancient governments, but, perhaps more than any document can, it provides us with an unfiltered view of how society at large reacted to forces that were largely out of its control.

8. The passage is primarily concerned with

    Ⓐ explaining the appearance of graffiti

    Ⓑ arguing that scholars should take graffiti more seriously

    Ⓒ suggesting that graffiti was censored by ancient societies

    Ⓓ indicating the hypocrisy of contemporary archeology

    Ⓔ evaluating a scholar's position

9. As used in the context of the passage, "exegesis" (line 8) most nearly means

    (A) explanation
    (B) debate
    (C) pronouncement
    (D) illumination
    (E) deliberation

10. The author's attitude toward graffiti as a subject of scholarly study can best be described as

    (A) ambivalent
    (B) repentant
    (C) enthusiastic
    (D) confused
    (E) disapproving

In Questions 11 to 14, for each blank, select the two answer choices that (1) complete the sentence in a way that makes sense and (2) produce sentences that are similar in meaning.

11. Though the occupational landscape of the city has generally been thought of as industrial, the diversity of the citizens' jobs _____ this categorization.

    A undermines

    B deflects

    C conflates

    D diminishes

    E subverts

    F presages

GO ON TO NEXT PAGE ➤

12. With so many divergent opinions in the field, it was unreasonable for the scientist to expect that his theory, however sound, would not encounter _____.

    A expression

    B resentment

    C resistance

    D comprehension

    E criticism

    F intelligibility

13. With the proliferation of the Internet has come _____ people's attention spans: unless users receive immediate stimulation from what is in front of them, they will quickly seek novelty on another page or website.

    A an attenuation of

    B a distortion of

    C a reinforcement of

    D an amelioration of

    E a decrease in

    F a reprisal of

14. Despite most people's professed _____ psychotherapy, people are seeking the help of these professionals in record numbers.

    A skepticism of

    B curiosity about

    C ignorance of

    D investigations in

    E aversion toward

    F confusion about

Questions 15 to 17 refer to the passage below. For each question, select <u>one</u> answer choice, unless the instructions state otherwise.

The idea to use Navajo for secure communications came from Philip Johnston, the son of a missionary to the Navajos and one of the few non-Navajos who spoke their language fluently. Reared on the Navajo reservation, Johnston was a World War I veteran who knew of the
5 military's search for a code that would withstand all attempts to decipher it. He also knew that Native American languages, notably Choctaw, had been used in World War I to encode messages.

Johnston believed Navajo answered the military requirement for an undecipherable code because it is an unwritten language of
10 extreme complexity. Its syntax and tonal qualities, not to mention dialects, make it unintelligible to anyone without extensive exposure and training. It has no alphabet or symbols and is spoken only on the Navajo lands of the American Southwest. One estimate indicates that fewer than 30 non-Navajos, none of them Japanese, could understand
15 the language at the outbreak of World War II.

Early in 1942, Johnston met with Major General Clayton B. Vogel, the commanding general of Amphibious Corps, Pacific Fleet, and his staff to convince them of the Navajo language's value as code. Johnston staged tests under simulated combat conditions, demonstrating
20 that Navajos could encode, transmit and decode a three-line English message in 20 seconds. Machines of the time required 30 minutes to perform the same job. Convinced, Vogel recommended to the Commandant of the Marine Corps that the Marines recruit 200 Navajos.

15. The author most likely mentions the fact that Navajo "has no alphabet or symbols" in order to

    Ⓐ emphasize how difficult it is to decipher Navajo language
    Ⓑ suggest a potential drawback of the use of Navajo for secure communications
    Ⓒ explain why so few non-Navajos can speak the language
    Ⓓ highlight the differences between Navajo and other Native American languages
    Ⓔ suggest that Johnston's ambitions were impractical

16. The passage is primarily concerned with

    Ⓐ examining the complexity of a language
    Ⓑ profiling someone's search for a solution to a problem
    Ⓒ analyzing the benefits and drawbacks of an approach
    Ⓓ explaining why a certain strategy was adopted
    Ⓔ dissecting the origins of a certain methodology

GO ON TO NEXT PAGE ➤

17. Select the sentence in the second or third paragraph of the passage that provides empirical evidence in favor of using Navajo for secure communications.

> [   ]

Question 18 is based on the passage below. Select <u>one</u> answer choice.

Studies show that an individual suffering from insomnia is more likely to be a smoker than is a non-insomniac. Clearly, lack of sleep induces insomniacs to smoke.

18. Which of the following, if true, most weakens the argument?

- Ⓐ Nicotine is known to have relaxing properties.
- Ⓑ Little is known about the causes of insomnia.
- Ⓒ Most insomniacs report developing a smoking addiction after having developed sleep problems.
- Ⓓ Many of smoking's physical effects, such as irritability and anxiety, are associated with insomnia.
- Ⓔ Many insomniacs whose sleep patterns return to normal report quitting smoking.

Questions 19 to 20 refer to the passage below. For each question, select <u>one</u> answer choice, unless the instructions state otherwise.

Islam, in part because of its ban on figural representation, has contributed certain characteristics to art that have been seen since the seventh century. Artists have to rely on vegetal motifs, calligraphy, and geometric patterns for ornamentation. According to a 2007 article
5 in the journal *Science*, physicists Peter Lu and Paul J. Steinhardt discovered that Islamic artists as far back as the 15th century were using the concept of quasicrystalline geometry, symmetrical polygonal shapes in patterns that can be extended indefinitely without repetition. The polygons are actually mathematical principles that are appreciated
10 both as science and art; however, the math precedes the shape. "They made tilings that reflect mathematics that were so sophisticated that we didn't figure it out until the last 20 or 30 years," said Lu in a 2007 interview with Reuters.

19. According to the passage, why do Islamic "artists have to rely on vegetal motifs, calligraphy, and geometric patterns for ornamentation"?

   (A) Because they did not have the necessary resources for other forms of expression,

   (B) Because other forms of expression were banned.

   (C) Because they did not have the mathematical sophistication for other forms of expression.

   (D) Because it was believed that abstract forms of representation were more aesthetically pleasing,

   (E) Because it was believed that indecipherability was fundamental to their art.

20. Which of the following could most properly be inferred from the passage?

   (A) Islamic art was the first art to use mathematical principles.

   (B) Prior to the seventh century, there were no recorded geometric patterns for ornamentation in art.

   (C) The math in Islamic art is incomprehensible to modern scholars.

   (D) Were there no ban on figural representation, Islamic artists would never have used mathematical principles in their art.

   (E) Early Islamic artists were not aware of the relationship between art and mathematics in their creations.

—————————— **STOP.** ——————————
This is the end of Section 3.

SECTION 4

Verbal Reasoning

20 questions—30 minutes

This section includes three types of questions Reading Comprehension, Text Completion, and Sentence Equivalence. Read the following directions before you begin the section.

Directions

Reading Comprehension Questions
- *Multiple-Choice Questions—Select One Answer Choice*: Select one answer choice from a list of five choices.
- *Multiple-Choice Questions—Select One or More Answer Choices:* From a list of three answer choices, select all that are correct.
- *Select-in-Passage*: Select the sentence in the passage that meets a certain description.

Text Completion Questions
- For each blank, select one choice from the corresponding list of choices. Fill all blanks in the way that best completes the text.

Sentence Equivalence Questions
- Select the two answer choices that (1) complete the sentence in a way that makes sense and (2) produce sentences that are similar in meaning.

In Questions 1 to 6, for each blank, select the choice that best completes the text.

1. The (i) _____ that the executive employed to hire the employee eventually backfired. Once the employee understood that such underhanded tactics had led to her hiring, the (ii) _____ that made her so qualified for the job devolved into indifference and even resentment.

Blank (i)	Blank (ii)
Ⓐ courage	Ⓓ enthusiasm
Ⓑ cunning	Ⓔ idolatry
Ⓒ rancor	Ⓕ garrulity

2. Advances in digitization, with its emphasis on speed and effectiveness, are a(n) _____ byproduct of a capitalistic society. When a society places a premium on efficiency, any developments that can decrease the amount of time and energy expended will be embraced.

Ⓐ curious

Ⓑ inexorable

Ⓒ incidental

Ⓓ deleterious

Ⓔ incremental

3. The author wrote the letter with a(n) (i) _____ tone, her feelings (ii) _____ by a pride that rendered her inborn sensitivity inaccessible.

Blank (i)	Blank (ii)
Ⓐ indecipherable	Ⓓ accentuated
Ⓑ muted	Ⓔ obscured
Ⓒ effusive	Ⓕ emboldened

GO ON TO NEXT PAGE ➤

4. It would be wrong for the student to conclude that the inherent complexity of the problem makes it (i) _____. Through (ii) _____, other seemingly insolvable problems have been unraveled. What remains to be seen is whether the student has the requisite resolve to arrive at the right answer.

Blank (i)	Blank (ii)
Ⓐ intractable	Ⓓ intuition
Ⓑ profound	Ⓔ serendipity
Ⓒ incorrigible	Ⓕ persistence

5. The bees' tendency to sacrifice themselves for the clan (i) _____ biologists operating under the assumption that all organisms behave out of (ii) _____.

Blank (i)	Blank (ii)
Ⓐ validated	Ⓓ self-interest
Ⓑ angered	Ⓔ responsibility
Ⓒ flummoxed	Ⓕ isolation

6. Amateur writers, equating (i) _____ with depth, will often write unnecessarily verbose prose, not realizing that doing so is often (ii) _____ to conveying their thoughts.

Blank (i)	Blank (ii)
Ⓐ superfluity	Ⓓ sympathetic
Ⓑ perspicacity	Ⓔ detrimental
Ⓒ verbosity	Ⓕ secondary

Question 7 is based on the passage below. Select <u>one</u> answer choice.

Evidence indicates that the wavelengths emitted by distant stars in the galaxy are longer than would be expected, given the atmospheres of the stars. Most astrophysicists agree that **a longer wavelength emitted by a star signifies an increased distance.** From this information, **scientists**
5   **claim that the universe is expanding.**

7. The two items that appear in **boldface** play which of the following roles?

   Ⓐ The first boldfaced phrase provides evidence in support of a claim; the second boldfaced statement is that claim.
   Ⓑ The first boldfaced phrase provides a claim in opposition to another claim; the second boldfaced statement is that claim.
   Ⓒ The first boldfaced phrase provides a claim in support of a larger claim; the second boldfaced statement is that claim.
   Ⓓ Both boldfaced phrases provide evidence in support of a major claim.

Questions 8 to 10 refer to the passage below. For each question, select <u>one</u> answer choice, unless the instructions state otherwise.

Historic buildings are often regarded as energy inefficient in measurement systems that focus solely on annual energy usage. This approach ignores two important factors: (1) the annual energy use in an appropriately rehabilitated historic building is not measurably
5   greater than for a new building; and (2) 15 to 30 times as much energy is used in the construction of a building than its annual operation. For an existing building, the energy expended in construction has already been "embodied" in the structure. When the energy consumption analysis is approached from a life-cycle perspective, wherein both the
10 energy needed to construct the building as well as annual energy usage is included, the energy inefficiency claim against historic buildings largely disappears. This is an area, however, where more research and more widely dispersed research is necessary.

8. The passage suggests that which of the following are advantages of an "appropriately rehabilitated historic building" relative to a newly constructed building? (Indicate all that apply.)

   Ⓐ The historic building will use less energy on an annual basis.
   Ⓑ Rehabilitating a historic building uses less energy than constructing a new building.
   Ⓒ The life-cycle energy use of a historic building is no greater than that of a newly constructed building.

GO ON TO NEXT PAGE ➤

9. Select the sentence in the passage in which the author qualifies a major claim.

```
┌─────────────────────────────┐
│                             │
│                             │
└─────────────────────────────┘
```

10. In the context of the passage, the word *embodied* most nearly means

    Ⓐ encapsulated
    Ⓑ anthropomorphized
    Ⓒ accounted for
    Ⓓ explained by
    Ⓔ justified by

In Questions 11 to 14, for each blank, select the two answer choices that (1) complete the sentence in a way that makes sense and (2) produce sentences that are similar in meaning.

11. Daniel lived the _____ life of an academic, moving from city to city and never living in one location long enough to settle down.

    Ⓐ peripatetic

    Ⓑ disillusioning

    Ⓒ itinerant

    Ⓓ frugal

    Ⓔ prolific

    Ⓕ profligate

12. The fact that plants, unlike most animals, lack a central nervous system has erroneously led to the more extreme conclusion that, unlike animals, plants do not behave _____ to stimuli in their environment.

- A haphazardly
- B predictably
- C systematically
- D observantly
- E subtly
- F erratically

13. The beleaguered politician saw a dramatic shift in her public perception. The diplomatic skills that had once been lauded as forthright were now less-charitably interpreted as acts of _____.

- A altruism
- B docility
- C pecuniousness
- D duplicity
- E artifice
- F bonhomie

14. Critics mistake for simplicity the _____ of the author's prose, neglecting to realize that verbosity is not a prerequisite for complexity.

- A concision
- B subtlety
- C convolutedness
- D nuance
- E terseness
- F concomitancy

Questions 15 to 17 refer to the passage below. For each question, select <u>one</u> answer choice, unless the instructions state otherwise.

If we ask ourselves wherein consists the immense superiority of Chaucer's poetry over the romance-poetry—why it is that in passing from this to Chaucer we suddenly feel ourselves to be in another world, we shall find that his superiority is both in the substance of his poetry
5 and in the style of his poetry. His superiority in substance is given by his large, free, simple, and clear yet kindly view of human life—so unlike the total want, in the romance-poets, of all intelligent command of it. Chaucer has not their helplessness; he has gained the power to survey the world from a central, a truly human point of view. We
10 have only to call to mind the Prologue to *The Canterbury Tales*. The right comment upon it is Dryden's: "It is sufficient to say, according to the proverb, that here is God's plenty." And again: "He is a perpetual fountain of good sense." It is by a large, free, sound representation of things, that poetry, this high criticism of life, has truth of substance;
15 and Chaucer's poetry has truth of substance.

15. In the context of the passage, "want" most nearly means

   Ⓐ deficit
   Ⓑ desire
   Ⓒ intelligibility
   Ⓓ avarice
   Ⓔ dedication

16. Which of the following would be an appropriate title for the passage?

   Ⓐ "Chaucer's Influence on the Romance Poets"
   Ⓑ "Romance Poetry: From Chaucer to Dryden"
   Ⓒ "Chaucer Versus the Romance Poets: An Examination of Chaucer's Supremacy"
   Ⓓ "Chaucer's Examination of Human Life"
   Ⓔ "*The Canterbury Tales* and Their Place in Chaucer's Ouevre"

17. Select the sentence in the passage in which the author uses evidence to support an assertion about the difference between Chaucer and the romance poets.

Question 18 is based on the passage below. Select <u>one</u> answer choice.

To reduce traffic congestion, town X has proposed increasing the
number of city buses. Most residents are in favor of the proposal and
have indicated that they will accept an increase in taxes to support it.
Thus, once the proposal is implemented, traffic congestion in town X
5 will decrease.

18. Which of the following, if true, most weakens the argument?

    Ⓐ Traffic congestion has only recently become a problem in town X,

    Ⓑ Most of the people commuting in town X are residents of town X.

    Ⓒ To finance the proposal, the council of town X is considering
diverting funds from other areas.

    Ⓓ Most of the residents in favor of the proposal have indicated that
they will continue commuting with their cars.

    Ⓔ By implementing the proposal, town X will reduce the amount of
exhaust emitted by its vehicles.

Questions 19 to 20 refer to the passage below. For each question, select <u>one</u> answer choice, unless the instructions state otherwise.

In 1919, a year before American women were given the right to vote,
Margaret Bourke-White wrote in her diary, "I want to do all the things
that women never do!" Just 10 years later, she was hired as the first
photographer for *Fortune* magazine. As a trailblazer in the nascent field
5 of photojournalism, Bourke-White became a person of many firsts,
including having her photograph of the Fort Peck Dam appear on the
first cover of the freshly released *Life* magazine in 1936, being the first
Western photographer allowed into the Soviet Union, the first woman
to fly with a U.S. combat mission, and the first woman allowed to fly in
10 a B-47 bomber. "Her accomplishments would have been significant in
any historical time, no matter who had done them—the fact that she
was a woman in those very early prefeminist years makes them all the
more remarkable," says author and professor Lynne Iglitzin.

19. In the context of the passage, "nascent" most nearly means

    Ⓐ emerging

    Ⓑ unwelcomed

    Ⓒ aesthetic

    Ⓓ controversial

    Ⓔ trailblazing

20. Professor Lynne Iglitzin would most likely agree with which of the following statements?

Ⓐ The fact that Bourke-White was female was central to her accomplishments.

Ⓑ Had Bourke-White worked in a different era, she would have been more successful.

Ⓒ Bourke-White's accomplishments are minimized by the fact that she had no competition.

Ⓓ Bourke-White's gender has little bearing on the importance of her accomplishments.

Ⓔ Bourke-White's notoriety as a female photojournalist contributed to her success.

—————————————— **STOP.** ——————————————
This is the end of Section 4.

Quantitative Reasoning

20 questions—35 minutes

This section includes four types of questions: Multiple-Choice Questions—Select One Answer, Multiple-Choice Questions—Select One or More Answers, Numeric Entry Questions, and Quantitative Comparisons. Read the following directions before you begin the section.

General Information

- Numbers: All the numbers shown in this section are real numbers.
- Figures: Assume that the position of all points, angles, and so on are in the order shown and the measures of angles are positive,
- All figures lie in a plane unless otherwise stated.
- All straight lines can be assumed to be straight.
- Note that geometric figures are *not necessarily drawn to scale*. Do not try to estimate lengths and sizes of figures in order to answer questions.

Directions

Multiple-Choice Questions—Select One Answer

- Select one answer choice from a list of five choices.

Multiple-Choice Questions—Select One or More Answers

- Select one or more answer choices following the directions given.
- You must select all of the correct answer choices and no others in order to earn credit for the question.
- If the question specifies how many answer choices to select, you must select that number of choices.

Numeric Entry Questions

- Indicate your answer in the box provided with the question.
- Equivalent forms of an answer, such as 1.5 and 1.50, are all correct.
- You do not have to reduce fractions to lowest terms.

Quantitative Comparisons

- These questions present two quantities, Quantity A and Quantity B. Information about one or both of the quantities may be provided in the space above the two quantities. You must compare the two quantities and choose

  Ⓐ if Quantity A is greater
  Ⓑ if Quantity B is greater
  Ⓒ if the two quantities are equal
  Ⓓ if the relationship between the two quantities cannot be determined

GO ON TO NEXT PAGE ➤

Each of the following questions consists of two quantities, Quantity A and Quantity B. You are to compare the two quantities. You may use additional information centered above the two quantities if additional information is given. Choose

(A) if Quantity A is greater
(B) if Quantity B is greater
(C) if the two quantities are equal
(D) if the relationship between the two quantities cannot be determined

x is a positive integer such that $x^2 > 50$

	QUANTITY A	QUANTITY B	
1.	x	7	Ⓐ Ⓑ Ⓒ Ⓓ

The number of hours Bob worked in December was 10% less than the number of hours he worked in November. Bob's hourly wage in December was 10% more than his hourly wage in November.

	QUANTITY A	QUANTITY B	
2.	The amount Bob earned in November	The amount Bob earned in December	Ⓐ Ⓑ Ⓒ Ⓓ

	QUANTITY A	QUANTITY B	
3.	The number of the multiples of 9 from 10–300, inclusive	32	Ⓐ Ⓑ Ⓒ Ⓓ

Circle c has a diameter of length d

	QUANTITY A	QUANTITY B	
4.	π	The circumference of circle c divided by d	Ⓐ Ⓑ Ⓒ Ⓓ

z is an integer such that $8 \le |z| \le 10$

	QUANTITY A	QUANTITY B	
5.	The number of possible values for z	3	Ⓐ Ⓑ Ⓒ Ⓓ

	QUANTITY A	QUANTITY B	
6.	$\dfrac{1}{\left(1 + \sqrt{\frac{1}{3}}\right)}$	$\dfrac{1}{\left(1 + \sqrt{\frac{1}{4}}\right)}$	Ⓐ Ⓑ Ⓒ Ⓓ

Lines *x* and *y* intersect to form a 90-degree angle, and
neither line is parallel to the *x* or *y* axis.

	QUANTITY A	QUANTITY B	
7.	The product of the slopes of *x* and *y*	-1	Ⓐ Ⓑ Ⓒ Ⓓ

$$a > b > k > 0$$

	QUANTITY A	QUANTITY B	
8.	$\dfrac{a}{b}$	$\dfrac{(a + k)}{(b + k)}$	Ⓐ Ⓑ Ⓒ Ⓓ

For Questions 9 to 20 select one answer choice, unless the instructions state otherwise.

9. If $(x + 3)^2 = 25$, which of the following could be the value of *x*?

Ⓐ -8
Ⓑ -5
Ⓒ -2
Ⓓ 5
Ⓔ 8

10. If *x* and *y* are integers, and $(x^{-3})(y^{-2}) = 72^{-1}$, then what is the value of $x + y$?

```



```

11. A manufacturer purchased an item at 30% less than its production cost and sold the item at a price that was $\frac{1}{7}$ greater than what the manufacturer paid for it. The price at which the manufacturer sold the item was what percent of the item's production cost?

Ⓐ 20%
Ⓑ 30%
Ⓒ 70%
Ⓓ 80%
Ⓔ 90%

12. If $\frac{1}{3^a} > \frac{1}{100}$, then the greatest possible integer value for *a* is

Ⓐ 1
Ⓑ 2
Ⓒ 4
Ⓓ 5
Ⓔ 33

13. If a is equal to the product of the positive integers from 1–30, inclusive, which of the following is not a factor of a?

   (A) 42

   (B) 51

   (C) 58

   (D) 56

   (E) 62

14. If $\frac{x}{y} > 1$ and $x + y < 0$, then which of the following must be true? (Indicate all that apply.)

   [A] $|x| > |y|$

   [B] $x < y$

   [C] $x > y$

   [D] $x^2 > y^2$

**Stated Order of Preference of
Phones X, Y, and Z**

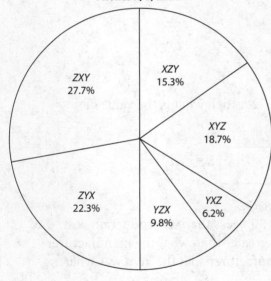

Total ratings: 1,000

**Ratings for Different Features
Phones X, Y, and Z**

	Usability	Value	Appearance
X	4.2	3.8	4.0
Y	3.7	4.0	3.6
Z	4.1	4.8	4.2

Questions 15–17 refer to the figures above.

15. The number of consumers who rated phone X as their preferred phone was how much greater than the number of consumers who rated phone Y as their preferred phone?

   (A) 160

   (B) 180

   (C) 220

   (D) 340

   (E) 360

16. The total number of points assigned to phone Z for value was what percent greater than the number of points assigned to phone Y for value?

   (A) 16.66%
   (B) 20%
   (C) 22.2%
   (D) 25%
   (E) 33.3%

17. In the pie chart, what is the approximate degree measure of the central angle corresponding to the preference YZX?

   (A) 10 degrees
   (B) 30 degrees
   (C) 35 degrees
   (D) 40 degrees
   (E) 45 degrees

18. If each of the edges of a cube increases by a factor of 2, the surface area of the resulting cube will be how many times the surface area of the original cube?

   (A) 2
   (B) 4
   (C) 6
   (D) 8
   (E) 36

19. If the length of a certain square increases by 10% and the width of the square decreases by 10%, the area of the resulting rectangle will be what percentage of the area of the original square?

   (A) 98%
   (B) 99%
   (C) 100%
   (D) 101%
   (E) 102%

20. A certain jar contains 5 marbles, r of which are red. If two marbles are to be selected at random, and the probability that both marbles will be red is $\frac{1}{10}$, what is the value of r?

   (A) 1
   (B) 2
   (C) 3
   (D) 4
   (E) 5

—————————————— **STOP.** ——————————————
This is the end of Section 5.

SECTION 6

Quantitative Reasoning

20 questions—35 minutes

This section includes four types of questions: Multiple-Choice Questions—Select One Answer, Multiple-Choice Questions—Select One or More Answers, Numeric Entry Questions, and Quantitative Comparisons. Read the following directions before you begin the section.

General Information

- Numbers: All the numbers shown in this section are real numbers.
- Figures: Assume that the position of all points, angles, and so on are in the order shown and the measures of angles are positive,
- All figures lie in a plane unless otherwise stated.
- All straight lines can be assumed to be straight.
- Note that geometric figures are *not necessarily drawn to scale*. Do not try to estimate lengths and sizes of figures in order to answer questions.

Directions

Multiple-Choice Questions—Select One Answer
- Select one answer choice from a list of five choices.

Multiple-Choice Questions—Select One or More Answers
- Select one or more answer choices following the directions given.
- You must select all of the correct answer choices and no others in order to earn credit for the question.
- If the question specifies how many answer choices to select, you must select that number of choices.

Numeric Entry Questions
- Indicate your answer in the box provided with the question.
- Equivalent forms of an answer, such as 1.5 and 1.50, are all correct.
- You do not have to reduce fractions to lowest terms.

Quantitative Comparisons
- These questions present two quantities, Quantity A and Quantity B. Information about one or both of the quantities may be provided in the space above the two quantities. You must compare the two quantities and choose

  (A) if Quantity A is greater
  (B) if Quantity B is greater
  (C) if the two quantities are equal
  (D) if the relationship between the two quantities cannot be determined

GO ON TO NEXT PAGE ➤

Each of the following questions consists of two quantities, Quantity A and Quantity B. You are to compare the two quantities. You may use additional information centered above the two quantities if additional information is given. Choose

Ⓐ if Quantity A is greater
Ⓑ if Quantity B is greater
Ⓒ if the two quantities are equal
Ⓓ if the relationship between the two quantities cannot be determined

$$6x + 8y > 36$$

	QUANTITY A	QUANTITY B	
1.	$3x + 4y$	18	Ⓐ Ⓑ Ⓒ Ⓓ

---

a, b, c, and d are positive integers such that $\frac{a}{b} < \frac{c}{d}$

	QUANTITY A	QUANTITY B	
2.	$\left(\frac{c}{b}\right)\left(\frac{a}{d}\right)$	$\frac{c}{d}$	Ⓐ Ⓑ Ⓒ Ⓓ

Set q consists of the integers from 1–99, inclusive.

	QUANTITY A	QUANTITY B	
3.	The probability that a number randomly chosen from set q is odd	The probability that a number randomly chosen from set q is even	Ⓐ Ⓑ Ⓒ Ⓓ

$$x^2 = x$$

	QUANTITY A	QUANTITY B	
4.	x	1	

	QUANTITY A	QUANTITY B	
5.	The sum of the exterior angles of a regular pentagon	The sum of the exterior angles of a regular hexagon	Ⓐ Ⓑ Ⓒ Ⓓ

50% of the students in a class are male, and 40% of
the students in the class have brown hair.

	QUANTITY A	QUANTITY B	
6.	The percentage of the students in the class who are boys with brown hair	20%	Ⓐ Ⓑ Ⓒ Ⓓ

	QUANTITY A	QUANTITY B	
7.	The number of 1-person groups that can be chosen from a group of five people	The number of 4-person groups that can be chosen from a group of five people	Ⓐ Ⓑ Ⓒ Ⓓ

Travelling at a rate of 125 meters per second, Bob travelled
more than 2 kilometers. (1 kilometer =1,000 meters.)

	QUANTITY A	QUANTITY B	
8.	The amount of time that Bob travelled	$\frac{1}{4}$ of a minute	Ⓐ Ⓑ Ⓒ Ⓓ

**For Questions 9 to 14 select one answer choice, unless the instructions state
otherwise.**

9. Next week, the probability of rain on any given day is $\frac{1}{4}$. What is
the probability that it will rain on Tuesday of next week, but not
on Wednesday?

10. Which of the following must be even?

    Ⓐ $x^2 + 6x + 9$
    Ⓑ $x^2 + 7x + 12$
    Ⓒ $x^2 + 4x - 21$
    Ⓓ $x^2 + 4x - 12$
    Ⓔ $x^2 + 8x + 15$

11. A used-car dealer purchases used cars for prices ranging from $8,000–$10,000 and sells used cars for prices ranging from $12,000–$18,000. If the dealer sold 10 cars yesterday, what was the maximum profit that he could have earned on all 10 cars?

    (A) $20,000
    (B) $40,000
    (C) $64,000
    (D) $80,000
    (E) $100,000

12. Two machines, working simultaneously at their respective constant rates, can print 400 sheets in 5 hours. If one machine can print 200 sheets in 3 hours, what is the rate of the other machine, in sheets per hour?

    (A) $\frac{40}{3}$

    (B) $\frac{80}{3}$

    (C) $\frac{100}{3}$

    (D) 80

    (E) 200

13. If a is b percent of z, and z is 200% of y, then what is y, in terms of a and b?

    (A) $50ba$

    (B) $\frac{50b}{a}$

    (C) $\frac{50a}{b}$

    (D) $\frac{ab}{50}$

    (E) $\frac{a}{50}b$

14. At a certain school, the ratio of students to teachers is 9:2, and the ratio of teachers to administrators is 5:3. Which of the following could be the total number of students at the school? (Indicate all that apply.)

    [A] 80
    [B] 90
    [C] 120
    [D] 180
    [E] 200

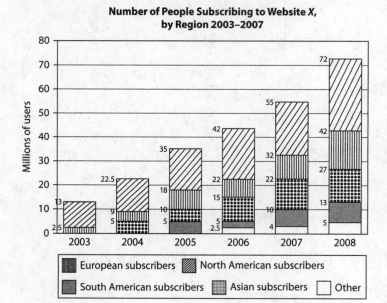

**Number of People Subscribing to Website X,
by Region 2003–2007**

Questions 15–17 refer to the figure above.

15. In which year did Asian subscribers account for the greatest percentage of all subscribers?

    Ⓐ 2004
    Ⓑ 2005
    Ⓒ 2006
    Ⓓ 2007
    Ⓔ 2008

16. The number of North American subscribers in 2008 was approximately what percent greater than the number of North American subscribers in 2006?

    Ⓐ 20%
    Ⓑ 25%
    Ⓒ 30%
    Ⓓ 33.3%
    Ⓔ 50%

17. In 2007, each subscriber spent an average of approximately 1,210 minutes per year on the website. In 2008, each subscriber spent an average of approximately 1,400 minutes per year on the website. For 2007 and 2008 combined, what was the average number of minutes per year that a subscriber spent on the website?

18. $(\sqrt{3} + \sqrt{2})(\sqrt{3} - \sqrt{2})(\sqrt{7} - \sqrt{5})(\sqrt{7} + \sqrt{5})$

   Ⓐ 1
   Ⓑ 2
   Ⓒ 3
   Ⓓ 4
   Ⓔ 5

19. If $5^{-x} + 5^{-x} + 5^{-x} + 5^{-x} + 5^{-x} = 1$, then x must equal (numeric entry)

   ┌─────────────────┐
   │   │
   └─────────────────┘

20. If $0 < a < 1 < b$, then which of the following is greatest?

   Ⓐ ab
   Ⓑ $\dfrac{a}{b}$
   Ⓒ $\dfrac{b}{a}$
   Ⓓ $\dfrac{a}{(b^2)}$
   Ⓔ $\dfrac{b}{(a^2)}$

─────────────── STOP. ───────────────
This is the end of Section 6.

Answers and Explanations

Section 1. Analytical Writing: Analyze an Issue

Use the following scoring rubric to grade your essay. Grade yourself as honestly as possible regarding the organization, structure, fluency, and accuracy of your writing. Then compare your essay to the sample high-scoring response that follows.

Analyze an Issue: Scoring			
SCORE	FOCUS	ORGANIZATION	CONVENTIONS
0	Does not address the prompt. Off topic.	Incomprehensible. May merely copy the prompt without development.	Illegible. Nonverbal. Serious errors make the paper unreadable. May be in a foreign language.
1	Mostly irrelevant to the prompt.	Little or no development of ideas. No evidence of analysis or organization.	Pervasive errors in grammar, mechanics, and spelling.
2	Unclear connection to the prompt.	Unfocused and disorganized.	Frequent errors in sentence structure, mechanics, and spelling.
3	Limited connection to the prompt.	Rough organization with weak examples or reasons.	Occasional major errors and frequent minor errors in conventions of written English.
4	Competent connection to the prompt.	Relevant examples or reasons develop a logical position.	Occasional minor errors in conventions of written English.
5	Clear, focused connection to the prompt.	Thoughtful, appropriate examples or reasons develop a consistent, coherent position. Connectors are ably used to mark transitions.	Very few errors. Sentence structure is varied and vocabulary is advanced.
6	Insightful, clever connection to the prompt.	Compelling, convincing examples or reasons develop a consistent, coherent position. The argument flows effortlessly and persuasively.	Very few errors. Sentence structure is varied and vocabulary is precise, well chosen, and effective.

Sample Response with a Score of 6

Engineers are fond of pointing out that scientific applications are essentially what makes science worthwhile; they scoff at theoreticians who spend their days "contemplating" and "pontificating" without producing real-world results. And while it can't be denied that applied research is vital to continued societal progress, I disagree with the statement that most of the money devoted to basic scientific research should instead be diverted to applied scientific research. Funds should be used in a balanced manner to support both types of research, because both are highly important.

If most of the money now used for basic science research was diverted away, this might cause the progress of basic science research to dwindle, which could thwart scientific advancement. Funding should continue to be devoted to basic scientific research, because it has value in its own right. On a fundamental level, basic scientific research enables us to expand our base of scientific knowledge. This type of research is responsible for the discovery of compounds and principles; it is responsible for teaching us about the properties of various elements; and it is crucial for identifying cause/effect relationships between factors in the physical world. Imagine where modern medicine would be without the fortuitous accident that enabled the discovery of penicillin by Alexander Fleming. Had Fleming not conducted basic research to confirm the action of penicillin and identify its properties, many of us would not be here today.

Basic scientific research is also a necessary precursor to applied scientific research; without it, there would be no knowledge to apply. When a compound or concept is discovered, it can often take years of learning before the scientific community is ready to put that principle into action. Electricity was discovered many years before Samuel Morse and colleagues used it in the 1830s to create the first electric telegraph—yet without the basic research conducted on electricity as far back as Benjamin Franklin's day, Morse would not have had the building blocks necessary to apply in constructing his machine.

Basic scientific research is also a necessary component of progress using the scientific method. Great leaps in science tend to progress in paradigm shifts. Scientists will begin to examine an area and develop new knowledge in it until eventually, a large-scale "shift" happens in the predominant beliefs about that subject, and the scientific community as a whole comes over to a new way of thinking. An example of this is the shift in popular thinking regarding the idea that the earth revolves around the sun. It took many years from the time that Copernicus first conceptualized the sun-centered model before this perspective was accepted by society as a whole, and the shift would never have happened without the help of key inventions, such as the telescope. Discoveries that are made now, about basic and fundamental ideas, may lead to scientific applications down the road that would not be accepted by the scientific community at the time the original ideas are formed. Science progresses in increments, and basic science research provides the building blocks necessary for applications that can only manifest later, when popular opinion is ready to adopt the new ideas.

At the same time as money should be devoted to basic science research, funds should also be used to support applied scientific research. Applied scientific research is vitally important for multiple reasons. First, applied scientific research is necessary for the growth and technological advancement of our society. Without applying what we know, we would never be able to advance and make significant gains. The researchers who experimented with Fleming's new discovery of penicillin took medicine to an entirely new level by applying what Fleming and his associates had learned.

In addition to being necessary for advancement, applied science research is also important because it is the route through which financial returns on our original scientific investments are made. Applied science leads to the production of new beneficial tools and technologies, which in turn may become revenue-generating products. This allows society to benefit financially from the investment made in the original research. Without studies that help us determine how knowledge can be successfully applied, the investment in basic scientific research would not be likely to reap as many gains.

Finally, applied scientific research is of value because it is vital for protecting our health and safety. The use of new products always brings with it a degree of unknown. Compounds that appear safe in one application may be quite destructive in the next. Applied scientific research can help us to determine which products are safe to use in which environments. The element mercury, for instance, historically had numerous uses in applications ranging from construction equipment to thermometers and dental fillings. But numerous scientific experiments on the toxicity of mercury have proven it to pose dangers for humans and animals, helping to increase awareness of its potential problems in medical applications.

It is tempting to conclude that applied scientific research is what matters most to progress, and that funds should be devoted to scientific applications instead of to basic knowledge development. In fact, however, basic science research continues to be an important part of how knowledge is developed, and it is a critical component that precedes application. Funds should therefore be devoted to research in both basic and applied sciences, because both disciplines are of value to human advancement.

Section 2. Analytical Writing: Analyze an Argument

Use the following scoring rubric to grade your essay. Grade yourself as honestly as possible regarding the organization, structure, fluency, and accuracy of your writing. Then compare your essay to the sample high-scoring response that follows.

Analyze an Argument: Scoring			
SCORE	FOCUS	ORGANIZATION	CONVENTIONS
0	Does not address the prompt. Off topic.	Incomprehensible. May merely copy the prompt without development.	Illegible. Nonverbal. Serious errors make the paper unreadable. May be in a foreign language.
1	Little or no analysis of the argument. May indicate misunderstanding of the prompt.	Little or no development of ideas. No evidence of analysis or organization.	Pervasive errors in grammar, mechanics, and spelling.
2	Little analysis. May instead present opinions and unrelated thoughts.	Disorganized and illogical.	Frequent errors in sentence structure, mechanics, and spelling.
3	Some analysis of the prompt, but some major flaws may be omitted.	Rough organization with irrelevant support or unclear transitions.	Occasional major errors and frequent minor errors in conventions of written English.
4	Important flaws in the argument are touched upon.	Ideas are sound but may not flow logically or clearly.	Occasional minor errors in conventions of written English.
5	Perceptive analysis of the major flaws in the argument.	Logical examples and support develop a consistent, coherent critique. Connectors are ably used to mark transitions.	Very few errors. Sentence structure is varied and vocabulary is advanced.
6	Insightful, clever analysis of the argument's flaws and fallacies.	Compelling, convincing examples and support develop a consistent, coherent critique. The analysis flows effortlessly and persuasively.	Very few errors. Sentence structure is varied, and vocabulary is precise, well chosen, and effective.

Sample Response with a Score of 6

The author of the statement concludes that Elmrose Corporation can increase its profits by relocating all of its operations and personnel to one office. The evidence cited concerns moves that the corporation made after 2010. In 2010, the company housed all of its operations and employees in one office. After 2010, the company moved to multiple locations and saw its profits decline. In fact, the author states, the profits of the company declined steadily each year after the expansion to multiple locations, leading the author to assume that the expansion to multiple locations was sole the reason for the profit decline.

When looking at this argument and the evidence given, we cannot say with certainty whether the move to different locations was responsible for the decline in profits, and whether reversing this would reverse the profit decline. In order to establish that the author's argument is valid, we would need to analyze additional evidence.

The first piece of additional evidence concerns the status of the company's profits before the expansion. We know that company profits declined steadily after 2010, but what were they before the company's moves? Were profits high overall? Or were they inconsistent, reflecting an up and down pattern? If profits were high consistently in the years during which the company was in one location, assuming all other factors were equal, this would strengthen the argument that the move to multiple locations might have hurt profits. If profits were low or inconsistent before the moves, this would weaken the argument, suggesting that some factor other than the company's location is responsible for its profit decline.

Along with examining Elmrose's profits before its expansion, we also need to gather evidence regarding the status of the company's sales revenue and business expenses both before and after the expansion. If sales go down or costs go up, or both happen at once, profits can be decreased. To really understand which factors are affecting profits, we would need detailed records regarding both revenue and expenses to see what, if anything, had changed.

If there was a decrease in sales or an increase in costs (or both) that could not reasonably be attributed to any other factors other than the expansion, this would strengthen the author's argument. In this case, the new locations of the company might be responsible for the reduced revenue, since perhaps customers might not want to shop at the new locations. Alternatively, the expansion might be responsible for increased costs, since maintaining multiple locations is likely to make it more expensive for a company to operate. If, however, revenue or cost changes could be attributed to other factors not linked to the company's moves, this would weaken the argument considerably.

Another area where we might gather evidence concerns advertising. Specifically, we would need to compare the status of company advertising efforts before and after the expansion. If advertising efforts had been reduced in scope after the moves, this would weaken the author's argument, since the reduction in advertising might be responsible for lost profits. If, however, advertising efforts had remained the same or increased after the moves, this would strengthen the argument, since additional advertising would be expected to result in increased profits, all other factors being equal.

The author makes a leap in stating that profits could be boosted if Elmrose took the simple step of moving back to one office. While this argument might be valid, we would need more evidence to establish that it was so. This would involve looking at the status of the company's profits before the expansion, its revenues and costs in the years before and after the moves, and also the extent of its advertising during both time periods.

Section 3. Verbal Reasoning

1. **A and F** The contextual clue is "in prioritizing efficiency." If society emphasizes efficiency, then it downplays other traits. Of the choices, the best word is *idealism*. "In favor of" indicates that the word in the second blank is in line with "efficiency." Of the choices, the best word is *pragmatism*.

2. **B** The contextual clue "despite" indicates that Wasselman's ability to attract followers was in contrast to the nature of his evidence. What would characterize the evidence of a theory that *shouldn't* attract followers? A good word is *absence*. Of the choices, the word closest in meaning to "absence" is *dearth*.

3. **C and D** The first blank is easier, so start there. The phrase "turn from" indicates that the word in the blank is the opposite of "self-seriousness." Of the choices, the best word is *irony*. The word in the second blank elaborates on the concept of irony. The best phrase is *a mused detachment*.

4. **C, D, and H** Start with the first blank. The word in the blank should be the opposite of "central." A good prediction is "peripheral." Of the words in the blank, the word closest in meaning to "peripheral" is *superficial*. The clue for the second blank is "even when it's intended," which implies that the word in the first blank means "unintended." Of the words in the choices, the best is *incidental*. The clue for the last word is "outside of the scope." Of the choices, the word closest in meaning to "out of scope" is *irrelevant*.

5. **B, F, and H** There are the most clues for the word in the second blank, so start there. The clue is "wariness of human motives." Of the choices, the word closest in meaning to this is *cynicism*. Now, use cynicism to determine the word in the first blank. The trigger "though" indicates that the writer explores more than just cynicism; thus, he is not a cynic. Of the choices, the word closest in meaning to cynic is *misanthrope*. Finally, "though" also clues us in to the meaning of the last word. It should characterize behavior that contrasts with what a cynic would expect. A simple word here is "good." Of the choices, the word closest in meaning to good is *benevolence*.

6. **C and E** The words in the blanks determine each other, so you need to look at the choices in pairs, instead of individually. The best pair is *inability* and *effectiveness*.

7. **B** Based on the given information, class A must have had more students who scored between 80 percent and 90 percent than did class B. .

8. **B** The passage states that "graffiti . . . can lend insight into the powerless voices that would otherwise have been censored by most ancient societies." This is in contrast to traditional academic perceptions of graffiti. The best answer is thus B.

9. **A** The author mentions "exegesis" when discussing the fact that the concise nature of graffiti makes its study more difficult than what scholars are used to. The best answer is "explanation."

10. **C** The author's point is that scholars *should* study graffiti to gain insight into the culture in which the graffiti originated. The author is thus "enthusiastic" about the prospects of graffiti as an academic subject.

11. **A and E** How does the "diversity of the citizens' jobs" relate to the city's classification as "industrial"? Since there are a multitude of jobs, the nature of the jobs is more than simply industrial. Thus, this "diversity" *undermines* and *subverts* the categorization.

12. **C and E** What the scientist encounters is based on the "divergent opinions in the field." If there are divergent opinions, then his theory would most likely encounter *resistance* and *criticism*.

13. **A and E** The word in the blank describes what the Internet has done to people's attention spans. The phrase after the colon provides context for this word by indicating that people will not view a page unless it provides "immediate stimulation." If people need "immediate stimulation," then their attention spans must have suffered a diminishment. Of the choices, the words closest in meaning to "diminishment" are *a decrease* and *an attenuation*.

14. **A and E** The fact that people seek psychotherapy contrasts with their views of it. Among the choices, the words that best express a contrast are *skepticism of* and *aversion toward*.

15. **A** The author mentons the fact that Navajo "has no alphabet or symbols" in support of the larger claim that "Johnston believed Navajo answered the military requirement for an undecipherable code because Navajo is an unwritten language of extreme complexity." The lack of alphabet or symbols is one example of this complexity.

16. **D** The purpose of the passage is to explain why Johnston recommended using Navajo for secure communications.

17. **Sentence 9: Johnston staged tests under simulated combat conditions, demonstrating that Navajos could encode, transmit and decode a three-line English message in 20 seconds.** This is the only sentence mentioning a study conducted to demonstrate the benefits of using Navajo.

18. **D** To weaken the argument, we should show that smoking leads to insomnia or that some third factor leads to both. Choice D suggests that the symptoms of smoking lead to insomnia.

19. **B** The first sentence of the passage states that the artists had to rely on other means "in part because of its ban on figural representation."

20. **B** In the first sentence, the author introduces "geometric patterns for ornamentation" as one of the examples "of art that have been seen since the seventh century." This statement implies that these patterns did not exist before the seventh century.

Section 4. Verbal Reasoning

1. **B and D** The word in the first blank describes the tactic that the executive used. This is clarified by "underhanded." Of the choices in the first column, the word closest in meaning to underhanded is *cunning*. The second blank describes a trait that "devolved into indifference." This implies that the original trait was the opposite of indifference. Of the words in the blank, the best match is *enthusiasm*.

2. **B** What kind of "byproduct" is digitization? It's speedy and effective, and capitalistic societies embrace such traits. It is thus most likely an "inevitable" byproduct. Of the choices, the word closest in meaning to inevitable is *inexorable*.

3. **B and E** Start with the second blank. If the pride "rendered her . . . sensitivity inaccessible," then what did it do to her feelings? A good prediction is "masked." Of the choices, the word closest in meaning is *obscured*. Now, move on to the first blank. What kind of tone would a letter have if the feelings are obscured? A good prediction is "guarded." Of the choices, the word closest in meaning is *muted*.

4. **A and F** Since other "seemingly insolvable problems have been unraveled," we can conclude that the "problem" in the first sentence is not insolvable. The word in the first column closest in meaning is *intractable*. Since the issue is whether the student has the "requisite resolve," we can infer that the other problems were solved through "resolve." The word closest in meaning is *persistence*.

5. **C and D** The words in the blank determine each other, so look for the best pair of words to fit into both. The pair that best fits is *flummoxed . . . self-interest*.

6. **C and E** If amateur writers "write unnecessarily verbose prose," then they must equate *verbosity* with depth. Since these words are "unnecessary," the effect of the verbosity must be negative. Of the choices in column 2, the word that best first is *detrimental*.

7. **A** The first boldfaced phrase provides the major claim of the argument; the second boldfaced statement provides a claim in support of that major claim.

8. **B** Choice A contradicts the passage and is thus incorrect. Choice B can be inferred from the following sentence: "When the energy consumption analysis is approached from a life-cycle perspective, wherein both the energy needed to construct the building as well as annual energy usage is included, the energy inefficiency claim against historic buildings largely disappears." Thus, choice B is correct. Choice C is too extreme. Though the author mentions that "the energy inefficiency claim against historic buildings largely disappears," the last sentence leaves open the possibility that differences might exist.

9. **Sentence 4** In sentence 4, the author presents the passage's major claim: "When the energy consumption analysis is approached from a life-cycle perspective, wherein both the energy needed to construct the building as well as annual energy usage is included, the energy inefficiency claim against historic buildings largely disappears." In sentence 5, the author qualifies this claim by stating that more research is necessary.

10. **C** The author uses "embodied" to explain the fact that the energy costs of building historic buildings have already been absorbed. These costs have thus been *accounted for.*

11. **A and C** The clues for the blank follow the comma. What would characterize a life in which one is "moving from city to city and never living in one location long enough to settle down"? A good prediction is "nomadic." Of the choices, the words closest in meaning are *peripatetic and itinerant.*

12. **B and C** The "extreme" conclusion erroneously drawn is based on the fact that plants lack a central nervous system. If plants lack such a nervous system, it would seem to follow that they don't behave in any "consistent" way to their environment. The choices most similar in meaning are *predictably* and *systematically.*

13. **D and E** The word in the blank describes the new characterization of the politician's diplomatic skills. They were once considered "forthright," but now they are interpreted more negatively. The word in the blank should thus contrast with forthright. A good prediction is "dishonest." The choices closest in meaning are *duplicity* and *artifice.*

14. **A and E** The key context clue is "neglecting," which indicates that the critics do not realize that writing does not have to be wordy to be complex. If they do not realize this fact, then they most likely think the author's prose is simple because it uses few words. Of the choices, the words that match the meaning of "using few words" are *concision* and *terseness.*

15. **A** The author uses "want" in reference to the "intelligent command" that Chaucer has and that the romance-poets lack. The word closest in meaning to "lack" is *deficit.*

16. **C** This is a main idea question. The correct answer will address the scope of the passage. in the first sentence, the author introduces his main point, which is to explain Chaucer's superiority.

17. **Sentence 4: We have only to call to mind the Prologue to *The Canterbury Tales.*** The author uses the selected sentence to support the following assertion: "He has gained the power to survey the world from a central, a truly human point of view."

18. **D** If no one uses the buses, then the proposal won't achieve its goal.

19. **A** The author uses "nascent" to describe photojournalism at the time that Bourke-White entered the field. Since Bourke-White accomplished many "firsts," we can infer that "nascent" is closest in meaning to *emerging.*

20. **D** Professor Lynne Iglitzin states that "her accomplishments would have been significant in any historical time, no matter who had done them." This statement implies the belief that Bourke-White's gender had little bearing on her accomplishments.

Section 5. Quantitative Reasoning

1. **A** Backsolve. If $x = 7$, then $x^2 = 49 < 50$. 7 is too small of a value for x. Thus, Quantity A must be greater.

2. **A** Plug in values. Assume that Bob worked 100 hours in November and made $10/hr. In this case, Bob earned $100 \times \$10 = \$1,000$ in November. In December, he thus worked 90 hours and earned $11/hr. In this case, he earned $90 \times 11 = \$990$ in December. Since he earned more in November, Quantity A is greater.

3. **C** To determine a value for Quantity A, use the formula for evenly spaced sets. The smallest multiple of 9 in the set is 18, and the last multiple of 9 in the set is 297. Plug these values in:

$$\frac{297 - 18}{9} + 1 = 32$$

4. **C** The circumference of the circle is $\pi \times d$. $\frac{\pi d}{d} = \pi$. Thus, the quantities are equal.

5. **A** Based on the prompt, z must be between 8 and 10 units away from zero. Thus, the positive values of z can equal 8, 9, or 10, and the negative values of z can equal -8, -9, and -10. There are 6 possible values for z. Quantity A is greater.

6. **B** Since the fractions we're comparing have the same numerator, the fraction with the smaller denominator will be larger.

    The comparison is thus:

    $$\sqrt{\left(1 + \sqrt{\tfrac{1}{3}}\right)} \text{ versus } \sqrt{\left(1 + \sqrt{\tfrac{1}{4}}\right)}$$

    To simplify the comparison, square both quantities to arrive at:

    $$1 + \sqrt{\tfrac{1}{3}} \text{ versus } 1 + \sqrt{\tfrac{1}{4}}$$

    Simplify further by subtracting 1 from both quantities:

    $$\sqrt{\tfrac{1}{3}} \text{ versus } \sqrt{\tfrac{1}{4}}$$

    Simplify further by squaring both quantities:

    $$\tfrac{1}{3} \text{ versus } \tfrac{1}{4}$$

    Since $\frac{1}{3} > \frac{1}{4}$, the denominator in Quantity A is greater, which means the fraction in Quantity A is smaller.

7. **C** If two lines are perpendicular, then their slopes must be negative reciprocals, meaning their product is -1.

8. **A** Plug in values: Let $a = 4$, $b = 2$, and $k = 1$. In this case, Quantity A $= \frac{4}{2} = 2$, and Quantity B $= \frac{5}{3}$. With these values, Quantity A is greater. Now, choose new values: Let $a = 100$, $b = 2$, and $k = 1$. In this case, Quantity A $= \frac{100}{2} = 50$, and Quantity B $= \frac{101}{3}$. Quantity A is still greater.

9. **A** Square-root both sides: $(x + 3) = 5$ or $(x + 3) = -5$. Solve for x in each equation:

$$x = 2 \text{ or } x = -8$$

10. **5** First, get rid of the negative exponents by expressing each base as its reciprocal:

$$\frac{1}{x^3} \times \frac{1}{y^2} = \frac{1}{72} \rightarrow (x^3)(y^2) = 72$$

Next, break 72 down into its prime factors: $72 = 3 \times 3 \times 2 \times 2 \times 2$. $x = 2$ and $y = 3$. $x + y = 5$.

11. **D** Choose a value for the production cost: $1,000. The purchase price was thus .7($1,000) = $700. The selling price was thus $(\frac{8}{7}) \times 700 = 800. 800 is 80% of 1,000.

12. **C** Since the numerators of the fractions are the same, it must be true that $3^a < 100$. The greatest integer, a, that satisfies this inequality is 4.

13. **E** The correct answer will be a value whose prime factors are not contained within the prime factorization of 30!. The prime factors of 62 are 2 and 31. 31 is not contained within the prime factorization of 30!.

14. **A, B, and D** Choose values that satisfy both constraints. Let $x = -3$ and $y = -2$. For these values, choices A, B, and D all hold true. Now, choose new values for x and y that satisfy the constraints: $x = -\frac{1}{2}$ and $y = -\frac{1}{3}$. For these values, choices A, B, and D still hold true.

15. **B** Look at Diagram 1. In two of the sectors phone X was rated as the preferred phone. The sum of these percentages is 15.3% + 18.7% = 34%. 34% of 1,000 is 340. In two of the sectors, phone Y was rated as the preferred phone. The sum of these percentages is 9.8% + 6.2% = 16%. 16% of 1,000 is 160. 340 − 160 = 180.

16. **B** Since these ratings are averages, you may be inclined to get the sum of the value ratings for each, and then use the percentage change formula. However, we don't need to get the sum, since the number of ratings is the same for both groups. Instead, use the average rating in the percent change formula:

$$\frac{4.8 - 4.0}{4.0} \times 100 = 20\%$$

17. **C** The preference YZX represents 9.8% of the entire circle. 9.8% × 360 degrees = 35 degrees.

18. **B** Surface area of a cube = $6e^2$. Plug in values. Let the original edge = 2. The original surface area is thus 24. The new surface area is thus 96. The new surface area is thus four times the original surface area.

19. **B** Plug in numbers. Let the original length = 10 and the original width = 10. The new length is this 1.1(10) = 11, and the new width is thus .9(10) = 9. The new area is thus 99. The original area was 100. 99 is 99% of 100.

20. **B** (probability of choosing r) × (probability of choosing r again) =

$$\frac{1}{10} \rightarrow \frac{r}{5} \times \frac{r-1}{4} = \frac{1}{10} \rightarrow \frac{r(r-1)}{20} = \frac{1}{10} \rightarrow r(r-1) = 2 \rightarrow r = 2$$

Section 6. Quantitative Reasoning

1. **A** Simplify the given inequality. $6x + 8y = 2(3x + 4y)$. Thus: $2(3x + 4y) > 36 \rightarrow$ $3x + 4y > 18$. Quantity A is greater.

2. **D** Rewrite quantity A as $(\frac{c}{d})(\frac{a}{b})$. Next, divide both quantities by $(\frac{c}{d})$. The new relationship is thus: $\frac{a}{b}$ vs 1. Without knowing the relationship between a and b, we cannot determine a relationship.

3. **A** In the set of integers from 1–98, inclusive, half of the numbers are even and half are odd. Therefore, in the set of integers from 1–99, inclusive, there are more odd integers than even integers. The probability of choosing an odd integer is thus greater than the probability of choosing an even integer.

4. **D** Since the equation $x^2 = x$ is quadratic, set it equal to zero, and determine the possible values for x: $x^2 - x = 0 \rightarrow x(x - 1) = 0 \rightarrow x = 0$ or $(x - 1) = 0 \rightarrow x = 0$ or $x = 1$. The relationship cannot be determined.

5. **C** The sum of the exterior angles of any regular polygon is 360 degrees.

6. **D** Without any information about the overlap between the percentage of students that are boys and the percentage of students that have brown hair, a relationship cannot be determined.

7. **C** The number of ways to select 1 person from 5 people is equivalent to the number of ways of selecting 4 people from a group of 5.

8. **A** Use the RTD formula: $\frac{125 \text{ meters}}{\text{second}} \times$ (# of seconds traveled) > 2 kilometers. Convert kilometers to meters: $\frac{125 \text{ meters}}{\text{second}} \times$ (# of seconds traveled) $> 2{,}000$ meters $\rightarrow$ # of seconds traveled $> \frac{2000}{125} \rightarrow$ # of seconds traveled > 16.16 seconds $> \frac{1}{4}$ of a minute. Thus, Quantity A is greater.

9. $\frac{3}{16}$ Since multiple events must be satisfied, we should multiply the probabilities of each individual event. The probability of rain on Tuesday is $\frac{1}{4}$. The probability of no rain on Wednesday is $\frac{3}{4}$. $(\frac{1}{4}) \times (\frac{3}{4}) = \frac{3}{16}$.

10. **B** Plug in values for x. First, choose an odd value, then choose an even value. The only choice that yields an even for both conditions is choice B.

11. **E** To achieve a maximum profit, the cost of an item should be as low as possible and the revenue on the item should be as high as possible. The least possible cost of the car is \$8,000, and the greatest possible selling price of the car is \$18,000. The greatest profit on one car is thus \$18,000 − \$8,000 = \$10,000. The greatest profit on 10 cars is thus \$10,000 × 10 = \$100,000.

12. **A** The combined rate of the two machines is 400 sheets/5 hours = 80 sheets/hour. The rate of the first machine is $\frac{200}{3}$. Let the rate of the second machine be y. Thus, $\frac{200}{3} + y = 80$. Solve for y: $y = 80 - \frac{200}{3} \rightarrow y = \frac{240}{3} - \frac{200}{3} \rightarrow y = \frac{40}{3}$

13. **C** Plug in values that satisfy the given constraints. Let $a = 50$ and $b = 25$. If 50 is 25% of z, then $z = 200$. If $z = 200$, then $y = 100$. Now, plug in 50 for a and 25 for b into the choices, and see which choice yields a value of 100.

14. **B and D** Whenever a question provides multiple ratios with a common element, manipulate the ratios so that the common element has the same value in both ratios. In this case, the common element is teachers, so we should manipulate the ratios so that the number of teachers is the least common multiple of 2 and 5: 10. In the first ratio: students/teachers $= \frac{9}{2} = \frac{45}{10}$. In the second ratio: teachers/administrators $= \frac{5}{3} = \frac{10}{6}$. The ratio of students to teachers to administrators is thus 45:10:6. The number of students must therefore be a multiple of 45. Any choice that is a multiple of 45 is a potential value for the number of students.

15. **C** Although the greatest *number* of Asian subscribers was in 2008, that is not the answer, because Asians formed a smaller percentage of subscribers in that year than they did in 2006. In 2008, there were roughly 15 million Asian subscribers and roughly 72 million total subscribers. The percentage of Asians in 2008 was therefore $(\frac{15}{72}) \times 100 = 20.8\%$. In contrast, in 2006, there were roughly 10 million Asian subscribers and 42 million total subscribers. $(\frac{10}{42}) \times 100 = 23.8\%$.

16. **E** Use the percent greater formula: percent greater = percent of − 100%. The number of North American subscribers in 2008 was approximately 30 million. The number of North American subscribers in 2006 was approximately 20 million. 30 million is 150% of 20 million. Thus, 30 million is 50% greater than 20 million.

17. **1,322** Use the weighted average formula: (average of 2007) × (weight of 2007) + (average of 2008) × (weight of 2008). We are given the averages, so let's find the weights. The weight of 2007 is approximately $\frac{55}{(55 + 72)} = .43$. The weight of 2008 is thus approximately .57. Now, use the formula: $1{,}210(.43) + 1{,}400(.57) = 524 + 798 = 1{,}322$.

18. **B** The first two factors form a difference of squares:

$$(\sqrt{3} + \sqrt{2})\,(\sqrt{3} - \sqrt{2}) = \sqrt[2]{3} - \sqrt[2]{2} = 3 - 2 = 1$$

The last two factors form a difference of squares:

$$(\sqrt{7} - \sqrt{5})\,(\sqrt{7} + \sqrt{5}) = \sqrt[2]{7} - \sqrt[2]{5} = 7 - 5 = 2.$$ Then multiply the $1 \times 2 = 2$

19. **1** Notice that all the terms on the left side of the equation are equal. We can thus combine like terms to arrive at: $5(5^{-x}) = 1$. Since $5 = 5^1$, we can rewrite the equation as: $5^1(5^{-x}) = 1 \rightarrow 5^{(1-x)} = 1$. If $5^{(1-x)} = 1$, then $1 - x = 0 \rightarrow x = 1$.

20. **E** The easiest way to answer this question is to choose values for a and b. Let $a = .5$ and $b = 2$. When we substitute these values into the choices, we arrive at:

    a) $(.5)(2) = 1$

    b) $\frac{(.5)}{2} = .25$

    c) $\frac{2}{.5} = 4$

    d) $\frac{.5}{4} = .125$

    e) $\frac{2}{(.25)} = 8$

Choice E yields the largest value.

Sample Scaled Scores

The following table gives an approximate idea of the scaled score that you would receive for your performance on the diagnostic test. The figures are approximations because the scaling is different for every form of the GRE test. (This process is necessary to ensure that scores on each test form are equivalent to scores on every other test form.) So do not assume that the scaled scores shown below are exactly the ones that you would receive on the real GRE. Use this information only to get a general idea of how your performance would be rated.

Sample Scoring for Quantitative and Verbal Sections	
NUMBER OF CORRECT QUESTIONS	SCALED SCORE
0	130
1	131
2	132
3	133
4	134
5	135
6	136
7	137
8	138
9	139
10	140
11	141
12	142
13	143
14	144
15	145
16	146
17	147
18	148
19	149
20	150
21	151
22	152
23	153
24	154
25	155
26	156
27	157
28	158
29	159
30	160
31	161
32	162
33	163
34	164
35	165
36	166
37	167
38	168
39	169
40	170

CHAPTER 16

Practice Test 2

SECTION 1

Analytical Writing

Analyze an Issue

30 minutes

For this task, you will be given a brief quotation that states or implies an issue of general interest. You will also be given instructions on how to respond to that issue. You will then have 30 minutes to plan and write a response.

Be sure to follow the instructions that you are given. In writing your response, support your ideas with reasons and examples drawn from your reading, your studies, and/or your personal experiences. Your response will be evaluated based on how well you organize and express your ideas, how well you support your opinions with reasons and examples, and how well you follow the rules of standard English grammar and usage.

Take a few minutes to plan your response. When you are finished writing, make sure to review your work and make any necessary revisions.

ISSUE TOPIC

For a society to truly flourish, dissent should be encouraged.

Respond to the above topic by composing an essay that states how much you agree or disagree with the given claim. Be sure to use evidence to support your stance and to consider evidence that would challenge your stance.

Analytical Writing

Analyze an Argument

30 minutes

For this task, you will be given a brief passage that presents an argument. You will also be given instructions on how to respond to the passage. You will then have 30 minutes to plan and write a response in which you evaluate the argument according to the instructions that you are given. Be aware that you are **not** being asked to present your own personal views on the topic.

In writing your response, be sure to support your ideas with reasons and examples. Your response will be evaluated based on how well you analyze the argument presented in the prompt, how well you organize and express your ideas, and how well you follow the rules of standard English grammar and usage.

Take a few minutes to plan your response. When you are finished writing, make sure to review your work and make any necessary revisions.

GO ON TO NEXT PAGE ➤

ARGUMENT TOPIC

Since Herald's Hardware began advertising on the radio, its revenues have increased by 13%. This is obvious evidence that advertising on the radio will make your business more profitable.

Write a response in which you discuss the soundness of the author's claim. Be sure to address any information that would strengthen or weaken the argument.

_____

_____

_____

_____

_____

_____

_____

_____

_____

_____

_____

_____

_____

_____

_____

_____

_____

_____

_____

_____

GO ON TO NEXT PAGE ➤

SECTION 3

Verbal Reasoning

20 questions—30 minutes

This section includes three types of questions; Reading Comprehension, Text Completion, and Sentence Equivalence. Read the following directions before you begin the section.

Directions

Reading Comprehension Questions
- *Multiple-Choice Questions—Select One Answer Choice*: Select one answer choice from a list of five choices.
- *Multiple-Choice Questions—Select One or More Answer Choices:* From a list of three answer choices, select all that are correct.
- *Select-in-Passage*: Select the sentence in the passage that meets a certain description.

Text Completion Questions
- For each blank, select one choice from the corresponding list of choices. Fill all blanks in the way that best completes the text.

Sentence Equivalence Questions
- Select the <u>two</u> answer choices that (1) complete the sentence in a way that makes sense and (2) produce sentences that are similar in meaning.

In Questions 1 to 5, for each blank, select the choice that best completes the text.

1. Attempts at rigorous literary analysis must accommodate the inherent _____ of interpretation. Unlike the sciences, where truth is arrived at by the accumulation of evidence, the arts have no external standard against which claims can be evaluated.

   - Ⓐ controversy
   - Ⓑ implausibility
   - Ⓒ ambiguity
   - Ⓓ debatability
   - Ⓔ discernibility

2. Novice readers often (i) _____ the point of satire. Believing that the purpose of exaggeration is purely comical, they often overlook the darker social commentary (ii) _____ in such stories.

Blank (i)	Blank (ii)
Ⓐ misunderstand	Ⓓ forgotten
Ⓑ enhance	Ⓔ implicit
Ⓒ undermine	Ⓕ denied

3. His writing is at once illuminating and (i) _____: He uses his talents to take the adventurous reader onto (ii) _____ detours, but these same detours will frustrate the reader accustomed to direct and (iii) _____ argumentation.

Blank (i)	Blank (ii)	Blank (iii)
Ⓐ exasperating	Ⓓ irrelevant	Ⓖ circumstantial
Ⓑ ambiguous	Ⓔ ill-construed	Ⓗ duplicitous
Ⓒ bellicose	Ⓕ edifying	Ⓘ unequivocal

4. Her actions call into question the belief that those in powerful positions forgo (i) _____. Since taking office, she has prioritized (ii) _____ over platitudes, even if doing so meant (iii) _____ some of her party's supporters.

Blank (i)	Blank (ii)	Blank (iii)
(A) reticence	(D) forthrightness	(G) vindicating
(B) candor	(E) triteness	(H) alienating
(C) loyalty	(F) felicity	(I) ingratiating

5. Unfortunately for the new employee, the _____ that served him so well in his prior job is inadequate for his present one, since success in his new role is predicated more on analytical skills than raw work ethic.

(A) industriousness
(B) discord
(C) prolixity
(D) tact
(E) subterfuge

6. The athlete's self-assurance should not be mistaken for (i) _____: throughout his career, his professed self-confidence has been (ii) _____ the skills he displayed at any point in time.

Blank (i)	Blank (ii)
(A) humility	(D) disproportionate to
(B) hubris	(E) commensurate with
(C) conviction	(F) allied with

Question 7 is based on the passage below. Select <u>one</u> answer choice.

Five years ago, Terlandia instituted a program to increase the savings rates of its older citizens. This year, the total savings by residents aged 50–65 was 10 percent more than the year before the program was instituted. It is thus obvious that Terlandia's program has
5 been successful.

7. Which of the following, if true, undermines the author's conclusion?

Ⓐ The savings rate in Terlandia is greater than the savings rate in neighboring Burlordine.

Ⓑ During the time period mentioned, the savings rate of residents between the ages of 20 and 30 increased.

Ⓒ During the time period mentioned, the number of Terlandian residents aged 50–65 increased by 15 percent.

Ⓓ Some components of Terlandia's program caused controversy among its younger residents.

Ⓔ Terlandia has unsuccessfully implemented similar programs in the past.

Questions 8 to 11 refer to the passage below. For each question, select <u>one</u> answer choice, unless the instructions state otherwise.

Volunteering has long been a common ethic in the United States, with people each year giving their time without any expectation of compensation. While these volunteer activities may be performed with the core intention of helping others, there is also a common wisdom
5 that those who give of themselves also receive. Researchers have attempted to measure the benefits that volunteers receive, including the positive feeling referred to as "helper's high," increased trust in others, and increased social and political participation.

  Over the past two decades we have seen a growing body of research
10 that indicates volunteering provides individual health benefits in addition to social benefits. This research has established a strong relationship between volunteering and health: those who volunteer have lower mortality rates, greater functional ability, and lower rates of depression later in life than those who do not volunteer. Comparisons
15 of the health benefits of volunteering for different age groups have also shown that older volunteers are the most likely to receive greater benefits from volunteering, whether because they are more likely to face higher incidence of illness or because volunteering provides them with physical and social activity and a sense of purpose at a
20 time when their social roles are changing. Some of these findings also indicate that volunteers who devote a "considerable" amount of time to

volunteer activities (about 100 hours per year) are most likely to exhibit positive health outcomes.

These findings are particularly relevant today as Baby Boomers—
25 the generation of 77 million Americans born between 1946 and 1964—reach the age typically associated with retirement. Based on U.S. Census data, the numbers of volunteers age 65 and older should increase 50 percent over the next 13 years, from just under 9 million in 2007 to more than 13 million in 2020. What's more, that number
30 can be expected to rise for many years to come, as the youngest Baby Boomers will not reach age 65 until 2029.

8. The passage is primarily concerned with

    (A) introducing the benefits of a practice and its relevance
    (B) questioning the methodology used to reach a conclusion
    (C) making a recommendation for a certain group
    (D) analyzing reasons for the increase in a certain practice
    (E) debunking a common perception

9. Based on the information in the passage, which of the following would most likely receive the greatest benefits from volunteering?

    (A) a college student with a small window available each week to volunteer
    (B) an elderly woman with a supportive social group and no known illnesses
    (C) an elderly man whose children recently moved to a different state
    (D) a middle-aged woman who volunteers with her choir group
    (E) a high school student who volunteers to receive credit for coursework

10. The author most likely states that "the youngest Baby Boomers will not reach age 65 until 2029" in order to

    (A) explain why volunteering is not as popular as it once was
    (B) suggest that volunteering will achieve its greatest popularity in 2029
    (C) support the point that volunteering rates will continue to rise
    (D) undermine a commonly held belief about volunteer demographics
    (E) examine the consequences of long-term volunteering

11. All of the following are the mentioned as potential benefits of volunteering EXCEPT

    (A) emotional well-being
    (B) increased social engagement
    (C) reduced risk of illness
    (D) longer life span
    (E) increased financial success

In Questions 12 to 15, for each blank, select the <u>two</u> answer choices that (1) complete the sentence in a way that makes sense and (2) produce sentences that are similar in meaning.

12. Because the artwork was damaged beyond recognition, traditional methods at determining its _____ proved fruitless.

   A origin

   B inspiration

   C value

   D provenance

   E controversy

   F detritus

13. Among the many myths perpetuated by the dieting industry is the notion that weight-loss is solely a function of a dieter's _____, with genetic factors playing no role in one's success.

   A restraint

   B heredity

   C inheritance

   D self-control

   E transience

   F fecundity

14. Behavior psychologists have long been puzzled by the coexistence of _____ and self-interest: How, they ask, can a human sometimes exhibit complete selflessness and other times behave with complete disregard for others' feelings?

   A altruism

   B malfeasance

   C indifference

   D turpitude

   E beneficence

   F lethargy

15. One of the more _____ side effects of the digitization of books is the constant accessibility of outside distractions: When a novel is paired side-by-side with other technological functions, the attention devoted to the novel is inevitably inadequate.

   A overlooked

   B satisfactory

   C deterministic

   D technocratic

   E pernicious

   F deleterious

GO ON TO NEXT PAGE ➤

Questions 16 to 17 refer to the passage below. For each question, select <u>one</u> answer choice, unless the instructions state otherwise.

The growth of aquaculture, or fish farming, may affect the levels of certain contaminants in consumable fish and shellfish. Dense colonies can increase stress and disease transmission among fish, in some cases requiring the administration of antibiotics. Studies have also found
5 higher levels of certain contaminants in farmed fish than in their wild counterparts, possibly due to differences in diet. For example, several studies have found higher concentrations of PCBs, organochlorine pesticides, and polybrominated diphenyl ethers (PBDEs) in farmed salmon.
10 Overharvesting also can affect the condition of fish and shellfish—not only the species being harvested, but also the species that prey on them—by disrupting the food web. Because of depleted food sources, predators can become more susceptible to disease (such as infection of rockfish by mycobacterial lesions). These infections are often confined
15 to internal organs and may not be apparent to anglers, although in some cases they are associated with external sores as well. Some types of mycobacteria can also infect humans who handle diseased fish if the infection comes into contact with an open wound. The slow-developing infections are usually not severe in humans, but in some cases they can
20 cause major health problems, especially in people with compromised immune systems.

16. Based on the information in the passage, which of the following can be concluded? (Indicate all that apply.)

   A   It has consequences for species other than the ones being fished.
   B   Anglers have no way of identifying when a fish is infected.
   C   Stress has an impact on a fish's immune system.

17. The author most likely mentions "PCBs, organochlorine pesticides, and polybrominated diphenyl ethers (PBDEs)" in order to

   Ⓐ   explain how differences in the diets of wild fish and farmed fish have arisen
   Ⓑ   support a claim about the relatively high levels of contaminants in farmed fish
   Ⓒ   illustrate the consequences of the diet of a typical farmed fish
   Ⓓ   provide examples of measures to counteract the consequences of fish farming
   Ⓔ   explain the use of antibiotics on farmed fish

Question 18 is based on the passage below. Select <u>one</u> answer choice.

A recent study of airborne illnesses in Belorussia showed that regular subway riders had a 10 percent chance of contracting influenza, while regular bus riders had a 15 percent chance of contracting influenza. Clearly, if the government of Belorussia wants to decrease the influenza
5 rate among its citizens, it should encourage bus riders to start using the subway.

18. Which of the following, if true, most weakens the argument?

   (A) Regular bus riders are, on average, older than regular subway riders, and susceptibility to disease has been linked to old age.
   (B) The costs of encouraging people to use the subway will put a strain on the government's budget.
   (C) If more people begin using the subway, some bus drivers will be out of employment.
   (D) For most routes, buses are as fast as subways.
   (E) Many bus riders prefer buses because they let the riders see outside occurrences.

Questions 19 to 20 refer to the passage below. For each question, select <u>one</u> answer choice, unless the instructions state otherwise.

Though Locke's *tabula rasa*—the theory that all behavior is learned—was long ago debunked by experimental psychologists, only recently have scientists found neuroscientific evidence supporting the position of instinctive thoughts and behaviors. Fundamental to these
5 investigations has been the use of fMRI, which enables scientists to "peer" into the brain of subjects and identify the brain regions activated by certain tasks. In direct contradiction of the Enlightenment myth of a *tabula rasa*, recent evidence shows that pre-verbal infants' brains demonstrate much of the same neural activity during social
10 interactions as do the brains of fully mature adults. One of the most illuminating studies in this field measured the activation in infants' brains when they observed an actor grasp a toy. Scientists found that infants who grasped a toy after observing someone else grasp a toy exhibited substantial activity in the motor regions of their brains,
15 whereas infants who observed the same actor but subsequently did not grasp the toy did not reveal such activity. These findings strongly support a hard-wired, instinctive capacity for empathy in infants, one that mirrors the same capacity in adult humans.

19. The primary purpose of the passage is to

  (A) suggest a difference between two groups of infants
  (B) explain a scientific methodology
  (C) offer evidence to support a position
  (D) contradict a widely held belief
  (E) contrast different approaches to studying a phenomenon

20. Select the sentence in the passage that highlights a scientific finding's significance.

—————————————————— STOP. ——————————————————
This is the end of Section 3.

Verbal Reasoning

20 questions—30 minutes

This section includes three types of questions; Reading Comprehension, Text Completion, and Sentence Equivalence. Read the following directions before you begin the section.

Directions

Reading Comprehension Questions

- *Multiple-Choice Questions—Select One Answer Choice*: Select one answer choice from a list of five choices.
- *Multiple-Choice Questions—Select One or More Answer Choices:* From a list of three answer choices, select all that are correct.
- *Select-in-Passage*: Select the sentence in the passage that meets a certain description.

Text Completion Questions

- For each blank, select one choice from the corresponding list of choices. Fill all blanks in the way that best completes the text.

Sentence Equivalence Questions

- Select the <u>two</u> answer choices that (1) complete the sentence in a way that makes sense and (2) produce sentences that are similar in meaning.

In Questions 1 to 6, for each blank, select the choice that best completes the text.

1. The editorial was just another example of her trademark _____:
   its claims were grand, and, at least superficially, appeared sound. But
   beneath this veneer of cogency lay arguments with no grounding in fact.

   - Ⓐ bombasticism
   - Ⓑ self-involvement
   - Ⓒ deflection
   - Ⓓ asperity
   - Ⓔ illegitimacy

2. Attempts to explain the arts through a scientific lens—be it economics,
   psychology, or physics—are inherently _____, since such efforts
   inevitably overlook the features that distinguish art from these other
   disciplines

   - Ⓐ encompassing
   - Ⓑ problematic
   - Ⓒ enthralling
   - Ⓓ eclectic
   - Ⓔ verbose

3. Complaints about _____ in pay are often grounded in misconceptions of basic economics: in a capitalistic society, a worker's salary is invariably a function of the impersonal workings of supply and demand.

   Ⓐ hostilities

   Ⓑ obscurities

   Ⓒ inequities

   Ⓓ irrelevance

   Ⓔ determinism

4. Despite making numerous attempts to (i) _____ the situation, the colleagues still had (ii) _____ dynamic, though they were less likely to outwardly express this contentiousness.

Blank (i)	Blank (ii)
Ⓐ rectify	Ⓓ an amicable
Ⓑ assail	Ⓔ an adversarial
Ⓒ circumvent	Ⓕ a stupefying

5. Always (i) _____, the professor demanded all the facts before coming to a decision. Once arriving at a decision, however, she was (ii) _____ in its defense.

Blank (i)	Blank (ii)
Ⓐ mystified	Ⓓ steadfast
Ⓑ skeptical	Ⓔ impecunious
Ⓒ circumscribed	Ⓕ bellicose

GO ON TO NEXT PAGE ➤

6. His occasional instances of self-denial should not be mistaken for wholesale (i) _____: those who have known him often comment on his (ii) _____ tastes and predilection for excess.

Blank (i)	Blank (ii)
(A) reconciliation	(D) indulgent
(B) deference	(E) discordant
(C) abnegation	(F) minimalist

Question 7 is based on the passage below. Select <u>one</u> answer choice.

In Verduria, many people who want to quit smoking use nicotine gum. Recently, a new pill has been released, and proponents of this pill claim that it is just as effective as nicotine gum in helping people quit smoking. **Although the overall cost of using the pill is no less than**
5 **the cost of using the gum,** researchers predict that the pill will become the primary mode of nicotine cessation.

7. The portion in boldface plays which of the following roles?

   (A) It states the main conclusion of the argument.
   (B) It provides evidence in support of the argument's main conclusion.
   (C) It states a potential objection to the main conclusion of the argument.
   (D) It provides an intermediate conclusion in support of the argument's main conclusion.
   (E) It provides an intermediate conclusion in support of a larger conclusion that goes against the argument's main conclusion.

Questions 8 to 10 refer to the passage below. For each question, select <u>one</u> answer choice, unless the instructions state otherwise.

[Sigmund] Freud was also a social critic. He believed that society, which has been fashioned by man, reflects to a great extent man's irrationality. As a consequence, each new generation is corrupted by being born into an irrational society. The influence of man on society
5 and of society on man is a vicious circle from which only a few hardy souls can free themselves.

Freud felt that the situation might be ameliorated by the application of psychological principles in raising and educating children. This would mean, of course, that parents and teachers would have to
10 undergo a psychological reeducation before they could be effective agents of reason and truth. Freud did not minimize the immensity of this task, but he did not know any other way by which to create a better society and better people. Freud's social criticism is presented in his book *Civilization and Its Discontents*.

15 What then was Freud? Physician, psychiatrist, psychoanalyst, psychologist, philosopher, and critic—these were his several vocations. Yet, taken separately or together, they do not really convey Freud's importance to the world. Although the word "genius" is used indiscriminately to describe a number of people, there is no other
20 single word that fits Freud as well as this word does. He was a genius. One may prefer to think of him, as I do, as one of the few men in history who possessed a universal mind. Like Shakespeare and Goethe and Leonardo da Vinci, whatever Freud touched he illuminated. He was a very wise man.

8. The passage is primarily concerned with

    (A) explaining how Freud wanted to change society
    (B) identifying the appropriate categorization for Freud
    (C) analyzing Freud's beliefs about society
    (D) discussing ways to reeducate society
    (E) comparing Freud to other great thinkers

9. The author most likely mentions "Shakespeare and Goethe and Leonardo da Vinci" in order to

    (A) give examples of people whose impact on the world was comparable to Freud's
    (B) suggest that it is impossible to truly define a genius
    (C) highlight the uniqueness of Freud's way of thinking
    (D) underscore the sorts of impact that deep thinkers can have on society
    (E) support the claim that Freud was a genius

10. In the context of the passage, "ameliorated" most nearly means

   (A) improved
   (B) trivialized
   (C) ignored
   (D) refashioned
   (E) intensified

In Questions 11 to 14, for each blank, select the <u>two</u> answer choices that (1) complete the sentence in a way that makes sense and (2) produce sentences that are similar in meaning.

11. In hindsight, it appears self-evident that the physicist's _____ the university was based not on the character of the other scientists, but, rather, with his frustration over the university's preference for research rather than teaching.

   A curiosity over

   B disaffection with

   C dereliction with

   D miscegenation with

   E denouement with

   F alienation from

12. Fortunately, the board members' _____ over other issues has not prevented them from consistently reaching a consensus on the all-important advertising budget.

   A dispersion

   B divergence

   C confusion

   D discord

   E monetization

   F frustration

13. The executive disputed the notion that the two companies are rivals, arguing that his company's success did not _____ that of the other company.

    A preclude

    B antecede

    C proper

    D hamper

    E encourage

    F miscalculate

14. A sport's _____ has little bearing on the skills needed to excel at it; indeed, many of the most neglected sports feature athletes whose abilities would easily transfer over to some of the better-known athletic endeavors.

    A popularity

    B dexterity

    C competitiveness

    D reputation

    E redundancy

    F duplicity

GO ON TO NEXT PAGE ➤

Questions 15 to 17 refer to the passage below. For each question, select <u>one</u> answer choice, unless the instructions state otherwise.

The features that ultimately came to characterize Hawaiian-style building—which also included breezy lanais, generous overhanging eaves, and textured exterior surfaces—came about as the hold of the Big Five weakened. The Pan-Pacific movement was gaining
5   sway, and the polyglot population began finding its many voices and architectural idioms. Churches responded to the "one Blood" sentiment of many of their parishioners by constructing verandah-like lanais on either side of the naves that symbolically welcomed all believers. Architects of the time in general often blended Eastern and
10 Western styles, ushering in a pagoda, for example, to sit in for a bell tower in the task of calling the congregation to service. For a long time, Hawaiian-style building seemed to have little to do with the architectural tastes the Islands' original settlers brought with them from the Marquesas Islands more than 800 years ago. For example,
15 the highly specialized skill needed to tightly weave the thatch that made their structures waterproof began disappearing in the 18th century, when the population declined by 90 percent, the result of diseases imported from Europeans. Evolving innovations, such as hipped roofs and airy lanais, had begun to make their appearance in
20 18th-century Hawaii just as the traditions that made them possible were being obliterated. It took longer than a century for some of the most fundamental aspects of Hawaiian architecture to find their way home again.

15. In the context of the passage, "idioms" most nearly means

   Ⓐ voices
   Ⓑ believers
   Ⓒ styles
   Ⓓ constructions
   Ⓔ edifices

16. According to the passage, why did churches begin "constructing verandah-like lanais on either side of the naves that symbolically welcomed all believers"?

    (A) to reflect the styles of other buildings constructed during the era
    (B) to display their wealth to the parishioners
    (C) to reflect a belief of their parishioners
    (D) to appease members of the Pan-Pacific movement
    (E) to incorporate the blending of Eastern and Western styles prominent in other buildings.

17. Select the sentence in the passage that introduces an ironic aspect of the evolution of Hawaiian architecture.

    ☐

Question 18 is based on the passage below. Select <u>one</u> answer choice.

At the end of each school year, University Z requires all students who enrolled in calculus to take a standardized final. This year, students in Professor Doyle's course scored higher, on average, than did the students in any other course. Since student placement in calculus
5   courses is randomized, the superior performance of Doyle's students is clearly attributable to his teaching ability.

18. Which of the following, if true, would most weaken the argument?

    (A) Calculus is the most advanced math course offered at University Z.
    (B) Because of the rigor of Professor Doyle's course, a greater percentage of students dropped his course than did the students in any other Calculus course.
    (C) Professor Doyle is known to have an unorthodox teaching style.
    (D) Student ratings of Professor Doyle were no greater than the average rating for other calculus professors.
    (E) University X has a nationally ranked mathematics program.

Questions 19 to 20 refer to the passage below. For each question, select <u>one</u> answer choice, unless the instructions state otherwise.

Some regional identities always have been partly the result of isolation. But I tend to think that other regional cultures flourish in their interaction with people of different minds around the world. We can see New England's regional identities developing not from its distance,
5 but from its engagement with other people. New Englanders were much involved, through shipping and migration, with other cultures around the world. But that didn't make them less of New England. They would travel around the world and establish their New England societies wherever they went, and their identities would be deepened by
10 it. It is partly the growth of global communications that makes people more conscious of their regional identities. It is not just a function of insularity.

19. In the context of the passage, "insularity" most nearly means

   Ⓐ superiority
   Ⓑ deflection
   Ⓒ confusion
   Ⓓ isolation
   Ⓔ communication

20. Select the sentence that provides evidence of New England's "engagement with other people."

   +----------------------------------+
   | |
   | |
   +----------------------------------+

———————————— **STOP.** ————————————
This is the end of Section 4.

Quantitative Reasoning

20 questions—35 minutes

This section includes four types of questions: Multiple-Choice Questions—Select One Answer, Multiple-Choice Questions—Select One or More Answers, Numeric Entry Questions, and Quantitative Comparisons. Read the following directions before you begin the section.

General Information

- Numbers: All the numbers shown in this section are real numbers.
- Figures: Assume that the position of all points, angles, etc. are in the order shown and the measures of angles are positive,
- All figures lie in a plane unless otherwise stated.
- All straight lines can be assumed to be straight.
- Note that geometric figures are *not necessarily drawn to scale*. Do not try to estimate lengths and sizes of figures in order to answer questions.

Directions

Multiple-Choice Questions—Select One Answer
- Select one answer choice from a list of five choices.

Multiple-Choice Questions—Select One or More Answers
- Select one or more answer choices following the directions given.
- You must select all of the correct answer choices and no others in order to earn credit for the question.
- If the question specifies how many answer choices to select, you must select that number of choices.

Numeric Entry Questions
- Indicate your answer in the box provided with the question.
- Equivalent forms of an answer, such as 1.5 and 1.50, are all correct.
- You do not have to reduce fractions to lowest terms.

Quantitative Comparisons
- These questions present two quantities, Quantity A and Quantity B. Information about one or both of the quantities may be provided in the space above the two quantities. You must compare the two quantities and choose

    (A) if Quantity A is greater
    (B) if Quantity B is greater
    (C) if the two quantities are equal
    (D) if the relationship between the two quantities cannot be determined

Each of the following questions consists of two quantities, Quantity A and Quantity B. You are to compare the two quantities. You may use additional information centered above the two quantities if additional information is given. Choose

Ⓐ if Quantity A is greater
Ⓑ if Quantity B is greater
Ⓒ if the two quantities are equal
Ⓓ if the relationship between the two quantities cannot be determined

$$a^2 - b^2 > 1$$

	QUANTITY A	QUANTITY B	
1.	a	b	Ⓐ Ⓑ Ⓒ Ⓓ

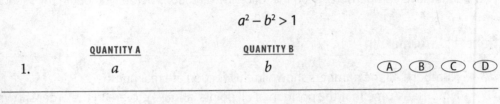

In the diagram, the sum of the diameters of the two smaller circles is equivalent to the diameter of the larger circle.

	QUANTITY A	QUANTITY B	
2.	The circumference of the larger circle	The sum of the circumferences of the smaller circles	Ⓐ Ⓑ Ⓒ Ⓓ

$$x^3 > x^5$$

	QUANTITY A	QUANTITY B	
3.	x	0	Ⓐ Ⓑ Ⓒ Ⓓ

$$b^2c < 0$$
$$abc > 0$$

	QUANTITY A	QUANTITY B	
4.	ab	0	Ⓐ Ⓑ Ⓒ Ⓓ

The probability that a certain event will occur is x.
The probability that the event will not occur is y.

	QUANTITY A	QUANTITY B	
5.	$x + y$	1	Ⓐ Ⓑ Ⓒ Ⓓ

n and q are positive integers, and n is a multiple of 5

QUANTITY A	QUANTITY B	
6. q^{n-5} | $q^{n/5}$ | Ⓐ Ⓑ Ⓒ Ⓓ

QUANTITY A	QUANTITY B	
7. The measure of angle ABC | The measure of angle DEF | Ⓐ Ⓑ Ⓒ Ⓓ

The retail price of a bookshelf is y dollars. The retailer will either add $5 to the retail price and then mark the price down by z%, or will mark the price down by z%, and then add $5 to the new price.

QUANTITY A	QUANTITY B	
8. The price of the bookshelf after the retailer adds $5 to the retail price and then marks the new price down by z%. | The price of the bookshelf after the retailer marks the original price down by z%, and then add $5 to the new price. | Ⓐ Ⓑ Ⓒ Ⓓ

For Questions 9 to 14 select one answer choice, unless the instructions state otherwise.

9. $4a^2 - 4b^2$ is equivalent to which of the following?

   Ⓐ $(2a - 2b)(2a - 2b)$
   Ⓑ $(4a - 4b)(4a - 4b)$
   Ⓒ $(2a + 2b)(2a - 2b)$
   Ⓓ $(2a + 2b)(a - b)$
   Ⓔ $(4a + 2b)(4a - 2b)$

10. If each of the sides of a certain square is doubled in length, by what factor will the area of the square increase?

11. On Tuesday, a salesman made four sales. On the first three sales, the salesman received a commission of $2,100, $1,500, and $1,800. If the salesman's average commission for all four sales was $2,000, what was the salesman's commission on the fourth sale?

Ⓐ $2,100
Ⓑ $2,300
Ⓒ $2,400
Ⓓ $2,500
Ⓔ $2,600

12. If $2a < 6$, and $3b > 27$, then $b - a$ can equal all of the following EXCEPT

Ⓐ 6
Ⓑ 7
Ⓒ 8
Ⓓ 9
Ⓔ 10

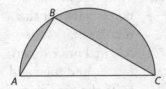

13. Triangle ABC is inscribed in the semicircle above. If the length of side AB is 10, and the length of side BC is 24, what is the area of the shaded region?

Ⓐ 169π
Ⓑ 84.5π
Ⓒ $169\pi - 120$
Ⓓ $84.5\pi - 120$
Ⓔ 120

14. An asteroid travels through space at a constant rate of 2.6 million feet per day. If the distance between the asteroid and a certain planet is 10.2 million feet, approximately how many seconds will it take the asteroid to reach the planet?

Ⓐ 80,000
Ⓑ 120,000
Ⓒ 200,000
Ⓓ 250,000
Ⓔ 350,000

Questions 15 to 17 are based on the data below. For each question, select one answer, unless the instructions state otherwise.

**Percentage Change in Student
Majors at University X**

Major	2015	2017
Biology	−12	8
Psychology	−10	10
Mathematics	6	11
English	−3	−10
Philosophy	11	−3

15. If 1,000 students majored in Philosophy in 2015, how many students majored in Philosophy in 2017?

  (A) 1,060
  (B) 1,077
  (C) 1,073
  (D) 1,078
  (E) 1,133

16. Based on the chart provided, which of the following statements must be true? (Indicate all that apply.)

  (A) The number of students who majored in Psychology in 2017 was less than the number of students who majored in Psychology in 2015.
  (B) The number of students who majored in Mathematics in 2017 was more than 17% greater than the number of students who majored in Mathematics in 2015.
  (C) In 2017, more students majored in Mathematics than in any of the other majors in the chart.

17. If the number of students who majored in Biology in 2015 was double the number of students who majored in English in 2015, then the number of students who majored in Biology in 2017 was what percent greater than the number of students who majored in English in 2017? Round your answer to the nearest integer.

For Questions 18 to 20, select one answer choice, unless the instructions state otherwise.

18. The population of State X is double that of State Y. If the population concentration (people per square mile) of State X is triple that of State Y, then what is the ratio of the area of State X to the area of State Y?

19. If x and y are unique nonzero integers such that $x + y = 0$, then which of the following CANNOT be true? (Indicate all that apply.)

    A) $|x| = |y|$
    B) $x < y$
    C) $xy > 0$
    D) $x^2 + y^2 = 0$
    E) $x^3 + y^3 = 0$

20. A survey of voter preferences showed that, rounded to the nearest tenths digit, 14.2% of voters expressed a preference for an independent candidate. If 80,000 voters responded to this survey, which of the following could equal the number of voters who expressed a preference for an independent candidate? (Indicate all that apply.)

    A) 11,315
    B) 11,321
    C) 11,390
    D) 11,399
    E) 11,400

———————————— STOP. ————————————
This is the end of Section 5.

SECTION 6

Quantitative Reasoning

20 questions—35 minutes

This section includes four types of questions: Multiple-Choice Questions—Select One Answer, Multiple-Choice Questions—Select One or More Answers, Numeric Entry Questions, and Quantitative Comparisons. Read the following directions before you begin the section.

General Information

- Numbers: All the numbers shown in this section are real numbers.
- Figures: Assume that the position of all points, angles, etc. are in the order shown and the measures of angles are positive,
- All figures lie in a plane unless otherwise stated.
- All straight lines can be assumed to be straight.
- Note that geometric figures are *not necessarily drawn to scale*. Do not try to estimate lengths and sizes of figures in order to answer questions.

Directions

Multiple-Choice Questions—Select One Answer

- Select one answer choice from a list of five choices.

Multiple-Choice Questions—Select One or More Answers

- Select one or more answer choices following the directions given.
- You must select all of the correct answer choices and no others in order to earn credit for the question.
- If the question specifies how many answer choices to select, you must select that number of choices.

Numeric Entry Questions

- Indicate your answer in the box provided with the question.
- Equivalent forms of an answer, such as 1.5 and 1.50, are all correct.
- You do not have to reduce fractions to lowest terms.

Quantitative Comparisons

- These questions present two quantities, Quantity A and Quantity B. Information about one or both of the quantities may be provided in the space above the two quantities. You must compare the two quantities and choose

  (A) if Quantity A is greater
  (B) if Quantity B is greater
  (C) if the two quantities are equal
  (D) if the relationship between the two quantities cannot be determined

Each of the following questions consists of two quantities, Quantity A and Quantity B. You are to compare the two quantities. You may use additional information centered above the two quantities if additional information is given. Choose

(A) if Quantity A is greater
(B) if Quantity B is greater
(C) if the two quantities are equal
(D) if the relationship between the two quantities cannot be determined

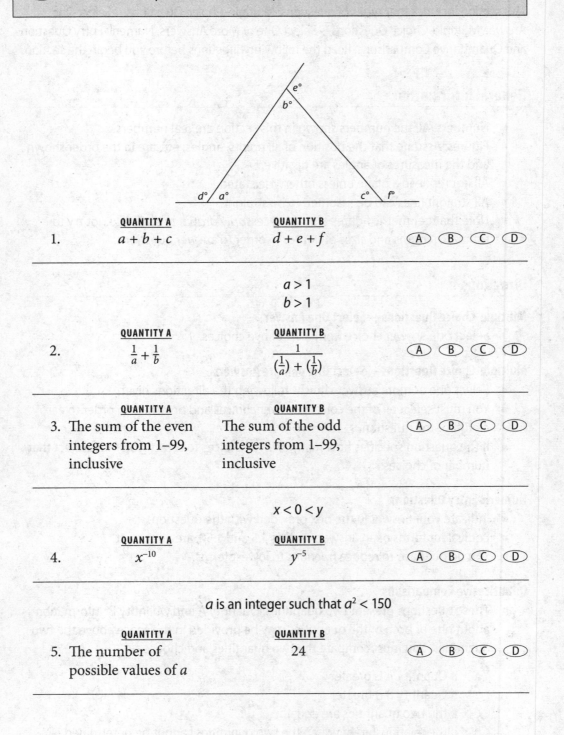

	QUANTITY A	QUANTITY B	
1.	$a + b + c$	$d + e + f$	(A) (B) (C) (D)

$$a > 1$$
$$b > 1$$

	QUANTITY A	QUANTITY B	
2.	$\frac{1}{a} + \frac{1}{b}$	$\dfrac{1}{\left(\frac{1}{a}\right) + \left(\frac{1}{b}\right)}$	(A) (B) (C) (D)

	QUANTITY A	QUANTITY B	
3.	The sum of the even integers from 1–99, inclusive	The sum of the odd integers from 1–99, inclusive	(A) (B) (C) (D)

$$x < 0 < y$$

	QUANTITY A	QUANTITY B	
4.	x^{-10}	y^{-5}	(A) (B) (C) (D)

a is an integer such that $a^2 < 150$

	QUANTITY A	QUANTITY B	
5.	The number of possible values of a	24	(A) (B) (C) (D)

At University X, 30% of the professors are tenured. More
than half of the tenured professors are men.

	QUANTITY A	QUANTITY B	
6.	The ratio of male to female professors at University X	1	Ⓐ Ⓑ Ⓒ Ⓓ

	QUANTITY A	QUANTITY B	
7.	$\dfrac{16^{-a}}{4^{-b}}$	4^{b-2a}	Ⓐ Ⓑ Ⓒ Ⓓ

$\frac{1}{7}$ of the x devices produced by a manufacturer were defective and
thus discarded. 70% of the remaining devices were sold.

	QUANTITY A	QUANTITY B	
8.	The number of non-defective devices that were not sold	$\frac{1}{4}x$	Ⓐ Ⓑ Ⓒ Ⓓ

For Questions 9 to 14, select one answer choice, unless the instructions state otherwise.

9. If $16a = 64^b$, then what is a, in terms of b?

Ⓐ 4^b

Ⓑ $2^{(6b/4)}$

Ⓒ $2^{(6b-4)}$

Ⓓ $4^{(6b/4)}$

Ⓔ $4^{(6b-4)}$

10. Last season, a certain basketball team won $\frac{7}{10}$ of its first 50 games and $\frac{1}{2}$ of its remaining games. If the team won $\frac{5}{8}$ of all of its games, how many games did the team play last season?

Ⓐ 75

Ⓑ 80

Ⓒ 85

Ⓓ 90

Ⓔ 95

11. If a, b, and c are integers such that $3a + 4bc$ is even, then which of the following CANNOT be true?

    Ⓐ b is odd
    Ⓑ bc is odd
    Ⓒ ab is even
    Ⓓ ac is odd
    Ⓔ $a + c$ is even

12. The length of a certain rectangle is four greater than its width. If the length of the diagonal of the rectangle is 20, what is the area of the rectangle?

$$\boxed{}$$

13. Wheel A and Wheel B start rotating at the same time. Wheel A makes 10 revolutions every minute, and Wheel B makes 6 revolution every minute. After how many hours will Wheel A have made 480 more revolutions than Wheel B?

    Ⓐ   0.5
    Ⓑ   1
    Ⓒ   1.5
    Ⓓ   2
    Ⓔ   2.5

14. At a certain organization, the average salary for the male employees is $50,000, and the average salary for the female employees is $60,000. If more than $\frac{3}{4}$ of the employees are female, which of the following could be the average salary of all employees at the organization? (Indicate all that apply.)

    Ⓐ $55,000
    Ⓑ $56,000
    Ⓒ $57,000
    Ⓓ $58,000
    Ⓔ $59,000

Questions 15 to 17 are based on the data below. For each question, select one answer, unless the instructions state otherwise.

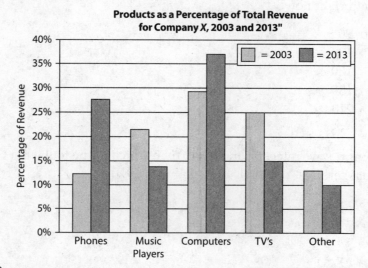

Products as a Percentage of Total Revenue for Company *X*, 2003 and 2013"

15. If $\frac{3}{4}$ of the computer revenue in 2003 was from laptops, then non-laptop computers accounted for approximately what percentage of all revenue in 2003?

   (A) 4%
   (B) 7%
   (C) 9%
   (D) 12%
   (E) 20%

16. If, In 2013, the amount of revenue from phones was approximately $25 million dollars, then the amount of revenue from computers in 2013 was closest to which of the following?

   (A) $29 million
   (B) $32 million
   (C) $36 million
   (D) $40 million
   (E) $42 million

17. The percentage of revenue that music players accounted for in 2013 was approximately what percent less than the percentage of revenue that music players accounted for in 2003?

   (A) 10%
   (B) 15%
   (C) 40%
   (D) 60%
   (E) 75%

GO ON TO NEXT PAGE ➤

18. Bob is 30 pounds heavier than Sara. If Bob and Sara each gain 30 pounds, Bob's weight will be 25% greater than Sara's weight. How much does Bob weigh right now?

    Ⓐ 90
    Ⓑ 120
    Ⓒ 150
    Ⓓ 180
    Ⓔ 210

19. If x and y are integers, and $y \neq 0$, then which of the following CANNOT equal zero?

    Ⓐ xy
    Ⓑ $x + y$
    Ⓒ $x - y$
    Ⓓ $xy - y^2$
    Ⓔ $x^2 + y^2$

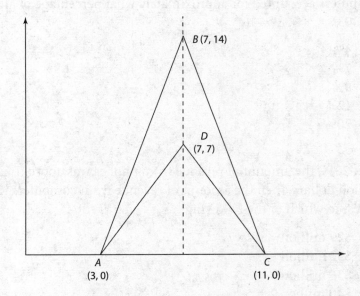

20. In the diagram above, the area of triangle ADC is what fraction of the area of triangle ABC?

    Ⓐ $\frac{1}{8}$
    Ⓑ $\frac{1}{4}$
    Ⓒ $\frac{1}{2}$
    Ⓓ $\frac{2}{3}$
    Ⓔ $\frac{3}{4}$

───────────── **STOP.** ─────────────
This is the end of Section 6.

Answers and Explanations

Section 1. Analytical Writing: Analyze an Issue

Use the following scoring rubric to grade your essay. Grade yourself as honestly as possible regarding the organization, structure, fluency, and accuracy of your writing. Then compare your essay to the sample high-scoring response that follows.

Analyze an Issue: Scoring			
SCORE	FOCUS	ORGANIZATION	CONVENTIONS
0	Does not address the prompt. Off topic.	Incomprehensible. May merely copy the prompt without development.	Illegible. Nonverbal. Serious errors make the paper unreadable. May be in a foreign language.
1	Mostly irrelevant to the prompt.	Little or no development of ideas. No evidence of analysis or organization.	Pervasive errors in grammar, mechanics, and spelling.
2	Unclear connection to the prompt.	Unfocused and disorganized.	Frequent errors in sentence structure, mechanics, and spelling.
3	Limited connection to the prompt.	Rough organization with weak examples or reasons.	Occasional major errors and frequent minor errors in conventions of written English.
4	Competent connection to the prompt.	Relevant examples or reasons develop a logical position.	Occasional minor errors in conventions of written English.
5	Clear, focused connection to the prompt.	Thoughtful, appropriate examples or reasons develop a consistent, coherent position. Connectors are ably used to mark transitions.	Very few errors. Sentence structure is varied and vocabulary is advanced.
6	Insightful, clever connection to the prompt.	Compelling, convincing examples or reasons develop a consistent, coherent position. The argument flows effortlessly and persuasively.	Very few errors. Sentence structure is varied and vocabulary is precise, well chosen, and effective.

Sample Response with a Score of 6

American society is built on the idea that people have a right to free speech. Indeed, our country was founded in part due to the fact that the colonists were taxed by the British crown without representation; they were never given the option to disagree with British taxation laws, and ultimately they went to war to protest this violation. So it might seem likely that many Americans would agree with the statement that dissent should be encouraged in order for society to flourish, since our founding principles are rooted firmly in this belief. I myself must agree with the statement as well, both because of my personal values and because history reveals that this is so. You wouldn't have to look very far for historical data that shows that when dissent is not allowed, society declines. One prime example of this is Soviet Russia. From the time that the Communists took power until the fall of the Berlin Wall in 1992, the Soviet Union was a highly repressive regime. Dissent was quashed at every turn, and propaganda was put forth to support the ideas of the Soviet leadership. Over time, due in part to the lack of new ideas being allowed in to stimulate the system, the Soviet economy declined to the point where citizens were miserable. The repression of the empire was an important reason why this political unit ultimately collapsed.

Even the United States has seen times of political repression, despite our belief in the value of free speech. This repression has led also to fear and turmoil within the nation. One example is the McCarthy Era that occurred in the U.S. during the Cold War. For about 10 years at the height of the Cold War, immediately after World War II, tensions were high between the U.S. and the Soviet Union, and potential sympathizers with communism were sought out and persecuted. Senator Joseph McCarthy led the pursuit, interrogating thousands of citizens and civil servants about their alleged subversive activities. The wave of terror that swept the nation as a result kept people afraid to express themselves and has been recorded as a dark period in our nation's history.

Perhaps the worst example of what can happen when dissent is discouraged can be found in Nazi Germany. Under Hitler's rule, not only was dissent prohibited—it was prohibited to even exist as a member of certain groups. This totalitarian regime required the strictest allegiance to reigning political principles, going so far as to penalize people for being born into groups other than the Aryan race. Millions of innocent people were exterminated for not ascribing to Nazi beliefs. The genocide that resulted under Hitler reveals the stark picture of what can happen when a ruling ideology is upheld at the expense of all opposing ideas.

These examples show the grave results that can be expected when dissent is discouraged or prevented by political leadership. When dissent is allowed, however, in many cases society grows and vastly improves. The Civil Rights Era in the United States provides an example of the results when citizens are allowed to voice dissenting opinions. The nonviolent protests of Dr. Martin Luther King, Jr. and his supporters were instrumental in swaying the U.S. government to adopt policies that respected the rights of African-American citizens and upheld equal treatment under the law. The changes brought about by these protests have taken many years to implement and are still a work in progress, but the civil disobedience of the 1960s was instrumental in bringing about positive results.

The growth of the city of Providence, Rhode Island, represents another case where dissent was encouraged and society flourished as a result. During the 1600s, Providence was settled by Roger Williams, a dissenter who had fled religious persecution in Massachusetts. After Williams established the colony, Providence became a refuge for many individuals who did not believe in the prevailing religious ideas of the day. Providence eventually grew to become the capital of the state of Rhode Island and flourished in both its culture and economy. Its roots as a haven for dissenters no doubt set the foundation for social and political diversity that enabled the community to thrive.

Although much criticized by many on both sides of the political spectrum, the two-party political system in the United States is another example of how the encouragement of dissent can promote societal progress. Many people feel that the predominance of the two-party system does not allow Americans a great deal of latitude to affect policy when they vote, because the parties are highly polarized and the political options supported by each are fairly predictable. Yet, the system does encourage an ongoing debate between conservative and liberal ideas that prompts policy to evolve, albeit sometimes quite slowly. The dissent promoted by the two-party system may only support incremental change, but it is change that occurs through the exchange of ideas in an open political forum. The capacity for such change is one of the hallmarks of our society.

In sum, the value of dissent for promoting societal growth cannot be understated. When dissent is prohibited, as has been the case with fascist dictatorships such as Hitler's, calamity often results. When dissent is allowed and even encouraged as part of a political system, the proliferation of conflicting ideas often gives rise to much-needed change, enabling societies to progress and, ultimately, to flourish.

Section 2. Analytical Writing: Analyze an Argument

Use the following scoring rubric to grade your essay. Grade yourself as honestly as possible regarding the organization, structure, fluency, and accuracy of your writing. Then compare your essay to the sample high-scoring response that follows.

Analyze an Argument: Scoring

SCORE	FOCUS	ORGANIZATION	CONVENTIONS
0	Does not address the prompt. Off topic.	Incomprehensible. May merely copy the prompt without development.	Illegible. Nonverbal. Serious errors make the paper unreadable. May be in a foreign language.
1	Little or no analysis of the argument. May indicate misunderstanding of the prompt.	Little or no development of ideas. No evidence of analysis or organization.	Pervasive errors in grammar, mechanics, and spelling.
2	Little analysis. May instead present opinions and unrelated thoughts.	Disorganized and illogical.	Frequent errors in sentence structure, mechanics, and spelling.
3	Some analysis of the prompt, but some major flaws may be omitted.	Rough organization with irrelevant support or unclear transitions.	Occasional major errors and frequent minor errors in conventions of written English.
4	Important flaws in the argument are touched upon.	Ideas are sound but may not flow logically or clearly.	Occasional minor errors in conventions of written English.
5	Perceptive analysis of the major flaws in the argument.	Logical examples and support develop a consistent, coherent critique. Connectors are ably used to mark transitions.	Very few errors. Sentence structure is varied and vocabulary is advanced.
6	Insightful, clever analysis of the argument's flaws and fallacies.	Compelling, convincing examples and support develop a consistent, coherent critique. The analysis flows effortlessly and persuasively.	Very few errors. Sentence structure is varied, and vocabulary is precise, well chosen, and effective.

Sample Response with a Score of 6

The author claims that the experience of Herald's Hardware is obvious evidence that advertising on the radio will make your business more profitable. This claim is based on the fact that Herald's revenues increased by 13% since it began radio advertising. The author's claim is not sound, because it relies on two problematic assumptions. Information pertaining to the store's advertising, sales, and costs would help to strengthen or weaken the argument.

The first problematic assumption of the argument is the idea that radio advertising alone is responsible for the increase in Herald's revenues. In reality, the increases could have been caused by other factors. Perhaps the radio advertising coincided with other forms of advertising that Herald's launched at the same time. It might have occurred during the spring or summer seasons, in which homeowners are likely to do more maintenance, thus leading to an increase in hardware sales. The neighborhood around Herald's might have experienced weather-related problems, such as damage from hail or flooding, that could have required residents to buy more supplies. Until we've analyzed other factors thoroughly, we can't assume that radio advertising alone helped boost Herald's sales.

The second problematic assumption of the argument is the idea that revenue increases equate to increases in profits. This assumption is not true. Profit is not simply a matter of the revenues earned by a company; it is calculated by subtracting costs from sales. Based on what the author has told us, we can't know whether the store's profits increased after the radio campaign began. Profits might have increased, if the store's overall costs remained stable or decreased and revenues improved. But if the radio advertising was expensive, and it increased costs for the store, Herald's profit might have declined.

Additional information could help to strengthen or weaken the author's argument, by providing more detail on advertising, sales, and costs. The argument would be strengthened if it could be shown that the advertising campaign was conducted only over radio, and that no other types of advertising occurred that might have boosted Herald's sales. This argument could also be strengthened if it were shown that advertising was the only significant factor that might have affected revenues during the time period in question, and that all other factors remained constant. Finally, the argument would gain strength if cost data showed that business expenses for the store remained level or even decreased while sales went up. This data would document that Herald's did in fact experience increased profit.

Contrary to the information that might strengthen the argument, certain pieces of information might also weaken it. Looking again at Herald's advertising, if it turned out that radio advertising was conducted simultaneously with advertising in other media, this would weaken the author's claim. Regarding sales, if other factors such as weather or seasonal changes could in fact account for the store's increase in revenue, the author's claim would be further weakened. Similarly, if cost data showed that the store's business expenses increased during this time period due to the advertising itself or other factors, leading to reduced profit for the store despite increased sales, this would weaken the author's argument as well.

The author of the statement jumps to a quick conclusion about the relationship between radio advertising and store profits, based on limited evidence about the timing of an increase in sales. It could be that the increase in revenue was not influenced by the radio advertising, and that Herald's store did not actually increase its profits. We would need to know more about the store's advertising, sales, and business expenses—among other factors—to determine whether this argument is valid.

Section 3. Verbal Reasoning

1. **C** Since literary analysis lacks evidence, its interpretations are most likely *ambiguous.*

2. **A and E** If novice readers overlook the darker social commentary, then they *misunderstand* the point of satire. Since this "social commentary" is part of the satire but is overlooked, it must be *implicit.*

3. **A, F, and I** The easiest word to begin with is the second blank. The writing is "illuminating" for the adventurous reader. Of the words in blank 2, the word closest in meaning to "illuminating" is *edifying.* Now, look at blank 1. If these detours "frustrate" some readers, then they are *exasperating.* Now, look at blank 3. The frustrated readers do not like detours, and are used to "direct" argumentation. Of the choices, the word closest in meaning to "direct" is *unequivocal.*

4. **B, D, and H** Start with the second blank, which is the opposite of "platitudes." The best choice is *forthrightness.* Now, move on to the first blank. If the politician prioritizes forthrightness, then her actions question the belief that politicians forgo "honesty." The closest choice is *candor.* Now, look at the third blank. The phrase "even if" indicates that her actions might have a negative effect. They might *alienate* her supporters.

5. **A** The trait that served him well in his prior job was his "work ethic," Of the choices, the word closest in meaning to "work ethic" is *industriousness.*

6. **B and E** The word in the first blank is a more extreme form of "self-assurance." The best choice is *hubris.* The word in the second blank serves the purpose of indicating that his self-confidence is justified by his skills. The best choice is *commensurate with.*

7. **C** To undermine the conclusion, we want to show that 10 percent increase in the savings of citizens aged 50–65 does not indicate that the savings rate of these citizens went up. If choice C is true, then the ratio of savings/person went down during the time period.

8. **A** The passage's primary purpose is to explain the benefits of volunteering.

9. **C** The passage states that volunteering is especially helpful for elderly people. One reason is that it provides "a sense of purpose at a time when their social roles are changing." The choice that most closely meets these conditions is C.

10. **C** The author states that "the youngest Baby Boomers will not reach age 65 until 2029" in order to support the point that the number of volunteers "can be expected to rise for many years to come."

11. **E** All of the choices are mentioned as potential benefits of volunteering except for "increased financial success."

12. **A and D** Since the artwork couldn't be identified, it was probably impossible to determine where it came from. The words that best fit the blank are *origin* and *provenance.*

13. **A and D** The word in the blank is a factor in dieting that contrasts with genetic factors. A good prediction is "willpower." Of the choices, the words closest in meaning to "willpower" are *restraint* and *self-control.*

14. **A and E** The word in the blank should match the meaning of "selflessness." The best choices are *altruism* and *beneficence.*

15. **E and F** Since technology results in an "inadequate" amount of attention paid to the novel, the side effect of digitization is negative. The choices that best satisfy the context are *pernicious* and *deleterious*.

16. **A and C** Choice A is supported by the first sentence of the second paragraph. Choice B may look tempting, but it can be eliminated based on the fact that in some cases, the diseases "are associated with external sores as well." Choice C is supported by the second sentence, which states that antibiotics are necessary because of the stress of the dense colonies.

17. **B** The author mentions these examples to support the fact that "studies have also found higher levels of certain contaminants in farmed fish than in their wild counterparts."

18. **A** Choice A shows that the high influenza rate among bus riders has nothing to do with the fact that they ride the bus. Instead, it has to do with their age and consequent susceptibility to influenza. Thus, encouraging these bus riders to take the subway will not reduce the spread of influenza.

19. **C** The passage mentions that Locke's theory is unfounded and then goes on to explain a recent study supporting this fact. Thus, the passage's primary purpose is to support the position that the *tabula rasa* is an unsound theory.

20. **Sentence 6** Sentences 4 and 5 give an example of a study that supports the position that infants have "instinctive thoughts and behaviors." The following sentence, sentence 6, explains why these findings are important.

Section 4. Verbal Reasoning

1. **A** What would characterize an editorial with "grand" claims? A good word is *bombasticism*.

2. **B** If the efforts "inevitably overlook" certain features, then the efforts are *problematic*.

3. **C** The word in the blank concerns what the complaints are about. Since they concern a worker's salary and are addressing misconceptions about salary, the best choice is *inequities*.

4. **A and E** Start with the second blank; "contentiousness" is a good clue. The word closest in meaning is *adversarial*. The word in the first blank refers to something they attempted but failed at. If the relationship was still adversarial, then they failed to *rectify* it.

5. **B and D** The first blank describes someone who "demanded all the facts." The best choice is *skeptical*. "However" indicates that her defense is the opposite of her skepticism. The best choice is *steadfast*.

6. **C and D** The word in the first blank is a synonym for self-denial: *abnegation*. The word in the second blank supports the claim that the person in question did *not* practice self-denial. What kind of tastes would such a person have? A good choice is *indulgent*.

7. **C** The portion in bold is a consideration against the argument's main conclusion that "researchers predict that the pill will become the primary mode of nicotine cessation."

8. **B** The author discusses how Freud might be a social critic to lead up to his larger point that the only appropriate categorization for Freud is as a "genius."

9. **A** The author provides these examples in the context of the discussion of Freud's genius. These examples serve to highlight what the author thinks constitutes genius.

10. **A** The author uses "ameliorated" in reference to the impact that the application of psychological principles would have on the situation in the first paragraph. Since the situation in the first paragraph is negative, the use of these principles would be to "improve" the situation.

11. **B and F** The physicist's relationship with the university was based on his "frustration." A good prediction is "dissatisfied." Of the choices, the words closest in meaning to dissatisfied are *disaffection with* and *alienation from*.

12. **B and D** The word in the blank contrasts with "consensus." Of the blanks, the best words are *divergence* and *discord*.

13. **A and D** The word in the blank clarifies the executive's claim that "the two companies are not rivals." If they are not rivals, then his company's success did not "prevent" the other company's success. The words closest in meaning to "prevent" are *preclude* and *hamper*.

14. **A and D** The word in the blank describes the relationship between a sport and the skills of that sport. The point of the second part of the sentence is that the skills of athletes in *neglected* sports are similar to those of athletes in well-known sports. Thus, the sport's *popularity* and *reputation* are irrelevant.

15. **C** "Idioms" is used in reference to the different architectural styles that developed during the period.

16. **C** The author mentions that the churches made these constructions to reflect the "one Blood" sentiment of their parishioners.

17. **Sentence 7** The fact that these innovations arose as the traditions that made them possible were obliterated suggests irony.

18. **B** The argument concludes that Professor Doyle is a superior teacher because his students performed better than the students in any other class. What would weaken this? B is a good answer. It shows a different reason for the superior performance of his students—specifically the students who couldn't handle his curriculum dropped out, leaving only the better-equipped students. Their superior performance may thus be attributable to their mathematical aptitude rather than Doyle's teaching abilities.

19. **D** In the last sentence, the author uses the word "insularity" to emphasize his point that "some regional identities always have been partly the result of isolation."

20. **Sentence 4** The only instance in which the author provides concrete examples of New Englander's engagement with other people is when he discusses "shipping and migration."

Section 5. Quantitative Reasoning

1. **D** Consider values that satisfy the given information. Case 1: $a = 2$, $b = 1$. In this case, $a > b$. Case 2: $a = -2$, $b = 1$. In this case, $a < b$. A relationship cannot be determined.

2. **C** Choose values. Let the diameter of the larger circle = 10. In this case, the circumference of the larger circle is 10π. Let the diameter of the medium-sized circle be 6 and the diameter of the smaller circle be 4. In this case, the circumference of the smaller circle is 6π, and the circumference of the smaller circle is 4π. $6\pi + 4\pi = 10\pi$. The two quantities are equal.

3. **D** Test different numbers that would satisfy the prompt. If $x = \frac{1}{2}$, then $\frac{1}{2^3} > \frac{1}{2^5}$. Thus, $\frac{1}{2}$ is a possible value for x. In this case, Quantity A is greater. What about negative numbers? If $x = -2$, then $(-2)^3 > (-2)^5$. Thus, -2 is a possible value for x. In this case, Quantity B is greater.

4. **B** Deduce what you can from the given information. The first inequality: b^2 must be positive because of the even exponent. Thus, if $b^2 c < 0$, then $c < 0$. Now, for the second inequality: If $c < 0$, and $abc > 0$, then $ab < 0$. Thus, Quantity B is greater.

5. **C** Since x and y are mutually exclusive, the sum of their probabilities must be 1.

6. **D** Choose numbers. If $q = 1$ and $n = 5$, then the value of both quantities is 1. If $q = 2$ and $n = 10$, then the value of quantity A is greater. A relationship cannot be determined.

7. **C** Note that each side of the larger triangle is double the corresponding side of the smaller triangle. These are thus similar triangles. One property of similar triangles is that corresponding angles are equal. Since angles ABC and DEF are opposite the largest side of their respective triangles, the measurement of these angles must be equal.

8. **B** Choose values. Let $y = 100$, and let $z = 20$. Now, evaluate Quantity A. With these values, a $5 increase will lead to a bookshelf that costs $105. After a 20% discount, the price of the bookshelf will be $.8(105) = 84$. Now, evaluate Quantity B. With these values, a 20% reduction in the retail price will result in a new price of $.8(100) = 80$. $80 + 5 = 85$. Quantity B is greater.

9. **C** The expression in the question is in the form of $x^2 - y^2$, where $4a^2$ corresponds to x^2 and $4b^2$ corresponds to y^2. Since $x^2 - y^2$ factors to $(x + y)(x - y)$, $4a^2 - 4b^2$ factors to $(2a)^2 - (2b)^2 = (2a + 2b)(2a - 2b)$.

10. **4** Plug in numbers. Let the original side length of the square = 3. In this case, the original area is 9. If the length of each side is doubled, then the length of each side is 6 and the corresponding area is $6^2 = 36$. $\frac{36}{9} = 4$

11. **E** $2,600 was the salesman's commission on the fourth sale. Since the average of the four commissions is $2,000, the total must be $2,000 \times 4 = $8,000. Subtracting the total of the other three commissions from $8,000 gives the commission on the fourth sale.

12. **A** First, isolate each variable. $2a < 6 \rightarrow a < 3$. $3b > 27 \rightarrow b > 9$. Now, assume that $a = 3$ and $b = 9$. In this case, $b - a = 9 - 3 = 6$. Since $a < 3$ and $b > 9$, the difference between the two must *be greater* than 6. Thus, 6 is not a possible value for $b - a$.

13. **D** Since triangle ABC is inscribed in a semicircle, it must be a right triangle. The area of the triangle is thus $\frac{1}{2} \times 10 \times 24 = 120$. Using the Pythagorean Theorem, the diameter of the circle = $AC = 26$. The area of the circle is thus (π) $r^2 = (\pi)13^2 = (\pi)169$. The area of the semicircle is thus $\frac{169\pi}{2} = 84.5\pi$. The area of the shaded region = area of the semicircle − area of the triangle. This can be expressed as $84.5\pi - 120$.

14. **E** Plug the given values into the R × T = D formula. The rate is 2.6 million feet per day and the distance is 10.2 million feet. Thus: 2.6 million × T = 10.2 million → T = $\frac{10.2 \text{ million}}{2.6 \text{ million}}$ = approximately 4 days. Now, convert days to seconds. 1 day = 24 hours = 60(24) minutes = 60(60)(24) seconds = 86,400 seconds. So, the number of seconds in 4 days is 86,400 × 4 = 345,600 seconds. The closest answer is 350,000.

15. **B** The number of students majoring in Philosophy in 2015 was 1.11(1,000) = 1,110. The number of students majoring in Philosophy in 2017 was thus (.97)(1,110) = 1,076.7 or approximately 1,077.

16. **A and B** The easiest way to confirm each choice is to plug in numbers.

    Choice A: Choose 1,000 for the number of Psychology majors in 2015. The number of Psychology majors in 2017 was thus 1,000(.9)(1.1) = 990. Choice A is correct.

    Choice B: Choose 1,000 for the number of Mathematics majors in 2015. The number of Mathematics majors in 2017 was thus 1,000(1.06)(1.11) = 1,176. The change was 176. 176 is more than 17% of 1,000, Thus, choice B is correct.

    Choice C: We have no values for any of the majors, so we cannot infer any relationships about the number of students in each major.

17. **117%** Choose values. Let the number of English majors in 2015 = 1,000. The number of biology majors in 2015 was thus 2,000. The number of Biology majors in 2017 was thus (2,000)(.88)(1.08) = 1,900.8. The number of English majors in 2017 was (1,000)(.97)(.9) = 873. Now, use the percent greater formula: % greater = % of − 100%. Plug in the numbers: (1,900.8/873) × 100 − 100% = 117%.

18. **$\frac{2}{3}$** Plug in numbers: Let 1,200 = population of State X and 600 = population of State Y. Let the population concentration of State X = 12, and the population concentration of State Y = 4. The area of State X is thus $\frac{\text{population}}{\text{area}} = \frac{1,200}{\text{area}}$ = 12 → area = 100. The area of State Y is thus $\frac{\text{population}}{\text{area}} = \frac{600}{\text{area}} = 4$ → area = 150. The ratio of the area of State X to the area of State Y is thus $\frac{100}{150} = \frac{2}{3}$.

19. **C and D** If $x + y = 0$, and neither x nor $y = 0$, then it must be the case that x and y are different numbers with the same absolute value. For example, $x = -2$ and $y = 2$. Based on this example, choices A and B are possible. For choice C to be possible, x and y would have to have the same sign. But they cannot have the same sign since they must cancel each other out. Choice C cannot be true and is thus a possible answer. Choice D cannot be true because any non-zero number raised to an even exponent will yield a positive result. Positive + positive > 0. Choice E is always true, since odd exponents preserve the sign of the base. Because x and y have different signs, x^3 and y^3 will also have different signs.

20. **B, C, and D** If the percentage, when rounded to the nearest tenth, is 14.2%, then the actual percentage, p, is such that $14.15 \leq p \leq 14.249$. We can use this percentage range to yield a range for the number of voters who expressed a preference for an independent candidate. The lower bound will be 14.15% of 80,000 = 11,320. The upper bound will be 14.249% of 80,000 = 11,399.2. Any value that falls between these two endpoints will be an answer. Among the choices, the values that fall in this range are B, C, and D.

Section 6. Quantitative Reasoning

1. **B** Since a, b, and c are the angles inside a triangle, the sum of their measures must be 180. Since each of angles d, e, and f are supplementary to angles a, b, and c, respectively, $d + e + f = 540 - 180 = 360$.

2. **D** Plug in numbers. First, let $a = 2$, and $b = 2$. In this case, the value of Quantity A is $\frac{1}{2} + \frac{1}{2} = 1$. The value of Quantity B is $\frac{1}{\frac{1}{2} + \frac{1}{2}} = \frac{1}{1} = 1$. In this case, the two quantities are equal. Now, let $a = 10$ and $b = 10$. In this case, the value of Quantity A is $\frac{1}{10} + \frac{1}{10} = \frac{2}{10} = \frac{1}{5}$. The value of Quantity B is $\frac{1}{\frac{1}{10} + \frac{1}{10}} = \frac{1}{\frac{2}{10}} = \frac{1}{\frac{1}{5}} = 5$. In this case, Quantity B is greater. A relationship cannot be determined.

3. **B** Don't calculate! The number of terms in the set in Quantity A is $\frac{98}{2} = 49$. The number of terms in Quantity B is $\frac{98}{2} + 1 = 50$. Each term in Quantity A is one more than the corresponding term in Quantity B, Thus, up until 98, the sum of the terms in Quantity A is 49 greater. However, this is offset by the additional 99 in Quantity B. Thus, Quantity B is greater.

4. **D** Plug in values. First, let $x = -1$ and let $y = 1$. In this case, the two quantities are equal. The correct answer must be C or D. Next, let $x = -1$ and let $y = 2$. In this case, the values in the quantities are different.

5. **A** Answer: Since a is an integer, the greatest possible value for a is 12, since $12^2 = 144$ (note that 13 is too large since $13^2 = 169$). The least possible value for a is -12, since $(-12)^2 = 144$ (note that -13 is too small since $(-13)^2 = 169$. We can express a's range as: $-12 \leq a \leq 12$. In this range, there are 12 negative integers (-12 thru -1), 12 positive integers (1–12), and zero. Therefore, there are 25 possible values for a.

6. **D** The given information is insufficient to conclude any relationship between *all* male professors and *all* female professors.

7. **C** Simplify Quantity A by expressing the numerator as base 4: $16^{-a} = (4^2)^{-a} = 4^{-2a}$. Therefore, $\frac{16^{-a}}{4^{-b}} = \frac{4^{-2a}}{4^{-b}} = 4^{(-2a + b)}$ or 4^{b-2a}. The two quantities are equal.

8. **A** If $(\frac{1}{7})x$ of the products were defective, then $(\frac{6}{7})x$ were not defective. Of these nondefective devices, $30\% = \frac{3}{10}$ were not sold. $(\frac{3}{10})(\frac{6}{7})x = (\frac{18}{70})x = (\frac{9}{35})x$. $(\frac{9}{35})x > (\frac{1}{4})x$. Quantity A is greater.

9. **C** Solution: To isolate a, divide both sides of the equation by 16 to arrive at:

    $$a = \frac{64^b}{16}$$

    Next, express the bases in base-2. $64 = 2^6$, so the numerator $= (2^6)^b = 2^{6b}$. Expressed in base-2, the denominator $= 2^4$. So the equation simplifies to:

    $$a = \frac{(2^{6b})}{2^4}.$$

    Since we're dividing terms with the same base, we'll keep the base and subtract the exponents to arrive at: $2^{(6b-4)}$.

10. **B** Let t = total games played. The number of games won = $\frac{7}{10}(50) + (\frac{1}{2})(t - 50)$. Since the team won $\frac{5}{8}$ of all games played, we can create the equation:

$$\frac{7}{10}(50) + (\tfrac{1}{2})(t - 50) = \tfrac{5}{8}(t)$$

Simplify:

$$35 + \tfrac{t}{2} - 25 = \tfrac{5}{8}(t) \rightarrow 10 + \tfrac{t}{2} = \tfrac{5}{8}(t) \rightarrow 10 = \tfrac{5}{8}(t) - \tfrac{t}{2} \rightarrow 10 = \tfrac{5}{8}(t) - \tfrac{4}{8}(t) \rightarrow 10 = \tfrac{t}{8}$$
$$\rightarrow 80 = t.$$

11. **D** To yield an even sum, the terms being added must both be odd or both be even. Since $4bc$ has a factor of 4, it must be even. Therefore, $3a$ must be even. For $3a$ to be even, a must be even. If a is even, then it is not possible for ac to be odd.

12. **192** Let w = the width. Thus, the length is $w + 4$. Since the diagonal of a rectangle forms a right triangle whose legs are the sides of the rectangle, we can use the Pythagorean theorem: $w^2 + (w + 4)^2 = 20^2 \rightarrow w^2 + w^2 + 8w + 16 = 400 \rightarrow 2w^2 + 8w + 16 = 400 \rightarrow w^2 + 4w + 8 = 200 \rightarrow w^2 + 4w - 192 = 0 \rightarrow (w + 16)(w - 12) = 0 \rightarrow w = 12$ (since w must be positive), and the length = 16. Therefore, the rectangle's area is $16 \times 12 = 192$.

13. **D** Wheel A makes 4 more revolutions each minute than does Wheel B. Thus: $4t = 480 \rightarrow t = 120$. 120 minutes = 2 hours.

14. **D and E** Assume that $\frac{3}{4}$ of the employees were women. In this case, the average salary for all employees would be $\frac{3}{4} \times 60{,}000 + (\frac{1}{4}) \times 50{,}000 = \$57{,}500$. Since the number of female employees accounts for *more* than $\frac{3}{4}$ of all employees, the average for all employees must be greater than \$57,500.

15. **B** In 2003, computer sales accounted for approximately 27% of all revenues. If laptop computers accounted for $\frac{3}{4}$ of these sales, then non-laptop computers accounted for $\frac{1}{4}$ of these sales. $\frac{1}{4}(27\%) = 6.75\%$. Among the choices, the value closest to 6.75% is 7%.

16. **B** Since phones represented 27.5% of all revenue in 2013, you can create the equation: \$25 million = $.275x$, where x = the total revenue in 2013. Solve for x: \$25 million/.275 = \$90.9 million. Finally, since revenue from computers account for approximately 36% of all revenue in 2013, take 36% of \$90.9 million: $.36(90.9) = \$32.7$ million. Among the choices, the value closest to 32.7 million is 32 million.

17. **C** In 2003, music players accounted for approximately 22% of all revenue. In 2013, music players accounted for approximately 13% of all revenue. 13 is what percent less than 22? Use the percent decrease formula:

$$\left(\tfrac{\text{difference}}{\text{original}}\right) \times 100 = (\tfrac{9}{22}) \times 100 = 40.9\%$$

Among the choices, the value closest to 40.9% is 40%."

18. **B** Let b = Bob's weight and s = Sara's weight. If Bob is currently 30 pounds heavier than Sara, then $b = s + 30$. If they each gain 30 pounds, then Bob's new weight will be $b + 30$ and Sara's new weight will be $s + 30$. After these changes, Bob's weight will be 25% more than Sara's. We can translate this as: $b + 30 = 1.25(s + 30)$. To solve for b, we should use the first equation to express s in terms of b: $b = s + 30 \rightarrow b - 30 = s$. Substitute $(b - 30)$ for s in the second equation and solve for b:

$$b + 30 = 1.25(b - 30 + 30) \rightarrow b + 30 = 1.25\,b \rightarrow 30 = .25b \rightarrow b = 120.$$

19. **E** Use the given constraints to determine whether each choice could equal zero.

    A: If $x = 0$, then $xy = 0$. Eliminate A.

    B: If $x = 3$, and $y = -3$, then $x + y = 0$. Eliminate B.

    C: If $x = 3$, and $y = 3$, then $x - y = 0$, Eliminate C.

    D: Factor: $xy - y^2 = y(x - y)$. For $y(x - y)$ to be zero, either y must be zero or $x - y$ must be 0; y cannot be 0, but $x - y = 0$ if $x = y$. Eliminate D.

    E: When a value is raised to an even exponent, the result must be greater than or equal to zero. Thus, $y^2 > 0$, and $x^2 \geq 0$. The sum of y^2 and x^2 is thus greater than 0.

20. **C** The base of both triangles has a length of 8. The height of triangle ADC is 7. The area of triangle ABC is thus $(\frac{1}{2}) \times 8 \times 7 = 28$. The height of triangle ABC is 14. The area of triangle ABC is thus $(\frac{1}{2}) \times 8 \times 14 = 56$

Cracking the

PHYSICS C EXAM

2017 Edition

By the Staff of The Princeton Review

PrincetonReview.com

Penguin
Random
House

The Princeton Review, Inc.
24 Prime Parkway, Suite 201
Natick, MA 01760
E-mail: editorialsupport@review.com

Published in the United States by Penguin Random House LLC, New York, and in Canada by Random House of Canada, a division of Penguin Random House Ltd., Toronto.

ISBN: 978-1-101-91997-2
eBook ISBN: 978-1-101-92023-7
ISSN: 1937-6391

The Princeton Review is not affiliated with Princeton University.

AP and Advanced Placement Program are registered trademarks of the College Board, which is not affiliated with The Princeton Review.

Editor: Selena Coppock
Production Editors: Beth Hanson and Liz Rutzel
Production Artist: Deborah A. Silvestrini

Printed in the United States of America on partially recycled paper.

10 9 8 7 6 5 4 3 2 1

2017 Edition

Editorial
Robert Franek, Senior VP, Publisher
Casey Cornelius, VP Content Development
Mary Beth Garrick, Director of Production
Selena Coppock, Managing Editor
Meave Shelton, Senior Editor
Colleen Day, Editor
Sarah Litt, Editor
Aaron Riccio, Editor
Orion McBean, Editorial Assistant

Random House Publishing Team
Tom Russell, Publisher
Alison Stoltzfus, Publishing Manager
Jake Eldred, Associate Managing Editor
Ellen Reed, Production Manager
Kristin Lindner, Production Supervisor